Discovering Gifts
in Middle School

LEARNING IN A
CARING CULTURE
CALLED TRIBES

Discovering Gifts
in Middle School

LEARNING IN A
CARING CULTURE
CALLED TRIBES

BY JEANNE GIBBS

IN COLLABORATION
WITH TEACHERS AND
ADMINISTRATORS EXTRAORDINAIRE

CenterSource Systems, LLC   Windsor, California

Published in the United States of America by
CenterSource Systems, LLC
7975 Cameron Drive, #500
Windsor, California 95492

Library of Congress Cataloging-in-Publication Data
Gibbs, Jeanne
    Discovering Gifts in Middle School : learning in a caring culture called Tribes / By Jeanne Gibbs in collaboration with teachers and administrators extraordinaire.
        p. cm.
    Includes bibliographical references (p. 423) and index.
    ISBN 0-932762-50-6 (pbk. : alk. paper)
    1. Middle school education—United States. 2. Group work in education—United States. 3. Classroom environment—United States. 4. Adolescent psychology—United States. I. Title.
    LB623.5 .G53 2001
    373.236—dc21
                                    2001001951

Illustrations: Pat Ronzone, Sausalito, CA
Photographs: Nita Winter Photography, Sausalito, CA
Book design: Lynn Bell, Monroe Street Studios, Santa Rosa, CA

PRINTED IN THE UNITED STATES OF AMERICA
10   9   8   7   6   5   4   3   2

Contents

Acknowledgements

The writing of this book from start to finish has been an exciting inquiry—leading to discovery after discovery of studies and people also dedicated to creating caring school communities that are responsive to the developmental and learning needs of young adolescents. Among the many is an expert cadre of administrators, educational specialists, teachers, trainers, research groups and students who have contributed ideas, articles, studies, stories, poems and words of wisdom to this book. The importance and timeliness of the topic were affirmed repeatedly whenever friends, associates—even strangers on planes—heard the title, *Discovering Gifts in Middle School*.

As old friends know, the cooperative learning process known simply as "Tribes" now is also recognized as a way to re-culture and re-structure whole school communities for educational excellence. The author is indebted to hundreds of teachers, administrators and district specialists whose comments and assessments continue to help CenterSource Systems to augment and refine both the content and process of Tribes TLC® (Tribes Learning Communities). I particularly thank Bonnie Benard for writing the special article in Chapter 4 on "engaging the developmental wisdom of adolescence." Bonnie's conceptual frameworks on resiliency and youth development have enriched Tribes throughout many years. Her brilliance as a thinker, competency as a writer and spirit as a caring human being shine through every word of her writing and presence.

I especially also want to thank Thomas Armstrong, Ph.D. for permission to adapt the adult multiple intelligences check lists from his book, 7 *Kinds of Smart,* to a version for young adolescents. Thanks to Tom and his publisher, students in the most formative period of their lives now will be able to discover their most special of all gifts… their own unique intelligences and possible paths to successful futures. Tom's work has long been a vital component of Tribes, and we thank him again.

Readers will find a lovely poem from caring administrator, Carroll Killingsworth, a profound poem from a reflective ten-year-old student, Andrew Whyte, and a touching song by Red Grammer. I know there is hope for peace in the world when gentlemen take to writing such caring poems and songs. Carroll, Andrew, and Red, thank you for the sharing of your hearts.

My appreciation is boundless and enduring to the twelve dedicated teachers, administrators and trainers who have contributed their perspectives and stories. The sharing of their own experiences in using the process of Tribes has long been a priceless gift. These colleagues are: Art Beaman, Ph.D., Michele Cahall, Beverly Edwards, Ph.D., Judi Fenton, Annette Griffith, Nancy Latham, Nancy Lindhjem, Mary Palin, Linda Reed, Marilyn Sumner, Betty White and Caroline Wong.

The background music connecting all of the words comes from the joyous artistry of Pat Ronzone's illustrations and Nita Winter's fine photographs. It is a privilege to include the work of these two well-known artists whose delightful and poignant images always convey their own deep love of children. And Lynn Bell, ingenious designer! Thank you for handling the complexities of the computer layout for this book. Lynn's cheerful patience with the many changes was remarkable. No one could have done it as well. Carolyn Rankin of CenterSource Systems took on the overwhelming task of writing and rewriting the 140 active learning strategies and energizers. She also worked as an editor with Jeanne Mancour of CenterSource. Jeanne is congratulated for wrestling the author's stack of references and bibliography into order.

Finally, I thank my fine family for their patience in watching and helping me to drag this laptop computer and boxes of materials around for almost two years… back and forth from seashore to mountains to offices and homes.

The journey of writing this book has been filled with the discovery of unexpected gifts and many new perspectives. It has given me a deeper understanding of the words of Marcel Proust, who wrote, *"Truly, the voyage of discovery is not in seeking new lands, but seeing with new eyes."* Due to the wisdom of all of your eyes, this has been the essence of my journey. Thank you one and all.

—Jeanne Gibbs

Discovering Gifts in Middle School by Learning in a Caring Culture Called "Tribes"

HERE WE ARE!

Please look at us carefully! We are those ten to fifteen year old want-to-be people in your middle school. We're the ones not sure of who we are. It seems as if our parents and teachers also are not quite certain what we are like beyond a collection of adjectives. The consensus is that we are every community's

active, noisy, restless,

impetuous, stubborn, compliant,

caring, compassionate, idealistic,

shy, worried, bored,

persistent, imaginative, courageous,

curious, inventive and spirited

middle school kids.

We are the group once so easy to manage and teach back in the early grades. We are the in-between-ers longing to be cool high schoolers. We are, as many people say, "caught in the middle."[1] Most of our schools are trying to homogenize us to make us "like everybody else." Most are trying to standardize what and how we learn even though we are all very different. The bells, schedules, hallway rush, lockers, lectures, worksheets, papers, pencils, and straight-row classrooms make us feel disconnected, boxed-in and bored.[2] We're caught in the middle in an impersonal production system.

LOOK AT US AGAIN!

We want you to see who we really are... and can become. Somehow we know we all have special strengths and gifts. We hope that once our schools recognize this they will announce that 100% of their students are "gifted students!"

Sometimes when we look bored and our thoughts drift out the classroom window, we probably are pondering some of the deep-down questions of our caught-in-the-middle years. We're silently asking...

"Am I competent?"

"Am I normal?"

"Am I loveable?"

We need a way to discover that the answers are YES!

Viewpoint

A true human being is never what he or she appears to be. Rub your eyes and look again.[1]

　　　　　　　　　　　　　　　　　—Rumi

"Look at us again," call out the diversity of middle school adolescents. "Tell us why so many of us feel school is frustrating, not very meaningful and just something to get through."

This question, phrased one way or another, also is being asked by concerned adults throughout the nation. Looking back, we realize the same question has haunted us throughout the last twenty years of school reform. Each new wave promised to establish educational excellence. "World class schools" would result from focusing on tougher discipline policies, behavior modification, high tech schools, computers, a new reading program, smaller classes, site councils, character education, more homework, less professional development, more teaching time… and now standards and testing.

Our viewpoint is that it is time to be courageous enough to raise three rarely discussed questions:

- *What proof did we ever have that educational excellence could be achieved through wave after wave of singular reform initiatives?*
- *Why is the field of education, unlike all other professions, resistant to staying current—to learn and implement valuable cognitive research, developmental studies and effective pedagogy?*
- *More than all, why are school communities not concerned with the growth and development of the full spectrum of children's development in addition to academic (intellectual) learning?*

Our viewpoint parallels that of innumerable respected educational leaders. Listen to some of the voices.

The failure of schools to address the full range of children's growth and development—their social, psychological, emotional and physical—in addition to their intellectual development— clearly is undermining the nation's efforts to achieve academic excellence.[2]

　　　　　　　　　　　　　　　　　—James P. Comer

Middle school grades—junior high, intermediate, and middle schools—are potentially society's most powerful force to recapture millions of youth adrift, and help every young person thrive during early adolescence. Yet all too often these schools exacerbate the problems of young adolescents. A volatile mismatch exists between the organization and curriculum of middle grade schools and the intellectual and emotional needs of young adolescents.[3]

　　　　　　　　　　　　　　　　　—The Carnegie Council on Adolescent Development

Our educational systems continue to teach intellectual development rather than intrinsic worth.[4]

—Jean Piaget

Young adolescents who are pushed through schools that are not responsive to their developmental needs, fail to discover their identity, unique gifts and interests that motivate learning into the future. They are the teenagers who enter high school unprepared. Lacking in self-knowledge and social and emotional competency, they are less likely to achieve academically. In contrast, schools that are *developmentally responsive* send middle level students onward with a sense of excitement as a result of having discovered themselves and gifts purposefully to pursue.

Schools that are focusing on the full-range of adolescent growth and development first transform the culture and structure of the school into caring learning communities. They believe, as does Anne Wheelock, that...

building a culture for school-based reform means uprooting many old assumptions about learning—to make way for new beliefs about how students 'become smart.'[5]

School communities that focus on understanding the nature and existential needs of their students use a synthesis of developmental strategies and meaningful pedagogy. The synthesis that hundreds of schools are turning to is not a curriculum, not a program. It is an on-going renewal process, a caring and supportive culture, known as "Tribes"—Tribes Learning Communities.

Teachers are supported to move from traditional didactic teaching, workbooks and memorization to active group learning so that students gain meaningful and lasting knowledge through constructive thinking, collaborative problem-solving and responsible social interaction. Of utmost importance is the fact that the peer support within learning groups (tribes) helps middle level adolescents to recognize their gifts and interests. The *Tribes responsive teaching process* is research based, and verified by thousands of studies on ideal learning cultures, resiliency, cooperative learning, constructivism, thematic instruction and brain compatible learning. *Responsive education* is a daily community process lived by teachers, students and the whole school community. It is a caring democratic culture that includes values, and challenges everyone in the school community to participate, to learn and to develop their personal best.

Young adolescents, ten to fifteen years old, are striving to achieve four developmental tasks—whether they or their parents and teachers realize it or not. They are seeking autonomy and independence, social competency, meaning and purpose, and the right to solve problems on their own. Middle level teens need to be empowered to accomplish these essential tasks in order to be successful in high school and adult life. They are at the "Turning Point" referred to in the landmark document of the Carnegie Council on Adolescent Development. Moreover, this is the basis of the warning from the Carnegie Council that *too many middle level schools are exacerbating the problems of young adolescents—by being unresponsive to their developmental needs*.

Authentic standards are *what* need to be achieved.[6] *How* to do so takes a synthesis of what already is known about learning and teaching. Excellent middle level schools have a recognizable spirit that respected educator, Joan Lipsitz, describes well....

> *In excellent middle schools, there has to be [or is] evidence of student joy, as demonstrated by laughter, vitality, interest, smiles and other indications of pleasure.*[7]

Yes, this is the energy that is noticed throughout hundreds of schools who have become Tribes Learning Communities. They are living and internalizing a new way of being and learning together. We invite you to do the same.

—Jeanne Gibbs

1 Caught in the Middle

1 Caught in the Middle

IN THIS CHAPTER YOU WILL....

- Consider the many gifts that early adolescents are seeking and can discover
- Realize the importance of the mission and goal of Tribes for adolescent development, learning and success in life
- Understand why middle level schools need to focus on adolescent development
- Learn what a middle level school should be and not be

*To be nobody but yourself
in a world which is doing its best,
day and night,
to make you like everybody else
means to fight the hardest battle
which any human being can fight.[1]*

—e.e.cummings

WHAT GIFTS ARE THEY SEEKING?

What gifts will our children find when schools and families finally recognize that the period of early adolescence is key to children's identity, sense of competency, resiliency and path to the future? The inner restlessness of the age group is an indicator that in the most critical stage of children's development their needs are being ignored. The nation's current focus on testing to standards based largely on factual rote-learning curriculum relegates social, emotional, moral and physical development to a low priority. A serious consequence is that it undermines improving American education. One of this country's most respected educators, Linda Darling-Hammond, is convinced that....

Bureaucracy's need to employ procedures that will allow it to continue to function 'without regard for persons' turns out to be the ultimate source of its failure to manage the job of educating people well.[2]

It is time to take seriously the abundance of research and correlative studies connecting and recommending the integration of children's social and emotional developmental needs into traditional academics—not as an add-on, but as the foundation for motivation, comprehension and success in school.[3] It is imperative that young adolescents discover their individual gifts, talents and interests before moving into the high school years. Finding the unique ways one learns, uncovering a latent interest or inherent skill, and gaining recognition for unique qualities gives affirmation to the gnawing question, "Am I capable?" Such gifts are the links to loving school and life-long learning.

A youngster who constantly doodles may linger long while viewing a Chagall or Picasso on a visit to the Museum of Art. He or she sees in the masters a hint of his or her own gift. He has part of the answer to "Am I capable? Yes!" His gift takes on life… in sketching, studying artists, art history, geometry, drafting and perhaps architecture. The spirit of his discovered gift excites learning into a future. Studies on brain compatible learning verify how making a connection to a keen interest, experience or previous piece of knowledge is motivational. It's a bit like having an earlier file already in the hard drive in one's computer. New information can be readily tucked in or downloaded into the file. Moreover, the meaning and retention of new knowledge (academics) is far greater because it is linked to previous knowledge.

Sounds like a better way to improve test scores!

Gifts can be demonstrations of one's talent… a literary composition, a drawing, an invention, a stage performance, mediating conflict, facilitating a group or analyzing a complex problem. All of the multiple intelligences cited by Howard Gardner are hidden gifts to be explored. Life-long learning can be transformed when students recognize the unique ways in which they do learn.[4] What a joy for a bored middle-school student to find out that she learns best through interpersonal dialogue and collaborative projects with peers! One of her fine personal gifts then is discovered. Who knows—it may lead her to be a production team manager at Intel!

Sure! Math, science, literature and the arts would become more meaningful!

Gifts are also the positive human qualities of character. The national concern that school violence and other adolescent problems are increasing has catalyzed funding for character education programs. The list of qualities (values or virtues) to be taught or promoted may vary from state to state or school to school, but are essentially:

Honesty	Integrity	Respect
Kindness	Persistence	Truthfulness
Responsibility	Compassion	Service
Justice	Empathy	Caring

Educators must be sensitive to the entire spectrum of these young people's capabilities.[5]
—ANNE WHEELOCK

The big question is: "To what degree can these qualities be internalized if only admonished or taught as a cognitive curriculum?" If it is our hope that the character qualities become behaviors in children, it is not enough to drill and exhort the qualities. They must be lived moment by moment in the culture of the school. Respected educator, John Goodlad, points out, "There is little need to invoke caring for one another if caring for one another is as present in what we do as in the air we breathe."[6]

Alfie Kohn also is convinced that exhorting and drilling students in specific behaviors is not enough, but that we must engage them in deep critical reflection about certain ways of being.[7] Within Tribes TLC® schools students and teachers reflect many times a day upon the ways they are working together. The inherent values of the caring community embrace and quickly develop valued character qualities. This type of learning is intrinsic and lasting.

THE GIFTS OF RESILIENCY also are kindled and strengthened through caring environments. In recent years the impressive longitudinal studies on resilience have brought enlightenment and hope to parents, educators, child caregivers and youth serving systems. Just as the caring community culture of Tribes embodies positive character qualities, it also fosters the social and emotional development of children and resilience. Early adolescence is our last best chance to nurture the development of enduring resilient qualities. Self-discipline, empathy, altruism, persistence, autonomy, a healthy outlook, positive expectations and a sense of humor are some of the invaluable qualities that have been proven to enable youth and adults to withstand and overcome the inevitable stress and adversity met during any lifetime.[8]

THE SHARED MISSION AND GOAL OF TRIBES LEARNING COMMUNITIES (TRIBES TLC®)

The philosophy and concepts urging a focus on the full range of child and youth development (intellectual, social, emotional, physical and spiritual) always have been and are the foundation of the process of Tribes. Recognizing that human development and learning are influenced by the ecology and interaction of the many systems in children's lives (family, school, peers and community groups), a shared mission and goal statement is used throughout Tribes schools.[9]

THE MISSION OF TRIBES IS: to assure the healthy development of every child so that each has the knowledge, competency and resilience to be successful in a rapidly changing world.

THE GOAL OF A TRIBES SCHOOL IS: to engage all teachers, administrators, students and families in working together as a learning community that is dedicated to caring and support, active participation and positive expectations for all students.

The mission and goal give the school community not only a focus on student development but a new way of being and learning together. Many have said, "It's as though everyone is finally singing the same song—in harmony!"

STUDENT FAILURE IS ABOUT SCHOOLS FAILING

Our educational systems continue to teach intellectual development, rather than intrinsic worth.[10]
—Jean Piaget

The statement above by child psychologist Jean Piaget was made more than thirty years ago! Yet his concern is still being ignored by a majority of educators, parents, policy-makers and standard-setters seeking educational reform. A majority of school systems continue to deal with parts of kids rather than their integral wholeness. How many times have you heard...

"Improve their knowledge (intellect) with new standards."
"Next month we'll work on social skills."
"Hire more counselors for their psychological problems."
"Send them out to recess to work off physical energy."
"Emotional? Spiritual? Intrinsic worth?
Don't go there at all."

Dr. James Comer, one of the nation's chief architects for school change, has also for more than thirty years urged educators to make children's development the foundation of education. Regretfully, he says:

Many in the school reform movement are concerned about issues of power (matters of choice, charters, vouchers, privatization), test scores and what parents, teachers, administrators, politicians want—not what children need to grow, develop, and meet their adult tasks and responsibilities.[11]

Unless reform is child centered, children and the society alike are going to be hurt—are being hurt.[12]
—JAMES COMER

19

The failure of schools to address the full range of children's growth and development—their social, psychological, emotional and physical—in addition to their intellectual development—clearly is undermining the nation's efforts to achieve academic excellence. More importantly, it is sabotaging the future well-being and success in life for millions of students. It has been estimated that 7 million young people—one in four adolescents—are extremely vulnerable to high-risk behaviors and school failure, and another 7 million may be at moderate risk.

Caught in a vortex of changing demands, the engagement of many youth in learning diminishes, and their rates of alienation, substance abuse, absenteeism, and dropping out of school begin to rise. As the number of youth left behind grows, and opportunities in the economy for poorly educated workers diminish, we face the specter of a divided society: one affluent and well-educated, the other poorer and ill-educated. We face an America at odds with itself.[13]

—Turning Points

The Troubled Journey, a 1996 survey of 250,000 youths from sixth through twelfth grade in more than 460 urban, suburban and rural mid-western communities, found that only one in ten adolescents met a set of criteria for "optimal healthy development." Peter Benson, President of the Search Institute which published the survey, recently concluded that "America has forgotten how to raise healthy kids."[14]

> The massive failure of schools to reach and teach to the developmental needs of millions of young people affects all aspects of society and the future of the nation.
>
> —CARNEGIE COUNCIL ON ADOLESCENT DEVELOPMENT

The landmark document Turning Points warned us more than ten years ago!

Professor of Human Development, Urie Bronfenbrenner, also raised the very serious question about the impact upon our nation:

How can we judge the worth of a society? On what basis can we predict how well a nation will survive and prosper? ...If the children and youth of a nation are afforded opportunity to develop their capacities to the fullest, if they are given the knowledge to understand the world and the wisdom to change it, then the prospects for the future are bright. In contrast, a society which neglects its children, however well it functions in other respects, risks eventual disorganization and demise.[16]

WHAT A MIDDLE LEVEL SCHOOL SHOULD NOT BE...
AND SHOULD BE

Middle level schools, just like their students, are also "caught in the middle" between two very differently organized systems... the elementary and the high school. Their dilemma is how much to mimic one or the other rather than defining systems that meet the early adolescent's needs... and to find the "yes" to the haunting questions, "Am I capable, normal and loveable?"

Peter Scales writes in his book, *Boxed In and Bored,* "too many school students too often feel boxed in and bored. Too many young adolescents are lectured to just when they need to explore and interact in small groups. Too many are left without effective guidance and connections with caring adults just at the time when their physical, emotional, social, spiritual and cognitive selves are undergoing great change. Too many are given curriculum that is less challenging and rules that are more strict than they experienced in elementary school, just when they need more academic challenge and a greater sense of participation in developing and enforcing the rules that regulate their behavior."[17]

A MIDDLE LEVEL SCHOOL SHOULD NOT BE

...a watered down high school

...a place where a student becomes a number

...a place where failure is accepted.

Respected researcher, Joan Lipsitz, reported more than a decade ago that:

Successful schools for young adolescents base all procedures, all policies, all practices, on a deep understanding of early adolescent development, especially the great variations within individuals and across individuals of the same chronological age. Knowing what the latest research says about early adolescent development is the first step in ensuring that schools—and communities—adjust to and become more challenging and supportive places for young adolescents.[18]

If an unfriendly foreign power imposed upon America the quality of education it has, we would have considered it an act of war.[15]
—JOHN GARDNER

A successful middle school is a unique place that supports children's development from childhood to adolescence. It is a place where...

- a caring culture assures learning and success for every child
- every child can experience success
- all feel a sense of belonging and of being valued
- all of the developmental needs of students are the priority
- children are not put down, ignored or fear harm
- children enjoy caring and support, meaningful participation and high expectations
- cooperation is emphasized and competition de-emphasized
- students explore a variety of their gifts, ways of learning and interests
- an interdisciplinary curriculum and teacher-based guidance program catalyze excellence
- professional development and collegiality among teachers is a priority
- a variety of groups study, plan, take action and assess on-going strategies
- the faculty is committed to working as reflective practitioners
- teachers enjoy middle school children and prefer teaching in a middle school
- there is high level of parent and community involvement supporting the caring culture and goals for student learning and development.

2 Getting to Know You—
The Developmental Characteristics of Young Adolescents

2 Getting to Know You—
The Developmental Characteristics of Young Adolescents

IN THIS CHAPTER YOU WILL....

- Realize how schools ignore and limit adolescent development
- Learn the importance of considering the contextual basis of human development
- Review the unique characteristics of early adolescents
- Learn what a responsive middle level school is like

Truly, the voyage of discovery is not in seeking new lands, but seeing with new eyes.[1]

—Marcel Proust

PERPETUATING A PATTERN

The majority of schools have become drastically out of synch with the developmental needs of young adolescents because, in the words of Joan Lipsitz, the age group is comprised of "the most severely neglected, underserved and hardly studied" children in American schools.[2] Schools that respond poorly or ignore student needs add stress to young lives and actually may perpetuate a vicious circle of underachievement.[3] Stress limits cognitive performance. Teachers become convinced certain students are not capable. They expect less and provide less challenge. Students caught in the cycle question their abilities, give up academically and drift into paths of risk that do offer identity though ultimately destructive.

A false assumption that all adolescents, whether 10 to 18 years old, are the same also has blinded educators to the developmental needs of early adolescents, 10 to 15 years old. This assumption led to the creation of junior high schools back in the 1920's and again in the 1940's for the stated purpose of preparing younger students for the high school system. True to that mission junior highs adopted the less personal high school structure of many periods, many teachers, direct instruction, increased homework, standardization of curriculum, competition and few connections to teachers or peers. The priority need of early adolescents, 10 to 15 year olds, is not to be prepared over several years for high school but to discover their individual strengths—and become themselves. Their developmental needs are very different than those that confront teenagers who are 16 to 19 years old. It is critical that all adult stakeholders begin "seeing with new eyes."

Theories abound on how to manage them, fix them, and improve them, as if they were products off an assembly line: just tinker with the educational system, manipulate the drug messages, impose citywide curfews, make more rules, write contracts, build more detention centers, be tough. Maybe if we just tell adolescents to say no, no, no to everything we disapprove of, maybe then they will be okay. But the piecemeal attempts to mend, motivate, or rescue them obscure the larger reality. We don't know them.[4]

— Patricia Hersch

To know them means moving beyond the assumptions, labels, symptomatic behaviors and adjectives of despair or amusement. We must walk in the shoes of a twelve year old today. Being twelve is not the same as a few decades ago. The impact of technology, the media, the explosion of information, communication, population mobility, economics and a restless multiethnic society has transformed the ecology of human development for today's children. That Psych 101 child development course of some years ago may not have touched upon the environmental variables that affect human development. It certainly did not include those faced by young teens today.

LOOKING AT THE BIG PICTURE OF HUMAN DEVELOPMENT

If we begin seeing children's development with new eyes, we'll understand that the path is not a neat predictable one. It is affected by each young person's....

- interaction in the settings of his/her daily life: family, school, community and peer groups
- the cultural norms, languages, beliefs, and mores of the surrounding systems
- and the wider impact of institutions, government, economics, mass media and religion.[5]

The adjacent graphic illustrates that human development is an ongoing transaction between an individual and many surrounding systems. It depends upon one's conception of an ever-widening world and one's interaction with it—as well as a growing capacity to discover, sustain, or change it.[6]

It is the last sentence that is especially significant for the work we need to do with our early adolescents. Recognizing that they are moving into ever-widening worlds, they need to be encouraged to manage their lives—and to discover, sustain or change situations and systems in which they find themselves. As fledgling idealists they have come to believe in democracy—not as represented by political parties but as their right to participate and influence decisions and common goals. As teachers and parents we need to welcome the indicators of their development—rather than leap to control their ideas and opinions. The age group's new strident behaviors, judgments and resistance are emerging out of a very natural quest to develop independence. Decades ago John Dewey asserted that the primary goal of education was....

- to teach the young to influence their environment, and
- to gain the insight to make choices beyond past experiences.[7]

Looking at children's development as an on-going process that is interactive with many daily systems means that we must learn how to challenge and support each child's ever-widening explorations and interests into worlds beyond "self." It means helping early adolescents to move beyond their childhood perspective of "me" to identifying with others as "we" in recognition of the common good of their community. Young people who fail to do so continue to live throughout most of their adult lives in small ego-centered worlds centered on "me and mine." Moreover, primary identification with self is a straight road to living in loneliness, intolerance, conflict, alienation, high-risk behaviors, periods of despair and failure throughout life. Mental institutions, alcoholism/drug treatment centers, jails and prisons are filled with "me first—me only" people. This is not a moral or "lack of character" problem. It is a failure to develop beyond the "me" stage of early childhood. It is a failure to grow socially, emotionally and spiritually as an adolescent and to become a responsible and caring human being.

We must ask, "Is this what has limited the futures of so many young people in our country today?" Are they the ones who were never challenged to discover their innate gifts, never to feel confident to relate in wider worlds of "we" as well as "me?" Those who stay passive, preoccupied with self, and resigned to circumstances have difficult lives. Studies on pre-school children have shown that a child who, at an early age, can demonstrate that she is capable of relating to others and helping to change a frustrating situation, later tends to be active and competent in grade school.[8] What if educational reform finally focused on the development of wholeness in children—calling forth their gifts of promise, personal power and life potential?

That's why I became a teacher!

We urge you to challenge other teachers, educators and parents in your school to form small *learning groups* or *learning communities*. Set aside enough time to envision how making a focus on the development of your early adolescent students could make a big difference. Discuss the material of these two chapters and then decide (democratically, of course!):

What changes in attitude, motivation, behavior and positive qualities would you expect to see?

How would it change your school? Approach to teaching? Relationships with parents? Staff development? Setting meaningful standards?

How would it change your day as a teacher or administrator?

Ultimately, how would it impact national concerns?

The philosophy and methodology of the process of Tribes has always been a "systems approach to support positive human development." It focuses on reculturing and restructuring the whole school community, so that the whole "village" learns how to contribute to kids' growth and development. There is no longer any doubt that creating caring learning communities in schools is the proven way to support children's development and achievement.[10]

Our work is not about a curriculum or teaching method... it is about nurturing the human spirit with love.[9]

—RON MILLER

THE CHARACTERISTICS OF YOUNG ADOLESCENTS

In order to be developmentally responsible, middle schools must be grounded in the diverse characteristics and needs of these young people. It is this concept that lies at the heart of middle level education.[11] — National Middle School Association

The years of "early adolescence" now are considered to fall in the range of 10 to 15 years due to the earlier onset of puberty in children today. The wide variation among students in physical maturation and their resulting anxiety even has led the National Middle School Association to suggest that early adolescents should be grouped by developmental age rather than by a chronological age graded system. Developmental age means readiness for learning based on specific characteristics of the learner, irrespective of chronological age. Children of the same developmental age may vary two to three years in chronological age. Early or late maturation affects a student's self-perception. Just as physical development varies among young adolescents, their intellectual, social, emotional and moral development also range widely. Overall, the primary anxiety for early teens is a need for identity and belonging. Much as we imagine it otherwise, academic success is dependent upon other developmental needs being met.[12]

The summary profiles that follow were defined from the literature on early adolescents and confirmed by groups of experienced (and still jovial) middle school teachers.[13]

INTELLECTUAL DEVELOPMENT

Young adolescents are in a transition from relying on concrete cognitive skills to abstract reasoning skills. The gradual development of abstract thinking skills gives them the ability to imagine hypothetical situations, to reconcile contradictions, to predict long-term consequences of immediate behavior, and to view situations from other people's perspectives. Although they are moving beyond their childhood orientation of present time, their attention span is still often short-lived and unfocused.

The age group is intensely curious and enjoys a wide range of intellectual pursuits—few of which are sustained. They prefer active over passive learning experiences and learning in interaction with peers. To the consternation of teachers they may show disinterest in conventional academics but are intellectually curious about the world and themselves. Though inquisitive about adults, they often challenge their authority.

MORAL DEVELOPMENT

Our young friends are generally idealistic, wanting to become socially useful and make the world a better place in which to live. They also are in a transition from a focus of "what's in it for me" to considering the feelings and rights of others. At the same time it is easier for them to see flaws in others than to acknowledge their own flaws.

The group often shows compassion for people who are suffering or downtrodden, and shows special concern for animals and environmental problems. Increasingly they begin to assess moral matters in shades of gray instead of the black and white terms of younger children. When facing a difficult decision, most rely on parents and significant adults for advice. They seek adult role models who will listen and affirm their moral actions. They are increasingly aware of and concerned about inconsistencies between values exhibited by adults and the conditions they see in society. The age group values direct experience in participatory democracy. They are very capable of offering their opinions and leadership.

PHYSICAL DEVELOPMENT

The rapid irregular growth, bodily changes and varying maturity rates of young adolescents often cause them to be awkward, uncoordinated, restless and fatigued. Girls tend to mature one and one-half to two years earlier than boys, and for that reason often develop a sexual awareness beyond the boys. The group is very concerned with bodily changes especially if they result in an increase in nose size, protruding ears, long arms and awkward posture. All sense an increase in energy and need physical activity several times a day. The need to release energy can cause sudden meaningless bursts of activity. In spite of new energy many lack physical fitness and have low levels of endurance, strength and flexibility. They may adopt poor health habits (junk food, experimentation with drugs and sex) and be physically vulnerable. More than all, young adolescents require the understanding of and connections to caring adults.

EMOTIONAL/PSYCHOLOGICAL DEVELOPMENT

Young adolescents are psychologically vulnerable because at no other stage of development are they more likely to encounter so many differences between themselves and others. Believing that their feelings and problems are unique to themselves, they can experience unpredictable and intense mood swings. They are highly sensitive to personal criticism, tend to be self-conscious and lacking in self-esteem.

Preoccupied with self, they are easily discouraged and have a strong need for approval. Peer acceptance and approval become increasingly more important as adult approval decreases in importance. Seeking to become increasingly independent and to act as an adult often provokes parents. It also can be the basis of resistance to teachers and other adults in authority.

Never doubt that the positive is also happening. Though caught in the middle, they are also experiencing many small joys as positive aspects of their personalities and character qualities are affirmed. As personal value systems develop, societal issues assume more importance. Physical energy and new moral judgment often become a way to achieve identity, increased self-esteem, acceptance and approval.

SOCIAL DEVELOPMENT

More than all, young adolescents have a strong need to belong to a group. Because their social skills frequently lag behind their mental and physical maturity, they may exhibit immature behavior. They tend to model their behavior after older, esteemed students or adults beyond the family. Though dependent on parental beliefs and values, they seek to make their own decisions. The age group wants attention and guidance from adults, but not necessarily with their friends watching. The drive for independence results in liking attention-getting fads (clothes, haircuts, earrings), new slang and phrases adults do not understand. Their big search is to have social acceptance and recognition in a peer group, especially a group that is well-respected by other young adolescents. This desire to have recognition within a peer group and work with peers is one of the reasons cooperative learning in on-going Tribes works well. And that is what this book is all about!

THE PATH TO SUCCESS

Indeed, it is time to view our young adolescents with new eyes. The characteristics that may at times drive parents and teachers crazy are not problems to be overcome. The age group's erratic energy, restlessness, drive for independence, bonding to peers, new capacity to see the needs of others, idealism, curiosity and need for identity are assets for learning. We must give up referring to the teenagers in the same way we talk about "the terrible twos." These kids are every bit as wonderful and precious—yet less understood! They are experiencing the most rapid self-conscious physical, emotional and social change that occurs in human life. Certainly there may be increased conflicts with parents, especially if parents do not understand the developmental issues (such as the need for more autonomy and decision-making). Just as with young children, moving through the years successfully depends upon the support of knowledgeable and caring adults. All adolescents need one or several adults who have "an irrational emotional attachment" to the young person. It is, as Bronfenbrenner states, "the illusion that comes with love."[14]

What would a responsive achieving middle school look like?

The benefits in schools of having a developmental student-centered focus are innumerable. The perspective:

- focuses the adults' attention on the children
- provides a framework for adults to consider children's behavior in a larger context
- enables adults to develop alternative strategies that promote children's health, self-esteem and learning
- helps the school community to develop supportive strategies that prevent problems before they develop.[15]

Hayes Mizell, Director of the Program for Student Achievement at the Edna McConnell Clark Foundation, recently stated:

It is a school whose mission, ethos, culture, structure, organization, curriculum, co-curriculum and instruction is explicitly dedicated to the achievement of every student and adult in the building… It is not a school where administrators and teachers assume they know all they need to know and that their work is limited to imparting their knowledge to students. In an achieving middle school the administrators, teachers and students understand that they all have something to teach and a lot to learn.[16]

In other words, the school must become an active **"learning community"** that involves every person at every level within the school. When that does not happen the mission may be given much lip-service but the structures, pedagogy and old cultural norms will undermine the support needed by students and the renewal of the system. Developmentally responsive middle level schools are characterized by having educators who enjoy young adolescents. Developmentally responsive schools have:[17]

• a shared vision based on research and practice
• high expectations for all (including teachers and administrators)
• a caring adult advocate for every student
• family and community partnerships
• and a positive school climate.

Now that's what Tribes Learning Communities are all about—how to make it happen!

You cannot have an achieving middle school unless it is an authentically caring school.

—HAYES MIZELL

31

3
Meeting Them Where They Are

3 Meeting Them Where They Are

It's 1:30 p.m. in Mrs. Scott's sixth grade class—admittedly not such a great time for the subject of math. But neither was morning. Mrs. S. is at the board working through beginning equations. Pencils are dropping on the floor, people are restless, many are whispering, sending notes, looking out the window and wondering how equations fit into the scheme of anything at all. Mrs. Scott raises her voice, "Class, pay attention. Joel stop talking. Pick up that book on the floor. You must give me your attention." The day drones on and on for students and teacher. Alone at last, Mrs. S. is worn out—much as she has been for the last ten years at the close of the day. "I cannot fight them anymore. The needs of this age group overwhelm me. Next year I just want to teach first grade."

A RESPONSIVE SCENARIO TO MEET STUDENT NEEDS

The vignette is not unique, and Mrs. Scott's frustration in reaching her students could be analyzed in many ways. The most obvious fact is that she is unaware that the restless behaviors and attitudes of her students are indicators that their new capacities and ways of learning are being ignored.

The challenge, therefore, is to find ways to engage the early onset of adolescence and its attendant freedoms and habits. How can we harness the ages thirteen to eighteen effectively for learning? The irony, of course, is that all these new realities, which only seem like problems are themselves powerful educational opportunities. The very qualities we deem destructive can be the sources of the motivation to learn.[1]
— Leon Botstein

Ultimately, Mrs. S. has only two options to manage her bored and restless students: (1) to control, to control, and lecture on; or (2) to create a responsive classroom culture and use participatory learning groups that engage them where they are. The latter option means Mrs. S. will become knowledgeable about the interlocking aspects of her students' intellectual, physical, social, emotional and moral devel-

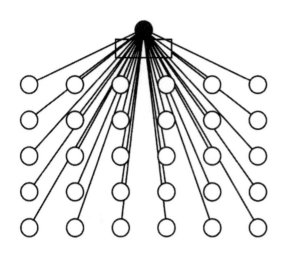

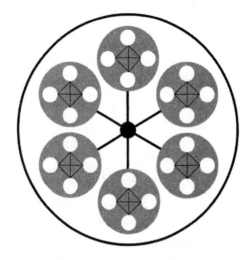

TEACHER-CENTERED INSTRUCTION   **STUDENT-CENTERED LEARNING**

opment. She will move from primarily relying upon teacher-centered direct instruction to student-centered active learning groups. Her classroom will look more like the illustration on the right.

The next chapters illustrate the big difference that this change makes for teachers and students, especially young teens.

The teacher-centered illustration above gives one a sense of what it takes for a teacher to maintain attention and control every moment every day. It is like trying to stand as a rock in a turbulent stream believing that the rigidity of the rock eventually will calm down the stream. The big secret (that liberates weary teachers) is that it is better to move along confluently with the river rather than to stand against it.[2] The cooperative approach of Tribes enables teachers to do that. It is similar to the philosophy and practice of Aikido, the Eastern art form that transforms conflict into harmony, and assures "win-win" outcomes for all parties. Aikido energy, known as "Aiki," consists of two gentle actions:

CONFLUENCE—empathizing and joining with an opponent, and

LEADING—utilizing a person's own energy to bring the person and one's self to balance.

The practice begins where the other person *is* and *centers on his or her welfare as well as one's own.*[3]

The Aikido metaphor illustrates one of the most effective relational skills. It assures "win-win" outcomes for students and teachers. Following are two brief scenarios on how the confluent approach could work in a "control" and "responsive" classroom.

CONTROL SCENARIO:

Mrs. S: "Joel, you must stop talking to Kelly and Scott."

Joel: "I just don't get what you're talking about."

Mrs. S: "Please be quiet. Pay attention. Ask me—not your neighbors."

Confluence means 'flowing with'—being the water and not the rock.
—TERRY DOBSON

CONFLUENCE SCENARIO:

Mrs. S: "Joel, I notice you talking to Kelly and Scott."

Joel: "I just don't get what you're talking about."

Mrs. S: "Would it be helpful to discuss and work on the problems with members of your tribe?"

Joel: "Yeah."

Mrs. S: "How many people would also like to work in groups after I finish the explanation?"

Unanimous show of hands.

In the example of Mrs. Scott's class, and probably your own, the students are being driven by two very natural developmental needs:

- to connect more closely to peers, and
- to solve problems independently of adults.

The traditional sit-in-straight-rows configuration and direct instruction question-answer talk is frustrating, no matter what time of the day math is taught. The structure is not confluent with the social and intellectual energy surging forth from the age group. There is no way to hold back the river of boredom and restless energy. It's more effective and enjoyable to tap the energy and swim with it.

The transfer of the learning process to student groups is responsive to where the students are in their stage of social and intellectual development. It provides active participation, and learning with peers and is student-centered.[4] It is the foundation of the Tribes Learning Community process.

CHANGING OUR VIEWPOINT

The wide range and diversity of early adolescent stages of development, characteristics, needs and assets could seem overwhelming enough for many teachers to go back to teaching first grade! But take heart! Remember we're seeing these 10-15 year olds' developmental needs in a different way—no longer as problems to squash or control. Rather than talking about the "needs" of the age group it is helpful to reframe our perspective from "adolescent needs" to "the tasks of adolescence." "Need" indicates a lack of something and denotes a deficit, whereas "task" is work to be accomplished. Understanding what tasks our students unconsciously are driving to achieve gives a perspective on the puzzling characteristics of the age group. Moreover, it helps educators and parents understand that rather than trying "to fix these kids" we need to fix the way we relate and work with them.[5]

The very qualities we deem destructive can be the sources of the motivation to learn.'

—LEON BOTSTEIN

THE TASKS OF EARLY ADOLESCENCE

The majority of the early adolescent characteristics and behavioral indicators fall into four tasks that our young friends, whether they realize it or not, are trying to achieve. The tasks are…

- autonomy and independence
- social competency
- a sense of purpose, and
- problem-solving—on their own.

Moving successfully into the adult world requires the fullest development of all four competencies—a good reason not to try to control all acting-out behaviors! They underlie the natural tasks that all 10 to 15 year olds are determined to accomplish. Amazingly enough, the four tasks of adolescence coincide with the characteristics of resiliency, which is the expressed goal of a Tribes Learning Community. Resiliency is the capacity to survive, to progress through difficulty, to bounce back and to move on positively again and again in life. This gives schools all the more reason to integrate the developmental tasks into the daily teaching and learning process. A comprehensive discussion on resilience is contained in Chapter 4.

Since adolescence is the age of the final establishment of a dominant positive ego identity, it is then that a future within reach becomes part of the conscious life plan.[6]

—ERIC ERICKSON

How does the process of Tribes help kids develop?

I'm so glad you asked!

The chart on the following pages details the components of the four tasks and how the process, culture and structure of Tribes TLC® supports their development.

HOW THE PROCESS OF TRIBES TLC® SUPPORTS THE TASKS OF EARLY ADOLESCENT DEVELOPMENT

ADOLESCENT TASKS	THE PROCESS OF TRIBES
AUTONOMY & INDEPENDENCE	
self-actualization	• builds personal identity • identifies skills, talents and gifts • empowers leadership • celebrates diversity
independence	• develops self-responsibility and resilience • teaches independent and democratic decision-making
internal locus of control	• uses reflection on behavior and interpersonal interactions • practices independent thinking within peer groups • affirms "right to pass" in group activity • teaches self-responsibility
self-esteem	• uses appreciation statements within peer learning groups • develops positive self-image • values respect for diversity
SOCIAL COMPETENCY	
pro-social behaviors	• trains adults to model and have students reflect on caring character qualities
communication skills	• teaches twelve communication/social skills
belonging	• structures long-term membership groups (tribes) in every classroom • assures inclusion of every student in a social learning group • uses many inclusion strategies
active participation	• trains teachers in use of cooperative and constuctivist learning methods • engages students actively through strategies that give influence and a sense of being valued
self-control/self-discipline	• involves peer groups to reflect upon and encourage helpful behavior • trains students in supportive peer-to-peer feedback

ADOLESCENT TASKS	THE PROCESS OF TRIBES
SENSE OF PURPOSE	
identity	• uses strategies for inclusion, presentation of self, and discovering gifts
positive expectations	• centers on high expectations for each and every person
personal goals	• encourages and practices attainment of personal and group goals, and service to others • centers on sharing, caring and community values
PROBLEM-SOLVING	
abstract thinking	• develops conceptual and contextual thinking • sets aside time to reflect on learning and group interaction
open-mindedness and flexibility	• seeks alternatives and builds creativity
emotional intelligence	• promotes conscious choice, social responsibility and resiliency
collaboration	• structures small groups and teaches collaborative skills so that learning groups work well together • teaches and practices democratic values, fairness and equity

Great! But I only have time to teach basics!

But what are "the basics" for these kids in the 21st century?

"THE BASICS" FOR THE NEW MILLENNIUM

Time out to think about it all! There have been only two other times in history when humankind moved through massive transitions that totally altered the world—two other times when humankind had to become competent in very different "basic skills" in order to survive. The ancient Age of Hunter-Gatherers gave way to the Age of Agriculture as nomads began to protect choice territories. The Age of Agriculture led to the Age of Industry as populations grew and mass production of goods and services were needed. Now the high-tech Information Age is impacting every aspect of life throughout the world.

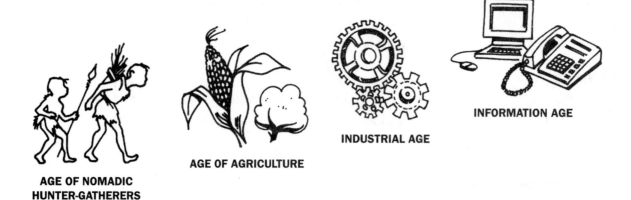

INFORMATION AGE

INDUSTRIAL AGE

AGE OF AGRICULTURE

AGE OF NOMADIC HUNTER-GATHERERS

The skills and knowledge developed in each of the Ages through time have been very different and critical to survival in the respective Age. The chart below highlights a few that people living in past Ages had to develop in order to live in their period of time.

KNOWLEDGE AND HUMAN STRENGTHS FOR THREE PAST AGES

HUNTER-GATHERERS	AGRICULTURE	INDUSTRY
Knowledge	*Knowledge*	*Knowledge*
survival in nature	survival from the land	survival in work organizations
making primitive tools	man/animal drawn tools	mechanization
tracking game	raising domestic animals	control of workers
fire building	planting/harvesting	mass production
		goods + services
sharing resources	trading/selling products	advertising
		reading, writing +mathematics
Strengths	*Strengths*	*Strengths*
physical	physical	physical, social and emotional
respect for nature	respect for family and land	respect for authority
independence	inter-dependence	co-dependence

Imagine what would have happened to people moving into the next new Age if they assumed the "basic skills and knowledge" of the past were sufficient for generations of the future. They would have continued to teach children...

- how to read animal tracks rather than literature
- how to use hand-plows rather than tractors
- how to communicate through oral legend rather than also writing
- how to use an abacus but not adding machines and calculators
- how to relate and live with one's own kind but not with a diversity of people in city workplaces.

Once again human beings must acquire totally different skills, knowledge and strengths in order to survive and thrive in an increasingly more complex world.

What should education be about today? The schooling that worked for yesterday? The Industrial Age of the last 150 years consisted of centralized workplaces in which people worked on pieces of prescribed tasks that required minimal communication with others, and little knowledge or influence over the end product, and therefore little satisfaction beyond paychecks. Systems that have prescribed methods had (and have) quantitative standards of output. The industrial authoritarian system, just like the DNA in cellular bodies, permeated all systems in American culture—particularly the schools which became factory models. Students were taught to be punctual, to follow orders and to do repetitive "seat-work" without making changes. Quantitative standards and tests were designed and redesigned to measure "out-put." Principles of participatory democracy were preached but seldom modeled as a way of relating, managing or teaching others.

DIFFERENT KNOWLEDGE AND SKILLS FOR A VERY DIFFERENT WORLD

The "basic skills," knowledge and people strengths of the Age of Industry out of necessity are being over-ridden today by this new Age of Information and Technology. People around the world are bombarded by instantaneous information, communication, changing systems, global world economics, global warming, multinationalism and multiculturism. The Age requires responsive, analytical, creative people at all socio-economic levels. Critical thinking is essential to sort out and synthesize complexities of information. Every bit as important are relational "people skills" for collaborative planning, collegiality, democratic leadership, mediation, team management, community development and teaching. Many years ago visionary writer Alvin Toffler coined the phrase "high-tech and high-touch," meaning that the coming era would usher into the world a balance of technology and relatedness. It has become evident this is the learning challenge now for humankind's survival.

Even the government is catching on! Each year the U.S. Department of Labor publishes what is known as the SCANS Report, the Secretary's Commission on Achieving Necessary Skills. The chart on the next page summarizes several years of their report for American education to consider. Notice that beyond what has long been considered the

SKILLS FOR THE 21ST CENTURY

BASIC SKILLS	THINKING SKILLS	PERSONAL QUALITIES
Reads, writes, performs arithmetic and mathematical operations, listens and speaks well	Thinks critically, makes decisions, solves problems, visualizes, knows how to learn and reason	Displays responsibility, self-esteem, sociability, self-management, integrity, and honesty

BASIC SKILLS

READING
locates, understands, and interprets written information in prose and in documents

WRITING
communicates thoughts, and messages in writing, and creates documents such as letters, directions, manuals, reports, graphs, and flow charts

ARITHMETIC/MATHEMATICS
performs basic computations and approaches practical problems by choosing appropriately from a variety of mathematical techniques

LISTENING
receives, attends to, interprets, and responds to verbal messages and other cues

SPEAKING
organizes ideas and communicates orally

THINKING SKILLS

CREATIVE THINKING
generates new ideas

DECISION MAKING
specifies goals and constraints, generates alternatives, considers risks, evaluates and chooses best alternative

PROBLEM SOLVING
recognizes problems, devises and implements a plan of action

SEEING THINGS IN THE MIND'S EYE
organizes and processes symbols, pictures, graphs, objects, and other information

KNOWING HOW TO LEARN
uses efficient learning techniques to acquire and apply new knowledge and skills

REASONING
discovers a rule or principle underlying the relationship between two or more objects and applies it when solving a problem

PERSONAL QUALITIES

RESPONSIBILITY
exerts a high level of effort and perseveres toward goal attainment

SELF-ESTEEM
believes in own self-worth and maintains a positive view of self

SOCIABILITY
demonstrates understanding, friendliness, adaptability, empathy, and politeness in group settings

SELF-MANAGEMENT
assesses self accurately, sets personal goals, monitors progress, and exhibits self-control

INTEGRITY/HONESTY
chooses ethical course of action

three basic skills, reading, writing and arithmetic, there are 13 other skills and personal qualities that are considered essential. The yearly reports emphasize that young people entering the adult world of work need to…

- know how to identify and organize information and resources
- relate well with others on teams
- understand social and organizational systems, and
- be ethical and responsible.

Schools focusing primarily on the traditional three academic R's with little concern for the other thirteen critical competencies may well be fulfilling the shocking prophecy contained in the SCANS Report:

More than half of our young people leave school without the knowledge or foundation required to find and hold a good job. These young people will pay a very high price. They face the bleak prospects of dead end work interrupted only by periods of unemployment.[7]

Moving between ages depends upon whether one is apprehensive and reactionary or knowledgeable and realistic. Clinging resolutely to "what was good enough for me in school" or "we just need more reading, riting and rithmetic" limits children of today to yesterday's world. Perhaps the predicament taking place now in American schools touches upon a warning given some years ago by social anthropologist, Margaret Mead:

So what will you teach the children?

We are now at a point where we must educate our children in what no one knew yesterday and prepare our schools for what no one knows yet.[8]

BETTER SCHOOLS JUST FOR GETTING JOBS?

Simplistic interpretation of the SCANS Report or going solely with the cry from business groups and many parents throughout the country that the primary purpose of schools is to prepare young people for the workplace shortchanges the higher and historic purpose of education. Better schools mean "better citizenship and richer, more caring lives."[9] Better schools that practice, indeed model, democratic principles and ethical relational values are the direct route to social justice and democracy.

AN EDUCATOR'S PERSPECTIVE

BY NANCY LINDHJEM

Nancy Lindhjem, Ed.S., is a school psychologist and a Tribes TLC® Trainer who has worked for more than 12 years in public school settings in Indianapolis, Indiana, using the Tribes process as the foundation for a wide range of middle and high school peer programs. She is in private practice with Children's Resource Group and, as a Tribes TLC® Master Trainer and Professional Development Consultant for Center Source, enthusiastically shares the philosophy and process of Tribes with educators across the country.

A TALE OF TWO SISTERS

During my last ten years as a Tribes trainer, whether in small rural communities or large urban areas, I have come to realize what may be the most important need for schools today… that is to develop positive school cultures. Nowhere does this need appear more critical than in our nation's middle schools, where the development of resilient students is an absolute must. This requires the implementation of three basic tenets: positive expectations for all students, a culture of caring and support, and active participation in learning. The process of Tribes clearly promotes and sustains these essential building blocks of education.

Recently, I had the opportunity to interact with two intelligent, independent, college-age women, one attending a college in Vermont, the other in Colorado. The insights I gleaned from these conversations will remain with me always. Their open and honest reflections on their middle and high school years speak volumes in regard to how to best educate and influence our youth of today.

Both of these young women strongly agreed that their middle school years were less than desirable. It seems that there were very few opportunities for them to develop relationships with their teachers. Both girls could only identify one teacher with whom they felt a real connection, one who took the time to know his students, who made them feel safe… and who engaged them in learning by practical applications to "real world" events. He held positive expectations for all of his students, not just a "chosen few."

In contrast, many of their other teachers often demonstrated attitudes that were perceived as critical, judgmental, and condescending. The girls reported seeing students being singled out and embarrassed in front of their peers, often for being different. The culture seemed to be one of competition and "looking good" in an authoritarian setting that seemed to reward compliant behavior over true learning. This only encouraged rebellion and resentment, which became a reality for these two young women.

Both girls had been in a segregated program for academically talented students, and over time found this practice more and more distasteful. They both felt it was unfair for certain segments of the school population to have opportunities that others didn't simply because of their intellectual abilities.

Due in part to these perceived inequities, the impersonal culture of their school, and the girls' need to be their "own person," they began to take on new identities—new friends, new habits (some illegal), new (and often negative) attitudes, new attire, and even new hair color (purple, green, flaming red). When these changes became obvious, no one but their parents seemed to notice. Adults at school who were expected to understand the behaviors of adolescence turned away. One guidance counselor who did notice, simply said, "We don't want people like you in our school."

The girls went on to tell the much more positive story of their high school experience. Fortunately, they managed to find their "niche" and came out of high school better people than when they went in. The differences from middle school to high school were dramatic. In middle school, when the girls were sent down to the office, they both felt scared and angry since the result was usually punishment, not understanding. In high school, however, they found concerned administrators and teachers who were willing to listen, problem solve, and who sought to understand these bright, young students. Genuine caring relationships began to replace the judgmental, critical comments and condescending attitudes they had experienced earlier. I was curious as to how these young women knew their teachers really cared. They both reported, "It showed." They knew their teachers as real human beings who cared about all of their students, regardless of their ability, attitude, or performance. Moreover, their teachers promoted deeper understanding of learning, not just rote memorization of facts to be recalled only long enough for a test on Friday.

As I completed my conversations with these amazing young leaders of tomorrow, I asked one of them if she could say one thing to her middle school teachers, what would that be? Her reply: "Please open your eyes. You're not living in the real world." Then I asked her what she would like to say to her high school teachers. Without missing a beat, she said proudly and gratefully, "Thank you!"

To all educators who recognize the value of your students and the myriad of gifts they have to offer, and to all who strive to provide them with a caring culture that ensures success, I say, "Thank you." To those educators who made a difference in the lives of the two young women highlighted here, I say an even louder, "THANK YOU"....because they are very important in my life. They happen to be my twin daughters, Anna and Ellie.

We cannot help but create better schools if we give attention to the balance needed between learning academics and assuring the development of teenagers in other basic competencies. The critical balance will be brought about as more and more schools recognize that becoming responsive and supportive of the natural inner drive of young adolescents for…

autonomy and independence

a sense of purpose and identity

social competency and

the right to solve their own problems

…is the path to excellence.

Ah! A Tribes School

4 *Assuring Futures of Promise*

4 Assuring Futures of Promise

IN THIS CHAPTER YOU WILL....

- Meet research-author Bonnie Benard who summarizes what smart schools can do to enable young adolescents to develop the attributes of resiliency
- Realize how the attributes are key to achievement, health and well-being
- Learn how your school can also assure futures of promise for students

So many kids come from neighborhoods and families with overwhelming problems. It's hard to know what to do....

Yes, poverty, unemployment, lack of health care, inadequate childcare, community crime, divorce, alcoholism, drug abuse and stress surround many young teens in our classrooms. True, today's world is harsh for many young people.

Yet there are those who somehow live through deprivation, adversity and stress more easily than others. Why do some children in a family do well while others raised in the same environment fail?

The answer is to be found in the exciting longitudinal studies on human resiliency, which finally are being brought to the attention of schools throughout the nation. Unlike the typical problem focused pathology approach which diagnoses what is wrong with kids (risk factors), resiliency research identifies the positive factors in children's lives that enable them to meet and overcome life stress. Throughout more than forty years, Dr. Emily Werner studied the lives of children who were growing up in high risk conditions such as neglect, poverty, war, parental abuse, physical handicaps, depression, criminality and alcoholism. A percentage of the children did develop various problems, but to the amazement of the researchers, a greater number moved into adulthood as competent and healthy adults. The greater number had developed the capacity to face and overcome life difficulties. Werner describes these children as "vulnerable but invincible."[1]

THE ATTRIBUTES OF RESILIENCY

The longitudinal studies of Emily Werner and other researchers highlight four human attributes that are evident in resilient children and adults. They have developed....

- **AUTONOMY:** an internal locus of control, a strong sense of independence, power, self-efficacy, self-discipline and control of impulses
- **SOCIAL COMPETENCE:** pro-social behaviors such as responsivess, empathy, caring, communication skills and a sense of humor
- **A SENSE OF PURPOSE AND FUTURE:** healthy expectations, goal directedness, belief in a bright and compelling future, motivation, persistence, hopefulness, hardiness, a sense of anticipation and a sense of coherence
- **A CAPACITY TO PROBLEM-SOLVE:** abstract and constructive thinking, a capacity to analyze and reflect on possibilities and creative solutions; flexibility.

It is no coincidence that (as we realized in the previous chapter) the same set of attributes are what young adolescents are striving to develop—consciously or unconsciously. These are the important "tasks of adolescence," remarkably enough also identified through studies on *human development*.

Take time out now and think of those times in your own life when somehow you were able to move through a difficult situation or period of time, when you were able to face and overcome a seemingly insurmountable difficulty due to your own resilient strengths.

I know it every day as a teacher!

A PERSPECTIVE ON RESILIENCE[2]

BY BONNIE BENARD

Bonnie Benard, MSW, is a Senior Program Associate at the WestEd Regional Educational Laboratory, School and Community Health Research Group. Since 1982 she has provided research support and conceptual frameworks for understanding and addressing prevention and youth development issues. In addition to her writing and consultation, she gives workshops and presentations internationally on the topic of resiliency and youth development. Bonnie's insights have long served as guiding principles for the caring culture of Tribes.

Resiliency requires changing hearts and minds.

—*BONNIE BENARD*

CREATING RESILIENT SYSTEMS BY ENGAGING THE DEVELOPMENTAL WISDOM OF ADOLESCENCE

In an age of standards–driven educational reform and "get tough on youth" social policies, we must ask, where is human development? We see, once again, human development (referred to as youth development during the adolescence years) pushed aside as a "nice" but nonessential concern for education and prevention. Ironically, this is happening at a time when the best of social and behavioral science research is consistently documenting that the most effective, efficient, and joyful approach to meeting standards and preventing health-risk behaviors in young people is by creating environments in our schools that meet adolescents' developmental needs and thereby engage their intrinsic motivation.

Brain science, multiple intelligence research, motivational psychology, effective schools research, child and youth development, and long-term studies of individual resilience in the face of risk and challenge are finding that healthy development and successful learning are the product of critical developmental supports and opportunities. However, it is to resilience research—the long-term studies of positive human development in the face of environmental threat, challenge, stress, risk, and adversity—that educators and preventionists can turn to find the most powerful research-based answer to what these supports and opportunities should look like for *all* young people in all schools.[3] They consist of three simple and common-sensical principles of effectiveness:

- caring relationships
- positive expectation messages and beliefs, and
- opportunities for participation and contribution.[4]

Whenever and wherever you find a school achieving positive academic outcomes for *all* children—not just the few—you will find this commonsense philosophy driving the mission of the school.

CARING RELATIONSHIPS

Caring relationships are the supportive connections to others that model and support healthy development and well-being. Ultimately, they weave the fabric of a safe and resilient school. Caring relationships have been identified by these longitudinal studies of human resilience, program evaluation research, the recent National Longitudinal Study of Adolescent Health,[5] qualitative studies, and personal stories as the most critical factor protecting healthy and successful child and youth development even in the face of multiple risks.

Caring relationships are those of mutual trust in which someone is "there" for a youth. This is demonstrated by having adults in the school who take an active interest in who the young person is, being respectful, having compassion for a youth's life circumstances, and paying attention and actively listening to and talking with the youth. During adolescence the peer group emerges as a critical provider of this essential support.

HIGH EXPECTATION MESSAGES

High expectation messages refer to the consistent communication of direct and indirect messages that the young person can and will succeed. These messages are at the core of caring relationships and reflect the adult's (and friend's) belief in the youth's innate resilience and ability to learn. The message, *"You can make it; you have everything it takes to achieve your dreams; I'll be there to support you,"* is a theme in resilience research and a pivotal protective factor in the family, school, and/or community environments of youth who have overcome the odds.

In addition to this challenge plus support message, a high expectation approach conveys firm guidance—clear boundaries and the structure necessary for creating a sense of safety and predictability—not to enforce compliance and control but to allow for the freedom and exploration necessary to develop autonomy, identity, and self-control. A high expectation

You can make it; you have everything it takes to achieve your dreams; I'll be there to support you.

approach is also individually-based and strengths-focused. This means identifying each youth's unique strengths, gifts, and callings and nurturing them as well as using them to work on needs or concerns.

OPPORTUNITIES FOR PARTICIPATION AND CONTRIBUTION

Resilience research has documented the positive developmental outcomes, including reductions in health-risk behaviors and increases in academic success factors, that result when youth are given the chance to belong to a group; to have responsibilities; to be involved in relevant, engaging, and respected activities; to have a voice and choice; to make decisions; to plan; and to have ownership and leadership. Most importantly, resilience research and outcome evaluations of service learning and cooperative learning find positive academic and social outcomes when youth are given the opportunity to give back their gifts—to be of service to other people, to nature, to their community and world. Providing young people with opportunities for meaningful participation is a natural outcome of schools and classrooms that convey high expectations.

It is no coincidence that resilience and other social and behavioral research continually identify these three characteristics as supporting healthy and successful outcomes. It is precisely through caring relationships, high expectation messages, and opportunities for participation and contribution that we engage our students' intrinsic motivation—their drive to meet their developmental needs for safety, love, belonging, respect, mastery, challenge, power and identity, and, ultimately, for meaning.

Having high expectations assumes that 'one size never fits all.'

The people and places most often identified in the resilience research as providing these three "protective" factors—thus meeting students' developmental needs—were teachers and schools. In the words of Emmy Werner:

One of the wonderful things we see now in adulthood is that these children really remember one or two teachers who made the difference. They mourn some of those teachers more than they do their own family members because what went out of their lives was a person who looked beyond outward experience, their behavior, and their often times unkempt appearance—and saw the promise. [6]

Resilience research has also found that schools that not only have these turnaround teachers but that have fair and equitably enforced rules, a lot of varied opportunities to succeed, and that give students a decision-making voice and opportunities to work with and be helpful to others, become safe havens for students to develop cognitively, socially, emotionally, physically, and spiritually. In the words of one student, *"School was my church, it was my religion. It was constant, the only thing that I could count on every day....I would not be here if it was not for school."* In other words, they become places where students' developmental needs are honored and placed centrally in the mission of the school. Let's look at what these mean for schools.

SAFETY refers to both physical and emotional safety. For healthy development and successful learning to occur our children must feel safe in their classrooms and schools. Brain research tells us that when children do *not* feel safe, their brain stays in a vicious fight-flight circuit. In order to engage higher order thinking skills and creativity, a child must feel safe.

The gut response measures often taken by politicians and some school administrations to school safety often become barriers to achieving real school safety. The hiring of more police officers and security guards; installing sophisticated weapon detection and student surveillance devices; toughening punishments for children who misbehave; and attempting to identify students at risk for becoming mass murderers often only further marginalize youth that are "different"—making them feel even more unsafe. And do you remember that Columbine High School students, Eric Harris and Dylan Kliebold, did not feel safe in their schools? Real safety only comes through building an inclusive school community in which diversity is honored and all students are welcomed into the circle. A first step in creating a safe classroom and school is inviting students to create their own agreements/ ground rules… such as occurs in schools using the process of Tribes.

LOVE AND BELONGING refers to basic *affiliation and attachment* needs—the need to be *connected to people and places* that ultimately gives all of our lives meaning and hope. Meeting academic standards requires starting with relationships. No quote has ever stated this more eloquently than the following words of Nel Noddings:

> *At a time when the traditional structures of caring have deteriorated, schools must be places where teachers and students live together, talk with each other, take delight in each other's company. My guess is that when schools focus on what really matters in life, the cognitive ends we now pursue so painfully and artificially will be achieved somewhat more naturally… It is obvious that children will work harder and do things—even odd things like adding fractions—for people they love and trust.* [7]

What does this mean for your school? It means we must put *relationships* at the heart of what we do in our classrooms and schools. There are hundreds of ways to do this: *making one-to-one connections* with a student—even for a few seconds is a powerful acknowledgement; shaking hands, actively listening, being available, showing an interest, noticing something they're doing right, and so on. In some schools, every student is assigned to an adult who checks in with him or her at least once a week.

Besides student-teacher connections, we have to create inclusive classroom communities where *all* students feel invited in. Cooperative learning groups and peer-helping in which *all* students can be helpers—even challenged students can help younger youth—are critical strategies for building belonging. This means paying special attention to who's not currently included and including them. Healthy development requires that students stay connected; relationships must be maintained and responsibilities honored.

Class size reduction can be an effective support for teacher-student relationship-building. It gives classroom teachers more and more opportunities to get to know and connect with their students. At the school level, it means breaking up large schools into smaller schools such as schools-within-schools, academies, and career magnets. In classrooms, it means that each student is a member in an on-going "tribe." Relationships cannot happen in large anonymous groups.

It is human nature to create our own small groupings because we are all seeking safety and belonging. As educators we need to create small heterogeneous groupings in which everyone has a place and diversity is honored as it is in Tribes Learning Communities. After school activities also provide a great opportunity to create small groupings with an adult serving as facilitator/mentor. These can range from support groups of all kinds to interest-based groups to community-service groups.

RESPECT The need or drive to be respected—to be acknowledged and honored for who we are—is a powerful motivator. Lack of respect—along with lack of caring and boredom—are usually the top three reasons school dropouts give for leaving school. May I suggest that if we want good outcomes in the traditional 3 R's: Reading, Riting, and Rithmetic, we need an additional 3 R's: Relationship, Respect, and Responsibility. Debra Meier's turnaround school, Central Park East in Harlem, put both relationships and respect at the heart of her school's mission. She wrote,

> *Maybe mutual respect is what we're all looking for—which means feeling sure the other person acknowledges us, sees us for who we are—as equal in value and importance. When there's enough respect, perhaps we're able to give up tight control over our youngsters, and give them more space to make their own decisions, including their own mistakes.*[8]

Once again, there are hundreds of ways school staff can show respect to students. Primarily, however, if we want students to be respectful to us, we must model it first. Attentive listening and speaking nonjudgmentally, shaking hands, using a Namaste greeting mean, "I greet the soul within you." Once again, a small group process like Tribes is a powerful structure for promoting a respectful climate in which teasing, harassment, bullying, and other forms of violence are not tolerated.

MASTERY AND CHALLENGE The drive for accomplishment—to be good at something—is inborn in all of us. Where we have our problems in schooling is when we have very narrowly defined what that "something" can be. We have assigned greater value to mathematical and linguistic intelligences, and in terms of the physical—to sports participation over dance—than the rest of these intelligences. This is what our culture values and yes, students need to learn. However, Howard Gardner and his disciples of multiple intelligences tell us that we need to use the strengths—the intelligences students are especially good in—to address the areas of

If we want good outcomes in the traditional 3 R's: Reading, Riting, and Rithmetic, we need an additional 3 R's: Relationship, Respect, and Responsibility.

challenge. To have someone with the power of a teacher acknowledge your gifts is an incredible motivator that facilitates learning in the challenging areas. I would like to point out that the strengths especially found in resilience literature include competencies in all these areas—especially the inter and intra-personal areas, creativity and outlets for the imagination.

So what does this mean for schools?

It means we have to create opportunities for success in each of these intelligences. We need to do activities in school in which we learn the interests, strengths, gifts, and dreams of each of our students. We need after school clubs *where students* can explore their interests in small groups. What about sports teams open to any student who wants to play? We need to value each of the gifts that our young people bring. Our artists need to have their work displayed and honored as much as the athletes have their trophies displayed. I might mention that in Columbine High School the sports trophies were showcased in the front hall—the artwork down a back corridor. Sports pages in the yearbook were in color, a national debating team and other clubs in black and white. The homecoming king was a football player on probation for burglary.

Challenge is a related drive to mastery but refers more to the idea of taking risks. Adolescents especially need to have opportunities to take *healthy* risks. Do you know that although *risk-taking* is often on lists of risk factors, it is also one of the characteristics of successful people? We now have a wonderful study of *adventure learning* that illustrates how this approach (also referred to as Outward Bound and other outdoor experience programs such as Adventures Cross Country and National Outdoor Leadership Program) not only helps adolescents achieve all of the developmental tasks—autonomy and independence, social competency, a sense of purpose, and problem-solving—it produces positive academic outcomes as well—even though it is a nonacademic program.[9] Why is this so powerful? Among many attributes, adventure programs create a restorative environment—especially through group process and support—in which most of adolescents' developmental needs are met.

Providing ropes courses and challenge courses through after school programming is one obvious approach. However, this research also makes the case for experiential learning—hands on, working in groups under adults' supervision and facilitation, and time for reflection. Sound familiar? These are also the characteristics of the process of Tribes.

POWER AND AUTONOMY are the needs not only to find one's *identity* but to discover oneself as an autonomous person. We're talking here about self-efficacy—knowing you can take action and influence your environment. Youth who feel a sense of their own worth and power don't need guns to feel powerful; they don't need to hurt others or themselves to prove they exist and matter.

How do we meet a student's need to have some power and control? We give them opportunities to participate and contribute in an ongoing way in our classrooms and schools. Once again, while approaches like cooperative learning, peer helping, and service learning meet this drive, the bottom line is having personal control—chances to make decisions about their own schooling. This means we as teachers and administrators don't impose our ideas of what students need—*we ask them*. This is the simple strategy of asking students their opinions, their needs, their ideas—and acting on them—not tokenizing them. Having your students create the governing rules of the classroom is a key strategy. When a problem develops, we can bring the students in on it, inviting their ideas of how we—as a classroom community—can solve it. In order to develop healthy psychological autonomy, adolescents need safety and the room to grow *within* the structure of a caring community.

MEANING Last—and certainly not least but probably the most important!—is the search for meaning that lies at the heart of every human life. Humans, including adolescents, have the need to find meaning in what they do. Our genetic code makes us meaning-makers, constructors of our own knowledge. We must find purpose and relevance in what we do or we experience a *disconnect*—a sense of alienation from our true *sense of calling*. The loss of meaning is probably one of the major underlying reasons that 40% of our teens have unmet mental health needs—especially depression and stress. Government figures from 1998 show reductions in almost all teen health-risk behaviors: violence, alcohol and tobacco use, and drug abuse. However, depression, suicidality, and suicide are statistics that are *not* going down.

Schools need to be safe places for the exploration of the critical existential questions that drive not only the adolescent search for meaning but all of our quests for a meaningful life.[10]

- *Who am I? What is my true nature?*—This is the search for identity.
- *What do I love? What are my interests, and dreams?*—This is the search for autonomy and meaning.
- *How shall I live? What values do I wish to live by?*—This is the search for morality.
- *What is my gift to the family of the earth? What are my strengths and gifts? How can I make a difference?*—This is the search for purpose.

These questions of purpose are not particularly comfortable for schools. In fact, purpose is primarily taught in the curriculum through goal-setting and decision-making, and career exploration—most often with strictly rational techniques. We need to include the spiritual dimension—the above questions—if we are to help students make the deepest connection of all—to see themselves as interconnected to others, to nature, and to life itself.

HOW DO SCHOOLS DO THIS?

Some schools use the Council process, a circle or group process that creates a climate of safety, respect, and honor to reflect and share in community these deep yearnings.[11] Others use Tribes Community Circles which accomplish the caring community culture of connectedness in a similar way.

Educators can also provide experiences that honor the questions and allow students to give their gifts to the world through creative expression—theater, dance, photography, video production, art, music, storytelling, and creative writing. Research on the arts is documenting the power of creative expression to achieve the developmental tasks of adolescence—as well as positive academic outcomes.[12] Similarly, research on *community service learning,* in which students can connect what they learn in schools to the real world and see themselves as active contributors, also achieves the developmental tasks and promotes academic success.[13]

The common denominator running through the above strategies and approaches that meet adolescent developmental needs and thus help youth achieve their developmental tasks is that of *small group process.* Group process *is* the vehicle for creating a caring community—for students and for educators. In fact, Thomas Sergiovanni writes, *"The need for community is universal. A sense of belonging, of continuity, of being connected to others and to ideas and values that make ourselves meaningful and significant—these needs are shared by all of us."*[14]

Schools will be transformed only when this community-building process is implemented for teachers as well as for students. The critical challenge for the 21st century does not lie in mastering this piece of information or that technology. It lies in creating connectedness—in building schools across the nation that tap the innate developmental wisdom that is our shared humanity, connecting us to each other and to our shared web of life.

See me beautiful…
Look for the best in me
It's what I really am
And all I want to be,
It may take some time
It may be hard to find…
See me beautiful.

See me beautiful…
Each and every day,
Could you take a chance—
Could you find a way
To see me shining through
In everything I do—
And see me… beautiful.
                    —Song by Red Grammer[15]

5 A Culture for Growing Early Adolescents

5 A Culture for Growing Early Adolescents

IN THIS CHAPTER YOU WILL LEARN THAT....

- Whatever becomes the focus of a school affects everything and everyone in the system
- A caring community culture is the essential first step toward school improvement… and schools being able to be responsive to the needs of young adolescents
- The process of Tribes TLC® not only establishes a positive culture but also structures a caring community of learners and active learning groups
- The recommended components of an ideal learning culture are incorporated in the process of Tribes TLC®

Creating a setting is one of man's most absorbing experiences, compounded as it is of dreams, hopes, efforts and thought.[1]
—Seymour Sarason

THE CRITICAL PARADOX

Today after more than forty years of debate on how to lift the nation's schools from mediocrity to a level of educational excellence the national consensus is that a rigorous focus on standards, curriculum and testing—and not children's development—is the solution. As compelling as the new mandate may be, there is little guarantee in research or practice that any prescribed "mechanical remedy" in and of itself will be successful.[2] Distinguished Professor Linda Darling-Hammond of Stanford University warns that "what looks like clarity at the top may contribute more clutter at the bottom."[3]

The paradox has been researched extensively and cited for years, in no uncertain terms, by James Comer. He firmly believes that the priority on academic curriculum and testing is what deeply ails American education.

Even people in education who are sensitive to child development focus on curriculum/instruction/assessment first, and I argue that it should be development first and that development should guide everything else.[4]

Inasmuch as Tribes is an active learning process, we would like you to take a few moments to prove something to yourself. Following are two circles each with three wider circles around them. The center of the circle on the left is labeled "SCT," "standards/curriculum/testing." The circle on the right is "AdDev," "adolescent development."

Ask yourself, "what would the culture (spirit and expectations) within the school be like if the focus had become "standards/curriculum/testing (SCT)?" Jot down a few descriptive words in the left side column on the next page. Now ask yourself what might the culture look like, feel like, sound like if the focus of the school had become "adolescent development (AdDev)?" Write a few words in the column on the right.

 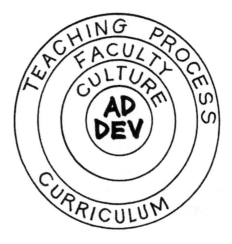

Beyond the culture in each school, ask yourself what would the faculties in the two different schools have to do, learn and work on? Finally, what would the teaching process and curriculum be like in each school?

SCT SCHOOL	ADDEV SCHOOL

Sure, it's okay to write in this book!

Whatever becomes the main focus of a school drives everything throughout the system. School culture, discipline policy, curriculum, teaching methods, assessment, supervision, use of resources, quality of relationships, professional development, staff morale... all are determined by the focus.

Never for a moment think that we do not urge all schools to define and assess learning and have standards. This is especially important for a middle level school committed to the fullest dimensions of development for its students. The question is: What are the standards about? Only academic achievement? Or, also the degree to which a student is developing as a smart and capable person in all aspects of his or her personhood? A middle level school that is committed to adolescent development, will define meaningful standards relevant to the abilities that students *demonstrate* as a result of learning. Assessments will reflect their capacity to apply concepts and information to real-life issues, to work collaboratively with peers, to mediate conflict, to problem-solve, to assess personal and group learning—and demonstrate self-responsibility, ethical character values and respect for others.

Nel Noddings, Professor of Child Education at Stanford University, also is a strong advocate of the developmental approach:

In direct opposition to the current emphasis on academic standards, a national curriculum and national assessment, I have argued that our main educational aim should be to encourage the growth of competent, caring, loving and loveable people. Our society does not need to make its children first in the world in mathematics and science. It needs to care for its children—to reduce violence, to respect honest work of every kind, to reward excellence at every level, to ensure a place for every child and emerging adult in the economic and social world, to produce people who can care for their own families and contribute effectively to their communities.[5]

The Big Idea!

Though often discussed, often written into mission statements, often highlighted at conferences and from podiums, the social, emotional and ethical/spiritual development of students as human beings is seldom recognized by educators, politicians and anxious communities as the pathway to academic learning. It is the business community that recognizes that more adults lose jobs, not out of a lack of workplace skills, but due to their inability to work well with others.

"Kids development as whole people = success!
What if everyone got it?"

That would raise a very different set of initial questions at the national level and in school communities. The first debate would not be "which reading or math curriculum should we purchase this year?" The school community would explore…

- Who are these children? How do they learn?
- What tasks of adolescence are they facing during the next few years?
- What strengths, skills and knowledge do they need in order to do well in tomorrow's world?
- How can they become life-long learners for this age of information?
- How does social and emotional development contribute to academic achievement?
- What do we as adults, the stakeholders in the futures of these kids, need to learn?
- What steps need to be initiated in our school?

These questions are not the usual list of school problems to be managed, solved or repeatedly funded. They are not about identifying the "kids-at risk." The questions flow out of the conviction that all students are "kids-at-promise"—and that our responsibility is to establish a motivational school environment in which all will experience success because they are growing into the fullness of their gifts and humanity.

Compelling studies point out steps to achieve high performance middle level schools.[6] How to take the first step of creating the ideal learning culture, we can immodestly say, is to follow the sequential process steps that hundreds of Tribes Learning Communities are taking.

THE DEVELOPMENTAL PROCESS OF TRIBES TLC®— AN OVERVIEW

The swirling circle illustration on the next page could be considered the synopsis of this book. It illustrates the renewal process that a school community deliberately establishes to maximize development and learning for middle school adolescents.

Yes! We visual learners like the next illustration! Thank you!

THE DEVELOPMENTAL PROCESS OF TRIBES

The goal of the school, which is represented in the center of the illustration, is to foster the full range of human development and meaningful learning for the young adolescents of the school. Three positive strategies, noted in the out-reaching circles, support the achievement of the school community goal.

CIRCLE 1: The whole school community establishes a culture of caring and challenge to support the goal of human development and learning.

CIRCLE 2: The whole school community is structured into collaborative learning groups that sustain the culture.

CIRCLE 3: Teachers trained in the process of TribesTLC® facilitate active learning strategies, experiences and projects that are student-centered, and responsive to the developmental tasks middle level adolescents are striving to accomplish.

You need to tell 'em more about the big picture.

Yes! Fly along here we go...

THE IMPORTANCE OF A SAFE AND CARING CULTURE

Growing healthy kids is somewhat like growing geraniums. Whether you have a green thumb or not, plants have little chance to grow unless they are in rich soil and watered well. It just won't do to bring home a bright new geranium and wedge it into the old pot of soil left by a plant that just withered and died.

Getting ready to develop the personal best in 10–15 year olds works the same way. For all to bloom and do well, nutrients for growth must be continually available and released all day long. Growing plants in good soil and students in a nurturing culture means they do not need one-by-one "fixing." The whole batch will bloom—perhaps at different times, but each in their own uniqueness and radiance.

Walk into any school or classroom and you will sense that each has a culture of its own. Some are caring and friendly, others harsh and dispassionate. All have impact on how people in the system live, learn and work together. The primary reason that efforts toward school renewal fail is because the nature of the school's culture is dismissed as unimportant. It needs to be recognized as the primary resource to be renewed or altered for adolescents' growth and learning.

Culture is the climate, the environment and spirit in a school that permeates everything that goes on within the classrooms, the staff and other groups. Culture is shaped out of the historical patterns that include the unspoken norms, values, beliefs, ceremonies, rituals, traditions and myths underlying how people think and how they act. The elements of the culture are seldom recognized or discussed though they affect everything that happens in the school. A great exercise is to have your faculty list some of the unspoken beliefs they may have about teaching, student learning, discipline, and the students of the school. Would you hear any of the following?

Those kids just can't learn.

As a faculty we don't ask each other for advice.

We don't need professional development.

Behavior on the playground won't improve.

Smart students do as they are told.

Awards are motivational.

Awards are not motivational.

The parents just don't care.

> *It is only by reculturing a school beforehand or along with any restructuring effort that meaningful improvement can be made.[7]*
>
> —MICHAEL FULLAN

Assumptions like these may or may not have factual basis, yet when they permeate a school for a long time they sustain a negative climate. If the staff assumes certain children cannot learn, one way or another the self-images of those students also will confirm just that. Never doubt that the myths, core beliefs, values, and unspoken relational norms are not an active influence on the school system every day.

The purpose of schools is to develop capable and healthy human beings. Studies on how the human brain works clearly show that threat, intimidation and emotional stress close down cognitive thinking and learning.[8] As one third grader told his teacher when asked why he gave up working with a new group, he said, "Oh, my brain downshifted—I got pushed and called a name." Whenever threatening negative behaviors become the daily norms of a classroom, the whole class can "downshift." Discovering gifts in middle school is impossible in an unfriendly stressful environment. Discipline policies, curricula, new buildings or an abundance of computers matter little if the school culture centers on institutional mandates and expediency rather than the very human needs of young adolescents. Whereas positive school cultures correlate strongly with increased student achievement, development and motivation—and also with teacher productivity and satisfaction!

THE COMPONENTS OF A POSITIVE SCHOOL CULTURE

Jerome Bruner, respected cognitive and developmental psychologist from Harvard, Oxford and New York University, writes:

> *What is needed in America—as in most countries of the developed world—is not simply a renewal of the skills that make a country a better competitor in the world markets, but a renewal and reconsideration of what is called **school culture.** On the basis of what we have learned in recent years about human learning—it is best when it is **participatory, proactive, communal, collaborative and given over to constructive meanings rather than receiving them.** We do even better at teaching science, math, and languages in such schools than in more traditional ones.*[10]

Those of you who already are familiar with the process of Tribes, will recognize that the Tribes Learning Community® process incorporates the components of the ideal school learning culture.

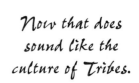

Now that does sound like the culture of Tribes.

It is difficult to think of a reform initiative of significance that can proceed successfully without understanding and attention to the culture of individual schools.[9]

—JOHN GOODLAD

IDEAL LEARNING CULTURE	THE TRIBES PROCESS
COMMUNAL	builds inclusion for all uses cooperative learning transfers responsibility to groups promotes caring and sharing celebrates community learning
PARTICIPATORY	reaches all students through meaningful participation uses interactive strategies encourages peer leadership
PROACTIVE	uses positive agreements to assure a caring culture reaches students of multiple intelligences, abilities and cultures trains teachers to use brain compatible methods and communication
COLLABORATIVE	invites influence uses consensus strategies promotes teacher collegiality
CONSTRUCTIVE MEANING	involves students in research and learning meaningful content uses student planning groups

Creating a positive school culture to support adolescent development and learning depends upon people agreeing how they will connect to and respect each other. Clear positive agreements need to replace negative norms. Shared beliefs on student development and learning, core teaching concepts, and a common vision for all students of the school are essential. Each day we need to ask, "Is the overall climate of our school supportive, challenging and caring?"

AN ADMINISTRATOR'S PERSPECTIVE

BY CAROLINE WONG

Caroline Wong, M.Ed., has over 30 years of experience in education as a teacher, principal and trainer. As the Principal for 10 years of the Moanalua Middle School in Honolulu, and now as a consultant and trainer for the Department of Education of Hawaii, she is striving to assist all schools to develop an integrated and comprehensive system to support the success of all students. Caroline believes that the process of Tribes is an essential key to proactive and preventive support for middle level students.

WHY TRIBES TLC® FOR MIDDLE SCHOOLS?

A warm aloha to all of you from Hawaii! I am in my tenth year as principal of Moanalua Middle School which is located on the island of O'ahu about three miles from Honolulu International Airport, crossroads of the Pacific. We have 890 seventh and eighth graders who reflect the ethnic and socioeconomic diversity of our community. About one-third of our students are military dependents and come to us from all over the United States and the world. Truly, our student body is like a rainbow, reflecting the beauty and color and cultural diversity.

Our school had been a traditional junior high school for more than twenty-five years. In the early 90's, as our student population began to change and reflect more challenging learning needs and behaviors, we clearly understood that "if we continued to do the same things, we would continue to get the same less than satisfactory results." A staff team was trained in the total quality improvement process and we began utilizing this process to focus on improved teaching and learning for all students. One of the key principles of the total quality process is systems change. School restructuring is dynamic change that is positive and purposeful and involves changing the system or model of how we do things. It goes far beyond tinkering and making adjustments.

All members of the staff became part of the learning community as we explored the research on early adolescent developmental needs; grappled with our basic core beliefs and philosophy about effective teaching and learning for middle schoolers; and created a shared vision of a restructured school that would best serve the needs of all kids. As we ventured forth on the challenging journey to create a supportive learning environment, we were guided by that compelling vision of achievement for our students.

Structural changes now: (1) support all students and teachers in heterogeneously grouped interdisciplinary teams; (2) provide daily planning and conferencing time for teacher teams; (3) include a half-hour daily advisory period called *Connections* with one of the team teachers; and (4) provide a framework for using time within a flexible block schedule where teacher teams, not bells, determine the time and structure of the class to best address student learning needs.

In addition to these structural changes, teaching practices that more effectively address the developmental needs of early adolescents have resulted in improved classroom interactions and learning experiences. Teaching and learning has moved from mostly paper and pencil activities to "hands-on" work in cooperative groups; and from specific assignments and projects in content areas to more comprehensive and integrated problem-based learning experiences.

Despite all of these restructuring and instructional improvement efforts, there was still a large missing piece—a process to create and sustain the desired positive culture in our "system" and in every classroom. Every school has a culture which can most often be felt by simply walking on the campus. As a former social studies teacher, I refer to culture in the broadest sense. The culture of a school reflects shared beliefs, values and practices; a common language and methods of communication; how members live, interact and work together; and what traditions are valued and celebrated. It is not dependent on the school leader, but is truly shared and woven into the fabric of school life, extending into our homes through partnerships with parents and community groups. Research results clearly demonstrate that the classroom culture and supportive learning environment have a direct impact on the learning process and contribute to improved student achievement.

At Moanalua Middle School, this heart-shaped vacuum has been filled through a schoolwide commitment to the Tribes TLC® process which has become our "new way of learning and being together." The entire staff, including clerical, custodial, and cafeteria staff, was trained in Tribes. Tribes now defines how everyone in our learning community interacts and grows personally and professionally.

To sustain the Tribes process, strengthen the teaching methodology and build capacity, three staff members have been trained as Tribes trainers. The character education program, based upon a set of identified core ethical values, has been integrated through the Tribes process to further intensify the positive school culture and extend it through service learning to others in the community. The daily half-hour *Connections* time provides a structure to address ever-changing burning issues for early adolescents. The goals for *Connections* are to improve student skills in communication, decision-making, and problem solving. *Connections* also provides the framework for systemic training in the Tribes processes, allows students to be active participants in their own learning, and supports the Tribes processes to be replicated in every classroom across content areas.

As a learning community, we have recognized: (1) that organizations do not change… people change, (2) that change is a process, not an event… and (3) that change is personal and developmental. The Tribes path has truly become an integral part of the journey for improved achievement for all students at Moanalua Middle School.

I get it! The culture of a school is its soul.

6 Creating the Learning Community

6 Creating the Learning Community

IN THIS CHAPTER YOU WILL LEARN....

- The importance and meaning of community to support the learning tasks of young adolescents
- How collaborative groups of learners can transform a school system
- How the four Tribes TLC® agreements guide the school community
- About the stages of group development that are the foundation of the Tribes process
- About traveling along the Tribes Trail Map

Establishing community in our school, meaningful relationships between adults and students, was as important as all the changes made in teaching, curriculum and assessment.[1]

—Deborah Meier

WHY COMMUNITY?

Follow any early adolescent for a day (exhausting—yes!) and it becomes obvious that making connections and belonging to a group is what drives their "energizer batteries." Slow a few of the skateboarders down and they will name friends in the skateboarder after-school community. The same will happen among other school groups, whether known as the computer nerds, jocks, cheerleaders, yardbirds (smokers), cools, weirdos, stars, regulars, and others of more unique nomenclature. Likes gravitate to likes within good and not-so-good groups, gangs, clubs or tribes. Belonging to a group may be more important than the interest in common. Underlying the very human need is to belong to "a place where everyone knows my name."

That, along with many other reasons, is why group learning has been proven effective for middle level students.[2] It is one of the important reasons that the Tribes TLC® process works so well with the population. Everyone is in an inclusive on-going learning group every day in every class.

Ah, now we're in the third circle— the community of learners!

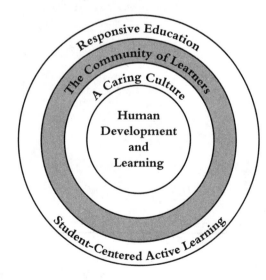

THE DEVELOPMENTAL PROCESS OF TRIBES

Hey, I need that too!

Me too!

Me too!

Connection and affirmation from mom, dad and grandma no longer is quite enough for young adolescents. They also desperately need connections to other caring adults, who reach out and encourage their emerging gifts of heart and mind. The studies on fostering resilience in children provide clear evidence that the most important factor in a young person's development and later success in life is the presence of an adult who cares.[3] More often than not, it is a person beyond the family system. Although our early adolescent friends are set on having increasingly more autonomy in making decisions, the majority verify that they still want to hear adult opinions and viewpoints. The reality is that it is difficult for many to make connections and find inclusion in traditionally organized middle level schools. Once a school becomes responsive to this critical need and reorganizes as a Tribes Learning Community, a web of caring relationships emerge—not only for students but for teachers, administrators and parents.

THE MEANING OF COMMUNITY

The word "community" stirs different memories in everyone. What cherished moments come to mind for you? An inclusive first step for a staff or parent group is to set aside time to share some of those moments when people felt a sense of belonging and value in a group. What made those experiences special? How did people relate to each other? Jot down your thoughts about community in the boxed space on the next page.

Different populations, ages and genders may define the meaning of community in different ways. The nightly news media uses the word to refer to collections of people, few of whom know each other: the medical community, the Hispanic community, the gay community, the northside community. Some of us think of commune communities, farm communities, retirement communities. How then can the spirit of community that we want in a school be defined? As you read the following definitions written by journalist, John McKnight, keep in mind how the descriptors would support the needs of young adolescents.[5]

Nearly everyone agrees that our schools and our society have a connection problem. And nearly everyone agrees that one way to renew connections is to help schools to become caring communities.[4]

—THOMAS SERGIOVANNI

Remember, it's okay to write in this book.

COMMUNITY

CAPACITY: Communities are built upon recognizing the whole depth, the strengths, weaknesses, and the unique capacities of each member.

COLLECTIVE EFFORT: Communities share responsibility to achieve goals for the common good, and to engage the diversity of individual talents and skills.

INFORMALITY: Transactions of value are based on consideration; care and affection take place spontaneously.

STORIES: Reflection upon individual and community experiences provides knowledge about truth, relationships and future direction.

CELEBRATION: Activities incorporate celebration, parties and social events. The line between work and play is blurred as people enjoy both at once.

Thomas Likona, respected author on moral development and education, crafted this definition which seems especially relevant for middle schools.

To build a sense of community is to create a group that extends to others the respect one has for oneself, to come to know one another as individual, to respond and care about one another, to feel a sense of membership and accountability to the group.[6]

STRUCTURING COMMUNITY

Imagine that you are our friendly pelican looking down through the glass roof of a Tribes school. "Reflection," which is her name, would see cellular structures throughout all of the classrooms. Each classroom is a community, and within each classroom are inclusive small community groups, tribes, teams or clubs. The culture within all of the classrooms and tribes is safe and kind because the students have made agreements with each other to be helpful friends. The tribes are places where everybody does "know my name." They are places where it is safe enough to be smart: to ask questions of teachers, to speak up in a group, to acknowledge and learn from mistakes, and to ask for help in completing a difficult task. Tribes are places where students know they will not be called names, suffer put-down remarks, or be disrespected for their cultural or individual diversity—all so prevalent in dispassionate impersonal schools. Comprehensive studies have proven that attention, learning, performance, retention and recall all diminish when stress and anxiety are high. Eric Jensen, respected author of *Teaching with the Brain in Mind,* confirms that excess stress and threat in schools may be the single greatest contributor to impaired academic learning.[7]

Reflection would also see teachers, administrators, parents and resource people relating and working in on-going small groups—all with meaningful tasks to achieve. Membership in collaborative groups gives everyone in the school community identity, inclusion and valued roles as they work to achieve common goals. The structure decentralizes planning, problem-solving, mentoring, monitoring and assessment. Everyone learns—everyone teaches. Collaborative groups, all living the positive culture of Tribes TLC®, can transform a dispassionate system into a spirited caring community. It is, we believe, what "school restructuring" should be all about.

Everyone learns— everyone teaches!

It's no mystery how to develop a caring classroom learning community.

That's right! Use the process of 'Tribes!'

ABOUT THE NAME, TRIBES!

Tribes? You smile and wonder when you hear the name. How did the name come about? It's hard to remember exactly when it happened. Throughout the early years teachers who were experiencing our group theory brand of cooperative learning would remark, "This is like being in a family." "It's like being a team." Inevitably, someone would counter, "No, it's like being a tribe." The feeling of being part of some type of caring small group may be what so many of us in Western society long for today. It also brings to mind the fact that for centuries indigenous people have lived in caring tribal groups for strength and survival.

At times, the question about the name, "Tribes," has been raised by Native American and First Nation people. Once having heard about the community culture of Tribes they are appreciative of the value placed upon their beliefs. When their teachers begin to experience the process in training, inevitably some smile and say, "This is our old way of being together... to talk and listen as the old ones still do."[8] It is then that with much chagrin, this author feels somewhat presumptuous to have titled the latest Tribes book, *A New Way of Learning and Being Together.* It is, however, with great pride that we let the reader know that Ojibwe, Navajo and Hopi schools are using the process of Tribes, and have had their own educators trained to sustain the "old way of being together."

TRIBES IS A PROCESS? WHAT'S PROCESS?

Never for a moment assume that Tribes is a curriculum or a set of fun activities to do as time-fillers on a dull day. Tribes TLC® is a specific democratic process. What is process? Process is a sequence of events or learning experiences that lead to the achievement of a specific outcome. The outcome of the process of Tribes in middle level schools is to maximize human growth and learning for early adolescents. "How," you ask, "can school leaders possibly make this happen?" "Can teachers do it easily?" Yes! Moreover, working with the age group becomes a pleasure.

Using the process of Tribes requires learning and facilitating a sequence of three group development (community building) stages and four positive agreements among the students in a classroom or the adults within groups in the school. The community agreements are:

- Attentive listening
- Appreciation/no put downs
- The right to pass
- Mutual respect.

People also learn to use specific collaborative skills, and to reflect on the learning and interaction occurring in their small groups and the larger community. The process not only establishes and sustains a caring environment for adolescent growth and active learning, but also provides an effective process for collaborative management of school and community groups.

Based on hundreds of research studies, Drs. David and Roger Johnson continue to emphasize the importance of school community to learning:

The theme that runs through all successful schools is that students, teachers, administrators and parents share a sense of community and a 'socially integrating sense of purpose.' Students are thought of as citizens while teachers are thought of as community leaders. A sense of belonging boosts the desire to learn.[9]

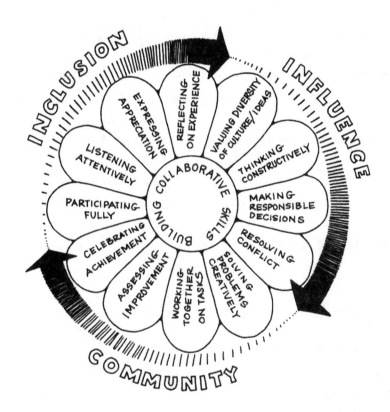

THE TRIBES AGREEMENTS—A NEW WAY OF BEING TOGETHER

Building the positive environment for a Tribes Learning Community begins by replacing negative norms of the school or organization with explicit positive agreements. All groups and organizations have unacknowledged norms, silent rules, that affect relationships and behavior, and convey "this is how we do things around here." In a dispassionate imper-sonal school the norms may be:

- Nobody listens anyway
- The more put-downs the more fun
- No one respects me or my things
- Never ask questions
- Nobody really cares
- Stay cool—don't let on how you feel!

There is no way to support, let alone reach and teach any age group of children, when negative norms are operant every hour of every day throughout a school. Admonitions by teachers and attempts to control abusive remarks and behavior consumes the energy of teachers. Students themselves need to identify the negative norms that are hurtful in their classrooms or the school. Count on our young adolescents wanting to problem-solve. Given the opportunity to define more supportive ways of being and working together, they readily remind each other of the positive agreements they have made. Inherent in our goal of adolescent development is the encouragement of self-responsibility and the internalization of ethical social principles. It begins by transferring responsibility to students to help each other live better ways—less hurtful ways—of being together. The idealism of early adolescents is a gift waiting to be used. Awakening the empathy within their hearts and constructive problem-solving within their heads is the most effective way to create safe, non-violent schools.

How to involve middle level students in summarizing their ideas into language similar to the four Tribes agreements is detailed in a later chapter. What is important to know is that when used consistently the four Tribes agreements have been proven to create and sustain a positive learning environment throughout thousands of classrooms and schools. The four agreements and their definitions are:

ATTENTIVE LISTENING: To pay close attention to one another's expression of ideas, opinions and feelings; to check for understanding; and to let others know that they have been heard.

APPRECIATION/NO PUT-DOWNS: To treat others kindly; to state appreciation for unique qualities, gifts, skills and contributions; to avoid negative remarks, name-calling, hurtful gestures and behaviors.

RIGHT TO PASS: To have the right to choose when and to what extent one will participate in a group activity; to observe quietly if not participating actively; and to choose whether to offer observations later to a group when invited to do so.

MUTUAL RESPECT: To affirm the value and uniqueness of each person; to recognize and appreciate individual and cultural differences; and offer feedback that encourages growth.

Some schools and classes may want to add additional agreements beyond the four. It is important, however, that the list isn't longer than five agreements or students will be more likely to ignore them, and not reinforce them with each other.

Tribes agreements need to be posted in a prominent place in classrooms and throughout the school. One dedicated leader, a bus driver at a Navajo reservation school, has the four agreements on the steps going up into his bus. He smiles and says, "Now, we have a peaceful bus!"

The idealism of early adolescents is a gift waiting to be used.

Whenever tribe groups begin to work together, the teacher or leader reminds everyone of the four Tribes agreements, or invites group members to review them aloud. The leader states that it is the responsibility of all of the members in each tribe to remind each other of the agreements so that their learning group can work well together. Transforming the classroom or school into a positive environment depends upon everyone monitoring and living the agreements.

A major difference between Tribes and some of the other classroom group methods is that people maintain membership in the same group for an extended period of time. This is based on research indicating that: [10]

- People perform better on learning tasks when they are members of "high cohesion" rather than "low cohesion" groups, and
- Students who feel comfortable with their peers utilize their academic abilities more fully than those who do not.

The difference between using randomly formed task groups and creating long-term tribes looks something like this:

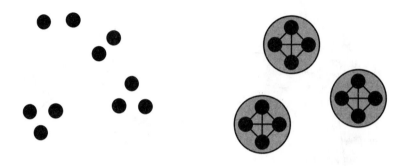

RANDOM LEARNING GROUPS   **THE TRIBES LEARNING COMMUNITY**

Random groups produce a scattered energy, and since they do not provide ongoing inclusion and trust, it is more difficult for students to work together. Long-term membership assures support for all members within each small group and throughout the learning community. The intentionally created structure supports social development, cooperation and achievement for students of all abilities.

STAGES OF GROUP DEVELOPMENT—THE TRIBES TRAIL

The strange map found after you turn the page is one of the main secrets to the magic that happens in Tribes. Okay, we know you think our map looks more like the cross-section of a gopher-infested garden! It really is our attempt to detail the important synchronization that takes place between the teacher, facilitator or leader, and the development of small learning groups. The success of any group's life together and the individual achievements its members make depend upon the leader's knowledge and ability to orchestrate learning strategies appropriate to the group's particular stage of development. It strikes us as sad that though all living takes place in groups, we seldom are taught how to make groups work well together. Think back to the times you have been in a meeting where you have heard....

*The meeting will come to order. Tonight's agenda was mailed to you. The secretary will read the minutes. The executive committee **has decided that all members will....***

Families, labor unions, churches, parent-teacher associations, management staffs, faculties and classrooms… all are in search of a reliable democratic process that assures fairness and equality in participation. Ignorant of any group development process, a majority of organizations struggle in limbo somewhere between a great guru theory of leadership and democratic process, waving Robert's Rules of Order to maintain control. As a member, you may never feel as involved as the leaders are. You may wonder why you are there at all, and how the group will ever really know what unique talents, skills, or resources you have to contribute. *You,* the real special "you," are seldom invited to express your expectations or opinions and may never become a possible resource to the organization. In time your interest wanes and you drift onward, hoping for more recognition, support, and a way to make contribution in some other group.

The reason that people become drop-outs—whether from families, work staffs, organizations—or for that matter from other relationships—is because they do not feel included or valued. Paid employees (yes, even teachers and administrators) also manage to drop out, but in subtle ways, such as not following through on responsibilities, taking many leave days, sabotaging a department's plans, caucusing with other disgruntled peers, manipulating meetings, or being apathetic. Students drop out by gradually moving to "flight or fight." Apathy, boredom, lack of participation, shyness, absenteeism, and inability to complete tasks are some of the ways of taking flight. Those that fight, or initiate acting out behaviors (such as teasing, hitting, stealing, using foul language, etc.), are delivering the same message: "I don't feel included… nobody cares about me." Few leaders are aware of a basic principle: **If a person does not feel included, he/she will create his own inclusion by grabbing influence.** He will attract attention, create a controversy, demand power, or withdraw into passive belligerence.

This organizational disease is a veritable plague in any system that is still managed through top-down authoritarian methods. Such organizations only provide inclusion and influence for the top leaders, and have great difficulty in developing participation. Meetings that are interrupted by angry staff members or strident parents indicate a lack of inclusion. Their frustration may lead to uproar and grabbing influence one way or another. In the same way, we need to get past thinking of disruptive students as behavior problems to control. The majority of acting-out kids are longing to be included. One of our country's major concerns, anti-social behavior among youth, can be turned around once schools, families and local communities understand that all adolescents are seeking places of belonging—and significance in the worlds of their daily lives.

When one has no stake in the way things are, when one's needs or opinions are provided no forum, when one sees oneself as the object of unilateral actions, it takes no particular wisdom to suggest one would rather be elsewhere."

—SEYMOUR SARASON

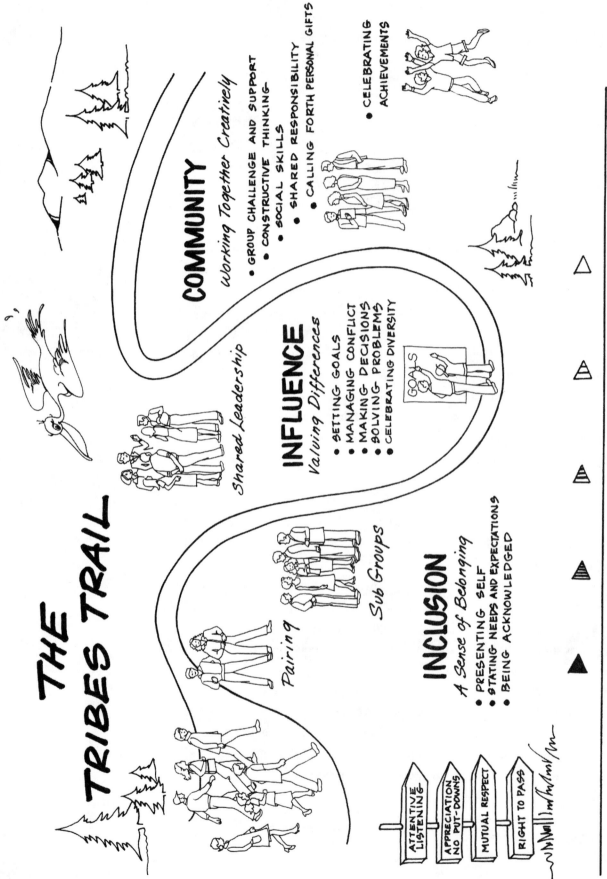

THE TRIBES TRAIL

COMMUNITY
Working Together Creatively
- GROUP CHALLENGE AND SUPPORT
- CONSTRUCTIVE THINKING
- SOCIAL SKILLS
- SHARED RESPONSIBILITY
- CALLING FORTH PERSONAL GIFTS
- CELEBRATING ACHIEVEMENTS

Shared Leadership

INFLUENCE
Valuing Differences
- SETTING GOALS
- MANAGING CONFLICT
- MAKING DECISIONS
- SOLVING PROBLEMS
- CELEBRATING DIVERSITY

GOALS

Sub Groups

Pairing

INCLUSION
A Sense of Belonging
- PRESENTING SELF
- STATING NEEDS AND EXPECTATIONS
- BEING ACKNOWLEDGED

ATTENTIVE LISTENING
APPRECIATION NO PUT-DOWNS
MUTUAL RESPECT
RIGHT TO PASS

FACILITATOR'S ROLE: TRANSFER RESPONSIBILITY TO GROUP

THE TRIBES TRAIL MAP

Every guide taking people into a wilderness needs a map so that the community of people traveling together arrives at their hoped-for destination. As a teacher or school leader, it is essential that you understand some simple stages of group development and the major issues that are bound to arise as people learn to work well in collaborative groups.

The Tribes Trail Map illustrates the sequential stages of group development that you, the teacher-facilitator, will follow to develop your learning community. Notice the bottom line. It shows a gradual shift in your role from being directive, providing much structure, to becoming less directive and transferring leadership to tribes within the community. After initial activities that develop inclusion, you will be encouraging students to assume leadership in their tribes and within the classroom. The net effect of this subtle process is that responsibility is transferred to students themselves. This is why the Tribes process is effective in calling forth the potential talents, gifts, and resources of group members. The process elicits a multiplicity of resources and gifts in the learning community, and enables tasks to be accomplished by all in satisfying and creative ways.

It is this intentional transfer of leadership in the midst of a positive and caring environment that makes the Tribes program different from other cooperative learning approaches. This transfer, the calling forth of gifts, is the big secret to building self-worth and motivation among early adolescents. No matter what the age level, it gives a loud and clear message—you are capable people who can indeed manage yourselves and help each other!

THE STAGE OF INCLUSION

Now let's look more closely at how this works. Notice on the Tribes Trail Map the separate individuals coming into a classroom, the staff or organizational meeting. As mentioned previously, the scale at the bottom of the map indicates the degree of structuring that the teacher or leader needs to facilitate for people as they come from their many separate paths. Each person entering the group is unique in his or her life experience, and perceives the new classroom situation or meeting out of a personal complex of diverse needs and expectations. Newcomers to any group feel an initial anxiety and have many unspoken questions:

- I wonder if I'll like this classroom?
- Will the teacher and other kids like me?
- How will they get to know me? I feel scared.
- Why am I nervous?
- What will we be doing?
- I wish this were the end of the day, not the beginning.

Knowing this, your responsibility is to live up to the name "facilitator," which means "one who makes it easy." If people stay immersed in these initial anxieties, they cannot learn and in time will act-out or drop-out. Remember how the brain works? Fear and

INCLUSION

In order to have inclusion, three opportunities must be provided:

1. Each person needs to be able **to introduce herself,** not just by stating her name but by offering a short description of her feelings, interests, resources, talents or special qualities.
2. Each person needs to be able **to express his hopes or expectations** for what will happen during the group's time together.
3. Each person needs **to be acknowledged** as having been heard, appreciated, and welcomed.

anxiety sabotage rational thinking and learning. Immersed in anxiety, students will take to their own comfort zones—which may not be positive for either themselves or others. A student may simply show restlessness, shuffle papers, get a stomach ache, or in time become regarded as one more learning disability. A teacher who never feels comfortable among faculty members may be inattentive at meetings, irritable with students, and simply suffer through to the end of the year.

In a classroom it may take several days or weeks for all students to present themselves to the total class or within a small group. In organizational settings, like faculty meetings, initial inclusion means gaining adequate recognition and the same opportunity to present oneself prior to tasks and agendas. **It means balancing persons and tasks.** This is what makes the big difference in how people finally are able to work together productively.

As soon as possible the facilitator begins to model and discuss the basic four agreements that make the Tribes process work well. By having people first meet in small temporary groups (pairs or triads), initial anxiety is alleviated and inclusion begins to happen. Observe any organization of more than six people. People very naturally sub-group or arrive at a meeting with one or two others in order to feel less anxious. The intentional use of small temporary groups (sometimes called

Invite the pelican that soars over the Tribes Trail to be your constant companion. Her name is Reflection. She will tell you, rather immodestly, that she makes the Tribes process work well anywhere. At times, you will want to ignore her calls: "timeout," "stop the action, teacher," "time to reflect," or "what's happening now?" Reflection knows that if you watch from the bird's eye view, classroom management goes more smoothly. Reflection is a wise bird who can describe just what she saw or heard while people worked together. You will find her questions on the pages of every Tribes strategy. Reflection clears up confusion and helps everyone soar to greater heights.

"trial tribes") early in a meeting makes it easier for all to feel included at least with a few others before relating to a larger group of people. Using our process, leaders of large conferences sub-group hundreds of people early in the gathering to guarantee that no one is isolated. Agenda items can even be submitted from all of the small groups in order to include everyone's expectations.

Inclusion is a basic human need, and unless it is met people feel vulnerable and defensive. The saying "a camel is a horse designed by a committee" most certainly refers to a committee whose members attempted to undertake a task without first having achieved inclusion together. Time spent up front, building inclusion and trust is the most valuable commitment a group can make. Although it takes a bit longer at first, the pay-off in trust, motivation and achievement makes all the difference!

THE STAGE OF INFLUENCE

As mellow as the stage of inclusion can be, in time a very natural restlessness may be observed throughout the community. The restlessness is a positive sign. It indicates that people do feel included and are ready to work together. You will begin to notice that....

- members are taking more initiative and speaking up; they may be making suggestions, asking confronting questions, and even resisting leadership
- people are discussing or questioning group goals, ways to work together, and how decisions are made
- people are not being as polite or as patient with each other
- conflicts are beginning to arise.

Rather than panic and decide that groups just don't work, recognize these indicators as positive signals. The new restlessness means that the time spent in building inclusion, trust, kindness, and a sense of belonging has been achieved. People are now ready to really work on tasks together... the stage of influence has arrived. Congratulations!

The Influence stage centers on these questions:

- How can each person influence the goals, tasks, and decision-making process of the group?
- How can members assert their individuality and value in the midst of the group?
- How can leadership be shared so that the resource and potential of each member is called forth?

To feel "of influence" is to feel of value (worth, power, individual resource) to the group. To the extent that each person does not feel important in a classroom or organization, commitment and motivation decrease.

The responsibility of the teacher-leader is also to provide methods for resolving the inevitable different issues and concerns. Conflicts and misunderstandings are a natural part, a vital dynamic, of any group or organization—and cannot be ignored. They can be resolved through a variety of strategies, such as:

To feel "of influence" is to feel of value.

- Reflecting on and discussing the incident or situation that is happening
- Helping people to state their feelings clearly
- Assisting the group to give constructive feedback
- Facilitating problem-solving methods
- Role-playing, using role-reversal techniques
- Negotiating the priorities of individual members.

If issues are ignored, the energy of the group is deflected away from its capacity to accomplish tasks together!

The sensitive classroom teacher recognizes that continuing to focus on subject matter in the midst of interpersonal or group issues is neither academically nor emotionally helpful. Having people meet in their tribes to resolve a disruptive issue not only transfers responsibility to the class, but promotes a sense of value for the students. Once the conflict has been resolved by students, people will go back to their work on tasks with renewed energy.

INFLUENCE

Rather than allowing group members to wrestle for ways to have influence, the skilled teacher or leader provides a selection of strategies that help people to….
- Express diverse attitudes, opinions, positions, and personal feelings
- Put forth ideas without others passing judgment; help people to respect individual differences
- Use participatory methods for decision making so that all members feel they are influential and of value to the group
- Help members share leadership responsibilities.

During the influence stage the teacher supports the tribes to work as much as possible on their own. Contact with the groups is maintained by requesting periodic reports and circulating casually among the tribes to determine whether assistance is needed. However, if a teacher sits down within a group, the dynamic changes immediately. Group members will center on the teacher and cease to participate with each other. As the influence stage progresses and issues become resolved, shared leadership begins to emerge from group members. What a delight it is to see the shy child of the class lead an activity in her tribe! And what a relief it is to see the dominant member sit back as the others in the tribe demonstrate their unique skills and talents. Some folks have called the Tribes process magic. It simply is a community learning process—a reality that can be achieved by any dedicated teacher or school leader.

THE STAGE OF COMMUNITY

Who does not long for a sense of community in the midst of a city, an organization, a staff, a school, the classroom… the impersonal crowd? The deep human longing is our need to be known, to belong, to care and be cared for. Community is the spirit that happens when many minds and hearts come together to work toward a common good. Community happens through inclusion and the appreciation of individual differences. One can tell when community has become a reality. It is the delightful surprise one day that those we are with, no matter the differences in age, gender, race, culture, intelligence, or talent—all are indispensable and beautiful.

The possibility for community, whether in a classroom, school, or any organization, depends upon the belief that interdependence and connection to others is key to human development, learning, and the accomplishment of task.

At this point in the Tribes process, the classroom, faculty, or school community needs to ask itself the following:

- How well do we know the unique strengths and weakness of each of our members?
- Do we share responsibility for accomplishing common goals and tasks?
- Are we freely using our diverse talents and skills?
- Are we expressing our caring and consideration for one another?
- Do we take time to tell stories and reflect on our experiences together?
- Do we laugh, play, and enjoy each other as we create new approaches to solve old problems together?
- How well do we recognize contributions and celebrate our community accomplishments and shared traditions?

The caring community we long for doesn't just happen. It can be intentionally developed by any group of people deliberately creating *inclusion* for all members, and working through the nitty-gritty issues of *influence*.

Once a group has gone through adversity together, its members become filled with the confidence that they can handle whatever comes their way. This is the path to resilient relationships, creativity and outstanding results!

You will know that you are in a community if you often hear laughter and singing. You will know you are in an institution or bureaucracy if you hear the silence of long halls and the intonations of formal meetings.[12]

—JOHN MCKNIGHT

COMMUNITY

Creating Community requires....
- Dedication to resolving rather than avoiding uncomfortable problems and conflicts that begin to separate members
- Learning and practicing the skills that enable collaboration
- Agreements about how we will treat each other
- Time to reflect on how well we are doing.

THE SPIRAL OF RENEWAL

Each time the members of a learning community or classroom tribe come together they need some type of inclusion activity before they begin to focus on task; and influence issues always need to be addressed. A helpful way of visualizing the continuing growth and evolution of a tribe is to imagine an ascending spiral that moves up through the levels of inclusion, influence, and community as it rises. One full "loop" represents a group meeting so that each time the spiral completes a cycle, it goes through the three stages again. But each time a tribe meets, though it still needs to begin with inclusion, it moves on to a slightly higher level of positive interaction. The spiral is continuous and a never-ending process. Graphically, it looks something like this:

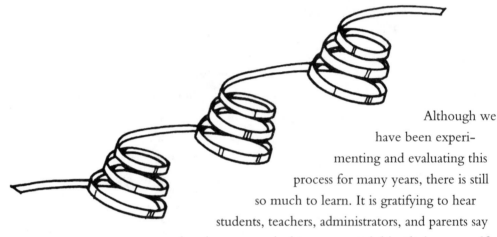

Although we have been experimenting and evaluating this process for many years, there is still so much to learn. It is gratifying to hear students, teachers, administrators, and parents say that they emerged a bit more **special in their own self worth** because they had the opportunity to be part of a tribe somewhere. It does take a commitment and time to integrate the Tribes cooperative learning process into a classroom or school community, but a surprising array of benefits do come about whenever **inclusion** leads the way.

BUILDING BRIDGES BETWEEN NATIONS

A PERSPECTIVE FROM INTERNATIONAL SCHOOL EDUCATORS

BY JUDI FENTON AND ART BEAMAN

We, as educators, must find that balance between the world of the mind and that of the heart and soul. It is the mind that preoccupies our time and that will take us to the information age. But it is the heart and soul that will allow us to remain connected to our own humanity, that will build that bridge between us… and create a good society.[13]

—Paul D. Houston

Imagine entering an international school in a third-world country where over 40 languages are spoken and where almost nothing in your new surroundings is familiar to you. Imagine going to a school where the instruction is in English, a language you neither speak nor understand. Imagine having no friends, in a country where you do not feel comfortable, safe, or accepted. Imagine having your special belongings and keepsakes packed away at home, in storage. Imagine your parents working long hours for a corporation or an embassy, gone from home for extended periods of time. You are left at home to be cared for by someone who does not speak your language. Imagine entering your new school… vulnerable, scared, and alone. These are typical experiences for students stepping into a classroom in a foreign country for the first time.

We began our overseas careers as seasoned educators from the United States who were totally sold on the process of Tribes. However, it wasn't until we began teaching in China, and subsequently in the Dominican Republic, that we particularly realized the importance of human resilience. The need to be resilient and to feel connected is especially important for students whose support systems are fragmented or destroyed.

During our first year in China we team-taught a small group of middle and high school students in grades 6–11. Five of our students were brothers and sisters. Instruction was in English, yet only 25% of our group were native English speakers. We quickly realized the task ahead of us went well beyond teaching our students content and using the English language. Our students desperately needed to feel included… to feel a part of a community. Brothers and sisters in the same classroom, high school students mixed with middle school students, adolescents, multi-cultural diversity, language barriers… a challenging combination. Would the Tribes process be effective here?

Each morning we held a community circle and each day our students worked in cooperative groups using the Tribes TLC® learning experience format as a guide to lessons. The Tribes agreements proved to be a powerful tool, as they gave all students an understandable framework with which to relate. It didn't take long for the students to begin to support one another—and for our non-English speaking students to begin to feel safe. Not surprisingly, the right to pass was the agreement most used at first… it ensured safety. We will never forget the joy our class felt when our most timid student, a boy from North Korea, risked speaking for the first time during community circle! The following year, as a ninth grader, this same boy ran for a student body office and won. The protective factors of caring and support, positive expectations, and active participation

Judi Fenton, M.Ed., is the Assistant Superintendent of Curriculum and Instruction at the Carol Morgan International School (K-12) in Santo Domingo, Dominican Republic. She has been a teacher, principal and state coordinator for gifted programs, and has worked with teachers, students, administrators, and parents in four different countries. Judi is convinced that educational reform can only come about through a spirit of trust, caring, and mutual understanding—a philosophy she lives in every aspect of her life.

Art Beaman, Ph.D., teaches high school Advanced Placement Psychology, Calculus and other math courses at the Carol Morgan School. Art has worked as a university professor, researcher and consultant in the U.S. and Australia. He uses the process of Tribes in all of his classes, and with his wife, Judi, conducts on-going training at Carol Morgan and other international schools.

were fully realized through the implementation of the Tribes process in our classroom. We saw the effects of this daily. The Tribes agreements used by brothers and sisters at school spilled over into their homes. High school students modeled kindness and sincerity when working with middle school peers. Strong, lasting friendships were forged. High levels of trust and mutual respect led to rapt attention when classmates shared information about their home countries. Students new to the classroom were embraced and made to feel welcome and safe. Laughter and learning developed as the norms.

It wasn't until the students became completely immersed in the stage of inclusion that we began to realize their full potential, not just as honorable caring citizens, but as human beings capable of building bridges to world peace and global interdependence. Our students were from many different cultures, with differing political perspectives. Yet they had become best friends, had mastered attentive listening, shared a common language, and demonstrated respect for differing points of view. When the class began moving into the stage of influence, we made a conscious effort to step back and transfer responsibility to the group. As the students gained more experience in solving problems and in resolving classroom conflicts, they began to branch out, bringing issues from outside of the classroom to the community circle. Problems that occurred on the bus and playground, as well as issues from the housing units where they lived, were discussed and resolved. Their ability to approach conflict in a non-aggressive manner was key to their growth as future leaders.

From our international schools will come young adults most likely to live and work abroad throughout their careers—resilient, fully bilingual, politically astute young people who possess world awareness and cross-cultural understanding. Having practiced and internalized the TribesTLC® collaborative skills in an atmosphere of mutual respect, they will also possess the problem solving skills, pro-social behaviors, and autonomy necessary to function as citizens of a multi-cultural, global society.

Will our students become global leaders? Will they be instrumental in bringing about world peace? Not all of them, but we feel certain some will. As their teachers, we know in our hearts that they are different. Along with their global perspective, we know that these students possess the ingredients needed to achieve a balance between the mind, the heart, and the soul…. the very ingredients needed to build bridges between nations.

COMMUNITY

Somewhere, there are people
to whom we can speak with passion
without having the words catch in our throats.
Somewhere a circle of hands will open to receive us,
eyes will light up as we enter, voices will celebrate with us
whenever we come into our own power.
Community means strength that joins our strength
to do the work that needs to be done.
Arms to hold us when we falter.
A circle of healing. A circle of friends.
Someplace where
we can be free.[14]

—Starhawk

7 Learning About Learning

7 Learning About Learning

Yes, we're flying into the fourth dimension— student-centered learning!

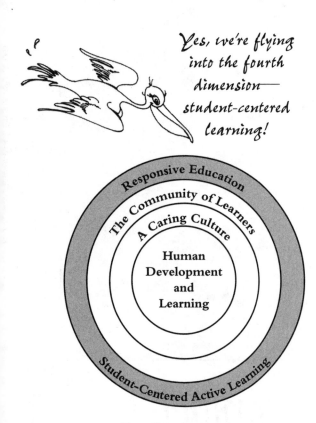

THE **DEVELOPMENTAL** **PROCESS OF TRIBES**

Instruction begins when you the teacher, learn from the learner; put yourself in his place so that you may understand what he learns and the way he learns it.

—Kierkgegaard

THE VOLATILE MISMATCH

Throughout the country hundreds of middle school educators are going back to their planning groups and boards, having finally recognized that achieving new levels of learning depends on how well their schools are addressing the whole interlocking entity of early adolescents' needs. Standards, curriculum and testing, apart from attention to the overwhelming social, emotional and intellectual changes driving the age group, sentences populations of children to life-long struggle and failure. Fortunately, smart schools have begun to take seriously the alarm sounded more than a decade ago in the respected Carnegie Council on Adolescent Development report, "Turning Points, Preparing American Youth for the 21st Century."

A volatile mismatch exists between the organization and curriculum of middle grade schools and the intellectual and emotional needs of young adolescents.[1]

The report detailed eight broad recommendations for restructuring middle level schools into learning environments suited to the needs of young adolescents. The very first recommendation was to **"create small communities for learning where stable, close, mutually respectful relationships with adults and peers are considered fundamental for intellectual development and personal growth."[2]**

Although the report was considered a blueprint for reform of middle level schools and many schools did reorganize during the last decade, national studies have indicated that life inside the classrooms for sixth through eighth graders remained relatively stable and uninspiring. The typical situation in the eighth grade reflected a continuing conflict between prevailing practices and the known needs of early adolescent students. Cooperative learning was honored more in intention than practice; exploratory curriculum was largely absent. The progress toward the implementation of the recommendations for the education of early adolescents has been extremely slow.[3]

It's as though the factories of standardization just keep turning out one size of coat no matter what the needs of their customers.

MOVING FROM 'SCHOOLING' TO MEANINGFUL LEARNING

Traditional "schooling" treats knowledge as "a commodity" that is stored in teachers' minds and texts, and that can be "delivered" into the heads of students. Like other commodities the assumption is that it also can be itemized and measured. Students are required to listen attentively, complete assignments alone, remember facts and concepts—and one way or another return the same information to the teacher.

Thus at a time when early adolescents are trying to become socially competent, the traditional classroom is set up to separate people and to minimize student-to-student interaction. At a time when early teens are struggling to become independent and self-directed, traditional middle school classrooms impose more controls, rules and restrictions. In today's world of rapid communication and change, compliance is rewarded over creativity. Too often the resulting student restlessness or inattention is diagnosed as "A.D.D." (attention deficit disorder) and is treated as a neurological disability or discipline problem. The system is rarely perceived as dysfunctional—**the students are.**

Now is the worst of times—and the best of times. It is the worst of times to urge schools to change the culture and pedagogy of their systems, indeed to tailor them, to match and support the growth and learning needs of their students... or to suggest that such an effort is a proven path to educational excellence. The standards-testing frenzy is all consuming.[5] Yet it is the best of times. Concurrent with the growing backlash, the voices of knowledgeable research groups and educators, though still a small band, are speaking out.[6] Though largely dismissed, a comprehensive research and knowledge base to establish educational excellence exists. It needs only to be synthesized and applied well within schools willing to become totally student-centered. The synthesis is woven by

With dismal regularity, we return to efforts to improve K-12 education. These efforts usually fail because education is conceived narrowly as 'schooling.'[4]
—MIHALY CSIKSZENTMIHALYI

implementing a caring and supportive culture, brain compatible teaching and learning, components for human development, resilience, cooperative group learning, constructivism, learning communities and effective professional development to name a few. Schools have scotch-taped one study, curriculum or program at a time—but seldom have become whole school or district "learning communities" to synthesize what works and apply it.

WHERE TO BEGIN

The majority of teachers and school leaders are deeply committed smart people who love kids, and are willing to learn about learning. The best place to begin is to schedule a Tribes course, of course! One of the first of their many ah-ha's will be understanding how the human brain takes in information and constructs knowledge. They will be relieved finally to know why direct instruction is incompatible with how the human brain acquires meaningful knowledge. A faculty gains motivation and new hope once they begin to learn together and to discuss questions such as....

• What determines how much can be remembered?
• What makes learning impossible at different times?
• Can test scores really be improved if we reach and teach kids in a different way?

HOW THE HUMAN BRAIN CONSTRUCTS KNOWLEDGE

Teachers and school leaders begin to rethink "the delivery of information" to students when they hear that neurophysiological data suggests that the nervous system is not capable of taking in everything! It can only scan for material it is prepared to find by virtue of its own past experiences and internal patterns.[8] The main function of the brain is to sort out and catalogue meaningful patterns of information. As with computers, the human brain enters relevant new information easily into previously created files. However, if previous files based on a student's interest do not exist, they must be actively developed. Given this fact, how can we imagine that any sizeable amount of unrelated academic material conveyed by direct instruction (teacher-talk) will be filed easily (down-loaded) and readily recalled later for a test?

It is beyond the scope of this book to provide all of the current fine material on the workings of the human brain. Nevertheless, it is important for teachers using the process of Tribes to understand some essential concepts that justify our active-learning student-centered teaching approach.

All sensory information comes into the brain from the body's senses (sight, hearing, touch/feeling, smell, taste), and zooms into one of two possible pathways depending upon whether a sense of threat or danger is perceived. The body and brain work, one might say, in a co-dependent partnership—so much so that recent researchers are using the term "bodybrain."[9]

Yes, this is what schools using the process of Tribes are doing!

I never let 'schooling' interfere with my education.[7]
—MARGARET MEAD

This is a bird's eye view!

When there is no sense of danger the information travels on a slow pathway to a sensory relay station, called the **thalamus,** onward to the **hippocampus,** the center of learning and memory, and then to the **cerebral cortex,** the center of long term memory and thinking. However, when there is a sense of danger the data zooms on a fast path to trigger mechanisms for survival. The sensory input goes directly to the **thalamus** relay station, which sends it directly to the **amygdala,** the center of all fear, threat and passion, which zings it into an internal regulator called the **hypothalamus** which shouts at the pituitary and adrenal glands to release a stress hormone called **cortisol.** Whoa! Instantaneously the hormone whips through the body and brain via the bloodstream and activates fight or flight behaviors. The story doesn't end there! The rational cerebral cortex never has a chance to think things through and emotional balance is destroyed. With persistent stress, cortisol can be devastating to the learning and memory system, the **hippocampus.**[10]

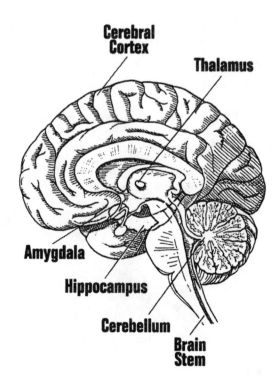

Knowing this, gives a better understanding why the climate of classrooms must be safe, caring and supportive learning environments. Somewhere in the novel "Dune" the frantic hero cries out, "Fear is a mind-killer!" Many kinds of fear kill minds daily in classrooms. There is the fear of asking a question, fear of not giving the right answer, fear of being teased, called a name, ridiculed for one's culture, gender or diversity. Minds are killed through loneliness, hostility and exclusion by peers. For some it may be intimidation from a teacher, a reprimand that seems unfair, boys being called on more often than girls, or "the smart people" more than others. Rational thought and memory become unavailable. Emotional balance is lost. The bodymind becomes swamped with the stress hormone cortisol, and one more adolescent gives up.

AN EDUCATOR'S PERSPECTIVE

BY BEVERLY EDWARDS

Beverly J. Edwards, Ph.D., is the Teacher/Trainer Coordinator for implementation of the Tribes TLC® process at the Fulton Teaching and Learning Academy of Tulsa Public Schools. She also is an Adjunct Professor at Langston University and Tulsa Community College. Bev's students and colleagues appreciate her enlightening insights from her knowledge in neurobiology, human development, and cognitive learning. Her interest and energy for learning is contagious.

THE BIOLOGY OF ADOLESCENT LEARNING

Each and every child comes into the world with enormous learning potential, and though all vary genetically, every single one basically has the same immense potential. Every human brain is unique and no brain is perfect; each of us has many learning gifts and probably each has some kind of learning "glitch." As dedicated teachers, administrators and parents, we continually seek ways to enhance our students' natural abilities so that all may maximize their extraordinary learning potential.

Recent discoveries about the human brain and the learning process continue to yield extremely exciting information. A wealth of knowledge from the biological and neurosciences now gives parents and educators a broad understanding of the essential physical, nutritional and emotional needs of young adolescent learners.

First and foremost is the number one brain food—water.

WATER is essential for the electrical and chemical action between the brain and the central nervous system in the distribution of oxygen and nutrition. Under normal conditions, teens and adults need to drink approximately one quart per hundred pounds of body weight each day.[11] The brain and body must be properly hydrated for optimal health and learning.

NUTRITION How well we know that most adolescents eat excessive amounts of saturated fats, simple carbohydrates (cookies, candy, cakes) and caffeinated drinks! Yet for optimal brain, bone and muscle growth, teenagers should be urged to eat more protein (in the form of eggs, dairy products, tuna, chicken, pork and yogurt); more fresh fruit for essential vitamins and minerals; and green leafy vegetables which help to reduce depression and improve mental activity.[12]

SLEEP Those memory lapses, attentional deficits, depressed moods and times of slowed reaction are some of the consequences of insufficient sleep. Recent research suggests that sleep patterns change fundamentally at the transition of adolescence. Most teens begin to feel sleepy 1–1½ hours later than adults and, requiring 9 hours sleep for optimal school participation, struggle to meet early morning school hours. Recognizing this, some secondary schools are scheduling later start times.

MOVEMENT AND EXERCISE Restlessness in the classroom? Of course!
Young teens need a lot of opportunities to move. Asking students to simply stand up increases the blood flow to the brain by 10–15%. A brisk walk around the perimeter of the school helps to increase alertness and elevates the mood. The Tribes TLC® energizers have the same impact on the body and brain system… there is a direct link from the cerebellum, which coordinates muscle movement to the pleasure centers in the emotional systems.[13] It's better to move them than to lose them!

EMOTIONS Yes, the time of adolescence is reigned by emotions. It is a time of tremendous need to "fit in" and to have a sense of belonging in one or more peer groups. Tribe classrooms help to fulfill this critical need by structuring safe and caring membership groups in which students thrive, and in which they learn valuable interpersonal skills that will serve them the rest of their lives. Over time, students grow in their ability to give compliments/appreciation to each other while their respect for others' unique ideas, gifts and talents grow. Emotional development grows through trust and sharing. The process is enormously valuable for a student's development into a happy, respectful, contributing adult.

THE VALUE OF GROUP DISCOURSE

More than 30 years ago respected educator Paolo Friere rejected this "banking" conception of knowledge based on evidence that what students understand does not correspond directly to what they have read in authoritative texts or have been told.[14] Years of impressive research on cognitive learning affirms Freire's evidence that knowledge cannot be transmitted from one mind to another. Individual knowledge is a synthesis of what a person hears and reads—and interprets through previous experiences, familiar symbols and language. Moreover, knowledge is created and recreated between people doing things together. It evolves out of group discourse on concepts and the opportunity to collaborate on the applications and meaning of concepts.[15] The assumption that a teacher's knowledge can be transferred into the minds of students is a fallacy that perpetuates direct instruction and undermines students acquiring long-term meaningful knowledge.

Disciplined students may take down information during a lecture hoping to keep it in memory until the next test, but the data will not become stored by the brain as significant knowledge. The fact that information is altered differently by each learner, depending upon his or her experience and discourse with others, also brings into question the efficacy of "check one-right-answer" standardized tests. Students who can memorize facts easily may score higher on some tests than students who have

The human mind is awesome— but not a dumpster!

97

had the opportunity to discuss and apply information to real-life problems and projects. Yet those in the latter group through active learning have acquired lasting knowledge for the future. They also score higher on tests designed to assess conceptual knowledge and constructive thinking applications.

Learning is not the result of will power or skills. Learning is the result of raising questions, generalizing across experiences, defining an hypothesis, discussing with peers, making real-world applications and reflecting on results. The teaching/learning process needs to be student-centered, inquiry-based, participatory and linked to meaningful real life and world situations.

THE PRINCIPLES FOR STUDENT-CENTERED ACTIVE LEARNING[17]

COGNITIVE AND METACOGNITIVE FACTORS

PRINCIPLE 1. Learning is an active process in which meaning is developed on the basis of experience.

PRINCIPLE 2. The learner associates and links new information to existing knowledge in memory.

PRINCIPLE 3. Strategies for "thinking about thinking" or reflecting on learning facilitate learning.

AFFECTIVE FACTORS

PRINCIPLE 4. Individuals are naturally curious and enjoy learning when in the absence of negative conditions and emotions.

PRINCIPLE 5. Curiosity, creativity and higher order thinking processes are stimulated by learning tasks of optimal difficulty, relevancy, authenticity, challenge and novelty for each student.

SOCIAL FACTORS

PRINCIPLE 6. Learning is facilitated by social interaction, discourse and collaboration.

PRINCIPLE 7. Learning and self-esteem are heightened when individuals are in respectful and caring relationships with others who genuinely appreciate their unique gifts and talents.

INDIVIDUAL DIFFERENCES

PRINCIPLE 8. Learners differ in their ways of learning, the pace at which they learn and capabilities in particular areas.

PRINCIPLE 9. Each learner constructs reality and interprets life experiences in different ways depending upon prior learning, beliefs, culture and external experiences.

THE PRINCIPLES FOR STUDENT-CENTERED ACTIVE LEARNING

Understanding how the human brain acquires knowledge helps to explain not only student boredom from teacher-talk work-alone schooling, but the failure of American education. It justifies taking bold steps that move well beyond adopting one more costly reading curriculum or pushing teachers to prepare students to score higher on State tests.

The principles for student-centered active learning, based on brain research, must be raised to discussion among teachers, administrators, parents, school boards—and especially politicians claiming they know how to improve education. The principles are especially important for teachers who truly want to reach and teach early adolescents in ways that are responsive to their stage of development. The adjacent chart listing nine research-based principles could revolutionize American education. Best of all, hundreds of thousands of uninspired students would no longer view school as "something just to get through."

RESEARCH-BASED TEACHING BOOSTS TEST SCORES

For some strange reason the field of education seems to maintain an institutional indifference to research more than other professions such as medicine, law, engineering, public health and the sciences. Thousands of comprehensive studies indicate how altering a teaching practice can boost standardized test scores. A study that one 8th grade math teacher read about made a huge difference to his students.

Best of all, hundreds of thousands of uninspired students will no longer view school as "something just to get through."

U.S. fails math

It was most likely that your favorite teacher attentively assisted you in solving arithmetic equations—but she probably shouldn't have. New research suggests that American educators don't let students learn to solve problems on their own—causing kids to score lower in math than their Japanese counterparts. In a 1997 study funded by the U.S. Department of Education, James Stigler, Ph.D., of the University of California at Los Angeles, and James Hiebert, Ph.D., from the University of Delaware, analyzed video tapes of 231 eighth grade math classes in Germany, Japan and the United States over one year. As reported in their recent book, The Teaching Gap (Free Press, 1999), the researchers found that American teachers spent 90% of class time going over proce-

dures, formulas and problem-solving techniques. In Japan, however, students spent over 50% of class time discussing concepts and inventing their own solutions to problems. Although the Japanese students frequently had incorrect answers, Stigler and Hiebert believe they achieved a better understanding of the material than American students who often quickly forgot their memorized facts.

Three years ago, a New Jersey based public school teacher, Bill Jackson, adjusted teaching of his math curriculum to reflect this research. That year, his eighth-grade students' standardized test scores increased by 20%; this year, an above-average number entered honors algebra. Jackson says: "To do math, kids must be given a chance to do math." [18]

The opportunity for students in Mr. Jackson's class to discuss concepts, create solutions and problem-solve on their own connects directly to: (1) how the human brain learns through group discourse; and (2) how the developmental needs of 8th graders contributed to success. The change in the teacher's style appealed to their developmental needs: *to gain autonomy, social interaction with peers, a sense of purpose, and problem-solving on their own.* Rather than individually memorizing a procedure demonstrated by the teacher, they discussed and "invented solutions to problems"—and as a result were able to score higher on standardized tests.

> *What students can do together today they can do alone tomorrow.*[19]
> —VYGOTSKY

LETTING GO AND MOVING ON TO GROUP LEARNING

Moving from the traditional pedagogy to research-based group learning also liberates teachers. A teacher in a large middle school acknowledged that one day she really saw her standardized self lecturing to her class of non-standardized teenagers, and was startled with the emotion she felt. She was lonely. There seemed to be an impenetrable wall between her and the young people—some restless and some sitting quietly—in rows in front of her. She had been noticing the wall ever since her faculty heard a presentation by a Tribes TLC® trainer several weeks earlier. She saw and heard about this diagram.[20]

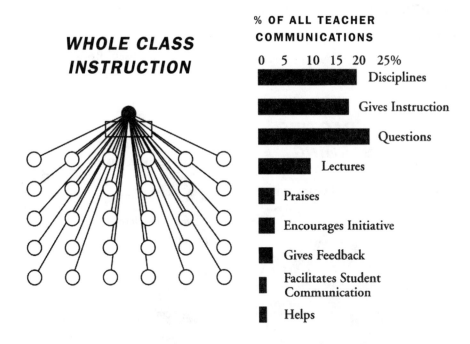

WHOLE CLASS INSTRUCTION

% OF ALL TEACHER COMMUNICATIONS

0	5	10	15	20	25%	

Disciplines

Gives Instruction

Questions

Lectures

Praises

Encourages Initiative

Gives Feedback

Facilitates Student Communication

Helps

Studies verify that when teachers depend upon "whole class instruction," more than 70% of their time is spent lecturing, giving instructions, asking questions and disciplining restless students. Only 30% of their time can be devoted to doing what the majority long to do… to praise, encourage initiative, give feedback and work supportively with students. Whole class individualized instruction causes students to be competitive and results in non-competitive students seeing themselves as low achievers. The structure cannot:

- transfer responsibility to students for inquiry, research and discourse on concepts together
- help students identify their own unique gifts, skills, interests and intelligences
- have students to hold each other accountable and to reflect and celebrate individual or group work done well
- awaken early adolescents to the joy of learning.

CREATING AN ACTIVE LEARNING CLASSROOM

In contrast to the previous diagram, the same studies show that when classrooms are reorganized into student learning groups, "teacher talk" time lessens from 70% to 25%.

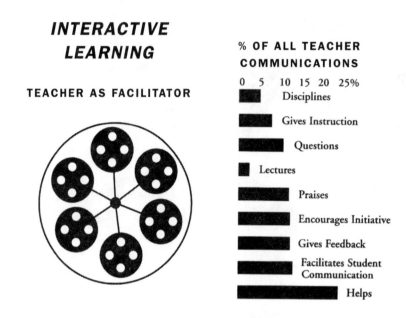

INTERACTIVE LEARNING

TEACHER AS FACILITATOR

% OF ALL TEACHER COMMUNICATIONS

| 0 | 5 | 10 | 15 | 20 | 25% |

Disciplines
Gives Instruction
Questions
Lectures
Praises
Encourages Initiative
Gives Feedback
Facilitates Student Communication
Helps

Now 75% of the teacher's time can be spent helping and encouraging students, giving feedback, facilitating student communication, praising and celebrating success. The transfer of responsibility to student groups to gather, interpret, and apply information and concepts makes a dramatic difference. When students become responsible to each other, accountability for individual performance and behavior becomes a group concern. Guided by the four Tribes agreements, teachers hardly ever have to intervene to manage behavior.

At best, the old structure gave each student five or ten minutes a day to speak about academic topics—mostly, in response to questions from the teacher. Dialogue with peers in groups minimally can provide ten times that amount of "air time." The image of the classroom changes from rigid straight rows to something like this:

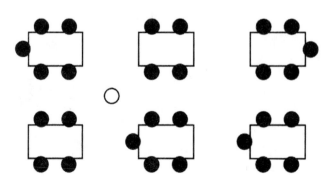

Tables replace desks and desks become centered so that four or five students can face each other and work together. Altering the physical environment of the classroom is step one toward making the classroom student-centered.

The pattern of interaction in classrooms (and also in faculty meetings) looks like this:

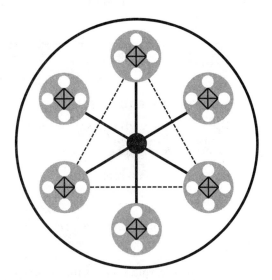

> *In America's best classrooms, again, the emphasis has shifted. Instead of individual achievement and competition, the focus is on group learning. Students learn to articulate, clarify, and restate for one another how they identify and find answers. They learn how to seek and accept criticism from their peers, solicit help, and give credit to others... This is an ideal preparation for life-times of symbolic analytic work.[21]*
>
> —ROBERT REICH

Thirty-two students of this class now have a sense of inclusion and belonging in learning groups. The eight tribes make classroom management easy for the teacher. It is similar to having eight departments in a business organization, each of which has the responsibility of managing their "personnel" and quality of work. Accountability first happens within "the department" (tribe) and then to the teacher. In the same way the tribes as well as the teacher provide support for learning, growth and discovering gifts. Management theory has proven that no one person can supervise and support more than 6–8 people. Why are teachers expected to do the impossible every day? However, one person can supervise and give support to 6–8 small departments. When tribes, guided by the four positive agreements, are given this responsibility, individual motivation and productivity increase immensely. Teachers hardly ever need to intervene to manage behavior.

The connecting lines in the diagram indicate that active learning takes place both within the tribes and between tribes as facilitated by the teacher. In the next chapter we will discuss the formation and types of cooperative groups that can be used to ensure the active learning of content and on-going support.

THE ROLE OF TEACHER CHANGES — THEY BECOME LIBERATED AND SMILE A LOT!

Moving to cooperative group learning transforms the role of teachers. They become facilitators, researchers and designers of active and meaningful learning experiences. Using cooperative groups melts the impenetrable wall between teachers and students. Best of all group learning is effective because it not only is brain compatible but is also responsive to the developmental needs of early adolescents. For those reasons it can be called "Responsive Education."

The chart that follows contrasts the differences between the two paradigms of traditional and responsive education.

A CONTRAST OF PARADIGMS[22]

TRADITIONAL SCHOOLING	RESPONSIVE EDUCATION
Based on ten decades of practice	Based on thousands of research studies
Competitive culture	Cooperative culture
Structure: teacher-centered	Structure: student–centered
Focus: intellectual development	Focus: human development
Emphasis: verbal/linguistic and logical/mathematical learning	Emphasis: multiple intelligences
Curriculum relies on texts and workbooks	Curricular learning relies on primary sources of data and manipulative materials
Teacher as information giver	Teacher as interactive facilitator— mediating learning environment
Teacher as expert authority	Teacher as a co-learner
Students viewed as blank slates	Students viewed as creative learners
Students as passive recipients of facts and concepts	Students as active constructors of knowledge
Curriculum presented part to whole with emphasis on basic skills	Curriculum presented whole to part with emphasis on big concept
Criteria and goals given by teacher, not-explicit before instruction	Shared development of goals and criteria for performance
Teachers seek correct answers	Teachers seek viewpoints and conceptions
Learning is decontextualized	Learning is grounded in "real world" contexts, problems and projects
Western bias	Multicultural, global views
Teacher tests	Students and teacher assess progress
Tests that test	Tests that teach

IDENTIFYING THE GIFTS OF MULTIPLE INTELLIGENCES

The work of Howard Gardner and other cognitive and behavioral scientists is bringing enlightenment to educators throughout the world. The reality is that human beings have a variety of different intelligences, unique ways that we perceive, prefer to learn, relate and meet life situations.[23] Moreover, we cannot be arbitrarily standardized so that one way of teaching or testing fits all.

Lynn Stoddard, author of the very fine book, *Redesigning Education: A Guide for Developing Human Greatness,* deplores the fact that "our fixation on curriculum development instead of human development is the enormous dam blocking educational reform."[24] It has caused us to ignore the work of those who reveal the individuality of human nature, how the brain works and how children learn. The result is that the discovery and development of each child's intelligences and gifts go unattended.

Gardner summarizes the diversity of intelligences as nine "ways of knowing." The illustrations and brief descriptions that follow highlight the ways. Remarkably, it is two of the nine intelligences, verbal/linguistic and logical/mathematical, that are focused upon in the majority of schools in the Western world. Before children enter school, they are busy discovering many ways of learning and exploring their environment. By second or third grade in school they discover that their active, physical, rhythmic, imaginative, relational and existential selves have to be set aside. This is especially difficult for children coming from other than Western Caucasian cultures, namely: Native American, Asian, Pacific Islanders, Hispanic and Afro-American.

In infancy and early childhood children begin learning through what Gardner calls "raw patterning" to perform simple tasks as the foundation of a given intelligence. Walking, running and jumping are the basics of body/kinesthetic intelligence; just as

A good school for adolescents must engage the attention of every young person.[25]
—LEONARD BOTSTEIN

Middle school kids especially must have the opportunity to discover the gifts of their own intelligences.

learning the alphabet is basic to verbal/linguistic intelligence. As children grow they move to greater levels of pattern complexity called "symbol systems," in which they may develop the ability to draw various shapes (visual/spatial intelligence) or make different tones (musical/rhythmic). Each intelligence has its own "notational language" that not only can be learned by others, but can also be recorded in some form, such as a musical composition (musical/rhythmic) or a graphic design (visual/spatial). The years of early adolescent development are especially important—it is at this period that children are becoming aware of their skills and preferences in ways of learning. Finally, in the secondary or college years a time is reached when a preferred intelligence may evolve into a career path.

David Lazear writes:

If we provide students the opportunity to develop the full range of their intellectual capacities and teach them how to use their multiple ways of knowing in the learning task, they will learn the things we are trying to teach more thoroughly than if we only permit them to learn in the more traditional verbal/linguistic and logical/mathematical ways.[26]

In Chapter 10 we will revisit the multiple intelligences to look at many ways to support the development of all nine intelligences in young adolescents.

WILL YOU TEACH ME?[27]

Will you teach me how to sail through space on a comet's tail?
Will you teach me how to fly, to sail the skies on wings untried?
Will you teach me how to soar, to see things as never before?
But most important of all, will you teach me how to fall?

Will you teach me how to cry, to release feelings deep inside?
Will you teach me how to laugh and travel off the beaten path?
Will you teach me how to dream, to face the future sight unseen?
Will you teach me how to be… the only thing I can be… me?

—Andrew Whyte, age 10
Norman Ingram Public School
Toronto, Ontario, Canada

8 Initiating Responsive Education—
The Tribes Community Circle

8 Initiating Responsive Education—

The Tribes Community Circle

The familiar life horizon has been outgrown, the old concepts, ideals and emotional patterns no longer fit—the time for the passing of a threshold is at hand.[1]

—Joseph Campbell

It is 3:10 p.m. in the teacher's lounge at the Westfield Middle School. The whole faculty has been moving on from the teacher-centered "threshold" of schooling to student-centered group learning in order to address the social, emotional and intellectual development of the school's young adolescent population. The teachers are talking about the positive changes they are observing in their students' self-control, social interactions and new interest in learning.

"I haven't had to send anybody to the office since they've been in Tribes."
"How are your special ed kids doing?"
"Great! Every day I notice improvement in their social skills."
"Those two difficult kids in my room no longer are zapping verbal bullets at people."
"The shy little girl is speaking now when in her tribe."
"There's a lot of caring going on."
"I'm beginning to love every hormonal one of them."

SOCIAL AND EMOTIONAL INTELLIGENCE SUPPORTS
ACADEMIC LEARNING

Perhaps as never before, a question that has persisted for more than 3000 years once again is being discussed by concerned educators, parents and even political leaders. It is heard within discussions on character education, youth problems, children's development and debates on curricula and pedagogy. Best of all, it raises local and national dialogue beyond standards and test scores! Invite your faculty to discuss this bigger question:

What really is most important in preparing young people to become active and constructive caring citizens?

Tougher courses in science and math? Computers for every child? Smaller class sizes? A longer school day or year? More federal $$$? Strong discipline policies? Awards? Uniforms?

These are the favored topics that consume most of the time and anxiety in school meetings rather than the central question from which all teaching should rightfully flow. Esteemed research educators such as Daniel Goleman, Howard Gardner, James Comer, John Goodlad and John Dewey to name a few—have agreed that the essential foundation for both academic learning and the capacity to become an active constructive citizen is having knowledge of ourselves—and others as well—and being able to use this knowledge to solve problems creatively.[2]

Unfortunately, educational practice today rarely connects teaching of the mind with social and emotional development. Good teachers have always recognized that how a person feels about himself cannot be separated from mastery of a subject. High grades and SAT scores do not predict satisfaction and productivity throughout life—nor a good citizen make. It is well documented that social emotional intelligence is predictive of academic achievement, productive experiences in the world of work, and better health.[3] For thousands of years humankind has ultimately recognized the truth of the mandate… "Know thyself."

Social intelligence is the capacity:
- to relate well to others
- to conceptualize and manage social relations, interpersonal problems and conflict
- to be empathetic, patient and considerate of cultural, racial and gender diversity
- to collaborate
- to enjoy working for the common good.

Social intelligence, to a great extent, depends upon the degree of one's emotional literacy which Daniel Goleman defines as the following five essential capacities:[5]
- self-awareness
- the ability to handle emotions
- self-motivation
- empathy
- social skills.

All are self-reflective capacities. They give one an ability to recognize what others are thinking and feeling, and dramatically affect children's ability to learn and succeed in life.[6]

> The most exciting breakthrough of the 21st century will occur not because of technology, but because of an expanding concept of what it means to be human.[4]
>
> —JOHN NAISBITT

Can social and emotional intelligence be taught?

Yes and no! Social skills and character values are being taught as curricula throughout many schools today. However, acquiring social and emotional intelligence depends on many factors in the developmental years of a child's life. The same protective factors that nurture resiliency, discussed in Chapter 4, lead to social emotional literacy when experienced daily in a child's environment. If you recall, Benard summarizes the factors as:

• caring relationships
• opportunities for participation and contributions, and
• positive expectation messages and beliefs.

This is why Tribes Learning Communities, unlike many other cooperative learning approaches, first establish a culture of caring. Living daily within a context of supportive relationships and repeatedly reflecting upon social learning experiences fosters the "habits of the heart"—empathy, respect, kindness and caring. Reflection on personal learning—self-reflection on discovered strengths, gifts and inner knowledge—is every bit as important to the development of the whole child as intellectual knowledge.

THE BENEFITS OF LEARNING THROUGH COOPERATION

It becomes obvious that there is no other way for schools to support young adolescents in becoming socially competent apart from working with peers in on-going cooperative groups. As discussed earlier, knowledge becomes meaningful for the human brain through social discourse with others. All of the four important tasks of adolescence—autonomy and independence, social competency, a sense of purpose and capacity to problem-solve—depend upon discourse, cooperation, negotiation, problem-solving, sharing and reflection with others. The immense benefits of cooperative group learning not only support the needs of American youth but also transform a middle level school when implemented throughout the system. Drs. Roger and David Johnson of the University of Minnesota have worked for years to assess and summarize more than 600 studies reporting the benefits of learning through cooperation with others rather than competitive or individualized instruction.[7] Among the many benefits are:

- Greater productivity and academic achievement
- Constructive thinking skills: planning, inferring, analyzing, gathering data and strategizing
- Social competency: trust in others, perspective taking, sense of personal identity, interdependence, sense of direction and purpose
- Motivation: high expectations of success and achievement; high commitment and persistence
- Social support: constructive management of stress; high quality relationships that extend life and are helpful to people
- Psychological health: the ability to develop, maintain and improve one's relationships and situation in life; success in achieving goals
- Self-esteem: improvement due to positive peer relations and achievement
- Positive interpersonal relationships: supportive friendships; appreciation of peers' skills and contributions
- Intergroup relationships: caring concern; acceptance of multi-cultural diversity; commitments to the common good.

Everyone needs Reflection!

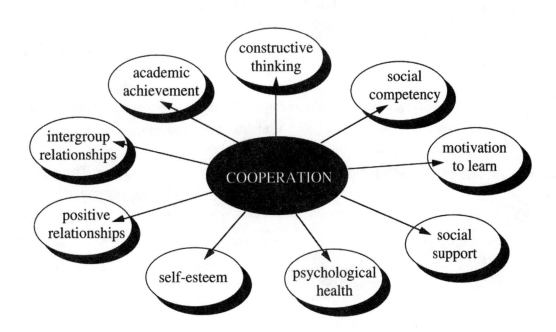

These benefits are healing components that can build community and democracy within schools, families, workplaces and the nation. We doubt that the many problems of youth—alienation, violence, drug abuse, gangs, school dropouts, suicide, delinquency and despair—will ever lessen unless school, family and community systems model cooperation and caring.

If you are trying to convince your school board, administrators, parents or other teachers that cooperative learning groups are effective, we urge you to lead discussions on the benefits of cooperation. The Tribes Learning Community process not only fosters development and learning for young adolescents but establishes a culture of caring and support, active participation, and high expectations for all groups of the school.

RESPONSIVE EDUCATION

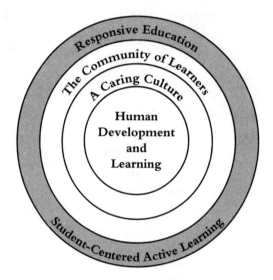

**THE DEVELOPMENTAL
PROCESS OF TRIBES**

Responsive education is an active learning process that supports the intellectual, social, emotional, physical and spiritual or inner development of young adolescents. The four essential tasks of adolescence—autonomy and independence, social competency, a sense of purpose and the capacity to problem-solve—are the compass points for teachers in Tribes TLC® middle level schools. The important tasks gain support daily through the social interaction and cooperation in tribes, and in the socially equitable classroom culture of caring.

*Oh, good, there's a chart
on the next page!*

STAGES TOWARDS EXCELLENCE THROUGH GROUP LEARNING

WHOLE CLASS INSTRUCTION	THE TRIBES COMMUNITY CIRCLE	COOPERATIVE LEARNING IN TRIBES	DISCOVERY LEARNING IN TRIBES
TEACHER: directs lectures facts and concepts	*TEACHER:* directs initiates activity	*TEACHER:* plans initiates strategy	*TEACHER:* selects topic/problem engages students through inclusion makes connections to past and present learning experiences lays ground work for group task
asks questions	asks questions		
seeks correct answers assigns desk work	affirms multiple answers	*STUDENT TRIBES:* discuss and work on task or problem seek ideas and report solutions to class	*STUDENT TRIBES:* 1. *engage* define inquiry questions and process select question to explore (teacher acts as resource facilitator)
manages behavior	manages behavior builds inclusion	manage task and interaction build inclusion and influence	2. *explore* implement activities to explore inquiry manage and assess group interaction
	STUDENTS: use agreements learn collaborative skills work in collaboration reflect on interaction	monitor agreements use appeciation	3. *explain* articulate observations and ideas share and clarify terms/language with facilitator (facilitator determines misconceptions and levels of understanding) present learning/project to whole class or parents justify conclusion based on academic knowledge
tests for facts		reflect on learning and group interaction assess for knowledge and learning	4. *elaborate* expand on concepts and make connections to real world
STUDENTS: learn alone	learn together	learn together	5. *evaluate* reflect on performance outcomes share appreciation students (and teacher) assess learning

The chart, **Stages Towards Excellence Through Group Learning,** illustrates the continuum of change in teaching practices that thousands of Tribes teachers are making to reach and teach students more effectively—and to improve test scores! The "stages towards excellence" are initiated as teachers moderate their use of whole class instruction and gradually use the Community Circle, Cooperative Learning and Discovery Learning. Curricula is increasingly taught through active learning group experiences… and transferring responsibility and leadership to student groups. Wherever you and your faculty are now on the continuum is truly okay. What is important is that teachers support each other, coach each other and reflect upon their progress along the way. Change takes time, but once the direction is clear, it builds a spirit of community, collegiality and excellence in learning throughout a school.

Active or hands-on learning is given nearly universal support from researchers and respected educators as the best, and perhaps only way, for students to develop capacities in critical thinking, problem-solving and decision-making. Recommended practices are cooperative learning, constructivism, instruction and practice in class discussion, responding to open-ended questions, research (using materials other than texts), writing projects, cooperative group projects, decision-making, problem-solving, brainstorming, role-play, simulations, perspective taking, on-site learning, observation, mock trials, case studies, town meetings, interaction with guest speakers and resource persons, and community service projects.[8]

Active learning must feel like flying!

ABOUT THE STAGES

As soon as teachers of a school have become trained in the basic Tribes Learning Community course, they are ready to implement the process by engaging students daily in a Tribes Community Circle. The objective of this first stage is to build inclusion, to learn to use the four Tribes agreements and to teach students to assess their participation and learning through group reflection. The community circle is, however, teacher-centered—all eyes and ears on the teacher while he or she introduces topics, asks questions and controls behavior. Unfortunately, some few teachers assume that they are "doing Tribes" because they have their classes meet in the circle configuration. The community circle stage, used consistently, does develop a caring community climate and social skills—but it is only the launching pad to the next stage, Tribes Cooperative Learning.

Once students are familiar with the Tribes community process, the agreements, and some of the collaborative skills, the teacher and students organize tribes for cooperative learning. The classroom takes on new energy and motivation among students as the teacher's style changes from whole class direct instruction to facilitating active group learning. Gradually increased responsibility is transferred to students to learn academic material, to monitor the agreements and to manage the interaction of their tribes. The transfer from teacher to students not only is motivational but especially meets the developmental needs of middle level adolescents. No longer do teachers spend 70% of their time lecturing, asking questions, giving instructions and disciplining. As facilitators of cooperative learning, teachers then have that much time to give support and encouragement to students. Best of all, they have time to know their students and tailor learning experiences to their interests and needs.

The move to Tribes Discovery Learning adds even a more significant dimension and promise for the education of today's children. The Tribes Discovery Learning process is based on decades of learning about teaching by such eminent leaders as John Dewey, John Piaget, Jerome Bruner, Howard Gardner and Lev Vygotsky, to name but a few. Even back to the 18th century, a Neapolitan philosopher, Gambattista Vico, asserted that humans can only understand what they have themselves "constructed." Today the concept has become known as constructivism, and is gaining ever-increasing validity from recent evidence in the brain and biological sciences.[9] The approach engages students in social dialogue to define questions for inquiry, research, problem-solving, and to challenge hypotheses, design projects, test/defend solutions and evaluate their collaborative results. It transforms academic concepts for young learners into meaningful real-world possibilities.

Most teachers have learned the hard way that placing socially unskilled students in a learning group and expecting them to cooperate will not be successful. Students must have learned essential social, communication and group skills so that they can work well together. Unfortunately, teachers who do not realize this give up group learning, and sacrifice the proven benefits their students and they could have.

Turn back to the last chapter to recall the student-centered classroom study.

Tribes is the glue that holds it all together...

...and makes group learning successful!

Sure, and that happens with adult groups too!

Tribes Discovery Learning is an integration of two frameworks:

1. the Tribes group development process of inclusion/influence/community, and the collaborative group skills and agreements; and

2. a constructivist instructional model, developed for the Biological Science Curriculum Study (Roger Bybee, Principal Investigator, Miami Museum of Science) and known as the "Five E's" standing for Engage, Explore, Explain, Elaborate, and Evaluate.[10]

The complementary frameworks make planning easy for teachers who are committed to being responsive to the learning needs of young adolescents.

We'll refer to the stages of the chart as we move through the "how-to-do-it" chapters. For now, just compare the first two columns: Whole Class Instruction and The Tribes Community Circle.

THE FIRST STAGE—THE TRIBES COMMUNITY CIRCLE

The special spirit of community doesn't just happen in a classroom or organization by dividing people up to work in small groups, or by using randomly selected group activities. Building community is a deliberate process that needs to be facilitated over a period of time. The daily community circle is step one in actualizing the culture of Tribes and the environment that builds resiliency... namely: caring relationships, positive expectation messages, and beliefs and opportunities for participation and contribution.

It begins by creating inclusion for every person within the intended learning community and by practicing the set of positive Tribes agreements:

- Attentive listening
- Appreciation/No put-downs
- Right to pass
- Mutual respect.

It takes several weeks for all students within a new class to be able to know everyone else. The purpose of the time is to give students many opportunities to present themselves in positive ways. During this time, the teacher not only will be using many of the Tribes inclusion strategies from this book, but will be teaching collaborative group skills and engaging students in honoring agreements. She will also be modeling the skills and agreements. Tribes teachers may have students meet several times each day in a community circle for discussions on curricula, learning skills, reflecting on the day, giving statements of appreciation and celebrating.

At the same time that a teacher begins to help students become familiar with the community circle process, he also begins to have people meet in pairs, triads, and groups of four or five, as an additional way to promote inclusion and to begin working together on academic topics.

INCLUSION EXAMPLE: "Find two people you still do not know very well and for five minutes share why you enjoy a favorite outdoor activity."

ACADEMIC EXAMPLE: "Turn to a neighbor and for a few minutes talk about what you would do if you ever became the President of the United Nations."

This use of temporary small groups helps to make the transition to long-term Tribe membership groups. It also gives the teacher an opportunity to see how different combinations of students work together.

GETTING STARTED

Remember the Tribes Trail Map in Chapter 6? Notice that in the beginning the teacher needs to be directive to help everyone become comfortable and feel included. The quality of the classroom environment is strongly influenced by a teacher's personal style, the behavior that he or she models and expects from his or her students. What is talked about during a community circle session may be less important at this point than how the class interacts together. The circle in which people are sitting needs to be large enough so that everyone can see each other. Begin by saying something like, "This year our class will be working together in some new ways—in small groups, so that people can help each other learn, and to learn from each other. We also will meet often as a whole class in a community circle like this."

During this first introduction, raise your hand and tell the class that this is how you will ask for attention. It is a non-verbal signal for everyone also to raise his or her hand and to stop talking. You might state that using the signal means they will never have to hear you shout.

"Now, how many people would like that?" (Ask for a show of hands.) "It is also a great test of our awareness, or consciousness."

GIVING INSTRUCTIONS

Describe the activity or task that the community will be doing, and give the purpose for doing it. Use initial strategies that promote inclusion. Some that may be appropriate are: Community Circle Topics, Something Good, or Wishful Thinking. The Matrix grid at the beginning of the section on learning strategies helps you to make selections. The primary purpose of active learning strategies is to serve as structures (formats) to teach academic material.

INITIATING SHARING

Initiate sharing by being the first to speak on the selected topic, and then invite others to do so by going around the circle. Remind everyone that they have the right-to-pass. When someone does pass, openly acknowledge the person with a nod or smile to convey that passing is okay. After going around the circle once, facilitate a second go-around to give those who hesitated to speak the first time a second opportunity.

KEEPING THINGS MOVING

It is best to refrain from repeating, paraphrasing or commenting on anyone's contribution. Make mental notes on what you may want to bring up later. However, if someone does get put down (derisive laughter, groans, etc.) deal with the incident in a direct but matter-of-fact way. "People, remember the agreement that we made about not putting anyone down." Or ask the group, "Which agreement do we seem to be forgetting?" Let the class identify it rather than you doing so.

LEARNING AND PRACTICING THE TRIBES AGREEMENTS

The second purpose of the community circle is to teach and practice the Tribes agreements and other collaborative group skills. At the same time that you introduce a discussion topic or an active learning strategy, also announce the skill to be practiced at the same time: "Class, we will also be practicing attentive listening during our ten minute discussion." Begin transferring responsibility to the class by asking one or two people to keep track of the time, and later reporting their observations on how well people listened to each other. The class also can discuss and list "Spotlight Behaviors" that time-keepers select, do not disclose, but look for during circle time. At the close of the circle discussion the time-keepers identify people who demonstrated a "Spotlight Behavior." The rest of the class guesses which behaviors were spotlighted.

ENCOURAGING FOLLOW-UP

After everyone has had a turn, allow time for questions and comments. Ask people to speak directly to one another and to use first names. Model this by saying something like, "Lisa, it would be exciting to hear more about the set design for the play."

Initiate the follow-up referring to some of those mental notes you were keeping. Invite others to do the same. Do not dominate the discussion yourself. Just facilitate and clarify as needed.

DEFINING COMMUNITY AGREEMENTS

It is important for early teenagers to enter into a discussion of what they need in order to feel safe or trusting in a group. Set aside time to do this even though you may have shared the Tribes agreements early. Your students will own them once they have brainstormed what they want their class to be like. This can be done as a brainstorm in small groups or as a community circle discussion. Typically, people will say things like:
- "I don't like it when people call me names."
- "I don't want to get pushed around."
- "I don't want to do something just because everyone else does."
- "I don't want our group to fight and hassle all the time."
- "I want people to like me."

After the brainstorm have the class or small groups synthesize and summarize the statements as closely as possible to support:
- Attentive listening
- Appreciation/No put-downs
- Right to pass
- Mutual respect.

Discuss any statements that do not seem to fit. It's okay if the class feels it needs one more agreement. However, since the purpose of these agreements is to build a positive learning environment—and to have students become responsible for sustaining them—the list should be no more than five. Agreements must not be seen as school or teacher rules. Tribe agreements are positive and relational, defining how people want to relate to and treat each other. Such rules as "No Running in the Halls" or "No Pushing in the Bus Line" are not what is meant by relational agreements. In time these types of behaviors will lessen as the community agreements of mutual respect and no put-downs are internalized by students. The point is to have your students "own" the agreements as much as possible. Even though you are tempted to make a sign or graphic of the agreements to post, invite students to do so. It may help to awaken new "gifts."

Your own modeling is absolutely the most essential factor in altering the learning culture. Modeling comes through to kids as authentic when it is congruent and heartfelt.

Owning and living the agreements yourself also means:

• Setting aside a lesson plan long enough to tune into a student's concern or pain

• Being non-judgmental, patient, and caring even with the more difficult ones

• Avoiding subtle put-downs in the midst of frustration or stress

• Standing on your own rights... to pass, to state your feelings, to say, "No, I choose not to do that. It would not be good for me."

• Affirming through warm eye contact or a gentle touch on the shoulder

• Laughing at your own mistakes; conveying your own fallibility and commitment to lifelong growth and learning.

ATTENTIVE LISTENING

Attentive listening is probably the most important social skill to be taught and practiced by everyone in the learning community. Unfortunately, for many young adolescents (as well as adults) the experience of being listened to in a caring way rarely happens.

Attentive listening is a gift to be given. It depends upon:

• Acknowledging the person who is speaking—giving him full attention and eye contact

• Withholding one's own comments, opinions, and need to talk at the time

• Paraphrasing key words to encourage the speaker and to let her know she has been heard

• Affirming through body language that the speaker is being heard

• Paying attention not only to the words but also to the feelings behind the words.

Being there means speaking, and listening with head and heart.

Too often we half-listen to each other, running the words through our heads that we want to say as soon as it is our turn. Most teachers assume that kids have learned at home how to listen. Most adults assume we all do it well—though we may never have been taught the principles.

The skill of attentive listening needs to be considered a priority within every school's curriculum because it affects children's ability to learn academic material. This is especially important as classrooms move toward cooperative learning, inquiry, collaborative projects and group discourse.

Begin by teaching students three essential listening strategies to be found in the section on learning strategies. Namely....

• Teaching listening

• Teaching paraphrasing

• Reflecting feelings.

you

eyes

undivided attention

ear

heart

APPRECIATION/NO PUT-DOWNS

Since one of our main objectives is to develop a sense of self-worth and self-esteem in early adolescents, the scores of derogatory remarks that bombard young people each day must be eliminated. Unfortunately, put-down remarks can be a basic form of communication among teenagers and adults themselves. At times they are used in families to convey affection: "You goof-off, you jerk, you crazy kid." Though off-hand or flippant, they not only damage self-esteem but undermine the level of trust within a group. A positive climate cannot develop unless we:

- Challenge students themselves to point out and object to put-down remarks, and
- Encourage students instead to exchange statements of appreciation.

One way to encourage your class to confront put-down statements is to teach them to respond with "I-Messages."

Example: "Michael, I feel angry when I'm called 'stupid.' It's a put-down and it hurts!" See the next chapter for a discussion on teaching "I-messages."

STATEMENTS OF APPRECIATION

Minimizing put-down statements is half of the step toward creating a caring community. Put-downs need to be replaced with statements of appreciation. Helping people of any age to express appreciation often can be like swimming against a strong current. It is a sad commentary on our society that in the course of a day we make five times as many negative comments as statements that affirm the value of others.

Statements of appreciation are invited at the conclusion of every group learning experience, and are modeled by the teacher throughout the day. It is very important that you search for truths to say. Kids know when something doesn't ring true—is not sincere and honest. To help people begin making statements of appreciation, use such sentence starters as these:

"I liked it when... (describe the situation)."

"I felt good when you..."

"I admire you for... (describe the quality)."

After completing a group activity, write the sentence starter on the chalk board and invite people to make statements. Your own modeling encourages the sharing of positive statements perhaps more than anything. It is important that you model being both a good giver and a good receiver.

Examples:

"I appreciate your kindness, Joel."

"The ideas that you came up with, Sandy, made our project special."

"I felt honored when you gave me a copy of your own poem."

THE RIGHT-TO-PASS

The right-to-pass means that each person has the right to choose the extent to which she or he will share in a group activity. It is the essence of our democratic system not to be coerced, to have a right to one's privacy, and to be able to take a stand apart from the majority. Without such guarantees, individual freedom within a group is not protected. Choosing the right-to-pass means that the community member prefers not to share personal information or feelings, or to actively participate in the group at the moment. It is his or her choice to remain quiet and to be an observer for a short period of time. This right must be affirmed repeatedly by teachers and peers: "Okay, you do have the right to pass. It's just fine to do so." Being a silent observer is still a form of participation. It also gives support to a student who at the time may be concerned with a social or emotional issue.

This protective agreement is essential within all organizational and group settings. It provides control to participants. It encourages adolescents to be self-determining and responsible among peers. It gives young adolescents the practice and courage to stand back from situations that are uncomfortable or contrary to their own values. Drug abuse prevention programs for secondary students have emphasized the teaching of refusal skills—and to "Just Say No." Urging socially conscious middle level students to just say "No" is somewhat simplistic. They need to have repeated opportunities to assert their right-to-pass in the midst of working with peers daily in school settings. It is part of becoming independent and autonomous whether in good or bad groups. It is an essential developmental task and resiliency strength.

Many teachers are anxious that if this agreement is used in classrooms, students will pass on learning subject matter. First of all, the agreement does not apply when individual accountability is required on learning tasks. Students do not have the right to pass on homework, taking tests, responding to the teacher, etc. They do, however, have the right to pass on peer-led interaction. It is important to keep in mind that…

- Temporarily withdrawing from activity does not mean a student is not learning.
- You can count on the tribe, or peer group, to draw the person who usually passes back into an active working role.
- Healthy human development and resiliency depend upon young people becoming inner-directed rather than remaining dependent upon outer control from others.

MUTUAL RESPECT

The purpose of the mutual respect agreement is to assure everyone that their individual cultural values, beliefs, and needs will be considered and properly honored. It also means that adults demonstrate respect for students' rights, needs, and differences. The rich multicultural diversity of our population is an invaluable resource for this country's future. Where better to learn to live it than within the school community? The agreement means respect for:

- Others—no matter what their race, gender, age, color, or learning ability
- Newcomers from other cities, states, or countries
- Teachers, parents, and other caring adults
- Personal property and individual privacy
- Individual skills, talents, and contributions.

This new agreement for the Tribes process was expanded from one once called "confidentiality/no rumors-no gossip," which we regard as one of the important aspects of mutual respect. Students will continue to need assurance of confidentiality—to know that others in their group will not disclose personal confidences. For students in classroom tribes, no-gossip does not mean that a student should not go home and tell her parents what she said or did in her tribe. It does mean that she does not have group members' permission to disclose what someone else may have said.

BUILDING COLLABORATIVE SKILLS THROUGH STAGES OF GROUP DEVELOPMENT

The Tribes process with its sequential stages of group development—inclusion, influence and community—is a pathway for the development of the essential collaborative skills that students (and all of us) need in order to live, love, play, and work well together. Collaborative skills don't just happen, even though we may use cooperative learning groups in classrooms, or have the intent to collaborate with others on a work project. The skills must be taught and practiced over and over in relation to others who share a common purpose and meaning in their lives. This could be a class, faculty, a work team, a board of directors, a neighborhood group, or city council. Collaborative skills are the constructive thinking and social skills set forth in the U.S. Secretary of Labor's report as necessary skills for the 21st Century. Whenever human systems do not work well or fall apart, one can be certain that essential people skills are missing.

The graphic on the next page illustrates the twelve skills taught and strengthened during the sequential stages of group development in a Tribes classroom. Inclusion skills prepare the class to handle the influence stage. The essential collaborative skills learned in the influence stage become the foundation for a vital community... working together with others from diverse backgrounds, solving problems, assessing for improvement, and celebrating their achievements. The ongoing practice of these key collaborative skills creates a classroom with high levels of participation on the part of all students and establishes a positive climate for teaching and learning.

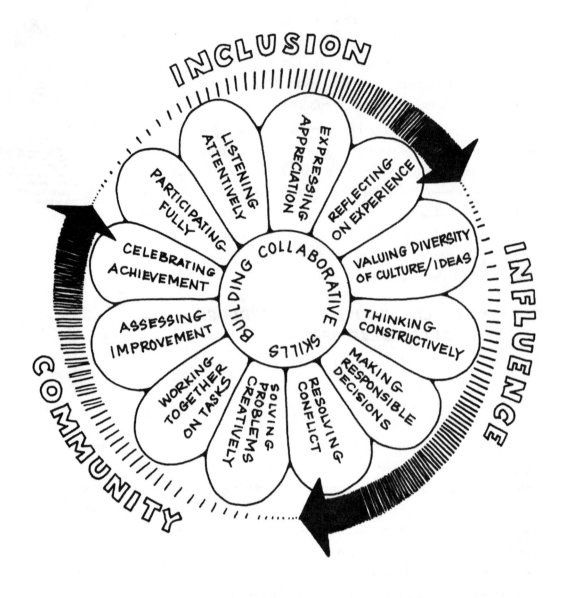

SEVEN STEPS IN TEACHING COLLABORATIVE SKILLS

1. Engage students in identifying the need for the skill (using discussion, role-play, story, or situation).

2. Teach the skill (using the Looks/Sounds/Feels-Like structure or other strategy).

3. Practice the skill regularly, and have students give feedback on how well it was used.

4. Transfer the responsibility to the tribes to remind each other to use the skill.

5. Ask reflection questions about the use of the skill in tribes, the class, the playground, at home, etc.

6. Point out times when you notice people using the skill well.

7. Notice and celebrate when the skill is "owned" as a natural behavior in the classroom or school.

TEACHING COMMUNITY AGREEMENTS

Invite students to sit together in a community circle. Pre-sketch or draw the following grid on the blackboard and have the class fill in the specific examples:

AGREEMENT: LISTENING		
LOOKS LIKE	**SOUNDS LIKE**	**FEELS LIKE**
heads together	talking one at a time	great
eyes looking	encouragement	I'm important
people nodding	good idea	people care
leaning forward	uh-huh	I'm smart
smiling	yes!	we're friends

1. Invite discussion on the need for the skill or agreement.
   Remember the cooperative learning way: Meet them where they are; Don't lecture or talk at them; Invite students to share what they already know and then add to it.
2. Ask people to call out words for the grid: "What does listening look like?" "What does it sound like?" "What does it feel like?"

The four agreements should be posted in a prominent place and reviewed whenever the community circle or tribes meet. When learning the Tribes agreements, affirm the behaviors whenever you see them happening, and in time ask students to do the same.

Example: "I can tell the Cyberfox tribe is listening well to each other... people are talking one at a time and their heads are together."

Now and then you may inadvertently overlook one of the agreements yourself. Do encourage the class to bring this to your attention. Accept such reminders graciously and without defensiveness. Kids can be great agreement and social skills reinforcers. You can count on them to monitor and help sustain the Tribes learning environment for the class.

ASKING REFLECTION QUESTIONS

The other key not only to have group learning be successful, but to have students move to new highs in academic achievement, is to follow every learning experience with "reflection" questions. Research studies as well as the experience of hundreds of teachers verify that the time taken to ask reflection questions can double the retention of the facts and concepts learned in an academic lesson.[11] See the appendix for an article on the impact of group "processing" or "reflection." In Tribes TLC® we prefer to use the word "reflection" rather than "process" in order to distinguish the learning experience questions from the Tribes group development process. We also want to teach and emphasize that reflection (meta-cognition) is a very necessary skill for living and surviving well in today and tomorrow's complex world of information and change.

Three types of reflection questions are used in Tribes Learning Communities.

THREE TYPES OF REFLECTION QUESTIONS

CONTENT (COGNITIVE LEARNING): Questions that are focused on the academic concepts, ideas and knowledge gained from the learning experience; also the constructive thinking skills that were used.

COLLABORATIVE (SOCIAL LEARNING): Questions that focus on the interaction and participation of members in the learning group; also the collaborative skills that were used.

DISCOVERING GIFTS (PERSONAL LEARNING): Questions that help to identify skills contributed to complete the task; also special gifts, talents, interests noticed by the tribe or the student individually.

"Here is an example of reflection questions I used with my 8th grade literature class. The class had been reading the short story, "The Advocates," by Franz Kafka.[12]

CONTENT: What does your tribe believe is the main message of the story? How did you go about analyzing the several messages?

COLLABORATIVE: How did you go about getting everyone's opinion? Is there a particular collaborative skill your tribe needs to practice next time?

DISCOVERING GIFTS: How did you help your tribe? Is this a skill you have noticed before about yourself?

You do not need to ask all three types of reflection questions after a learning experience, but do use at least two of the different types. Base your choice on what you believe will make the content meaningful and the social or personal learning significant for the majority of students in the class.

Time out for reflection also develops the capacity to learn from experience and understand the working dynamics of groups and systems. It supports all aspects of the definition of human development: the ability to discover, sustain, and alter "situations"—to move into ever-widening realms of knowledge and experience.

The questions suggested for each strategy in this book may not be the best ones to ask your own class. There simply are no sure-fire questions that are appropriate for all cultural populations and age levels. Your own intuition, creativity and judgment are needed to draw out meaningful learning for your students.

ENCOURAGING APPRECIATION

The power of the Tribes process on adolescent development also comes from the practice of giving students opportunities to express appreciation to each other after working together. To be able to hear one's peers acknowledge special qualities, skills, and contributions to the group is much more meaningful to most students than periodic affirmation from a teacher. Moreover, how many times a day can any teacher affirm each and every student in the class!

USING TEMPORARY SMALL GROUPS TO BUILD COMMUNITY

If you look at the Tribes Trail Map again, you will notice that pairs, triads, and temporary groups are also used to build inclusion in the community before people become members in long-term tribes. While your students are working together in these "trial tribes" you can observe how people get along with others. This serves as valuable information when you are ready to move students into long-term tribes.

BUILDING COMMUNITY CREATIVELY

Please do not feel limited to the active learning strategies contained in this book in order to develop a sense of community among all your students. An abundance of initial inclusion activities exists in many other books. Use your teacher ingenuity to create whatever will best reach your students. Good community building strategies....

- have win-win rather than win-lose outcomes—cooperation rather than competition
- provide inclusion for everyone—all can participate
- draw upon and highlight the contributions that people make in the course of the activity.

The best kind of learning is learning all together, in little groups or big groups; it's a really good way to teach kids. Learn with each other, not just alone. Kids who don't learn this way are really missing out. I think it's a privilege for us to be able to have this kind of education. People who just learn the traditional way, just by themselves, who don't get help, it's like, totally un-nineties. It's also scary.[13]

—Julia Devanthery Lewis, sixth grader
Cambridge, Massachusetts

9

Building Small Groups for Growth and Learning

9 Building Small Groups for Growth and Learning

I learned you have to get along with others to work in groups.
—James, 5th grader

No put-downs—that's a good agreement so no one will say mean stuff. I like all the agreements but I like no put-downs better than all of them...nice!
—James , 6th grader

I learned about attentive listening. You can learn more!
—Courtney, 5th grader[1]

*How do I know when my students are ready
to work in on-going small groups?*

READINESS FOR TRIBES

After several weeks of community strategies, your class is ready to be in tribes when you can say "yes" to the following questions:

1. Do students understand and respect the agreements?
2. Do they know one another from having worked in pairs, triads or other temporary groups?
3. Can you identify the leaders, the less popular students, the particular friendships, the possible behavior problems?
4. Have students had successful learning experiences working in practice groups?

Introduce the concept by having the class meet in a community circle and discuss their experience of working together, not only in the class circle but in many small groups. Invite them to discuss:

• groups they belong to—teams, families, clubs, departments, etc.

• the purpose of belonging to various groups

• what makes groups work well.

Tell the class that everyone will become a member of a learning group to work together on special projects, research, and curricula—and to help each other be successful. It may be helpful to share some of the proven benefits realized through cooperation (discussed in the previous chapter), and discuss how business and other organizations work in teams. Do what you can to help the class become invested in the idea of belonging to a learning group and working together rather than solely on their own. Of course, all will wonder how the groups will be formed and who will be in their tribe. State that each person will write the names of several people they would like to have in their learning group and assure your students that one or more of those named will be in their tribe.

SOCIOMETRY MADE EASY—HOW TO BUILD TRIBES

For middle level students, groups of 4, 5 and 6 are appropriate. Smaller groups of 4-5 work well for students 10-12 years old, and groups of 5-6 for 13-15 year olds. More than 6 people in a learning group, whether young adolescents or adults, can lead to more problematical dynamics and difficulties working in collaboration.

Following is a step-by-step process that you can use to achieve a sociometric balance in your classroom groups, without using any cumbersome instruments. The "Seven Friends" method of building tribes enables you to achieve the best mix of skills, cultures, and relationships. It has the added advantage of allowing your students some influence in determining who will be in their tribe. Be sure to give yourself enough time to do this thoughtfully.

SEVEN FRIENDS

1. Give each person a 5" x 8" index card. Have people print their names in the center of the card.

2. Ask each person to print the names of seven other people they would like to have in a tribe. Ask for at least 3 boys and 3 girls to be on the list.

3. Collect all the cards. Remind your students that they will each be in a tribe with at least one identified friend, but not with all of those listed.

4. Assuming that you will have five tribes, select the cards belonging to five leader types, those who have been named the most by others and who also enjoy learning. Spread these cards out on a table.

5. Select the cards of five students who exhibit quiet or less positive behavior. Place one of their cards next to each of the leader cards.

6. Add the remaining cards to each group, making sure that each card has a name requested by someone in the group.

7. Make any adjustments necessary to achieve a balance of boys and girls.

8. Check once more to be sure that each card is still matched with a friend.

FORMING TRIBES

Once you have determined the composition of the tribes, set a date when everyone will move into the groups. Advance notice builds great anticipation. When "T Day" arrives, choose an exciting way for people to discover who is in their tribe. Many teachers have used "People Puzzles" or the options found at the end of the strategy, "Cruising Careers." You can, of course, invent other ways to form tribes.

PEOPLE PUZZLES

1. Begin with sheets of poster board, one for each tribe.

2. Sketch a design on each sheet so that you can cut as many puzzle pieces as the number of students you want in a particular tribe.

3. Print a student's name on each piece. Make sure that all the members of a tribe are included in the same People Puzzle.

4. Hide the pieces around the classroom at a convenient time.

5. Tell the class to look for their own names and find people with matching pieces.

When everyone has found their tribe, assign the groups to different areas of the classroom. Desks or tables and chairs need to be rearranged so that tribe members face one another. Once the tribes have settled down, ask reflection questions. Examples:

- *DISCOVERING GIFTS:* What did you learn about yourself in finding members of your tribe?
- *CONTENT:* What made this strategy a good way for people to find group members?

After the tribes have done some initial inclusion strategies, tell the class that people will remain in these groups for at least one month. The class then will evaluate how their tribes are working and whether any changes need to be made. This defuses the inevitable remark, "I wanted to have someone else in my tribe!" At one time a survey was conducted to learn how many Tribes teachers actually had to alter the membership of their class tribes. Those who had students stay in the same groups for at least three weeks never felt the need to make any membership changes. The secret is that after that much time, the inclusion strategies, group process, and positive agreements have created a sense of belonging, caring, and trust. People have forgotten about wanting a particular friend—they have made several new close friends whom they like, and whom they do not want to leave.

BUILDING TRIBAL INCLUSION

Remember that Tribes Trail Map and discussion back in Chapter 6? Implementation of it moves into daily application. Although you did many inclusion strategies with the whole class to build community before forming tribes, the need for inclusion continues. Each time a new group forms, people sense the same "stranger anxiety." If this issue is not addressed, it limits the ability of a group to work well together. Inclusion must happen all over again with the new tribes.

As a facilitator of this group process, you need to select a series of inclusion strategies that will help people present who they are, what they do well, and what their expectations, hopes, and needs might be. Taking the time to do this during the initial days in tribes makes all the difference in managing the class and having cooperative learning work well. People are not ready to work together on curricula unless inclusion and trust have been developed within their learning groups. Disruptive behavior and inattention happens whenever students do not feel included.

That's what plagues teachers throughout the day and school year. Anti-social behavior gains attention—"someone notices 'me' and now cares." It is a way to feel important in the midst of many

A way to feel included is to grab influence.

others. The Tribes process decreases behavior problems in schools simply because everyone is included and valued.

On the day before the new tribes are to be announced, invite people to bring something meaningful to share at the first meeting of their new tribe. The item could be an award, a gift, a picture or something written or made. Sharing something symbolic helps each person to talk about self and initiates the identification of individual gifts, skills and interests. More than all it develops a sense of belonging and positive energy in the group.

STRATEGIES THAT BUILD INCLUSION

Though we have said it before and will say it again, it is important that you select inclusion strategies geared to the interests, age level, and culture of your particular class. Do read the preface to the section on Learning Strategies before leaping into using them. Hopefully, you are involved in an in-service training conducted by one of CenterSource Systems' certified Tribes TLC® District Trainers. If so, you will experience many good initial strategies that can be easily adapted to your class. Some of the favorites are...

- Wishful Thinking
- I'm Proud Circle
- Campaign Manager
- Interview Circle.

One teacher advises, "You need to be as flexible and creative as you are with all other curricula!"

THE FIRST DAYS OF USING TRIBES

1. Commit to begin and end each day with a community circle.
2. Ask students to review the class agreements.
3. Use an inclusion strategy for the whole community. Ask reflection questions. Give an overview of the day's schedule, work, and any announcements.
4. Have people move to their customary work areas.
5. Explain the objective of the learning experience or task, and the collaborative skills or agreements that people will later assess.
6. Give the directions one step at a time, using as few words as possible. Write the steps on the board if there are several.
7. If clarification is needed on instructions, ask that the group confer among themselves before asking you.
8. State how much time there will be to complete the task or strategy. Ask each tribe to make sure that every member participates.
9. While the tribes are working together, observe their progress. Intervene only if absolutely necessary.
10. Signal when time is up, and have each tribe report progress by responding to appropriate reflection questions. Reflection questions can be handled either in community circle or in tribes.
11. Invite statements of appreciation.

TRANSFERRING RESPONSIBILITY

One of the major objectives in using learning groups with early adolescents is to call forth their positive leadership qualities and self-responsibility. This means that an intentional transfer of control needs to be made from the teacher to the tribe, and from the tribe to its members. As a sensitive teacher you can look for opportunities to have the tribes increase their capacity to function independently. Here are some of the ways in which responsibility can be transferred:

- Intervene only as necessary while the tribes are working together
- Encourage members to remind one another about the agreements
- When students ask you a question, refrain from answering immediately; turn it back to the class or tribe, asking "Who can help to clarify the instructions?" "What ideas do other people have?"
- Ask tribe members to assume helpful tasks and roles
- Have tribes keep attendance, make contact with people who are absent, and help returning members to catch up with the tribe and class
- Have the class make a list of classroom maintenance tasks, and have the tribes assume different ones for a period of time
- Have the tribes plan parties, field trips, parent involvement, and other class activities
- Ask tribes for suggestions to improve lesson plans, academic projects, and the learning environment
- Have them give feedback to you as the teacher.

The process of transferring responsibility to students increases participation—and, if you recall, participation, caring, and high expectations contribute to the development of resiliency. It also supports the developmental adolescent tasks—encouraging independence, social competency, gaining a sense of purpose and problem-solving.

OBSERVING THE PROCESS

Admittedly, it can feel strange to be in the background while your tribes tackle a challenging, engrossing task or strategy. This, however, is not a time to sit idly by, or to catch up on grading papers! During these periods when your busy tribes cease to need you, you become the process observer, looking for the new skills, gifts and behaviors to be affirmed. It also gives you time to notice the dynamics within the tribes. Following is a list of some of the dynamics that you can observe and reflect upon while your tribes are working together.

OBSERVATION CHECKLIST

1. How are people sitting?
   Are they in a close working configuration, or are some people sitting back?
   Are they leaning forward attentively, or are they slouching, sprawling, or lying back?

2. How are people participating?
   Are a few doing all the talking or work? Is participation balanced?
   Are people lively and animated, or lethargic and tentative?
   Is everyone focused on what is happening, or are side conversations taking place?
   Are people passing?

3. How are people taking care of one another?
   Are they listening to one another?
   Are put-downs happening? If so, are they being confronted by group members?
   Are disagreements being resolved in satisfying (win-win) ways?
   Are kindness and cooperation being demonstrated?
   Is appreciation being expressed?
   Is the group drawing in the quieter people?

4. How are people feeling and behaving?
   Are they smiling and/or laughing?
   Is your intuitive response one of warmth and relaxation, or anxiety and tension?

5. Are they working well on the learning task?
   Who has assumed leadership?
   Are the less social or shy learners included?
   Do they seem mindful of the goal to complete the task on time?

6. What is happening for you?

7. Other

FACILITATING THE PROCESS

What happens when you observe breakdowns in the process? Let's use an example. You have given your 7th grade tribes the strategy, "Brainstorming," so that they will learn the process and use it later in a history lesson. One recorder in each tribe is furiously attempting to write down all the ideas being voiced by tribe members. While observing the behaviors in each tribe, you notice that Tanya, one of the recorders, is having a hard time getting all the information down on paper. People are saying things like, "Hey, you left out my idea!" "Slow poke!" Your impulse is to stride over to the group and take charge. Instead, you take a deep breath and reflect on all that is going on. You observe that only two students, Heidi and Jamal, are really "into" the strategy. They're leaning forward and putting forth many ideas. The other tribe members are sitting back rather apathetically, waiting for the time to run out.

What are your alternatives, other than intervening directively?

You could do nothing, in which case the situation would either:

1. Stay the same

2. Get better—someone might remind others of the agreements, or volunteer to help Tanya, or

3. Get worse—an argument might erupt.

A better alternative is to raise your hand and stop the action. Simply call out, "Time out," or "Stop the action!" Wait patiently until order and silence fill the room. Then ask "What's happening?" First ask everyone to look and listen back to what was going on in the classroom or tribes. Suggest that everyone "runs the movie backward" in their heads, and describe what people were doing. The first reflection and statement for each person to make should be, "I saw myself...." Tell students to describe their own behavior, not that of others. Then ask for descriptions of specific sounds and actions. Follow the "Time Out Reflection Cycle" below and lead the class into deciding what everyone can do to improve things.

USING THE TIME OUT REFLECTION CYCLE

- Stop the action—ask, "What's happening?"
- Give everyone time to reflect—don't start diagnosing the situation yourself. Wait until people begin to speak up.
- Ask for descriptions of specific sounds and actions.
- Ask how people felt and how the behavior or situation affects the class as a whole.
- Invite or brainstorm ideas to change the situation.
- Have everyone decide what to do to improve things.

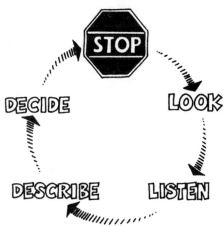

The repeated practice of reflecting on group and community interaction helps people to become aware of the impact of their behavior on others and the dynamic of the group. Reflection is emphasized in Tribes TLC® because it is essential for learning and development.

Of course, if Tanya's tribe does not report the behavior that you observed, you should comment on it. Not to do so would be interpreted as an indication that you were not paying attention, or that you did not think it was important.

KEEPING YOUR PURPOSE AND ROLE IN MIND

The Tribes process integrated with a Responsive Education approach has but one overall purpose:

to assure the growth and human development of every young adolescent in the school community so that each has the knowledge, skills, and resilient strengths to be successful in a world of rapid change.

Meaningful group learning teaches children to reflect upon and manage their own lives well.

This interactive approach to human development and learning makes the "here and now" of each day a laboratory. Through group interaction, this generation of young people will be able to move from a singular focus on "me" to "we"—and to a concern for our community, our nation, and the future of our world.

Our role as educators is to make the process of learning relevant, meaningful, exciting, and effective. Teachers need only to learn how to sustain caring learning environments and teach responsively to the developmental tasks all adolescents are struggling to achieve. Doing just that enables all schools to call forth the best within each and every child. There needs to be a new title for all of the dedicated teachers on the front line of American education—something like "leaders of learning" or "choreographers of human development." Do send us your ideas on this!

LEARNING HOW TO PREVENT AND RESOLVE CONFLICT

One of the most important collaborative skills for today's students and teachers to learn is how to manage conflict—a dynamic that inevitably arises within any group of people working, playing, or living together. Denial or avoidance of a conflict ultimately undermines relationships, the group environment, and the ability to work well together. There's a saying, "There is no way around—only a way through."

Conflict is a natural part of life because as individuals we differ in what we want, need, and think. Conflicts occur over these differences. But conflict itself isn't the problem—it's how we deal with it. Most people have not learned how to manage conflict constructively. As adults in an adolescent's world, we must learn to resolve conflict before we can teach the process.

Within each conflict there is an opportunity to gain new knowledge. If our intent is to learn, we will seek to understand why the conflict happened. In the process, each person discovers more about his or her own perceptions and unspoken assumptions, as well as those of other people. As a result, relationships will be more satisfying.

The capacity of people to live and work well together depends upon how well they learn to solve problems and manage conflict. When a group has the commitment and skill to resolve rather than ignore conflict, individuals feel free to contribute ideas, explore one another's assumptions, and raise questions. This is essential in the process of becoming a learning community of any kind.

Resolving conflict needs to begin with the assumption that a "win-win" solution is possible. Strong feelings often make defining the problem difficult, and what appears to be the problem may be just a superficial issue. Once the real problem is identified and agreed upon, it becomes possible for people who have been in opposition to work out a solution that will be fair to both of them.

Gail Whang, now Health and Safety Program Manager of the Oakland Unified School District in California, emphasizes how combining the process of Tribes and a conflict resolution process affected her former school staff. "Conflict resolution brought people out of their classrooms and together. Tribes built on that power. Not only were we involved together in a school wide program, but because of the nature of both trainings, it brought

> To create a classroom where students feel safe enough to challenge each other—and us—is to give them an enormous gift.[2]
> —ALFIE KOHN

the staff closer. We got beyond griping about students in the lunchroom and began talking to each other about what we valued and who we are. We began to change the culture of our school."

A CONFLICT RESOLUTION CURRICULUM

The outstanding school curriculum referred to by Gail is the Conflict Resolution process developed and published by the Community Board Program of San Francisco. It recommends a set of "building blocks" for the effective resolution of conflict:

• Awareness of conflict in our own lives and how we respond to it

• Appreciation for the differences between people

• Understanding of important feelings

• The ability to talk clearly to another person about a conflict

• The ability to listen to a person with whom we have a conflict.

A specific sequence of steps is suggested for use whenever two students become involved in a conflict:

STEP 1: Both students agree to the ground rules.
"I agree not to interrupt, not to call a name, and I agree to work to solve the conflict."

STEP 2: One person tells his/her side of the story using I-Messages, saying how s/he feels about what happened, and what s/he wants. The other person listens attentively and restates the problem.

STEP 3: The second person restates the problem for the first person. Suggestion: Begin with, "So the problem for you is..."

STEP 4: Steps 2 and 3 are repeated, with the 2nd student speaking.

STEP 5: Both people suggest possible solutions.

STEP 6: Both work to agree on a resolution that is:

• specific

• balanced—both people will be responsible for making it work

• realistic—and will solve the problem.

Many Tribes schools not only use the Community Board Program but also train groups of students as "Conflict Managers." They are identified by the T-shirts that they wear throughout the school—and on athletic fields, playgrounds and in neighborhoods to help kids resolve differences peaceably.[3]

TEACHING I-MESSAGES

It is also very important to teach middle level students (as well as adults!) how to express themselves in heated moments with I-messages. An I-message is a statement of the speaker's feelings in response to the behavior of others. Unlike a You-message, an I-message does not convey judgment, nor is it a put-down. Notice the difference between the following examples:

You-message:

"Kim, you dummy, you ruined my chance to be the pitcher. You make me angry."

I-message:

"Kim, I feel angry whenever a catcher isn't paying attention."

In the first example, Kim was rudely put down and blamed for the situation. In the second example, the speaker took responsibility for his feelings, stated them in strong terms... but did not put the blame on Kim. He defined the behavior that he perceived.

I-MESSAGES	YOU-MESSAGES
State and own the speaker's feelings	Hold another person responsible for the speaker's feelings
Describe the perceived behavior or situation; not a personal judgment	Blame others; judge and put people down

The purpose of an I-message is to communicate feelings in such a way that the other person is not forced to defend herself or avoid the situation. The impact of the You-message blames, shames, or intimidates the other person. It causes the other person to become resistant. The recipient of a You-message hears the message as "you are bad or wrong," and is less likely to consider resolution of the difficulty. Worst of all, You-messages escalate conflict.

You-messages can also masquerade as I-messages: "I feel that you are always a nuisance" is a disguised You-message because:

1. No feelings are stated or owned, even though the speaker says "I feel" (he really means "I think" or "I believe"), and

2. The phrase "You are always a nuisance" is a judgment, implying that the person is bad or incapable of being different.

In teaching people how to use I-messages, it is helpful to write this formula on the board:

I feel _____ (name the feeling)

when _____ (describe the situation or behavior).

Give examples:

"I feel confused when people shout at me."

"I feel scared when anyone threatens me."

I-Messages are also a good way to communicate positive feelings:

"I feel happy when I receive a compliment."

"I feel great when everyone participates."

Use the strategy "Teaching I-messages" from the Learning Strategy section to help your students learn this important life skill.

The I-message is a tricky concept to master even though it seems quite simple at first. This is another instance in which you need to be an appropriate role model. It may take some time, but with daily practice your students will begin to use them.

KNOWING WHEN TO TAKE CHARGE—YOUR CRITERIA

Yes, there are those crisis times when I-messages just won't work—for instance, when you encounter one student hurting another.

"Stop that this instant!" is much more appropriate for the moment than "I feel unhappy when you hit Aaron."

Handling antisocial or inappropriate behavior depends upon thinking through in advance what your own criteria will be:
- When to use additional inclusion activities
- When to encourage students to use I-Messages with one another
- When to use an I-Message yourself
- When to use group problem solving
- When to be directive and take charge.

RESOLVING GROUP ISSUES

The social climate in your classroom and your success with the Tribes process will be greatly influenced by the way in which conflicts and angry feelings are routinely expressed and resolved. As a Tribes teacher, your willingness to acknowledge, discuss, and resolve group issues in a caring, process-based manner will result in growth and learning for you and your students. All groups of people living, playing, or working together experience many predictable interpersonal issues. The chart on the following page gives an overview of typical questions that come up in a group's development, and it gives suggestions on how to resolve many situations.

In the beginning you may hear statements like these that indicate group issues.

"I pass!"
"I don't like my tribe."
"What about the new kid?"
"Hey, that's a put-down!"
"Let's form new tribes."

TRIBES ISSUE CHART

	ISSUES	QUESTIONS/FEELINGS	YOU, THE FACILITATOR, NEED TO
INCLUSION	**PRESENTATION OF SELF**	*Will I like this group?* *How will they get to know me?*	Be directive and provide structure; use many inclusion activities that permit each person to share who they are, what feelings, skills, qualities, and resources they have.
		I feel nervous with these new people. *Will they listen to me?* *Will they put me down?*	Have people work in pairs and triads; it feels less threatening. Teach listening skills. Make sure that people respect the Tribes agreements, especially "No put-downs" and "mutual respect."
	EXPECTATIONS AND NEEDS	*Will we finish by 3 o'clock?* *Can you help me with a problem?*	Provide opportunities for each member to state wants, needs and expectations for the time the group is together.
	ACKNOWLEDGMENT	*Will they like me?* *Do I dare tell someone I think she is a nice person?* *Does anyone else feel the way I feel?*	Be a good role model by giving and receiving appreciation easily. Provide opportunities for people to exchange statements of appreciation and good feelings. Ask reflection questions that encourage people to share thoughts and feelings about coming together as a group.
INFLUENCE	**ME VS. THE GROUP**	*Will my opinions be respected?*	Provide activities that help people share individual differences and cultural strengths.
	GOALS	*What are we to accomplish together?*	Introduce techniques that elicit input from each member in defining group goals. Model and encourage acceptance of all ideas before choosing group goals.
	DECISION MAKING	*How can we reach agreement?*	Introduce techniques for consensus decision making.
	CONFLICT	*How can we work this out?*	Introduce conflict resolution techniques (active learning, I-Messages, role reversal). Assist group members in reaching win-win solutions. Teach collaborative skills.
	LEADERSHIP AND AUTHORITY	*Do we need a leader?*	Encourage rotation of roles. Urge natural leaders to draw out more passive members.
		I resent it when someone tries to tell us what to do.	Ask reflection questions that help members discuss and resolve leadership problems. Use conflict resolution techniques as needed.
COMMUNITY	**CREATIVITY**	*I feel good about my abilities.*	Recognize individuals for unique achievements and gifts; encourage group members to do so with one another.
	COOPERATION	*Our group really works well together.*	Assign group tasks that require innovation, cooperation, and creativity.
	ACHIEVEMENT	*We did a great job!*	Assign projects: All group members receive the same grade or reward.
		What shall we tackle next?	Use groups for peer teaching, problem solving, planning and fun! Be alert for inclusion/influence issues; support groups in resolving them.
	CELEBRATION	*I really like our tribe and community.*	Take the time to celebrate—for whatever big or small reason!

1. "I PASS!"

Early in the tribe-building process, some people may be passing all the time, and others may not be participating. This type of behavior is usually an indication that some people feel unsafe with their groups. Suggestions:

- Discuss the reasons why some people are not participating, and then have the small groups discuss what to do.
- Have people work in pairs. Match a shy person with a more confident, outgoing one.
- Make sure that you are using appropriate inclusion strategies. (Try the strategy "Interview Circle" in tribes.)
- Spend some time with the habitual passer. Learn his special interests and talents; encourage him to share them with the tribe.
- Assign the passer a role or task in the tribe.
- Make sure that the agreements are being honored so that the environment is safe.

2. "I DON'T LIKE MY TRIBE."

A person who feels uncomfortable in his group may say things like:

"I don't like the people in my tribe."

"I get bored in my tribe."

"People in my tribe are dumb."

"I want to be in Sarah's tribe."

Rather than trying to talk a student out of a complaint, use your listening skills to find out what is really going on. Suggestions:

- Enlist the help of the tribe to give the person more inclusion.
- Gear some activities to her learning style and interests.
- Ask the person to "hang in" with the tribe for two or three weeks; by this time things usually work themselves out.

In some extreme cases, it may be advisable to transfer a student to another tribe, or to provide her with something to do alone while tribes are meeting. These are last-resort measures, only to be considered if all else fails.

3. "WHAT ABOUT THE NEW KID?"

When a new person enters your class after tribes have been formed, it is important to give her a special welcome. Her name is Robin....

ADOPTION CEREMONY

1. Introduce the new person and then ask the class how many people have ever moved to a new school like Robin is doing.

2. In tribes, ask people to share their newcomer experiences. Transfer the responsibility to keep time for sharing; five minutes is enough. Meanwhile, visit with Robin.

3. Then ask the question, "What ideas does your tribe have to help Robin feel welcome and included in our class?"

4. Ask each tribe to brainstorm lists of some helpful things its members could do. Allow five minutes.

5. Have the tribes take turns reading their lists to Robin.

6. After all the tribes have done so, ask Robin to choose which tribe she would like to join.

During this activity, build inclusion with Robin by interviewing her, letting her know a bit about tribes and that it will be her choice as to which tribe she'll join. The choice may be limited to those tribes having fewer people. If you prefer to assign the newcomer to a tribe, you can still ask all of the tribes to come up with creative ideas for helping the person feel welcome and included. Hundreds of parents have expressed their great appreciation to tribes schools that use this ceremony. In a very transient society, it is wonderful to have your child come home the first day and say, "I belong to a group already, and the kids made me feel real welcome!"

4. "HEY, THAT'S A PUT-DOWN!"

If you find that in spite of your most heroic efforts, people are still using many put-down statements, you may need to take some remedial action. Suggestions:

- Have each student write on a card something someone said to them that really hurt. Put all cards in the center and have each draw one and read it without comment. Then discuss how it would feel to receive them.
- Initiate an "anti-put-down" campaign.
- Challenge the put-down experts to create statements of appreciation that they would like to receive.
- Provide lots of opportunities for statements of appreciation.
- Be a good role model, both in giving and accepting statements of appreciation. Just make sure you are honest at all times.

5. "LET'S FORM NEW TRIBES!"

If your students begin agitating to change tribes, it is probably an indication that you need to do more full-group community inclusion and intergroup strategies. Suggestions:

- Remind everyone that they agreed to remain in the same tribes for at least three to four weeks before any changes are made.
- Combine two tribes for a strategy like "Interview Circle." Membership in tribes needs to remain as constant as possible. The long-term membership factor develops cooperation, trust and peer support for individual achievement.

NEED FOR INFLUENCE

Your students have been in tribes for over a month and things are going great. No more agitating to change tribes. Almost no put-downs. And talk about working independently! Then your smooth-running tribal classroom begins to get a little out of hand. Some of the people you counted on as positive role models are restless. You notice subtle and not-so-subtle indicators that disagreements are happening. I-messages and attentive listening are being forgotten. It seems like a terrible set-back and you say to yourself, "Forget group teaching!"

Congratulations! Your class is now ready to really go to work! The inclusion, or "honeymoon," stage of the Tribes process has run its course, and the stage of influence has arrived! The new restlessness is a sign that your students are comfortable with the group process—they feel included and safe enough to speak out, even those shy ones.

STAGE OF INFLUENCE

The stage of influence is not about fighting for control or power over others. It is an organizational stage in which people want to contribute value to their group or community. Take a few minutes before moving further into this chapter and review "The Stage of Influence" in Chapter 6.

You thought you had it made!

It's important to remember that if groups ignore the underlying issues of the stage of influence rather than working through them, their capacity to work well together will suffer, and they will never come to appreciate the diversity of group members. There is no way around—only through! Your job as a process facilitator is to recognize the restlessness as a sign of progress, and use strategies that help people express their individuality. A sense of value and positive power then becomes a reality. As soon as that happens, your class (or staff or organization) will be a strong learning community in which everyone participates, shares leadership, leaps ahead in learning—and discovers individual talents, skills and gifts.

It is time to empower middle level kids at this stage of group development. They all long to grow into their rightful autonomy, social competency, positive expectations/purpose and independent problem-solving. To confine them now back into whole class instruction and competitive individualistic learning is to dismiss their social and emotional developmental needs—that only can be supported well through interactive group learning. Your objectives for this stage are to...

- Provide many opportunities for people to state their differing opinions, values, and beliefs openly.
- Make respect for diversity (culture, gender and multiple intelligences) a focus in the classroom and school.
- Teach strategies for individual and group decision making.
- Teach strategies for individual and group problem solving.
- Allow time for students to define individual and group goals.

LEARNING TO STATE OPINIONS

It takes courage and trust to take a stand in the midst of peers and say, "I feel differently about this than the rest of you do." The more that students are given opportunities to state diverse beliefs, the stronger they will be able to do more than "Just say no."

Let's say you have a 9th grade history/civics class this year in which you've been using a theme such as "Self and Society." You've been building class community and have five classroom tribes, each composed of five students. Throughout the inclusion stage you also started to use some of the Tribes strategies as formats for academic content.

Today you have decided to tackle the first steps of the stage of influence. To do so begin with the four influence strategies listed below. Tailor the language and topics to fit the grade level and cultures of your students. The strategies are:

- Thumbs Up/Thumbs Down
- One, Two, Three
- Where Do I Stand?
- Put Yourself on the Line

Follow the directions as written, and remember: the strategy alone is not enough! Allow sufficient time for reflection questions so that in-depth learning happens. Use the strategies over several consecutive days. Begin by using topics of personal interest or controversial questions from material the class may have been discussing or studying.

Examples using the strategy, "Put Yourself on the Line:"
- "The only way to have a safe school is to have more rules, monitors and metal detectors. Where do you stand?"
- "The age that teenagers can vote and drive should be substantially lowered. Where do you stand?"

Ask several types of reflection questions. Although example questions are noted for all of the strategies in this book, craft your own special questions for the content of the experience.

The "Put Yourself on the Line" strategy can be followed up with many other learning opportunities.

Follow-up ideas:
1. People who agree on a position can form temporary new study groups to research and prepare a defense for their position.
2. The people on the extreme ends, who differ the most, can get together in debate and dialogue groups.
3. Students who learn through rhythm/music, visual/spatial, or body/kinesthetic intelligences may want to illustrate the various positions through role play, music, diagrams, or drawings. The next chapter discusses multiple learning styles and has hundreds of ideas to use.

The creative controversy that can evolve out of influence strategies not only can produce a wealth of learning in lesson content, but also challenges students' critical thinking and collaborative skills. Best of all, different opinions are affirmed and valued.

INDIVIDUAL DECISION MAKING AND PROBLEM SOLVING

Have you ever wondered why schools limit student choices to the extent that they do? Everything is so predictable for kids for twelve years—the classes one must take, the way the system works, the competition, the tests, the workbooks year after year. The opportunity to make choices is next to zero in traditional schools. If we truly want students to become self-directed and gain a sense of autonomy, learning how to make responsible decisions and solve their own problems is essential. Again, we recognize that this is one of the key developmental tasks middle level students are trying to achieve—to gradually gain a sense of power over their lives.

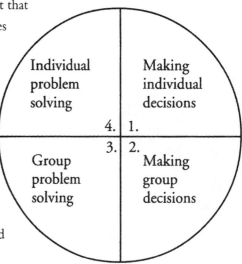

The distinction between decisions and problems is an important one:
- Decisions are judgments made concerning information as perceived by an individual or a group.
- Problems are dilemmas, intricate issues, and predicaments that need to be analyzed in order to reach resolution.

The difference between the two defines the preferred sequence to teach decision making and problem solving.

MAKING INDIVIDUAL DECISIONS

The strategies used to help students express different opinions also can help them practice making individual decisions.

Example strategy: Where Do I Stand?

"Our class will be working on four issues about the Civil War during the next three weeks. Stand by the sign of the topic you want to work on:
1. Roles of European countries
2. The Emancipation Proclamation
3. Lincoln's personal and political dilemmas
4. Economics in the South and North."

Individual decision making can be practiced throughout the teaching day by using many influence strategies and reflection questions. Reflection can happen in tribes or through writing in personal journals.

Individual decisions can also be made with the help of trusted tribe members, teachers, and parents through the Tribes strategy, "Let's Talk."

> Man ultimately decides for himself! And in the end, education must be education toward the ability to decide.[4]
>
> —VICTOR FRANKL

LET'S TALK

1. **Define the problem, situation, or concern**
   Example problem: "Whenever I go over to my friend's house after school, his mother is not home and he wants me to drink beer. I don't want to say 'No' because he won't like me if I do."

2. **Repeat the problem back (if in a discussion)**
   "You mean that you think you have to drink with your friend or he won't be a friend anymore?" Repeating back the problem usually brings elaboration.

3. **Think it through**
   "Would anybody lose respect for you if you did drink with your friend?"
   "Have you thought about the risks involved?"
   "Are you certain your friend will not see you anymore?"
   "Have you considered some alternatives?"

4. **Look at both sides**
   "What is the best thing that could happen if you said, 'No'?"
   "What is the worst?"

5. **Decide and act**
   "Having thought through the consequences, what is the most responsible choice you can make?"
   "Are you willing to accept the possible consequences by acting on your decision?"
   "If so, do it!"

6. **Evaluate the outcome**
   "What happened? What did you learn?"
   "Were you proud of your choice?"
   "Would you make the same one again?"

I'm good at barnstorming—must be the same as brainstorming!

MAKING GROUP DECISIONS AND ACTION PLANS

The stage of influence calls into question how tribes can make decisions together. Reaching agreement even on simple things (such as, "Who will report for our tribe?") often proves to be difficult.

First, teach the tribes how to use the strategies of Brainstorming, Consensus Building and Goal Storming. Keep in mind that once your students are familiar with the strategies, they can be used for lesson topics and real-time classroom decision making.

Practicing group decision making prepares young people to live in democracy—to work responsibly with others. The more that we give students the opportunity to reflect upon and analyze the dynamics that take place in their tribes, the better prepared they will be to "discover, sustain, and alter" systems, environments and situations in which they find themselves. This contributes to the development of resiliency and responsible autonomy.

Tribes that make group decisions to work on long term tasks or projects find it helpful to create "action plans" that designate tasks to be done, persons responsible for each task, and expected times for completion. The action plan can be posted, reviewed daily, and revised if necessary. Action plans are "group contracts," which remind people of their accountability to one another.

ACTION PLAN		TRIBE NAME:
WHAT	WHO	BY WHEN

GROUP PROBLEM SOLVING

The task seems simple, yet difficult even for adults to put into practice. Our immediate reaction is to suggest solutions, and then become aggravated when people care little about carrying them out. Our basic goal of preparing this generation to do well in today's world depends upon helping kids become responsible citizens. For this reason, Tribes trains teachers to transfer responsibility to student groups as much as possible. Having tribes rather than adult personnel solve classroom or school problems is also the key to sustaining a mellow environment. Let's look at two problems in need of student solutions.

PROBLEM #1: A few 6th grade students of the school have been seen spraying graffiti designs on the outside wall of the gym on weekends. Some of the offenders may be in the 6th grade class. Strategy: Tell the class about the problem. Then lead them through this Step-by-Step Process for Group Problem Solving.

STEP-BY-STEP PROCESS FOR GROUP PROBLEM SOLVING

1. Ask the tribes to discuss how they feel about people spraying paint on the wall of the school. Allow 3 to 5 minutes.

2. Pass out large sheets of paper and ask the tribes to brainstorm some ways that they could help solve the problem. Remind them of the rules for Tribes Brainstorming.

3. Ask each tribe to select their three best ideas or solutions to the problem. This can be done by consensus or by having each person write "1, 2, or 3" after three items of their choice. Stickers of three different colors may also be used. In this case, each student selects his/her top choices by placing a blue sticker on the first choice, red on the second choice, and yellow on the third choice. The totals on each suggested solution are counted (blue stickers 15 points, red stickers 10 points, yellow stickers 5 points).

4. Have two people record the three ideas from each tribe on the blackboard as they are read to the class.

5. Combine any duplicate or similar solutions.

6. Have all of the students approach the board, tribe by tribe, and vote for one solution.

7. Ask for two volunteers to add up the sticker points for each item. The solution receiving the most votes will be the one that the class will carry out.

What is remarkable in this example is that the identity of the 6th graders causing the problem is never discussed. They may, in fact, have participated (somewhat silently) in the problem solving.

Behavior problems can easily be handled whenever peers are given the opportunity to express how they feel about an annoying behavior. Have your tribes brainstorm "behavior that bugs me." Count on the power of peer feedback! Just going through the process of identifying conduct that is not approved by peers can cause a behavior to disappear rather quickly.

PROBLEM #2: You notice that the tribes are having various interaction problems. You want them to learn how to resolve group problems or issues. Strategy: Ask the class if they have noticed that people are having difficulties in working together. After hearing their replies, tell them that you also have observed some interaction problems, and that you would like them to figure out how to resolve them.

Then lead them through "Tribes Resolving Group Issues."

TRIBES RESOLVING GROUP ISSUES

1. Ask each person to reflect upon the group's interaction in their recent work together, and using a 3" x 5" card jot down any difficulties that kept the tribe from working well together.

2. Have each tribe place its cards face down in a pile.

3. Collect the stacks and exchange them among the tribes so that no tribe has its own.

4. Give the tribes 10 minutes to identify one issue from the cards and make suggestions on what a tribe might do to resolve the problem.

5. Have each group share suggestions with the whole class. The tribe being discussed can remain anonymous.

INDIVIDUAL PROBLEM SOLVING

There is an understandable concern about students sharing personal problems within groups in educational settings. We have always taken the position that it is inappropriate for educational groups to deal with any personal problems that border on the psychological, and that only qualified professionals should do so. Tribes are educational, not therapy, groups!

The more that students are involved in defining and solving a problem, the more likely they are to accept the responsibility to make the solution work.

It is inevitable, however, in these times of severe stress among children that family-oriented psychological problems become evident. The advice we give Tribes teachers parallels the majority of school district policies. If you notice or hear anything that indicates a serious disturbance in a child, it is an educator's responsibility to refer that student to the professional designated to handle such problems for the school.

Help your students understand that it is not the purpose of their tribes to deal with personal or family problems. Tribes may, however, help people think through concerns related to their school work, career questions, future goals, skill development, roles among peers, and friendships.

Two strategies in particular are helpful in supporting students to solve individual problems.

1. The "Client Consultant" strategy works well for educational, career, or personal interest concerns.
2. Personal journals can provide on-going reflection and assessment. Peers can choose to share or not with a trusted friend, teacher or parents—but only what they believe would be helpful in thinking through a problem.

SETTING GOALS AND MAKING INDIVIDUAL CONTRACTS

Schools and teachers who are committed to supporting the developmental tasks of adolescents also provide time for students to learn how to define purposeful positive goals—a key attribute of resiliency.

One way to start working towards this is to invite students to use the "Goal Storming" strategy independently. Ask people to choose something about themselves that they would like to pursue or improve (social or academic skills, attitudes, or behaviors) during the next weeks. Short time durations are better than long ones. Students may wish to share their goals with other Tribe members and write personal contracts, which can be signed by peers who agree to give encouragement and support. There is a format for the Personal Contract in the Learning Strategy section of this book. Positive peer support can work wonders!

Goals also can be recorded in the *Discovering Gifts* journals available from CenterSource Systems. Journals help students to reflect upon their experiences, document progress, and record changes. Personal journals are respected as private documents that are shared only if a student chooses to do so.

A TEACHER'S PERSPECTIVE

BY MICHELE CAHALL

Michele Cahall, M.A., has been a special education teacher of communicatively handicapped middle school students for more than 15 years for the El Dorado County Superintendent of Schools Office in California. She is a Tribes TLC® Master Trainer and a Professional Development Consultant for CenterSource Systems and has been deeply involved in the research and development of Tribes TLC® training and materials. She readily shares her primary purpose—"to improve the lives of kids and their families."

EVERY DAY IS DISCOVERY FOR SPECIAL NEEDS LEARNERS

I have been working with middle school special needs learners for my entire teaching career. When a child is placed in my program someone on the team usually mentions the benefits for that child because my program focuses heavily on social skills development. This discussion always causes me to wonder why all middle school classrooms aren't spending time on the social and emotional needs of their students.

Creating a positive social climate through the Tribes process provides an opportunity for my students to discover their gifts. Special needs learners need an environment where they feel safe. They need a sense of belonging to a group. When this happens, they can gain a sense of self through the direct instruction, repetition and practice of appropriate social interactions. Focusing on the developmental tasks—independence/autonomy, social competence, sense of purpose and problem solving—meets the needs of my middle school students.

At the beginning of each day, my students meet in a community circle. The community circle is comprised of sixth, seventh, and eighth grade students who have diverse abilities both socially and academically. The community circle is used to address all of the developmental tasks. After reviewing the agreements, the community circle students share their ideas about the topic of the day. We always conclude with reflection and appreciation. We often follow up with a written reflection in their *Discovering Gifts* journals. Written reflection helps to reinforce personal discoveries.

A typical week begins on Monday with the students sharing a highlight from their weekend. Special needs learners typically have a difficult time sharing an appropriate amount of information. Being able to practice in a safe environment promotes their social competency. Tuesday has been titled "Two for Tuesday." Each student shares two statements of appreciation about other classmates, teachers and their family members. Learning to give and receive statements of appreciation develops self-esteem and leads them to recognize their individual gifts. On Wednesday students share answers from a question of the day. The questions can reinforce a social skill or an academic concept. Thursday is used for problem solving or for the direct instruction of an effective communication technique. Peer groups reflect upon and encourage helpful behaviors. The week ends by having the students share their feelings about the school week. This is followed by verbal goal setting for the upcoming week and encourages the attainment of more personal goals.

I am certain that the big changes in behavior that occur for my students are due to the Tribes TLC® process. Such was my experience with Tom, an autistic boy, who was placed in my program. Tom was a sixth grade boy who appeared to have "lived in a box" for the first seven years of his schooling. He did not use eye contact nor greet people, and had limited spontaneous conversation. Early on, the students suggested that we brainstorm ways to help Tom move through his day more smoothly. A list was developed and each student signed up for a time in the day to help Tom. Tom was expected to have social interactions with peers for the first time. Over time, he learned to share his ideas, tell us when things weren't going well for him and give compliments to others. The active involvement of the students made all the difference.

The benefits of a Tribes TLC® environment in my Special Day Class are enormous. I am able to address the social and emotional needs of my students. I am able to teach my students effective communication techniques and we problem solve as needed. The process of Tribes not only enables special learners to learn social skills but also academic content because they are in trusting groups helping each other. For them every day is about discovery.

10 Creating Cooperative Learning Experiences

10 Creating Cooperative Learning Experiences

Help wanted

Motivated, caring, nurturing, creative, scholarly individual able to coordinate and communicate with colleagues of similar description… and able to inspire, motivate, and listen to early adolescents and their parents! Oh, and be willing to color outside the lines—because there are none. That's why our middle school is successful.[1]

—Jere Hochman

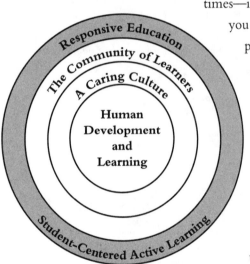

THE DEVELOPMENTAL PROCESS OF TRIBES

For more than 150 years few schools have been insightful enough to "color outside the lines" of the entrenched norms of traditional education. Although this may be the worst of times—it may be best of times finally to color outside the lines. As a reader, by now you know that we believe there is no excuse for not synthesizing the overlapping theoretical research on adolescent development, brain-based education, multiple intelligences, human resilience, ideal learning cultures, group theory, integrated thematic curriculum, reflective practice, cooperative education and constructivism. Educator Pat Burke Guild emphasizes that "each of these theories offers a comprehensive approach to learning and teaching, but is not a one-shot program. Each can be a catalyst for positive student learning. Each forces us to examine our values about people, learning and education to make the hundreds of daily decisions that put beliefs into practice."[2] Moreover, each of the theories is learning- and learner-centered. It is time to make a deliberate synthesis of all that is known about learning—especially throughout middle level schools.

Our circle illustration reminds us once more that this is what the developmental process, known simply as "Tribes," is all about. Smart middle level schools synthesize the best of learning studies by...

- making adolescent development, in all of its aspects, the focus of the school community
- establishing and sustaining a culture of caring throughout the school
- structuring the whole school community into supportive learning groups (communities)
- having well-trained teachers use educational pedagogy that is responsive to the learning and developmental needs of early adolescents.

RESPONSIVE EDUCATION IN MIDDLE LEVEL SCHOOLS

The four developmental tasks that young adolescents are determined to achieve—autonomy/independence, social competency, a sense of purpose and problem solving—help teachers and parents understand the restless and provoking behaviors of the age-level population both at school and at home. To become "responsive" in relating to and designing meaningful learning for the age depends upon adults in the middle school community deliberately setting aside time *to learn*. All need to understand not only the tasks of adolescence, but also deliberate initiatives that support the cognitive, social and emotional development of these students. Rich discussions and serious discourse can take place within on-going faculty and parent groups. The chart that follows suggests many "Responsive Education" initiatives. Small group meetings of your own teachers and parents, apart or together, will elicit many more appropriate initiatives.

MOVING TOWARDS EXCELLENCE THROUGH COOPERATIVE GROUP LEARNING

The full range of human development—intellectual, social, emotional, physical and personal/spiritual—from birth to death is an interactive journey made in community with others. There is no other way to promote the development of young adolescents in all of their potential and resilience apart from re-culturing and restructuring middle level schools into knowledgeable, responsive and caring communities. Mark Chasen, M.D., Director of the Mt. Sinai Medical Center in New York, cites the human physical system as a metaphor for organizational systems when he states, "You can't change the system unless you change the process. The results you get are the results of the system."[3] Respected educator Ted Sizer agrees, "For success to happen you have to change the entire system."[4]

> *For success to happen you have to change the entire system.*[4]
> —TED SIZER

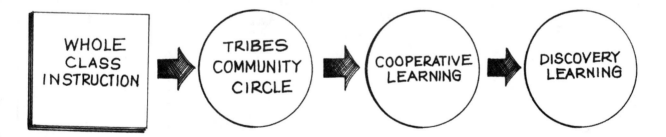

The journey we are taking—moving from the old 19th century model of didactic instruction to research-based practice—assures success and futures of promise for 21st century kids. The illustration above (a courtesy to all of us visual learners) is a reminder of the full page Chart: Stages Toward Excellence Through Group Learning in Chapter 8.

The shift does not mean that teachers need to completely abandon and never return to using a former practice. It means that the more they can use new active learning alternatives, the more the students will understand and retain academic material as meaningful learning.[5] The following chart summarizes the contrast in instructional practice.

RESPONSIVE EDUCATION IN CARING MIDDLE LEVEL SCHOOLS TO SUPPORT THE DEVELOPMENTAL TASKS OF YOUNG ADOLESCENTS

TASK	STAGE OF COGNITIVE DEVELOPMENT	STAGE OF SOCIAL AND EMOTIONAL DEVELOPMENT	RESPONSIVE EDUCATION INITIATIVES
AUTONOMY / INDEPENDENCE	Capable of cognitive problem solving Can think abstractly and hypothetically Integrates multiple factors to understand concepts	Oriented to peers and family Conflicted on degree of desired family involvement Seeks independence in decision making, although may lack judgment and experience Resists imposed control from adults	Classrooms are student-centered. Well-trained teachers engage students in multiple forms of cooperative and constructive group learning. Didactic teaching is minimized. Teacher teams integrate interdisciplinary thematic curriculum. Focus on relevance to current world, student lives, interests and future. Peer learning groups (tribes) plan, demonstrate and teach.
SOCIAL COMPETENCY		Seeks friends and belonging Attracted to peer leaders and role models Feels awkward with social skills May be motivated by social effects of drug or alcohol use May experiment with initial sexual intimacy	Promote peer leadership, peer helping programs, cooperative learning groups, and discovery of gifts Utilize peer role models for teaching skills Practice democracy and cultural/racial/gender equity Engage in constructivist approach Teach collaborative skills
SENSE OF PURPOSE		Pre-occupied with self-presentation, acceptance by peer group, physical maturity Risk-taking and experimental behavior in order to belong	Encourage acceptance of diversity, respect, and tolerance Nurture/enhance peer involvement and sense of community Involve students in community service activities
PROBLEM SOLVING		Oriented to present rather than future Egocentric Changing emotions, viewpoints, loyalties Differentiates between self and environment	Involve students in affecting immediate environment Teach management of group problems Teach appreciative inquiry

SHIFTS IN PRACTICE TO HELP STUDENTS DEMONSTRATE UNDERSTANDING

LESS	MORE
Whole class, teacher directed	Experiential, hands-on group learning
Worksheets, passive seatwork	Active learning
Transmission of information	Demonstration, coaching, mentoring
Coverage of curriculum	Deep study of a few topics
Textbooks and basic readers	Primary source material
Rate of memorization of facts	High-order constructive thinking
Tracking and leveling	Heterogeneous classes and groups
Reliance on standardized measures	Reliance on teacher descriptions and performance assessment

THE EFFECTIVENESS OF COOPERATIVE LEARNING

David and Roger Johnson not only are to be credited for their years of research and writing on cooperative learning but applauded for giving the field of education clear evidence that cooperative learning can be used at every grade level, in every subject area and with every task. They state on behalf of a host of other leading researchers, "We know more about cooperative learning than we do about lecturing, age grouping, departmentalization, starting reading at age six, or the 50 minute period. We know more about cooperative learning than almost any other aspect of education."[6] Both theoretical and demonstration research, documented in both scientific and professional literature, confirm the effectiveness of cooperative group learning. In the last 102 years (since 1898) over 550 experimental and 100 correlation studies have been conducted on cooperative, competitive and individualistic learning.[7] Meta-analysis of all of the studies on achievement show that cooperative learning results in significantly higher achievement and retention in contrast to competitive and individualistic learning and teacher-centered whole class instruction.[8] During the last 50 years, 106 studies have shown that cooperative learning promotes greater social support—which promotes achievement, productivity, physical health, psychological health and the ability to cope with stress and adversity.[9] Over 80 studies indicate the positive impact that cooperative learning experiences have on self-esteem, intrinsic worth and value of personal attributes to others.[10] The outcomes on achievement, psychological health, and social relationships are overlapping and influence everything else.[11] The reality is that...

Now we're flying over to Tribes Cooperative Group Learning.

159

Cooperative learning is here to stay.

> *Placing socially unskilled students in a learning group and telling them to cooperate obviously will not be successful. Students must be taught the social skills needed for collaboration and be motivated to use them.[13]*
>
> —DAVID AND ROGER JOHNSON

Cooperative learning is here to stay, because it is based on a profound and strategic theory and there is substantial research validating its effectiveness… there probably will never be a time in the future when cooperative learning is not used extensively within educational programs. It is important, therefore, that secondary school teachers understand the research on cooperative learning and academic achievement and know how to implement cooperative learning within the secondary school classroom.[12]

ACTIVATING ALL OF THE ELEMENTS OF COOPERATIVE LEARNING

Packaging kids into small groups of four, giving them work to do together, and telling them they need to cooperate is not cooperative learning. Too many teachers who try just that become convinced that "kids just can't work in groups!" "Forget cooperative learning—it doesn't work." They are right. It won't work well at all that way.

Students first must learn how to communicate and relate well by learning and using the four important Tribes agreements: listening, appreciation/no put-downs, right-to-pass and mutual respect. They need to have experienced inclusion, safety and trust in a Tribes community circle. Given that learning experience, students themselves can work well together in cooperative learning groups; they themselves will sustain the "conditions" or the following elements that have been identified as essential for group learning.

COOPERATIVE GROUPS DEMONSTRATE[14]

1. *Positive interdependence among members*
   People undertake a group task with a feeling of mutuality, each person contributing, doing his or her own part, knowing "we sink or swim together" and "together we can do it."

2. *Face-to-face promotive interaction*
   People help each other to understand the task, check comprehension and reflect on what was learned. They use helpful interpersonal and small group social skills.

3. *The use of interactive skills*
   Group members become adept at managing conflict, and developing trust and respect within their group.

4. *Individual accountability*
   Group members take personal responsibility for learning the material, contributing to the group, and assessing both individual and group achievement.

5. *Group processing*
   Members reflect upon and analyze group effectiveness; they define ways to improve group work together.

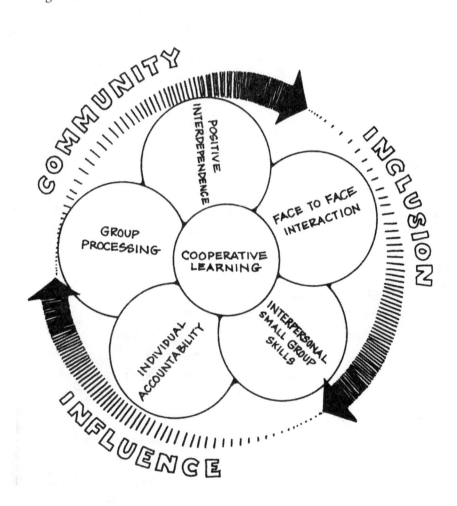

Many teachers say, "The process of Tribes is the glue that holds cooperative learning together." The five elements are *what* need to happen… the process of Tribes is *how* to have the elements happen.

DESIGNING AND FACILITATING COOPERATIVE LEARNING

You may have noticed that instead of talking about lesson plans, we're talking about designing learning experiences to achieve objectives and real-time discovery for students.

The example form on the next page, entitled "A Tribes TLC® Learning Experience," gives teachers an easy format to plan active learning experiences. The form can be used either to teach academic content by using a single Tribes strategy or to organize a sequence of strategies and group structures.

The Form is divided into the following five sections:

1. Provide for inclusion
2. Identify the content objective to be learned, and the collaborative skill to be practiced
3. Identify the strategy(ies)
4. Define reflection questions
5. Provide an opportunity for appreciation.

The Resource Section contains a blank Tribes Learning Experience form that you can copy for your own use.

PROVIDE FOR INCLUSION

Each time the tribes come together to work on a task, interest and participation is gained by introducing an inclusive question, strategy or active group activity. At the beginning of the Learning Strategy section there is a matrix that lists many inclusion strategies. They can be used as written, or tailored to respond to the culture, language and special needs of your students. Knowing that learning is accelerated whenever the human brain can link new information to previous knowledge and experiences, an inclusion question personalized as a "*You* question" can be used to connect students' experiences to an academic theme. Example: The content to be learned is about the California Gold Rush. After reminding everyone of the four agreements, or having the tribes do so, ask group members to respond to questions such as…

"Have *you* ever dreamed of finding a valuable treasure? Share what that may have been?"

"If *you* found a priceless treasure what would you do? Why?"

"If *you* knew you were going to explore a remote outdoor setting for a long time, what would help you to survive?"

The *You* question needs to be relevant to the possible personal experiences, interests, and knowledge of the learners. Such questions appeal to the imagination, recollections, opinions and previous felt energies of learners. Responses to *You* questions can be shared in pairs, triads or the whole tribe. They can be used in a writing activity (such as an imaginary letter to a friend), or recorded in personal journals. It is very important to give sufficient time for students to connect to the academic content before introducing it.

This is brain compatible.

A TRIBES TLC® LEARNING EXPERIENCE

1. PROVIDE FOR INCLUSION—A YOU QUESTION, ENERGIZER OR STRATEGY:

Energizer: I Like My Neighbor—call out topics based on culture, heritage, birth sites

2. IDENTIFY THE OBJECTIVES:

Content Objective:

To identify universal cultural concepts (geographical sites, historical and current family groupings, religions/beliefs, rites of passage, political governments and economic strengths and weaknesses).

Collaborative Objective:

To have all members: (check 1–3)

❑ Participate fully   ❑ Think constructively

❑ Listen attentively   ❑ Make group decisions

❑ Express appreciation of others' ideas   ❑ Work cooperatively on tasks

❑ Reflect often on group interaction   ❑ Respect and value different skills and opinions

❑ Other:

3. IDENTIFY THE STRATEGY(IES):

Group Inquiry: Each tribe will research a chosen population group and summarize concepts on a large chart to present to the class community. Task time: one week. Materials: Resource Lists from teacher

All We Have in Common: The class community will compare commonalities of the cultural populations. Task time: one period

4. ASK REFLECTION QUESTIONS BASED ON THE OBJECTIVES:

Content: *Reflect with your tribe on the three most important cultural concepts that may affect your own future and that of our country. Discussion time: 20 minutes. Task: write a 200-300 word paper on the meaning of the learning experience for you.*

Collaborative: *To work collaboratively on task. Ask tribes to discuss and share with community—What did your tribe do well in order to complete the task?*

Discovering Gifts: *Write in your journal—Which of my strengths or skills were helpful to my group? How?*

5. PROVIDE AN OPPORTUNITY FOR APPRECIATION:

In tribes: "I appreciate (name of person) for (describe the helpful behavior or skill)."

IDENTIFY THE LEARNING OBJECTIVES

There are always two objectives in a Tribes Learning Experience. The first is the academic objective: What is the content to be learned? The second is the collaborative objective: What social skill will be learned or practiced?

The content objective, of course, depends upon the curriculum you are to teach. However, just about any curricula can be raised to the level of "big ideas" or "meaningful themes." This is especially important for young adolescents, who are moving from concrete to complex thinking, and are anxiously seeking meaning and purpose—one of their four adolescent tasks. In recognition of this, an ever-increasing number of middle level schools are training teachers to integrate and elevate content to higher universal *concepts*. Marion Brady suggests four learning areas, which are based on their "probable contribution to human survival:"[15]

- Learning about our physical environment
- Learning about humans who occupy the environment
- Understanding states of mind that underlie human action
- Understanding how assumptions and beliefs manifest themselves in human behavior.

All of these study areas can be synthesized into meaningful themes on national and global issues affecting humankind.

A literature class studying Shakespeare plays could do so under the concept of *understanding power as a state of mind underlying human action*. Student groups and individual members within the groups would be responsible to research different aspects about power; how it affects public events today... and actively engage the whole class in all that they had learned. The time-line for the task could be brief or extensive. The concept could be repeatedly linked to real-life concerns or considerations students may have, and time set aside to write in personal journals. Shakespeare could become very real—perhaps a life-long, admired advisor and friend for many.

Our good friend and educator Susan Kovalik writes, "It is time to think of curriculum as an integrated meaningful whole... to see subjects in terms of meaningful concepts, and to utilize all the basic skills to support and clarify those concepts, giving students a once-in-a-lifetime opportunity to develop their personal learning power."[16]

Active conceptual learning is compatible with how the human brain learns and remembers. Teaching this way does not mean that basic academic curriculum is overlooked or ignored. It is woven into a richer more meaningful tapestry never to be forgotten.

CONSTRUCTIVE THINKING SKILLS

Youth moving into the high-tech information world of the 21st Century will be lost unless they are capable of thinking critically and constructively. The concepts and information that they may memorize today for the test tomorrow are quickly forgotten. Due to unprecedented rapid change in today's world and the mushrooming amount of new information in every domain, memorized information quickly becomes irrelevant. It is estimated that within 90 days students forget 90% of everything they have ever been

Start with what they know and build with what they have.

—LAU TAU, 100 B.C.

told.[17] These two reasons alone more than justify modifying or giving up lecturing, whole class instruction and memorization.

Our young adolescents (and all of us) need to become proficient in....

1. **Accessing information** from a wide array of resources: computers, libraries, newspapers, books, on-line data banks, public records and face-to-face people interviews

2. **Analyzing and interpreting** meaning through discussion, writing, graphics, music, drama or dance

3. **Synthesizing and linking** existing knowledge by comparing, integrating and summarizing concepts and information

4. **Planning and applying** acquired knowledge to real life issues, opportunities and problems

5. **Reflecting and evaluating** applied knowledge for on-going refinement, change and conclusions.

Oh no! Within 90 days students forget 90% of everything they have ever been told!

These very important constructive thinking skills are supportive of the direction in which our young teens are going one way or another... with or without school systems becoming more responsive! All are anxious and determined to achieve those key developmental tasks mandated by the very nature of their adolescence... problem-solving on their own, gaining a sense of meaning and purpose, becoming more independent, and gaining social competency by relating and working well with others.

The constructive thinking skills needed by young people in today's world may also be considered as collaborative skills in every sense of the word. The ability to contribute to a learning group, a work group, or a project team, depends upon clear thinking and expression.

COLLABORATIVE SOCIAL SKILLS

The second objective in the Tribes Learning Experience plan is extremely important. It supports the social and emotional development of young adolescents, and the age level need and task to become socially competent. Twelve collaborative skills are embedded and learned through Tribes TLC® strategies and the group process. The skills are social in nature for individuals, and collaborative within groups and organizations. The SCANS and other business reports verify that when critical social skills are undeveloped, adult workers face on-going loss of jobs, interpersonal conflict, personal stress and economic problems throughout their lives.[18] The illustration that follows shows twelve collaborative/social skills that are learned and lived within Tribes Learning Communities.

In addition, other communication skills, such as using "I-messages" to express one's feelings safely about the effect of another's behavior are learned and used. In effect, collaborative skills become part of the culture within a classroom, school, district, agency or other organization. They are the necessary foundation of any caring community.

COLLABORATIVE SKILLS

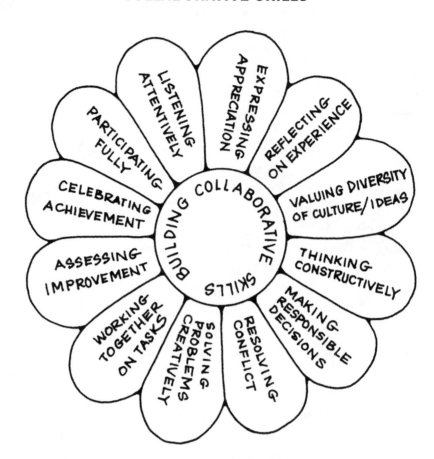

Cooperative learning promotes a great use of higher level reasoning strategies and critical thinking than do competitive or individualistic learning strategies.[19]

Each time you design a learning experience, select a skill that is timely and appropriate for the class. Begin with those, sweeping through the arrow of "inclusion" in the illustration on page 161, and as the tribes move into the stage of influence focus on problem-solving, decision making and so on. The Learning Strategy section contains ways for students to learn the invaluable life skills. Time taken for the learning contributes directly to time on task and enhancing academic learning.

Be certain that you always tell students the two objectives to be achieved and that they themselves will be reflecting, assessing and/or evaluating the degree to which they succeeded.

SELECTING STRATEGIES AND STRUCTURES

Knowing that we want the academic content to be learned in a meaningful way by students, one or several group interaction strategies are selected to carry the content. The content is *what* is to be learned... and the strategy is *how* it is learned. For example: content for a political science class may be "peaceful protest in democracy" that the teacher lectures about while students take notes. Peaceful protest is the content, the strategy is *"teacher-talk."* If the teacher had asked groups of students to research forms of peaceful protest, the content would be the same but the strategy would be *"group inquiry."* Dr. Spencer Kagan who uses the term "structure" rather than "strategy" writes:

As educators, we are faced with a range of educational objectives. Teaching is much more than simply imparting knowledge to our students. Students need to learn to be critical thinkers, how to share information, make decisions, reach consensus and get along with others. No single structure can accomplish this breadth of educational objectives... [edit]... Using many different structures makes teaching and learning more fun. Teaching and learning are then more characterized by novelty and exhilaration rather than by monotony and tediousness.[20]

The introduction to the Learning Strategy section in this book gives suggestions on making appropriate selections. Your plan may include several sequential Tribes group strategies to help students achieve the content objectives. We also urge teachers to become familiar with cooperative learning structures from other resources, such as *Cooperative Learning* by Spencer Kagan[21] and *Circles of Learning* by David and Roger Johnson.[22]

The Tribes strategies and/or cooperative learning structures that you select to carry the lesson content need to support the observed stage of group development. For instance, you would not want to use "Where Do I Stand," a strategy for the stage of influence, if the tribes still needed inclusion. Moreover, if they are to work on a task involving controversial issues, they should already have practiced a number of influence strategies. The exciting thing about the majority of the Tribes strategies is that they can be used over and over again as interactive formats for academic content.

We need only to be responsive to the direction in which these kids and the world are moving... to know how to transform teaching and learning.

I certainly can't create nine different lesson plans everyday!

Of course not!

REACHING STUDENTS OF MULTIPLE LEARNING STYLES

Picture nine students sitting in a semicircle in front of you. They may all have different learning styles because they all have different intelligences. Yet the traditional classroom reaches only two out of the nine, the 20 percent that learn through verbal/linguistic and logical/mathematical methods. National statistics tell us that at least three out of the other seven students will become dropouts if not reached academically in the elementary and middle school years. One thing is for certain—all of these kids cannot be written off as "learning disabilities" or "stupid." They simply have different ways of knowing and learning that are different from the 20 percent of students with verbal/linguistic and logical/mathematical intelligences. They are not failing—their schools are failing to reach them.

No, you do not have to create nine different plans. Become familiar with the descriptions of the nine multiple intelligences as defined over years through the remarkable research of Howard Gardner.[23] The various ways of knowing are also special gifts to be discovered! Most middle level students have recognized in their younger years that they have a preference or natural ability that is satisfying to use, and that perhaps it is very different from abilities of their siblings or friends. It is not the teacher's task to analyze or diagnose the specific intelligences of each student. In the Learning Strategy section there is a multiple intelligence checklist, adapted with permission from the work of Dr. Thomas Armstrong, that students themselves can use to discover their preferred ways of learning.[24] Teachers simply need to weave the many ways of learning throughout academic learning experiences.

The "Multiple Intelligences Idea Chart" that follows contains a wide range of ways to engage the diversity of your students. Many of the ideas evolved out of suggestions made by Dr. Armstong in presentations and many came from innovative teachers. The icons of the intelligences can be noted on your TLC® Learning Experience plans to help you keep track of your efforts each day.

MULTIPLE INTELLIGENCES IDEA CHART

VERBAL LINGUISTIC

Write story problems

Create TV advertisements

Compile a notebook of jokes

Debate current/historical issues

Play "Trivial Pursuit"

Explain a situation/problem

Create poems

Impromptu speaking/writing

Create crossword puzzles

Teach "concept mapping"

Learn a foreign language

Write instructions

Read stories to others

Describe an object for another to draw

Make up a story about a piece of music

Describe the steps to a dance

Write a role play/drama

Keep a personal journal

LOGICAL MATHEMATICAL

Create a time line

Compare/contrast ideas

Predict the next events in a story

Define patterns in history

Follow a recipe/instructions

Rank-order factors

Analyze causes and effects

Learn patterns

Analyze similarities/differences

Classify biological specimens

Create outlines of stories

Create computer programs

Use a story grid/creative writing

Create a "paint-by-number" picture

Read/design maps

Solve math problems

Teach calculator/computer use

Decipher codes

Compose music from a matrix

VISUAL SPATIAL

Make visual diagrams/flow charts

Illustrate a story/historical event

Design/paint murals

Imagine the future/go back in time

Play "Pictionary"

Teach "mind mapping" for note taking

Write/decipher codes

Graph results of a survey

Create posters/flyers

Create collages on topics

Draw maps

Study the arts of a culture

Make clay maps/buildings/figures

Create visual diagrams/machines

Illustrate dance steps/physical games

Teach Tribes energizers

Learn spatial games

Draw from different perspectives

Draw to music

INTERPERSONAL

Role play a historical/literary or
   class situation

Analyze a story

Tell stories

Read poetry using different moods

Teach arithmetic, math, computer

Review a book orally

Act out a different cultural perspective

Design and act out dramas/role play

Help tribe come to a consensus or resolve
   a problem

Facilitate participation in the tribe

Teach cooperative games

Help people deliver appreciation statements

Solve complex story problems

Discuss/debate controversial issues

Analyze group dynamics/relationships

Learn to sing and lead rounds

Plan and arrange social events

Find relationships between objects

BODY KINESTHETIC

Lead Tribes energizers and
cooperative games

Practice physical exercises

Lead students in stretching to
music deep breathing, tai chi, and
yoga poses

Learn dances of different cultures and periods
of history

Practice aerobic routines to fast music

Measure items or distances with thumbs, feet,
or hands

Illustrate geometrical figures (parallel lines,
triangles, rectangles, circles) with arms,
legs and/or fingers

Coach peers and/or younger children

Conduct hands-on experiments

Act out scenes from stories or plays

Design role plays

Invent a new household tool

Prepare food or snacks

Simulate various situations

Learn alphabet through physical movement

Learn/teach sign language

Make up a cooperative playground game

MUSICAL RHYTHMIC

Create "raps" (key dates,
math, poems)

Teach songs from different
cultures and eras

Play musical instruments

Make simple musical instruments

Learn via songs and jingles

Learn through drum beats/rhythm

Make up sounds and sound effects

Practice impromptu music

Create interpretive dance to music

Lead singing (songs from different cultures)

Write to music

Reduce stress with music

Teach rhythm patterns/different cultures

Compose music for a dramatic production

Teach dance steps

Identify social issues through lyrics

Illustrate different moods through dance steps

Lead physical exercise to music

Clap a rhythm for the class to repeat

EXISTENTIAL

Engage in reflection and self-study

Read books on the meaning of life

Attend some form of worship

Watch films on big life questions

Record thoughts in a journal

Listen to inspirational music

Study literature, art, philosophy

Discuss life/human issues in a group

Record dreams and mystical events

Paint while listening to music

Create a private "centering" space

NATURALIST

Keep a journal of observations

Collect and categorize data

Make a taxonomy of plants
or animals

Explain similarities among species

Study means of survival

Examine cellular structures with a
microscope

Illustrate cellular material

Take out-of-door field trips

Visit an aquarium

Camp outside to identify stars

INTRAPERSONAL

Keep a personal journal or feelings diary

Analyze historical personalities

Write on personal learning experiences

Evaluate personal and group strengths/
weaknesses

Analyze thinking patterns

Understand group dynamics

Use, design, or lead guided imagery

Write an autobiography

Analyze literary characters and historical
personalities

Define personal reflection questions

Imagine and write about the future

Dance different stages in life

Lead Tribes personal inclusion
activities

Practice relaxation techniques

Imagine self as character in history or story

Illustrate feelings/moods

Listen attentively

Draw self at different periods in life

Share how music affects feelings

Observe self (metacognition perspective)

ASKING REFLECTION QUESTIONS

The most important part of any Tribes TLC® learning experience may be
the reflection questions that you ask your students. If you didn't check
out the reference to a study on processing (reflecting) earlier, do so
now. It is in the Resource section. Asking good reflection questions within cooperative learning groups can double the rate of
retention of knowledge for students.[25] In other words, if we want
students to achieve higher test scores, reflection questions need
to be asked after every learning experience. Students begin to
understand that they are not just learning information but also
higher-order thinking, and social skills—competencies all critical
to their futures.

Well-chosen reflection questions are an immediate way to assess
how well your content and collaborative objectives were achieved.
You may recall from Chapter 8—Initiating Responsive Education—
that three kinds of reflection questions are used in the process of Tribes
in middle level schools.

CONTENT (cognitive learning) questions focus on academic knowledge gained from the learning experience.

COLLABORATIVE (social learning) questions focus on the interaction
and participation of members and the collaborative skills that were used.

DISCOVERING GIFTS (personal learning) questions help to identify
skills contributed to complete the task; special gifts, talents and interests
noticed by tribe members or the student individually.

*Now you'll especially see why
I am so prominent in this book
and in Tribes schools!*

You'll find examples of each type in the Learning Strategies of this book.

Plan the questions you will use, and jot them down on the TLC® Learning Experience Form. There will be times when you will want to change them due to events that happen during the class experience. Ask questions that will be most relevant and meaningful to the learning experiences.

APPRECIATION

Last but hardly least, opportunities need to be provided for people to express appreciation to those with whom they have worked. Never let a group finish work together without allowing time for statements of appreciation. The more that appreciation happens, the more cohesive the tribes will be—the more comfortable and cooperative they will become working together, the better they will accomplish learning tasks, and the greater will be every student's sense of self-worth.

ACCOUNTABILITY: ASSESSING CONTENT

Tribes TLC® teachers use a variety of ways to determine the degree to which learning objectives are being achieved by individual and group members. Standardized tests may not indicate the in-depth more meaningful learning that your students are acquiring through active group learning. The purpose of traditional tests ("what-is-the-right-answer") is to determine grades. The purpose of responsive education assessments and tests is to learn how to increase student learning.

The fact that reflection questions are being asked after every learning experience makes it more likely that more information and concepts will be retained. In addition, throughout the year do help your students to see their own progress, and involve the

Here's my bird's eye view.

IMPLEMENTING A TRIBES LEARNING EXPERIENCE IN FIVE STEPS

1. **Inclusion**

   Introduce the learning experience, as people sit either in the community circle or in tribes, with an inclusion strategy (content linked to lesson topic) or a *You* question.

2. **Objectives**

   Tell the students the content and collaborative skill objectives that are to be learned or practiced.

3. **Implementation of Strategies**

   Explain the task, group roles, and time available.

   Ask, "What questions do you have?"

   Observe and monitor the dynamics of the tribes working together, intervening only if they cannot resolve a situation or problem.

4. **Reflection/Accountability**

   Ask reflection questions. Use group and/or individual assessment for accountability.

5. **Appreciation**

   Invite statements of appreciation.

*Tests to learn?
Now that makes sense!*

tribes in viewing assessment not as ominous tests, but as snapshots of where they are on their journey of learning. Involve them in…

- Generating their own reflection questions for a learning experience
- Developing check lists with indicators of learning and giving them to the class or parents when giving presentations, speeches, group reports, role-plays, video productions, etc.
- Personal appraisal—using portfolios, writing in *Discovering Gifts* journals and sharing in tribes or with a buddy.

Teacher interviews with each tribe are also helpful. Don't quiz, but elicit what was learned. After a few times they will trust the discourse process with you, and be proud to share what they are learning. The purpose is not to jot down grades, but to take snapshots of where they are, and to determine the next step for them to learn even more.

ASSESSING COLLABORATIVE SKILLS

FORM A	FORM B	FORM C
STUDENT ASSESSMENT	**STUDENT ASSESSMENT**	**STUDENT ASSESSMENT**
Our Tribe's Work Together	*Participation in My Group*	*My Thinking Skills*

There are three assessment forms in the Resource section that can be used by students to assess their individual participation and thinking skills, and to determine how well their group is working together.

Form A—"Our Tribe's Work Together" can be used either by individual group members or by the whole tribe to reflect on how well they work together. If completed by individual members, the tribe can total and average all of the ratings for a group score.

Form B—"Participation in My Group" is used by students individually to reflect on their own participation in their tribe. They can monitor how well they are using certain skills, based on their own reflections over a period of time.

In addition, students can also use Form C—"My Thinking Skills" to reflect on the extent to which they feel capable of using various constructive thinking skills. This form and Form B are also contained in the Tribes TLC® personal journal, *Discovering Gifts,* so that students can use them repeatedly to determine their own progress and set on-going goals. The journal is available from CenterSource Systems.

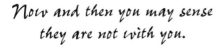

Now and then you may sense they are not with you.

There are those inevitable times when you realize your students have tuned you out. They are no longer listening, have a glaze in their eyes, and are drifting— beyond caring about what is going on in the classroom. You may have been working hard to have a more participatory classroom and are baffled whenever things seem to slip back. Not to worry... it is a signal to take time out, reflect on what is happening and take positive action. This checklist may help you to determine why attention is waning.

1. Are you connecting the topic or lesson to their personal experiences and previous learning?
2. Are you getting off the topic or talking too long?
3. How long have your students been sitting or working without physical movement?
4. Have you identified their stage of development and group issues so that you select appropriate strategies?
5. Are you using enough cooperative group strategies to maximize participation?
6. Are you hovering over the tribes, rather than giving them responsibility to work on tasks together, helping each other?

7. After an activity have you tried asking constructive/social reflection questions before asking content questions?

8. Is there a disturbing event that needs to be aired or resolved before learning can be resumed?

9. Are you sensitive to the loss-of-energy dynamic when it begins to happen?

10. Do you "stop the action" and ask students what is going on?

APPRECIATIVE INQUIRY

> *Appreciative inquiry touches something important and positive and people respond.*
>
> —SUE ANNIS HAMMOND

The fact that young adolescents thrive on acquiring on-going independence and opportunities to solve problems, makes them more than ready to assess how well their tribes are working together, and the extent of their own participation. In some of the Tribes Learning Strategies you will notice collaborative questions that suggest having students look at their tribe's performance. These "Appreciative Inquiry" questions are based on "What did we, as a group, do well?" rather than "What did we do wrong?" The latter is the traditional organizational management approach—look for a problem, diagnose it and find a solution. Even though a "fix-it" solution may be found, the assumption will persist that we need to keep looking for problems because *we are a problem group.* Appreciative inquiry looks for what works in an organization, based on the high moments of where we have been together. Participants, grounded in success, know how to repeat their success. The approach generates positive energy and increases the group's success.

You can use appreciative inquiry not only to define meaningful reflection questions but also to transfer the responsibility to tribes for problem solving. There is an appreciative inquiry problem solving strategy in the Learning Strategy section. The lists below show the contrasting scenarios.[26]

PROBLEM SOLVING	APPRECIATIVE INQUIRY
"Felt need"	Appreciating and Valuing
Identification of Problem	The Best of "What Is"
Analysis of Causes	Envisioning "What Might Be"
Analysis of Possible Solutions	Dialoguing "What Should Be"
Action Planning (Treatment)	Innovating "What Will Be"

DISCOVERING UNEXPECTED GIFTS

A TEACHER'S PERSPECTIVE

BY BETTY WHITE

The key is to expect the unexpected. As a classroom teacher, we need not know all the answers nor do we need to know what the wonderful "gifts" are that our students will bring. What we must do is believe that all students possess unique and wonderful unexpected gifts. Then we must provide the opportunity for them to be brought forth. Having taught sixth grade for over 15 years, I know that the process of Tribes is the perfect tool to facilitate the emergence of middle school students' gifts.

One year in early fall, the school's water supply was contaminated for several days and bottled water was brought in for students. The weather was very warm and teachers were to closely monitor consumption of this new commodity. I decided to bring water for my own 32 students. With much struggling and a lot of help, I filled with ice and water, the huge container my son's baseball team used and dragged it to the classroom. After watching for a couple of days, one young man informed me that I didn't need to bring so much the next day. His family worked in the fields and he had a large container. He told me he would bring enough water to take care of his Tribe! The unexpected gift of being responsible! That young man went on to become student body president of his high school!

Recently, a young Tribes teacher shared with me the story of a student who brought to her class on the first day of school, the reputation of a troublemaker and a loner. When asked what he liked to do, Jake said he liked to blow up things! He was only in her classroom nine weeks before his family had to move away, but during that time an amazing transformation took place. About four weeks into the school year, after working to get the agreements in place and using community circle for reflection and discussion, the students were drawing the names of States for social studies reports. When one girl was upset because she did not get the State she wanted, Jake suggested that maybe she could have his and he would take another one.

On his last day before moving, Jake sat in the center of the community circle in the teacher's swivel chair, and one by one the children shared an appreciation and said goodbye. The young man beamed with each comment. Just as the teacher dismissed the class to return to their desks, Jake asked if everyone could come back to the circle because he needed to tell them something. He then shared that he was really going to miss them all, thanked them for being friendly, and said he wished he didn't have to leave. The gifts of kindness, caring, and participation came forth! It happened by using the caring process of Tribes. The teacher had created an environment in the classroom that was safe—an environment that surfaced the unexpected gifts this student possessed.

Another one of my students, a sixth grade girl, used to take role and lunch count in our class, fill out the appropriate attendance slip and see that it got to the office on time. She was every bit as capable as I was! Whenever money had to be collected for field trips, class pictures, or the like, the class would suggest that Heather do it. They recognized her gift of being competent, efficient, and reliable!

Betty White is multifaceted! She is an expert teacher of many grade levels, a schoolwide reading facilitator at the Central Canyon Elementary School in Caldwell, Idaho, a national trainer traveling for two years for the John Hopkins University reading curriculum, Success for All… and a Tribes TLC® Master Trainer and Professional Development Consultant for CenterSource Systems. Wherever Betty goes, her competence and caring become long remembered as gifts to all.

Many times I have attended a meeting to confer on the staff's concern about a particular student. Too often the discussion goes around and around on the child's problems, which we probably have discussed before and have little ability or hope to fix. Finally, I have become convinced that if we focused more on discovering the gifts of these students and helped them to do the same—not only could we better the use of our energy and become supportive—but help to assure "futures of promise."

YEARS LATER—AN OUTCOME REPORT

Sometimes it takes years to discover the extent to which learning how to manage group process can influence the future of a young person. Melissa, the director of a city youth project, by chance met a former student whom she hadn't seen in more than twelve years. Later she received this note:

"…You know, after we talked, I remembered that I really wanted to tell you how much you taught me when I was involved in the Topeka Youth Project. You may not recall, but one of the things we really worked on was facilitating the group 'process' in our meetings. As a kid, I was always jumping in head first in moving things forward (and not always giving the group a chance to 'catch up'). Well, as it turns out, I use the group facilitation skills I learned back then everyday in my job at Sprint PCS. As a business analyst, I facilitate groups to gather information and help them understand their work process so we can develop better software. There are times when the group skips over important issues or moves too quickly, and I think back and ask myself, 'Now, hang on here. How would Melissa do this?' I really meant to tell you about this the other day, and we just got to talking about so many other things. Anyway, if I haven't said it before, I am saying it now—*Thank you very much* for all you taught me… and for the group experience."

I hear, I forget
I see, I remember
I do, and I understand!

11 Learning Through Discovery

11 Learning Through Discovery

All genuine learning is active, not passive. It involves the use of the mind, not just memory. It is the process of discovery, in which the student is the main agent, not the teacher.[1]

—Mortimer Adler

Human survival always has been based on discovery... the discovery of self and meaningful knowledge.

Right! That's why learning must be something a learner does... not something done to a learner!

DISCOVERY IS... "SOMETHING A LEARNER DOES"

Our effort to reach and teach young adolescents with education that is "responsive" to their developmental needs has progressed from whole class instruction to Tribes Community Circles, to Cooperative Group Learning and now to Discovery Learning.

The last three group learning approaches, all grounded in extensive research and the literature of over-lapping fields, clearly support the developmental needs of early adoles-

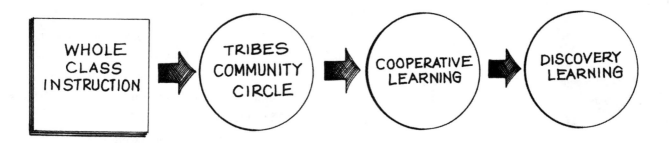

cent students. The progression represents a growing consensus about what needs to happen *more* and what needs to happen *less* in instruction. This does not mean that whole class instruction is completely abandoned. It does mean that the more that active group learning is used the more that students will attain higher levels of understanding, skills and knowledge.

A transfer of responsibility from teacher to students gradually has occurred, and the role of the teacher has changed from being the source of all information to being a facilitator of learning. Most teachers use all of the group approaches in the course of a day or period of time… convening community circles, facilitating cooperative learning experiences, and guiding student groups in learning through investigation and discovery. Teachers who take this journey do so because they also now believe "that a teacher-dominated instructional system that delivers information cannot work in an age of information explosion; and that the student who passively receives information has no notion of what it means to be a responsible citizen in a democratic society… or a worker who needs to take initiative and responsibility."[3] The culture of this new era requires a new kind of citizen.

Preparing a new kind of citizen to live and work in this new high tech era means that students of all ages need to learn how to:

Test and apply ideas… look at concepts from many points of view… develop proficient performances… evaluate and defend ideas with careful reasoning and evidence… inquire into a problem using a productive research strategy… produce a high-quality piece of work and understand the standards that indicate good performance… solve problems they have not encountered before.[4]

This kind of learning moves students beyond *memorization* and *recall* into constructive thinking, reflection and creativity. The purpose of education must be to empower today's middle level adolescents. It is our only hope of preparing kids for the future we ourselves have yet to know.

> *Rather than being powerless and dependent on the institution, learners need to be empowered to think and learn for themselves. Thus, learning needs to be conceived of as something a learner does, not something that is done to a learner.*[2]
>
> —CATHERINE FOSNOT

> Learning is not the result of development; learning IS development.[5]
>
> —CATHERINE FOSNOT

RECOVERING A WAY OF LEARNING

It is misleading to refer to the process of Tribes as "a new way of learning and being together." The community learning process is a very "old way" that has existed since the beginning of humankind. Communities of people have always survived by working together… to seek, to inquire, to search, to experiment, to observe, and always to search and try again. The path of learning corresponds to how the human brain works… constructing meaning over and over again and building upon previous knowledge and experiences. Somewhere in the mid-1800's this natural "old way" of learning was condemned to the past. It did not correspond to the standardized production needs of the Industrial Age appearing on the stage of time. Compliant people were needed to do repetitive work without making changes. There was little need for analytical thinking or conceptual problem-solving in the workplace. In general, the lives of most people in the 19th Century authoritarian period were prescribed by routine, hard work and absolutes. The period's way of autocratic rote learning… replaced learning through discourse and discovery in close community groups. It is amazing to realize that the dictates and norms of more than one hundred and fifty years ago still perpetuate the lecture model of instruction: teachers dispelling information, students taking notes, doing seat work and parroting back "right answers" to teachers and tests. Of serious concern to researchers and knowledgeable educators today is that the majority of classrooms throughout America have not changed.[6]

BACK TO THE FUTURE WITH DISCOVERY LEARNING

Discovery Learning, or constructivism, is a theory about learning—not a description of teaching activities. It is a philosophy and it is not new. Decades of studies and research on cognitive learning, neurobiology, social psychology, psychology and human development underlie its validity. Centuries of advocates as far back as Socrates, Jean-Jacques Rousseau (1762), Pestalozzi (1830), John Dewey (1896), Paolo Freire (1974), Jean Piaget (1941), Jerome Bruner (1960) and Lev Vygotsky (1962) have supported student-centered active learning rather than passive listening and mimicry. The work and voices of contemporaries such as Eliot Wiggington, James Comer, Shlomo Sharan, James Banks, Ted Sizer, James Beane, Linda Darling-Hammond, Deborah Meier, Howard Gardner, Eleanor Ducksworth, Catherine Fosnot, Thomas Lickona, Jonathan Cohen, Nel Noddings, Martin and Jacqueline Brooks, and Alfie Kohn (to name but a few)… advocate the same. Although they may express their viewpoints on learning in different terms, their theories and beliefs converge into most of the common perspectives:[7]

1. Knowledge is constructed by the learner.
2. Learning is the process of linking information to previous knowledge and experience—thereby enlarging one's representation of the world.
3. Each learner creates her own reality—assimilating new information into a living web that already exists in her mind—to understand the world.
4. Conceptual growth comes from the sharing of multiple perspectives, and the simultaneous change of one's personal interpretation in response to the perspectives of others.

5. The role of education is to promote collaboration and group discourse so that learners reach informed self-chosen positions.

6. Learning should occur in contexts that are reflective of real-world situations.

7. Testing should be integrated with the task rather than a separate activity.

MAKING A MIND SHIFT

Moving into Discovery Learning with the process of Tribes first of all means that teachers have to believe students are capable well beyond what they ever are able to demonstrate in passive direct instructional classrooms. They need to examine their traditional attitudes about middle level students and learning—and embrace a new set of beliefs such as the following. Check the ones that you believe and those you may need more time to consider.

Middle level adolescents…

• *can think* critically and constructively

• *need to believe* in their own abilities

• *are capable* of questioning, investigating, analyzing information and discovering for themselves

• *can develop* their own meaningful knowledge and learn to make decisions

• *have the ability* to take responsibility for their own learning.

Of greatest importance, do you believe that for a country to sustain democracy it must have citizens who can think independently?

Faculty members need to openly discuss these beliefs about learners and their roles as teachers. If the common philosophy and culture of constructivism is not addressed, teachers moving into the richness of Discovery Learning will have weak grounding. When asked, "Why do you teach that way?"—no matter the instructional approach—as classroom teachers we must be sufficiently knowledgeable to articulate and justify our choices.[8]

It is nothing short of a miracle that the modern methods of instruction have not yet entirely strangled the holy curiosity of inquiry; for this delicate little plant, aside from stimulation, stands mainly in need of freedom; without this it goes to wreck and ruin without fail. It is a very grave mistake to think that the enjoyment of seeing and searching can be promoted by means of coercion and a sense of duty.

—ALBERT EINSTEIN. 1949

It helps to ask every day…"Is my role just to dispense information or to develop independent thinkers!"

CHANGING THE CLASSROOM LANGUAGE

The language that most teachers use is the language they experienced when in school—however many years ago. It is a language of the traditional system that considers learning simply as the passive acquisition of information. The entrenched language makes it difficult for teachers to think in terms of creating student-centered classrooms, and to keep the emphasis on the learner and learning rather than the teacher and teaching. Here are some differences in language:

TRADITIONAL	CONSTRUCTIVIST
Today I will be teaching about…	Today you will be learning about…
This week I have to cover…	This week you will be discovering…
What unit are you working on?	What are you investigating or exploring?
I need to change my lesson plans.	Perhaps you need to modify your learning plan.
Are your reports ready?	Are your learning experiences ready?

KEEPING THE RESULTS IN MIND

As you begin to change your approach to working with young adolescents, and some days are tempted just to do 50 minutes of chalk-in-hand talking again, keep four well-proven results in mind:[9] When students are actively engaged in their own learning within inquiry (discovery) groups….

- they are motivated and they learn more
- they are building meaningful and lasting knowledge structures
- they are acquiring the ability to think constructively and to solve problems, and
- they are engaged in achieving the four developmental tasks of adolescence… gaining independence/autonomy, social competency, a sense of purpose/meaning, and the capacity to problem-solve on their own. It all comes together.

> *What students can do together today, they can do alone tomorrow.*[10]
> —LEV VYGOTSKY

Learning with your students is key to your success.

WHAT IS DISCOVERY LEARNING WITH TRIBES?

The literature and studies on constructivism, just as with cooperative learning, repeatedly emphasize that group learning has but limited success unless students have learned how to relate, monitor agreements, make collaborative decisions, manage group interaction and reflect on their progress. Otherwise, just admonishing middle level students to work "cooperatively" can be a nightmare. It is understandable why some frustrated teachers give up and go back to direct instruction and individual seat work. The tragedy is that active group learning, the most promising research-based technology capable of transforming American education, is written off. More often than not, it is the students who are blamed rather than the teaching process.

This is why we do not suggest initiating the constructivist approach (Discovery Learning with Tribes) until students have used the process of Tribes in cooperative learning groups for a period of time. It also is one of the reasons the process of Tribes has become highly valued—it assures success for learning groups.

THE FIVE E'S—A GROUP LEARNING FORMAT

The integration of the process of Tribes TLC® and an instructional model, known as "The Five E's," provides teachers and students an easy way to plan and conduct Discovery Learning. There are five sequential steps in the Five E approach: Engage, Explore, Explain, Elaborate and Evaluate.[11] Integrating the steps with the group process of Tribes is how to move smoothly from Tribes Cooperative Learning into Discovery Learning with Tribes.

The first step is to engage student interest in the *content* of the learning experience. In Tribes it also means *inclusion*. This step, unlike the next four, is teacher directed. The teacher identifies the academic content and task objectives, and plans how to introduce the instructional task.

CONTENT

The way that the learning issue, content or problem is defined influences the depth of understanding that students will achieve. In traditional schooling, curriculum is presented *parts-to-whole,* whereas in constructivist classrooms the emphasis is on the larger concept or issue, which is introduced first. In other words, curriculum is presented whole-to-parts. Here is an example of the traditional parts-to-whole class lesson.

The 8th grade biology class is studying fresh water fish. The instructor lectures about the parts of fish, students take notes, dissect fish and take a test about the fish. A week later the instructor lectures about the chemicals that kill fish in rivers, assigns chapters in the science book to read, and the task to memorize a list of chemicals. The next day, after a question/answer period led by the teacher, two students point out that the river "right here in River City" no longer has fish. Now the class is interested. People raise questions spontaneously. They want to learn what kind of fish once were there, what caused the pollution and whether something can be done to bring back the fish. After a few minutes the teacher interrupts the flurry of interest, announcing that there is no more time to spend on the subject. The class has to move on to the next unit. This exemplifies traditional parts-to-whole less-than-meaningful teaching.

The Discovery Learning experience would start with the real-time big idea—*pollution of our river*. Guided by the teacher, students would list many questions to research and investigate… questions about the river, its source, rainfall, currents, the fish, polluting chemicals, and industries contributing to the problem. Once the students are this engaged it is feasible that their investigation might become a local project involving other town people and authorities on cleaning up the river to bring back the fish. This is learning never to be forgotten.

The contrasting examples illustrate two important constructivist beliefs:
- learning is meaningful to students when it moves from a real-time idea (theme)—whole-to-parts, and
- it is better to go deeper on one topic—rather than skimming many.

Expecting students to build concepts from parts-to-wholes is like asking them to assemble a model airplane part by part without being able to view the big picture on the box. The human brain arranges (constructs) knowledge into pre-existing larger contexts rather than stacking piece by piece into unrelated boxes. This is why many students finally just focus on a few parts of a lesson without ever getting the big picture. The overall concept, its significance and meaning to them is lost.

CONCEPTUAL CLUSTERS AND POLAR CONFLICTS

In Tribes Discovery Learning conceptual themes such as in the example above and "polar conflicts" are excellent ways to initiate whole-to-parts learning experiences. The conceptual themes that follow were generated by people at the National Center for Improving Science Education as the "big ideas" of science:
- cause and effect
- change and conservation
- diversity and variation
- energy and matter
- evolution and equilibrium
- models and theories
- probability and prediction
- structure and function
- systems and interaction
- time and scale.

"Polar conflicts" also are helpful to initiate student reflection on the relationship of opposites. The list from one middle level school includes:[12]

- independence/interdependence
- impulsivity/reflection
- individual/group
- fantasy/realism
- freedom/responsibility
- reactive/proactive
- inhumanity/sensitivity
- chaos/cosmos
- objective/subjective
- static/dynamic.

A wealth of curriculum topics in all subject areas can be actively investigated, analyzed and reflected upon by beginning with polar conflicts and learning from whole-to-parts. Middle school teacher teams (tribes) enjoy generating their own rich themes for whatever the curriculum content may be. They recognize that as soon as students become engaged in reflection on a big concept, learning becomes more interesting, relevant, meaningful and fun.

School administrators intone that "in order for learning to take place, there must be order in the classroom." That may be true, but I feel the emphasis is in the wrong place, there should be something worth learning.[13]

—SUSAN OHANIAN

Use a "kid-grabbing" theme.

These are the words of our long-time friend and well-known educator, Susan Kovalik. Susan writes, "Theme building requires holistic thinking, a look at the forest, not just the trees.... It is something that you believe is critical for students to understand and to be able to do, a notion that is big enough and conceptually powerful enough that it can hold and organize a welter of ideas and thoughts, not to mention examples and facts by the barrel. Given that the brain is a pattern-seeking device, the theme is a general notion—big enough to reveal an important aspect of the real world, natural science or human action."[14]

THE INCLUSION QUESTION

Student interest is engaged in the instructional task by first setting the stage with an inclusion question that *contains* the big idea. In the example that follows, the big idea is conflict/recovery. Example: The task for 9th grade students is to compare the similarities and differences of the American Civil War and World War II. Before presenting the task, the teacher or students remind everyone to honor the four Tribes agreements. The teacher poses the inclusion question.

"ENGAGE"

Here's the 'how' to do it.

During the next two weeks, we're going to be learning about conflict and recovery from conflict. Is there anyone who has never been in some sort of conflict?

People laugh when one humorist raises a hand. The teacher continues, "Let's begin by sharing in your tribes—if you so choose—a conflict you know or read about and what people did to resolve it. Give everyone in your group equal time to share in the 10 minute discussion." Next the groups are asked to discuss and make lists of issues that can lead to conflicts that may result in war. The teacher has made connections to students' experiences, introduced the theme and promoted inclusion. The class could also be asked to connect the idea of conflict to previous learning, students could be invited to act out situations or the teacher could use an appropriate active learning strategy to elicit opinions and interest.

DEFINING THE OBJECTIVES AND QUESTIONS

Once the students are "engaged," the groundwork for the Discovery Learning task is explained. The teacher details the content and collaborative objectives, writing them on the board, flip chart or overhead. She clarifies the time for completion of the task and other requirements (reports, presentations, articles, assessment), and gives students the opportunity to ask questions. If this is an initial Discovery Learning experience for the class, the teacher also should describe her role as that of *a guide...* to consult on group plans, identify resources (materials, search sites, people to interview, etc.) and provide support as needed. The proven benefits for students to learn actively in this way could also be highlighted.

Next the tribes discuss topics and/or subtopics to be explored. They list specific *how or why* questions that they consider critical to investigate. Each tribe, after consulting with the teacher, selects a different manageable question to explore. It is the student inquiry process and the various group questions (on subtopics) that drive the exploration.

All of the small groups then *brainstorm* activities that they consider will give them information about their tribe's question. They make a written plan by listing the various activities under the respective questions, check with their *teacher-guide* on which ones are appropriate and feasible. This gives the teacher an opportunity to suggest learning activities and resources that also include required curriculum information and concepts.

The plan needs to be detailed specifying the activities that each student *will do* and *when*.

Here is an example.

THE SATELLITE TRIBE'S ACTION PLAN TO EXPLORE RACIAL PREJUDICE IN THE TWO WARS[16]

1. Bryan will meet with the school librarian on Tuesday at 2:30 p.m. to research and select two video tapes that highlight racial prejudice in the two big wars.

2. Colin will search the Web to find speeches that Abraham Lincoln and Franklin Delano Roosevelt gave at the end of the wars.

3. Kevin is going to research post-war recovery issues (reparations) in Germany and Japan after World War II—on Monday afternoon at the newspaper archives—and probably Tuesday too.

4. Kelly and Alexa are conducting a public citizen poll—interviewing at least 50 people at the Wallmart store on Saturday afternoon—on what people think causes prejudice and racial tension in our country today. Also on Monday at lunchtime they are meeting with Dr. Heathcliff, the psychologist at the Piney Road Stress Reduction Clinic, which conducts conflict management classes.

5. Our whole tribe will visit the veterans' retirement home on Saturday morning to interview some veterans from World War II.

6. Our tribe will read and also get information from Chapter 16: "Civil War in the United States" and Chapter 27: "World War II" in the book suggested by our guide.

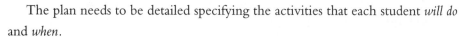

Once you have learned to ask questions—relevant and appropriate and substantial questions—you have learned how to learn and no one can keep you from learning whatever you want or need to know.[15]

—NEIL POSTMAN AND
CHARLES WEINGARTNER

Activities are implemented and discoveries are brought back for discussion in tribes. After levels of understanding and misconceptions are clarified with their teacher-guide, the tribes plan how to report or present their learning to the class community. Their conclusions must be justified by factual information and academic concepts. Their guide helps them to clarify explanations, information and terminology… and in the process, once again can determine levels of understanding and/or recommend additional material that may be needed to meet the learning objective well.

The students make presentations to the class community in various active learning ways that also have been discussed with their guide. A class familiar with multiple intelligence ideas and cooperative learning strategies can enliven their presentation… possibly also into a production for parents.

As part of their presentation they also need to involve the class community in expanding on the concepts they have learned, and make connections to current real-world issues. The connections can lead to further inquiry and new understanding for the class community.

Evaluate, the fifth "E," is an on-going diagnostic process that allows the teacher and students to determine how well the learners are attaining an understanding of concepts and knowledge, and how well they are working together in their learning groups. Assessment occurs at all points along the continuum of the discovery process through a variety of ways beginning with the *teacher-guide's* discussions with the tribes, teacher observations, performance assessments based on outcome expectations (including quantified rubrics), written group reports, individual reports, portfolios, and various types of tests to evaluate individual learning. The class community (and their guide) also should be the group to decide how to assess group presentations. There is a consensus in the literature that "viewing the evaluation process as a continuous one gives the constructivist philosophy a kind of cyclical structure. The learning process is open-ended and open to change. There is an on-going loop where questions lead to answers."[17]

The assessment of the on-going relational and learning process within the small groups has always been the Tribes way of learning and being together. The fact that the learning objectives (content/academic and constructive/social) are described for students at the beginning of every learning experience, and at the same time they are given the expectation that they will assess how well their groups attained the objectives… is in itself motivational. The time set aside at the close of every Tribes TLC® learning experience to express appreciation and to recognize peers for their contributions and gifts also is empowering. It sustains the culture of achievement and caring.

SUMMARY OF THE DISCOVERY LEARNING STEPS

1. ENGAGE

The teacher:

selects topic/problem

engages students through inclusion

defines the objectives and task of the
  learning experience

makes connections to past learning

lays groundwork for group task

describes role as a "guide"

2. EXPLORE

Student tribes:

review the four Tribes agreements

define inquiry questions

select question(s) to explore

discuss and list activities for questions

check with guide

make an action plan

conduct exploration

manage tribe interaction

3. EXPLAIN

Student tribes:

discuss their discoveries

plan presentations

clarify with guide

present learning to class

justify conclusions from academic
  information and concepts

4. ELABORATE

Student tribes:

involve class to expand on concepts
  and connect to real-world issues

discuss how connection can lead to
  future exploration

5. EVALUATE

Student tribes:

ask class prepared reflection questions

reflect/assess achievement of objectives

complete individual and/or group reports

give statements of appreciation

acknowledge members' gifts and
  contributions

A TEACHER'S PERSPECTIVE

BY MARY PALIN

Mary Palin, M.A., is a Tribes TLC® Master Trainer and a Professional Development Consultant for CenterSource Systems, as well as a teacher of a 6th grade Challenge Class— "kids who are a challenge or need one"—in the Lake Tahoe Unified School District, California. Mary says that she enjoys working with adolescents because of their spirit, creativity and energy—which coincidentally are qualities well matched in Mary.

TRIBES DISCOVERY LEARNING IS THE HOW TO MEET THE WHAT OF STANDARDS

What is happening in your classroom right now?

If you have read this book to this page, it is probable that you have made some changes in your classroom environment—perhaps you have incorporated some active learning strategies into your daily lesson plan. Most likely of all, you have said to yourself more than once, "I do that!" But to what extent are you making changes? Implementing what you may be learning in Tribes TLC® training? Infusing curriculum into Tribes TLC® strategies? Where are you in your transition to active learning? What is happening for your students that may not have been happening before?

GETTING STARTED

Speaking from my own experience of fifteen years of teaching through the Tribes process with 6th, 7th, and 8th graders, preparing learning experiences takes active organization, learning from mistakes, constant creation, recreation and reflection on what I teach and how I teach it… trying to help students make meaningful connections to real-life situations. Basically, to teach through a "discovery learning process," teachers must become on-going learners. That is why participating in training is such a helpful first step.

Just as the Tribes TLC® process is based on good teaching practice and research supporting student-centered active learning, so also is the foundation of Tribes Discovery Learning (constructivism). Tribes Discovery Learning integrates the group process of Tribes with the constructivist approach of student-directed learning. Active learning through dialogue, debate, hypothesizing, group investigation, projects, role-playing, and on-going reflection (assessment) enliven and motivate middle school students.

If you can say, "I do that!" as you read this book, you have started the process of Tribes Discovery Learning. Now, all you have to do is understand the framework and follow through.

HOW IT WORKS

You have been using the process of Tribes TLC® in your classroom. You have created an environment where students feel safe to ask questions, express opinions, and share from experience. Through the stages of group development, students have had multiple opportunities to work in groups, diverse in size as well as members. You know how to engage students in cooperative learning experiences that you even may have designed to meet the standards of your district and/or state requirements.

Choose a topic students must learn as part of the required curriculum. Using the "Five E" format explained in this Chapter, just start simple. Make it a goal to let go of some of the traditional teacher-directed routine—and see what happens!

AN EXAMPLE OF A "FIVE E" PLAN

ENGAGE: Use a Tribes inclusion strategy to introduce a topic. Let's say the topic that will be studied is "the European Renaissance," but don't announce it until after using an inclusion question that connects to the topic or its theme. The inclusion question below is a "You" question and the theme is "new beginnings."

Inclusion in tribes—Question: Have you ever wanted to change something in your life, or try something new or exciting? Share what it was and how it might affect your life. After time-limited sharing, introduce the topic, and the task objectives. List and explain the 5 E Steps. Clarify that your role is that of a guide helping all the groups on their discovery journey.

EXPLORE: Have the class (or tribes) explore specific questions (about people, discoveries, or inventions) that they want to discover about the Renaissance in Europe. Have each tribe select a question and make a plan of how they will get information. It is better to have them think in terms of exploring or researching a question rather than using the more traditional term of "topic." The teacher "guide" checks in to make certain the exploration is do-able and appropriate, and sets the time the tribe will have for their investigation.

EXPLAIN: Following the "Explore" time, ask the tribes to plan how they will present their discovery to the class (diagrams, map, role play, cooperative learning strategy, multiple intelligence involvements). The presenters must justify their conclusions and tell how they discovered the information. The guide checks the plan prior to the presentation and invites the group to add to what they may have missed.

ELABORATE: The presenters also invite students to ask questions, expand upon concepts and connections to real-world issues, and formulate additional questions that the class could pursue for further discovery.

EVALUATE: As a first step to determine what the class community has learned from the presentation, the presenters ask the class questions they have prepared, or they can take places in the other class tribes and use the questions to lead discussions.

Following each presentation, the presenting group reflects back to the task objectives, discusses what they have learned, documents highlights of their own learning (and discovery of gifts) in their journals, and writes individual reports.

Once you and your students are familiar and successful using the 5 E's in learning experiences, the doors are open. After students in my 7th grade classroom were familiar with the 5 E's, in definition and the context of their learning experiences, we took the next meaningful step: a two week learning project.

WHY IT WORKS

In case you still need convincing that this approach to learning is meaningful and long-term, consider how the essential elements of constructivism can be implemented through the 5 E's used in Tribes Discovery Learning:

ELEMENTS	TRIBES DISCOVERY LEARNING
A learner centered curriculum	Engage
Real-life interest	
Enriched environment	Explore
Inquiry, experimentation, investigation	
Interactive settings	Explain
Mediation and facilitation	Elaborate
Meta-cognitive reflection	Evaluate

In the face of educational "reform," it takes a little courage, new knowledge and an active learning approach to help students thrive on learning. It's not just about meeting standards. The concepts and information are WHAT we want students to learn, but not HOW they can and do learn.

IN A DISCOVERY LEARNING CLASSROOM[18]

STUDENT AUTONOMY AND INITIATIVE ARE ACCEPTED AND ENCOURAGED. Teachers help students attain their own intellectual identity. Students frame questions and issues and then go about analyzing and answering them. They take responsibility for their own learning and become problem solvers.

THE TEACHER ASKS OPEN-ENDED QUESTIONS AND ALLOWS WAIT TIME FOR RESPONSES. Higher level thinking is encouraged. The constructivist teacher challenges students to reach beyond the simple factual response, and encourages them to connect and summarize concepts by analyzing, predicting, justifying and defending their ideas.

STUDENTS ARE ENGAGED IN DIALOGUE WITH THE TEACHER AND WITH EACH OTHER. Social discourse in groups helps students to change or reinforce their ideas, and build a personal knowledge base that they understand. Only when they feel comfortable enough in a safe and caring environment to express their ideas will meaningful dialogue occur.

STUDENTS ARE ENGAGED IN EXPERIENCES THAT CHALLENGE HYPOTHESES AND ENCOURAGE DISCUSSION. The constructivist teacher provides opportunities for students to generate hypotheses and to test them, through group discussion of concrete experiences.

THE CLASS USES RAW DATA, PRIMARY SOURCES, MANIPULATIVES, PHYSICAL AND INTERACTIVE MATERIALS. The constructivist approach involves students in real-world possibilities and then helps them generate meaningful and lasting concepts.

Here's what it looks like, sounds like and feels like in a Discovery Learning classroom.

ASSESSMENT OF THE SCHOOL IMPROVEMENT PROCESS AND LONG-TERM OUTCOMES

Did you know? 150 years ago the first large scale standardized testing in the United States was initiated under the Secretary of the State Board of Education of Massachusetts by a renowned gentleman named Horace Mann. The goals were very much the same as standardized testing goals today:

- Accountability—to determine the effectiveness of systems and programs
- Feedback—to improve instruction by teachers
- Classification—to put students into categories, and
- Reform—to increase student learning.

Before that, evaluation was not standardized. In the little red schoolhouse it was individualized and left up to the teacher… who cared, observed, knew how her students were doing day by day, and helped them accordingly. The emergence of testing outside of the classroom changed the nature of educational assessment. Assessment no longer was a tool for the teacher to learn how students were doing, but became an instrument of public policy and politics.

Nevertheless....

This is the dilemma that exists today in the field of education. On one hand are the not-to-be disputed state mandates for high stakes testing *("criterion-referenced tests for specific content standards"),* and on the other hand are dedicated classroom teachers who know and care about their students, and cannot bear to short-change them by narrowing down learning to the memorization of information for the test… "to teach to the test." In ever-growing numbers, teachers want learning to be meaningful to empower students to handle complex problems and situations within real-life context. Specific content tests are irrelevant to this purpose. Assessments need to be performance based, reflective and take into consideration the full range of student intelligences and competencies. Unfortunately the dichotomy is difficult to overcome because the "outside" public and the "inside" educational community have different purposes and views of learning.

At the school site level all school communities want to know the degree to which various long-term outcomes (such as increases in academic achievement, decreased discipline problems, increased parent involvement, improved school climate, improved attendance, teacher collegiality, etc.) are achieved due to the use of the process of Tribes over a period of time. Prior to evaluating long-term outcomes, it is of great importance to conduct periodic *process assessments* to indicate the extent that key components of the process of Tribes are being implemented in classrooms.

Focusing only on outcome data, without simultaneously gathering data on the nature of students' school experiences provides very little leverage for improvement….Without evidence on processes, evaluation efforts are reduced to 'black box' inquiries with little potential to explain outcomes, whether good or bad.[19]

—Walt Haney

Process assessments are timely snapshots that point to areas to intensify for improvement. *For example:* A desired outcome for a school is to decrease conflict and racial tension among students. If a process assessment indicates that the agreement of *mutual respect* is not being practiced or demonstrated significantly in classrooms, teachers can focus on that Tribes agreement by implementing many mutual respect strategies throughout the school and classrooms. They also can have students identify and discuss the quality whenever discovered in curriculum content.

Tribes school communities can assess their school's progress by obtaining the Assessment Kit: Reflecting on the Tribes TLC® Process from CenterSource Systems. It consists of a reliable set of action research instruments designed and piloted by the Northwest Regional Educational Laboratory just for our use. It's purpose is to give teachers and students snapshots of the extent to which the components of Tribes are happening in classrooms, and then to plan together how to strengthen their use.[20] Periodic "reflection" along the trail results in goal attainment on any journey.

"I CONFESS....

I started out as a creationist. The first days of every school year I created; for the next thirty-six weeks I maintained my creation. My curriculum. From behind my big desk I set it in motion, managed and maintained it all year, lectured—systematic, purposeful, in control. I wanted great truths from my great practices. And I wanted to convince other teachers that this creation was superior stuff. So I studied my curriculum, conducting research to show its wonders. I didn't learn in my classroom. I tended and taught my creation.

These days, I learn in my classroom. What happens there has changed; it continually changes. I've become an evolutionist, and the curriculum unfolds now as my kids and I learn together. My aims stay constant—I want us to go deep inside language, using it to know and shape and play with our worlds. My practices evolve as eighth graders and I go deeper. This going deeper is research, and these days my research shows me the wonders of my kids, not my methods. But it has also brought me full circle. What I learn with these students, collaborating with them as a writer and reader who wonders about writing and reading, makes me a better teacher—not great maybe, but at least grounded in the logic of learning and growing."[21]

—Nancy Atwell

The inquiry method is not designed to do
What older environments try to do.
It works you over in entirely different ways.
It activates different senses, attitudes, and perceptions.
It generates a different, bolder
And more potent kind of intelligence....
It will cause everything about education—
To change.[22]

—Neil Postman and Charles Weingartner

12
Discovering Gifts
Throughout the Responsive Middle School

12 Discovering Gifts Throughout the Responsive Middle School

What we must reach for is a conception of perpetual self-discovery, perpetual reshaping to realize one's best self, to be the person one could be.[1]

—John W. Gardner

WHY EDUCATION? ARE WE MISSING ITS REAL PURPOSE?

Today it seems obvious that school communities, politicians, standards setters, curricula developers and hierarchies of funding sources have lost sight of the fundamental purpose of education. Throughout time, respected philosophers and educators from Plato to Albert Einstein, John Dewey, Jean Piaget, Urie Bronfenbrenner, John Gardner, James Comer, Daniel Goleman, Deborah Meier and Howard Gardner—to name but a few—have asserted that the fundamental purpose of education *is to develop greatness in human beings, active constructive citizens who are valuable contributors to society.* Howard Gardner shares his refreshing viewpoint,

> *I claim that an education for all human beings needs to explore in some depth a set of key human achievements captured in the venerable phrase 'the true, the beautiful and the good'.... I crave human beings who understand the world, who gain sustenance from such understanding, and who want—ardently, perennially—to alter it [the world] for the better.*[2]

The fundamental purpose of education is to develop greatness in human beings.

Unfortunately, schools today are facing unprecedented political pressure to achieve prescribed standards and test scores... quite apart from the humanizing purpose of education. Yet fortunately, the national crusade is causing networks of educators, parents, community and business groups to question whether this is all that education now means for children.

Keith Larick, Superintendent of one of the largest and fastest growing school districts in California, raises his concern on a videotape recently made for *Tribes Learning Communities.* He says,

> *As we look at the 21st Century we face great challenges. This will be an exciting time... we know that our young people are going to be exposed to more information than any generation before. They are going to have more knowledge and possess more insights than any group in our history. And at the same time that is not enough. They've got to have a sense of humanity.*

*They have to balance their lives between what they know and what they do to make this a better world. Having a program like Tribes brings that sense of humanity. I know that we have a greater responsibility, beyond self... collectively, to know what **we** [all] are going to contribute.[4]*

At first glance, the quotation from John Gardner heading this chapter clearly is addressed to our young adolescent friends, urging them to discover and become the best that they can be. As a second thought, it occurred to us to take the liberty of rephrasing Dr. Gardner's statement so that it might shed light on what we as educators and administrators in systems must do. The revised message then speaks loudly...

What we must reach for is a conception of perpetual discovery in the system, perpetual reshaping to realize its best, to be the responsive system it could be.

The only hope for young adolescents to be able to discover, reshape and realize their best selves clearly depends upon their middle level schools becoming the best that they can be. Just as in the quest for personal growth, a school must become a *reflective system* always open to *discovery and reshaping itself*. This is one of the reasons that the process of Tribes over time can lead to significant school improvement... and create a love of learning in students. No matter the type of group in the school (student tribes, faculty teams, parent groups, core planners, advisory groups), all in the Tribes Learning Community *practice reflection* in order to keep discovering, improving and achieving. The process becomes a norm of the whole system. It is a way for a school to become "the best it can be."

THE SHARED PRACTICE OF REFLECTION

Readers who have followed along this far are well aware that the Tribes Learning Community's intrusive pelican, "Reflection," is our meta-cognitive symbol calling attention in classrooms, among staff and throughout the community to what is being learned and what is taking place in a group, classroom or system. System change, school improvement and assessment... all depend upon this conscious practice becoming a norm throughout the school community. If in the daily rush no one says, "Stop the action... What's happening? What did we learn?," achieving significant school improvement will not happen.

Howard Gardner warns:

The push for action is powerful, particularly when it comes from impatient supervisors and parents. But unless one has the opportunity to think about what one is doing and to reflect on what went well, what went poorly, and why, the chances for a long-term improvement curve are slight. Time for individual and joint reflection must be built into the schedule; if it is not, then genuine change is most unlikely to occur.[5]

I'm a meta-cognitive symbol! Wow!

Test scores tell us nothing about the state of health of American education.[3]
— TED SIZER

The regular practice in Tribes of having student groups address "reflection questions" helps them to internalize this critical life-long learning skill.

DEMOCRATIC LEADERSHIP

Engaging parents, community leaders, resource persons, teachers and students themselves to support the transformation of their school into a high-performance system requires the development of democracy throughout the school. It is next to impossible to progress to responsive education for students if the school leader perceives the school as an organization to be controlled rather than a community to be inspired and led in a common cause. The majority of organizations are defined by management systems based on rules, regulations, imposed expectations, supervision and monitoring for compliance. Excellent middle schools are defined by the beliefs, values and sentiments that adults have concerning the students and their learning and development. Control driven business management practices may be effective in producing market products but they undermine the diametrically different purpose of schools—"to develop competent human beings to take constructive action in society." The values and cultures are completely incompatible to one another.[7]

> *Leadership is much more of an art, a belief, a condition of the heart, than a set of things to do.*[6]
> —MAX DE PREE

Leading a school community requires leadership that empowers all of the structured groups (teams and tribes) throughout the school to reflect, problem-solve, plan, initiate action and reflect (assess) again and again. The millennium school leader is a transformative leader—*a reflective practitioner* who affirms the gifts of others and empowers many in the mission of the middle school.

No longer a remote authority primarily juggling finances, personnel issues and problems, the effective middle school leader frees up time by distributing many traditional activities to a core group, lead teachers, teacher teams and support staff.[8] The change in role parallels the one that teachers are making in transferring responsibility to students in cooperative learning groups. The same principle applies: no one person can supervise and support more than five or six other people at any one time—but one person can empower and support cooperative teams of people. A growing number of "seasoned" administrators recognize the truth of organizational studies which indicate that "the only thing of real importance that leaders do is to create and manage the culture."[10]

Transformative leaders know the difference between power-over and power-to.[9]

After ten years as a principal I finally figured that out— and I found a life again!

According to Roland Barth, Director of the Principal's Center at Harvard University, the 21st Century administrator must be a transformational leader who not only is a *reflective practitioner but a learner. "To be a learner is to be able to admit, 'I do not know it all.' To be a learner is to admit imperfection. Who inspires more confidence? Who is the better leader? The principal who is learned and wise or the principal who is an insatiable life-long learner?"*[11] Think of a school leader that you consider outstanding. Ten to one you'll say the person is not governed by techniques, but by a desire to bring out the best in the people. The effective leader is able to stand back and be reflective in the moment of success or failure. He or she asks, "What am I learning that will help to lead the school community now?" This is especially important for middle level schools. Studies verify that the link between principal learning and the quality of teaching, in turn, affects the quality of student learning.[12]

TEACHERS IN REFLECTIVE PRACTICE

In the same way, middle school teachers must have self-reflective capacities so that they can continue to learn, to grow and to facilitate learning for today's adolescent students. Jonathan Cohen, author of the fine book, "Educating Minds and Hearts," states the need well:

Social emotional learning for educators is as important as social emotional learning is for our students. [edit] Our ability or inability to understand where the child is 'living,' and to empathize with and recognize the student's experience and our own, determines how successful any programmatic effort can and will be.[13]

Such professional growth does not happen simply in "now and then" in-service education, but through sustained on-site peer dialogue and support.[14] Expecting teachers to alter their traditional teacher-talk approach and move to active group learning is a big challenge. Throughout the years it has become clear that the Tribes TLC® schools that do well in sustaining the responsive process for student achievement, are those that schedule regular weekly study groups for teachers to think, share and work together as *reflective practitioners*.[15]

Such time is invaluable because it enables teachers to keep learning individually and collaboratively with colleagues. This cannot happen when teachers go out to professional development courses and conferences on their own.[16] Rich learning experiences evolve from topics, questions and cooperative learning in which the whole faculty participates in many meetings with questions such as…

- What are we doing to help these kids gradually achieve the tasks of adolescence?
- What gets in my way when I want to empathize and understand?
- What kinds of support or learning do I need?
- What helps us as teachers to work collaboratively and creatively?

Teachers quickly become aware that this kind of meaningful discourse helps to shape their thinking, knowledge, and ability to analyze, problem-solve and make decisions. Most of all it leads to the development of the "Three C's"—cooperation, collaboration and collegiality—all essential to sustaining a positive school culture and academic achievement.[17]

> *The new model of school reform must seek to develop communities of learning grounded in communities of democratic discourse.*[18]
>
> —LINDA DARLING-HAMMOND

Training in "the art of reflective practice" enables teacher teams to plan and progress through three invaluable stages: *reflection for action, reflection-in-action and reflection-on action*.[19] Indeed, the collegial practice is a vehicle for on-going assessment and action research throughout the school. The practice needs to be sustained as an essential component of the middle level school's professional development, improvement and assessment plans.

Carole Cooper, cooperative learning educator and professional development consultant, emphasizes the many types of reflective practice structures that can be used within a middle school.[20]

The good news is that teachers and school leaders trained in the process of Tribes TLC® are competent in facilitating productive collaboration in groups. Whether reflecting on student work, observing and mentoring each other, planning learning experiences, linking developmental learning goals or discovering their own gifts—they are collaborative and collegial. Moreover, there is a direct correlation of teacher collegiality to student achievement.

Discovering gifts means teachers too!

SUMMARY OF COLLABORATIVE REFLECTIVE PRACTICES

INDIVIDUAL REFLECTIVE PRACTICES

Self-contracting and monitoring

Portfolios

Journals

Case studies

PARTNER REFLECTIVE PRACTICES

Learning buddies

Mentoring

Peer coaching

Work exchanges or shadowing

SMALL GROUP REFLECTIVE PRACTICES

Action research

Study groups

Peer support groups

Professional dialogue groups

LARGE GROUP REFLECTIVE PRACTICES

Assessment centers

Exhibitions and panels

Presentations

Professional development schools

Teacher centers

Teacher institutes

Partnerships

Yes, middle school teachers also need to have caring support to be able to realize their own special gifts, and to be acknowledged for all that they bring to the learning community. Few enter the teaching profession without caring about children... without having a vision of being valued... without hoping they will be remembered for supporting and challenging the reluctant as well as the eager learners. Being in a school that has a caring community culture also brings the joy of discovery and celebration to their lives. Perhaps it is middle school teachers who, more than many other folks, symbolize "greatness as human beings... active constructive citizens who are valuable contributors to society!" May they all "discover gifts in middle school" with the process known as Tribes.

AN ADMINISTRATOR'S PERSPECTIVE

BY NANCY LATHAM

Nancy W. Latham, M.Ed., is the District Educational Specialist for Special Services in Central Oahu District, Hawaii. As a collateral responsibility, as a Certified Tribes Trainer, she also has coordinated training for teachers, administrators and support personnel in 41 schools. Throughout all of Nancy's professional work as a school renewal specialist, school counselor, elementary principal and middle school vice-principal, she has focused on the power of relationships in building resiliency for staff and students as a support for increased academic achievement.

SUSTAINING THE PROCESS: BUILDING DISTRICT-WIDE CAPACITY

Seven years after the process of Tribes was first introduced in the Central Oahu District in Honolulu, the philosophical beliefs and culture of caring have become the norm for District leadership and an integral part of more than 75% of the 41 schools in the district. Since 1993, more than 3000 teachers, administrators, and support staff have been trained in Tribes TLC®… providing enhanced learning environments for most of our students. There are seventy-two certified trainers on the island of Oahu; approximately thirty actively train and give ongoing support to school personnel in the four districts.

It is my pleasure to coordinate the ongoing development of the Tribes process throughout our district. Several factors have been critical to expanding and sustaining the use of the Tribes Learning Community process and institutionalizing the culture within our district: first, it was not a top-down initiative. Teachers and administrators recognized the value the process would have for our schools, and they shared their excitement with colleagues. Fortunately, we were able to secure funding from two Safe, Drug-Free Schools grants, which have paid all costs for the past four years. Staff members who participate in ongoing training may receive professional development credit. Our certified Tribes trainers continue to support teachers as they implement the process in classrooms and schools. Key to the support of the Tribes trainer network, are monthly meetings that are trainer-directed, providing time for sharing, planning, problem solving and collegiality. The trainer network also participates several times a year in their own advanced training conducted by Master Trainers from CenterSource.

Of great importance is the fact that our District Superintendents actively have supported the development of the process of Tribes as the basis for implementation of our Comprehensive Student Support Systems. The protective factors for resiliency now are the framework for a rubric to assess each school's provision of "Student Connectedness," as written in the school's annual improvement plan. The concept of resiliency is the basis of our current district multi-year Safe Schools—Healthy Students federal grant. New "high-risk" counselor positions have been intentionally renamed "Resiliency Counselors" within each of our middle schools. Fostering resiliency by implementing protective factors also has become the framework for the development of our school-based mental health system.

During the early years we hoped to be able to institutionalize the caring culture of Tribes throughout the Central Oahu District. Could there be recognizable indicators that somehow this was happening? Perhaps it was the day that the District staff realized that the Tribes Agreements, which are being used throughout our schools, could also serve as standards for our district staff. The standards that were defined and accepted are known as…

The Central Oahu District Staff Standards for Quality Support.

Our General Learner Outcomes:

- The ability to be responsible for one's own learning
- The understanding that it is essential for human beings to work together
- The ability to be involved in complex thinking and problem solving
- The ability to recognize and produce quality performance and quality products.

We will treat each other and all those with whom we interact with *mutual respect*.

- We will maintain confidentiality in all transactions.
- We will value diversity of opinions and ideas.
- We will respect others—no matter what their race, gender, age, color, or learning ability.
- We will respect personal property and individual privacy, individual skills, talents, and contributions.
- We will value each person's concern, taking personal responsibility for the resolution.

We will practice *attentive listening* in all communication.

- We will listen with our eyes, ears, and heart.
- We will withhold our own opinions and need to talk while others are talking.
- We will listen as an ally, with the intention to be supportive and helpful.
- We will approach challenges in a problem-solving mode, engaging in "I-statements" to take responsibility for our own feelings.

We will encourage and support *meaningful participation*.

- We will develop plans and programs to enhance the General Learning Outcomes.
- We will participate in the continuous improvement of Standards Based Education.
- We will share information in a timely manner to provide all who want to be involved the opportunity to be successful.
- We will share our own talents and skills with others to enable them to maximize their talents and skills.
- We will encourage and support teaming to learn with and from others.
- We will commit ourselves to quality in all that we do.

We will demonstrate our *appreciation*.

- We will celebrate the contributions of others.
- We will use verbal and nonverbal communication to express our appreciation.
- We will greet others in person and on the telephone with a smile.
- We will support our own resilience!

Yes, the process of Tribes has been philosophically "institutionalized" into our District's culture, and is being implemented by teachers, support staffs and district leadership. However, it is critical that we continue to seek opportunities to deepen our understanding of the caring process as the basis to continue to enhance academic achievement and resiliency. This expanded use of the Tribes process in every classroom in the Central Oahu District is our challenge and is our on-going commitment.

PARENTS IN REFLECTIVE PRACTICE

In Tribes Learning Communities parents also are engaged in reflective learning groups in which they can gain an understanding of the adolescent tasks their young teens are striving to achieve, principles on learning, developmental studies and forms of assessment. This cannot happen through large impersonal auditorium meetings. Parents also need inclusion in on-going small inquiry groups that are facilitated by other parents trained to implement the process of Tribes and active learning strategies. Once a school or district has its own certified Tribes TLC® trainers, they are able to train parent facilitators and help them to plan interactive meetings. The Resource Section of this book contains an example of an initial classroom parent meeting. Structuring the parent community in this way, into membership groups dedicated to understanding young adolescents, is one of the most effective ways to increase parent involvement. It also enables the responsive school to connect to the wider community of local services, business groups, family and youth organizations, colleges, universities, civic groups and professional networks. Every parent of every young adolescent needs inclusion and a sense of being valued by people in their teenager's school. They too have many undiscovered gifts, and are essential in carrying forward the middle school's important shared vision of *academic excellence, developmental responsiveness and social equity*.

STUDENTS IN REFLECTIVE PRACTICE... TO DISCOVER THEIR GIFTS

The regular practice in Tribes of having student groups respond to reflection questions enables young adolescents to identify their strengths, skills, gifts and interests throughout the day while working with peers. The hundreds of reflection questions in the Tribes Learning Strategies of this book not only help students to identify their own strengths but to acknowledge the strengths and contributions of others.

It is especially effective to have students record their reflections and discoveries in personal journals. An attractive journal designed for students in Tribes TLC® middle level schools is available from CenterSource Systems. The journal, "Discovering Gifts," contains:

- Reflection pages to record interests, gifts and skills
- Multiple intelligences checklists and descriptions
- Highlights on the tasks of adolescence
- Opportunities for discovering resilient qualities
- Reflection pages for making personal decisions
- Opportunities for looking at career choices
- Reflection on achieving personal goals
- Form: Participation in My Tribe
- Form: My Constructive Thinking Skills
- Monthly calendars and task organizer formats.

The multiple intelligences checklists also are contained in the Learning Strategy Section of this book so that all readers can help students identify their ways of knowing and learning. It is best not to have them do this until inclusion (belonging and trust) and

Reflection helps parents to understand the tasks of adolescence, learning approaches and forms of assessment.

influence (a sense of value) have been experienced in classroom tribes. Do follow the directions for using the checklists, as it is important for students to understand that all of the intelligences are wonderful and none better than others. We highly recommend that teachers, school leaders and parents read Dr. Thomas Armstrong's book, *7 Kinds of Smart—Identifying and Developing Your Multiple Intelligences,* in order to discover your own ways of learning and to improve your understanding of students who learn in ways different than your own.

A CULTURE OF SOCIAL EQUITY AND FAIRNESS

The responsive Tribes Learning Community that is focusing on adolescent development, *greatness* in its young human beings, must create and sustain a culture of fairness and equity. Anne Wheelock clearly states that it is the essential "ethos in which young adolescents feel safe enough to be their best selves and 'safe to be smart.'"[23]

It is as though many windows open all at once for our 10 to 15 year olds—to an awesome wider world that seemingly becomes theirs. They become idealistic and begin to see things from a different perspective... "schooling" being one. The world was more comfortable back in earlier childhood days in which concrete thinking (absolutism) reassured them that "this is how things are." Emerging from the mist of those years into abstract conceptual thinking shakes up just about everything. Now there is a need for a sense of purpose and meaning, questioning systems (particularly school and family values), personal worth, new opportunities, the relevance of school and the four underlying developmental tasks of adolescence. Since the most time is spent in school, sensitivity about social equity and fairness take on major importance. Who has not heard the questions?

> *Armstrong issues us a lifetime pass for honoring the intelligence we possess, and he also offers advice on how to add breadth and richness to experience. So long to boredom and living in ruts. We have permission to be free.*[22]
>
> —ROBERT SAMPLES

"It's not fair. The smart kids get to do special stuff!"
"How come we don't get a choice? Isn't that what democracy means?"
"Why do teachers call upon the boys more than the girls?"
"How come boys are always the group leaders?"
"Kids of my race aren't liked by some teachers."
"Why aren't the big tests about what we learned?"
"How come history is all about white people?"
"Why do we only have two Afro-American teachers here?"
"How come they cut out the music and art classes?"
"It's not fair..."

In the rush of a middle school's daily busy-ness, statements indicating unfairness are easily ignored simply because they have been heard so much before that they have become lost as unimportant norms in the culture of the school. Seemingly, the protesting voices have little to do with academic achievement, adolescent development or school improvement. This is not so! Indeed, if we want students to discover their gifts and be successful each in their own ways, the school culture must be a *culture of fairness*. The fairness that adolescents perceive as a right applies to gender, racial and cultural equity, equal opportunities, school policy, curriculum content, instructional strategies, classroom management, student rights and the extent that students can make decisions about their own learning. Being treated unfairly or treated differently not just by peers but also by teachers, principals or other adults in the school, especially at this overly sensitive age, can lead to paths of failure. Middle level schools may be perpetuating inequity and unfairness whenever…

- Multiculturalism, gender equity and multiple intelligences are seldom discussed, are not part of the school plan, and are not highlighted or integrated into curriculum
- Teachers have never participated in equity training, and unconsciously are more responsive to some students than others
- Teachers are not using cooperative learning
- Generalizations, labels and name-calling are ignored
- School policy contains biased language and rules
- Tests are perceived as biased or irrelevant to curriculum
- A caring community culture has never been developed.

It is well recognized that perceived injustice within a school breeds conflict, and destructive conflict in turn may give rise to more injustice. Middle school communities especially must model inclusion, respect, and a commitment to social justice.[24]

SEEKING A CULTURE OF FAIRNESS FOR GENDER EQUITY

Most pre-adolescent girls are interested in everything—people, animals, nature, sports, music and books. They play soccer, act out dramas, invent gadgets, sing and giggle a lot. Suddenly they become fragmented into contradictions. They are idealistic yet superficial, confident yet overwhelmed, noisy yet silent, wild with energy yet lethargic. One girl, breaking her silence, told psychologist Mary Pipher, "Everything good for me died in junior high school." The loss of self begins to encompass girls as they move into adolescence and are pulled by cultural forces to become attractive to boys while at the same time keeping up grades, being close to mom and dad—and living into their own gifts and dreams. Mary Pipher, author of the groundbreaking book, "Reviving Ophelia… Saving the Lives of Adolescent Girls," asserts that it is not simply new hormones that cause the deep emotional change—it is the culture. By the time girls reach the middle level years they have become aware that men manage the world as administrators, congressmen, bankers, corporate executives, scientists, writers, artists and musicians. They have learned that men have more power than women and usually dominate groups and organizations.

> *America today is a girl-destroying place. Everywhere girls are encouraged to sacrifice their true selves.*[25]
> —MARY PIPHER

Women should be attractive and helpful but not competitive. Eighth grade girls have to be attractive and helpful, but not competitive—or too smart. For the first time it begins to seem like an unfair game.

No wonder the football team gets everything. No wonder teachers call on boys more! No wonder I'm worrying all the time about my looks! No wonder....

It is at this time that young adolescent girls initiate different strategies to negotiate their school days and find identity. Three of the most prominent strategies are:[26]
- Speaking Out: Asserting themselves either positively or negatively; insisting on being heard; assuming positive leadership or becoming highly visible as a maverick leader or troublemaker.
- Doing School: Conforming to traditional expectations; doing what is asked; outwardly compliant whether to her advantage or disadvantage.
- Crossing Borders: Moving easily between different sets of norms and expectations; bridging between peers and adults or different racial and ethnic groups.

All young adolescent girls desperately need teachers who understand the subtle ways that girls are dis-empowered at this critical time in their lives. All need to be affirmed by caring adults that they are not lesser people meant to be in the background of life.

And what about the boys?

Boys too are trying to handle the conflicting cultural expectations that engulf them daily at school. Again, it is not just the hormones! Decades of history have imprinted "the warrior image" upon them. Real men, real boys are tough, competitive, aggressive, dominant, unemotional, physical, athletic, in charge and invulnerable. They also, especially at school, are supposed to be respectful, responsible, cooperative, considerate and compliant. Caught in the middle of these conflicting expectations—one set emanating from our Western culture and the other evolving from the school culture—boys often attempt to be not too compliant, not too feeling, not too reflective, or not too smart—all in order to appear "cool" in the eyes of their peers while trying to seek their own emerging identities.

Ever self-conscious at this age, many previously "high-achieving" boys will, in their early adolescent years, "dumb down" in order to fit in with the rest of the crowd. With the conflicting cultural pressure to be future leaders or "in charge," boys at times will assume cool, testy, or challenging "leadership" positions which are often misinterpreted or labeled by school systems that are not tuned in to the developmental tasks of early adolescence. Those that are perceived at school as non-compliant, too physical or intimidating, in time may be branded as troublemakers, and are disciplined repeatedly or suspended. Those who are overly active may become labeled as "ADHD"—having Attention Deficit Hyperactivity Disorder—and controlled with prescribed drugs.

It is in the middle school years that students begin to form opinions about how important school is to them. Similar to girls, young adolescent boys also begin to make choices and develop strategies "to negotiate" school. A few of the most prominent strategies are:

- Speaking Out or Acting Out: Asserting themselves either positively or negatively; either assuming positive leadership positions, or becoming highly visible by challenging authority and acting out in self-defeating ways.
- Doing School: Compliant, complacent, bored, "getting through by learning the game," they rarely protest or make their needs known; often become invisible.
- Dropping Out: Giving up; alone, lost or helpless; often socially isolated, shunned or unsupported with a multitude of unaddressed social or emotional needs.

Mary Pipher writes, "Boys need a model of manhood that is caring and bold, adventurous and gentle."[27] They have the same innate human qualities as girls, and need male mentors to assure them that being caring, considerate, cooperative, empathetic, kind and nurturing is tremendously important in the life of men.

We must challenge schools to address the conflicting cultural pressures that students face by adopting a priority focus on the human development issues that adolescents are struggling to attain, either consciously or unconsciously, at this critical age. The school culture must support all students by paying attention to inequities, empowering those who long for identity, supporting those who don't feel socially competent, inspiring those who search for purpose and meaning, and helping all to solve problems that come their way. Administrators and teachers must purposely develop meaningful practices and strategies to support and empower all students to reach the adolescent tasks that they long to attain.

Each person bears a uniqueness that asks to be lived and that is already present before it is lived.[28]

—JAMES HILLMAN

SEEKING MULTICULTURAL EQUITY

Through the years many have sounded the same wake-up call to the educational community as Spencer Kagan continues to do:

We are facing a severe crisis in education. If we do not change our educational practices, we are headed toward a break-down in race relations, both in our classrooms and in the society as a whole.[29]

It is predicted that by 2020, 48% of school-age youths will be students of color. Currently it is estimated that the majority of the school-age population in 50 or more major U.S. cities are from language minority backgrounds. Despite gains within the last decade, African American and Latino youths are still significantly behind Anglo mainstream youth on many indexes of academic achievement. They also have lower high school graduation rates and higher retention, suspension and dropout rates.[30] Biased conceptions of intellectual ability are reflected in academic tracking, differential access to resources and standardized informational tests that favor mathematical and linguistic learners.[31] Unfair conceptions about students of color also have led to a focus on individual characteristics and deficiencies of students rather than ways that school systems are failing them.

Whenever you hear or recognize name-calling, teasing, exclusion, meanness, fights or violence—know that the culture of the classroom and school needs rebuilding or treatment—not the kids. Know that when you see a teacher ignore a student of color (perhaps perceived as not having the right answer) or hear chatter in the teachers' lounge that "those kids can't learn," it is time to schedule professional development training and on-going staff discussions on multicultural, racial and gender equity issues.[32] All such bias has direct impact upon curriculum, pedagogy, classroom culture, learning, teacher-student and student-student relationships.

REVERSING INEQUITY

Years of research clearly show that cooperative learning reduces incidents of gender, racial and multicultural bias. The egalitarian social group structures create caring relationships, and a culture of respect in which diversities of people can work collaboratively to achieve common goals. Structuring on-going tribes assures inclusion for all students… the positive culture assures mutual respect and appreciation.

In addition to intensifying the use of Tribes TLC® cooperative learning, we strongly recommend that middle school staffs participate in multicultural and gender equity training so that everyone becomes more aware of the subtleties of bias, language and the disempowerment that routinely happens daily for too many students. A good way to gain a commitment from the faculty to work on these important issues is to schedule a series of meetings to reflect on what may be happening at your

Schools that are using Tribes cooperative learning are well on their way to reversing inequity.

school. The following chart, Matrix for Achieving Equity in Classrooms, provides a way to structure discussions. It also may be used as an assessment and planning tool.

If you really want to know what's happening have students design and conduct a survey!

Culturally responsive and gender equity teaching is validating and affirming because it teaches to and through the strengths of students. It....

- acknowledges the legitimacy of different ethnic groups
- builds bridges of meaningfulness between home and school experiences and socio-cultural realities
- uses a wide variety of instructional strategies that are connected to different learning styles
- teaches students to know and praise their own and each other's cultural heritages and gender strengths, and
- incorporates multicultural information, resources and materials in all subjects and skills being learned in schools.[33]

Linda Christensen, co-editor of *Rethinking Schools,* emphasizes,

As teachers, we have daily opportunities to affirm that our students' lives and language are unique and important. We do that in the selections of literature we read, in the history we chose to teach, and we do it by giving legitimacy to our students' lives as a content worth of study.[34]

MATRIX FOR ACHIEVING EQUITY IN CLASSROOMS

Use the following matrix to assess six forms of bias in a classroom or a school community. Strategies for reducing bias are included in each component.

	LINGUISTIC BIAS	STEREOTYPING	INVISIBILITY/ EXCLUSION	UNREALITY	IMBALANCE/ SELECTIVITY	FRAGMENTATION/ ISOLATION
WHAT TO LOOK FOR	Language which is dehumanizing or denies the existence of females or males; e.g., "Japs," "mankind."	Members of a group portrayed in one role or with one characteristic.	The lack of representation of a group.	Misinformation about a group, event or contribution.	Single interpretation of an issue, situation or conditions.	Separating contributions of females and ethnic groups from the mainstream.
POLICY— WHAT TO DO	Review policy for biased language.	Ensure nondiscriminatory discipline policy.	Recognize teaching performance which fosters equity.	Design proactive mission statement which corrects past bias.	Earmark money for equity classroom materials and training.	Design staff evaluations inclusive of equity criteria.
INSTRUCTIONAL STRATEGIES	Pluralize subjects to avoid a gender pronoun.	Encourage males and females to express a wide range of feelings, responses and sensibilities.	Encourage contributions from females and ethnic minorities.	Discuss controversial topics of discrimination and prejudice.	Engage students in analyzing and debating an issue.	Call on students equitably. Use cooperative learning.
CURRICULUM CONTENT	Set expectations for students to use non-sexist language.	Select readings that have the females and ethnic minorities in responsible, exciting leadership positions.	Have students count the numbers of male, female and ethnic group members to determine the proportion in relation to a population.	Engage students in conducting research.	Introduce collaborative ways to solve problems and make decisions.	Stress that learning is the result of collaborative efforts and contributions by many.
MANAGEMENT (SCHOOL AND CLASSROOM)	Engage all members in noticing and correcting biased language.	Intervene when slurs or jokes are made at another's expense.	Nurture cooperation among males, females and ethnically diverse students.	Facilitate shared decision making.	Create a supportive climate for differing perspectives to be discussed.	Establish ways of integrating groups during free time.
FAMILY AND COMMUNITY INVOLVEMENT	Attend council meeting and have students present on the use of non-biased language in newspapers, on road signs, etc.	Invite nontraditional role models to teach a lesson on their area of specialization.	Provide students with shadowing opportunities.	Examine the history of discrimination within local laws and history.	Establish advisory groups that are balanced by sex, ethnicity and disability.	Solicit volunteers from diverse groups to work with students.

FINDING FAIRNESS THROUGH AUTHENTIC ASSESSMENT

THE MEASURE OF A CHILD

Who knows the measure of a child,

The value of innocence,

The path of curiosity,

Or the depth of space the spirit reaches?

Who knows who will calm a fear

In a universe of unknowns,

Inspire a verse in the song of freedom,

Or weave a thread in the fabric of justice?

Take care… how you measure a child.[36]

—Carroll D. Killingsworth

Where is the standardized test that truly can measure the discovered gifts of our middle level learners? Jason, a special learner, now is writing poems. Terry, the aloof all "A" student, is coaching Anna and Peter in geometry. Dawn, usually so shy, is co-directing the spring play that she helped to write. Disruptive Gary and Gregory are working diligently and cooperatively with a team designing an energy efficient model town. But how well will these kids do on the next set of standardized State tests?

If the tests do not measure the meaningful learning students are acquiring in educationally responsive middle schools, but measure the recall of information from unrelated national curriculum, *are the tests fair?* An analysis of the most widely used standardized tests indicated that only 3 percent of the questions required "high level conceptual knowledge," and only 5 percent tested higher order thinking skills such as problem-solving and reasoning.[37] It is also significant that the questions on most tests primarily apply only to two intelligences, the linguistic and logical-mathematical, which are the predominant intelligences of only 20% of students. It comes as no surprise to hear Howard Gardner's warning: "Poor endowment or learning in one or both of these intelligences is likely to result in poor standardized test scores."[38] The spatial, musical, kinesthetic, interpersonal student learners mentioned above will not do well. In time, they will sense the unfairness, knowing that such tests have devalued their intelligences, constructive thinking, problem-solving abilities, social competency, respective gifts… and perhaps their futures.

It is not our purpose to further debate the pros and cons of high stakes standards and large scale tests. Our concern is that of other responsive educators who...

1. are committed to the full range of development in children, and

2. recognize that assessment is necessary, but that it needs to measure the incremental progress a student is achieving toward developmentally appropriate learning goals agreed upon by the school community.

We're caught in the middle— we have to do the State tests!

> *When you put in place a high stakes test that is not applicable to all students, clearly it is a discriminatory act.*[39]
>
> —LEONARD ATKINS

The purpose of standardized State tests is political... mainly to motivate schools to increase test scores in order to "achieve school reform." The purpose of authentic assessment is about children and their learning. The big decision is whether or not your middle school community wants to achieve meaningful learning and development for the diversity of kids in your school (beyond just prepping them for the State test)—and if so, how will you assess the degree that it is happening?

Assuming that responsive education is your goal, the following is a brief look at *authentic assessment*.

"TAKE CARE HOW YOU MEASURE A CHILD"

If we are genuinely interested in developing the abilities of a wider range of young adolescents, we must be able to easily diagnose the increments of their growth and learning, however small. It is what teachers of the little red schoolhouses did every day. They looked for defined indicators of student performance and learning. It wasn't difficult because their students were also involved in observing their own progress.

Authentic assessment does not rely on single tests or narrow samples of a student's learning. Teachers and students over time reflect upon and gather evidence on a definable set of academic activities, performances and processes that are considered essential to school and life success. Some examples would be: applying a mathematical theory to a complex problem, designing and conducting an experiment, reading and critically analyzing a text, writing a research paper, conducting and reporting an interview, planning a project, working productively with a team, or presenting a report to the class community.

Rather than testing for content facts and information, authentic assessment identifies what students have learned in applying academic concepts to contextual and real life situations.

Authentic assessment:

- is consistent with classroom practices and content; it asks questions about meaningful information, problems that students have solved and the process of doing so
- gathers evidence and reflects on indicators of student learning from multiple learning experiences
- promotes motivation, learning and teaching, and
- reflects local values, standards and control.

What is measured is valued and how it is assessed provides reliable indicators of student performance.[40]

The task of teachers is to make certain that assessments reflect the valued objectives of their curricula, and that they are aligned with the instructional methods being used… so that students regard the assessments as genuine and fair. To involve students in self-evaluating their own work and abilities, teachers use the following types of general classroom activities:

- portfolios
- surveys and inventories
- journals and letters
- various forms of conferences.

The dimensions of learning that the teachers of the school value are collectively identified by teachers. Students may also help to define appropriate indicators that class members will use to self-assess their own progress. Portfolios should not be collections of teacher-prepared worksheets and inventories, but collected samples of students' work and their reflections in many formats.

Countless studies verify that students are motivated, "self-regulated," to the degree that they are active participants in their own learning. When students are provided with choice, control and collaboration in their classrooms they are intrinsically motivated to learn.[41] This is one of the reasons that students need to know the objectives of the learning experience, work in cooperative groups and reflect upon the results of their learning… all of which are clear practices in Tribes TLC®.

Engaging middle level students in reflection and evaluation encourages understanding of what is expected, improves motivation, leads to pride in achievement and offers a realistic appraisal of weaknesses.[42] Self-assessment is a vital aspect of education in many countries, including England, Australia and New Zealand to name a few.

The matrix that follows compares three forms of assessment and the perceived consequences for students.[43]

The matrix can be used to help a faculty reflect on the big difference that happens for middle level students when a middle school uses self-assessments with students. Staff development that has high expectations, collegial support, and adequate resources to meet its goals is, for a faculty, the key to moving well into authentic assessment.[44]

FORMS OF ASSESSMENT

ISSUE	REPORT CARDS	TEST SCORES	SELF-ASSESSMENT
What are the outcomes?	Grades	Numbers	Motivation and learning
Who is being compared?	Class	Large populations	Student
Who is in control?	Teacher	Policymaker	Student
What is the student's role?	Passive	Passive	Active

Training teachers to use authentic assessment not only can balance a school's obligation to comply with standardized state testing, but significantly increases student motivation and achievement.

Authentic assessment is consistent with the philosophy of the landmark report, "Turning Points" from the Carnegie Council on Adolescent Development, the massive research studies on student-centered learning, cooperative learning, constructivism, brain compatible learning, multiple intelligences and resiliency. Moreover it supports the developmental tasks young adolescents are motivated to achieve.

It's time to decide! How should we measure these kids?

Authentically and fairly!

A PERSPECTIVE FROM ADMINISTRATORS

BY MARILYN SUMNER, ANNETTE GRIFFITH, AND LINDA REED

Marilyn Sumner, M.Ed., has been the Executive Director for Instructional Support Services for the Spring Branch Independent School District in Houston, Texas. Now retired, she is a private consultant.

Annette Griffith, M.A., is the busy Director of Guidance and Health Services, and the coordinator for Tribes in Spring Branch ISD.

Linda Reed, M.A., is the Area Superintendent for ten Spring Branch Schools: elementary, middle and high school.

All three are highly skilled administrators, Certified Tribes TLC® Trainers, and professional leaders not only in their own communities but nationwide.

A DISTRICT STORY— CREATING A CARING COMMUNITY

We often hear the question: "Why have schools of your district chosen to use Tribes?" Our response is very clear. First, we wanted to transform classrooms into interdependent learning environments that would increase the success for all students. Secondly, we recognized that the Tribes process provides a framework to actively link other instructional initiatives and align them through strategies and a common language across grade levels and subjects.

In less than two years from the first Tribes 24-hour training classes, we realized that the impact of Tribes would be bigger, more systematic and more powerful than we predicted. As teachers and other staff began to use the strategies and process, vivid success stories literally telegraphed from teacher to teacher and school to school. Without a district mandate and with limited district funding, Tribes grew from two schools investigating the process to implementation in all twenty-six elementary schools and a quarter of the middle schools.

Campus commitment was critical to the implementation at each school. Administrators, teaching staff and the Campus Advisory Team showed commitment through training activities, resources and follow-up support being written into their campus plans. Initial training was offered first to educators and schools who were ready to use Tribes. The district allocated resources for training and materials including CenterSource Systems training for a cadre of 44 Tribes district facilitators with the goal of having two per campus. A collaborative district network supports and sustains implementation. This collaborative structure addresses the needs of the trainers, including everything from training materials to study group meetings to the discussion of the progress of campus implementation and future needs.

Campus and district administrators were offered courses and urged to involve the entire community of students, parents, and staff in learning and using the process. Principal commitment was a key component to the implementation process. Principals and campus facilitators modeled the use of Tribes in faculty meetings, served as trainers and supported the development of trainers for their campus. Opportunities were created for staff to share successes, ask hard questions and reflect on their learning. Throughout the district, various departments began to voluntarily identify ways that Tribes related to their work. Assessments, formal and informal, have helped each campus and the district to improve its support of Tribes implementation each year. As a result, demand for Tribes classes is still greater than the number of classes that can be provided.

As greater proportions of the staff are trained, there is more and more observable evidence that behaviors and attitudes are changing among staff, students and parents. For example, we realized that many classroom discipline approaches adopted in the past endeavored to teach students responsibility, but did not transfer responsibility nor the monitoring and modeling of responsibility to students themselves. In district evaluation, teachers who have implemented Tribes indicated that they spent less time managing student behavior. Students in those classes reported that they got along better with others. By far the most exciting stories profile youngsters who have changed from "dropped out but present" in class to fully participating. Group behaviors have changed even at bus stops because students are accepting more responsibility for their behavior.

Our schools face daunting challenges that require new solutions, new ways to reach and teach all students and changes in behaviors for all stakeholders. Evaluations of these initiatives are critical to maintain community and administrative support. In the spring of 1999, 55 classroom teachers and their students, grades three through five, responded to an evaluation survey. The conclusion was that classrooms with Tribes trained teachers were different from the regular classroom where this process was not used. In Tribes classrooms mutual respect was consistently evidenced through behaviors. Students and teachers consciously were not a part of rumors or gossip. New people and visitors felt welcomed. Teachers indicated that they had more time for creative teaching, and students saw new learning as "fun." This Tribes evaluation process substantiated the many stories about teaching being more fun, students more focused.

Our most effective meetings look similar to the Tribes TLC® lesson components. Meeting plans incorporate time for inclusion, clear statements of purpose and objectives, strategies to accomplish tasks, reflection and appreciation. And yes, as educators we do need to refine our collaborative skills in order to work well together in different contexts. Even the routine of brief energizers enables adults to maintain focus longer. Work teams often comment on the emerging sense of community and positive energy as they produce results! As cross-functional teams of employees from diverse job roles work together, their inclusion and synergy develops common commitment to improve the work we do. It is no coincidence that the business world is engaged in a similar journey of organizational learning to meet the myriad of external forces of change.[45] A critical capacity building tool that we share is the power and productivity that can happen when the organizational culture is a caring community. Of course, we are deliberately building that culture through the process of Tribes.

Our schools' journey with Tribes is indeed weaving an amazing, stronger human fiber to improve the way we "do school." Talk about Tribes permeates through and around the system. The process not only develops a caring community but supports and aligns our work with powerful tools and a common language. Tribes has become the foundational framework for the selection, evaluation and meaningful connection to other initiatives critical to student success. Of course, Spring Branch schools are still in the midst of their Tribes journey heralded by celebrations all along the way. Wouldn't you also celebrate the day when the middle school teachers started asking each other why their sixth graders were acting kinder and more cooperatively? No need to answer! Just accept our invitation to join us in this journey that truly brings joy to learning and relationships.

BRINGING IT ALL TOGETHER

Reaching millions of young adolescents at the most crucial years of their development needs no longer to be a mystery. Innumerable schools have begun to do so… by synthesizing all that is already known about human development and learning. Discovering gifts in middle school is happening every day…

Wherever….

- The human development of young adolescents is the primary focus of a middle level school
- A caring culture of inclusion, respect, equity and fairness is created
- Students are engaged in and enjoying active meaningful learning
- Well-trained responsive teachers are using active group learning and are reaching the school's diversity of students
- Teachers, administrators and parents, committed to their own growth and development, learn together
- Reflective practice is used throughout the whole school community
- Leadership and planning is distributed to collegial teams
- Authentic assessment is valued and practiced, and
- Every student enjoys the support of one or more close caring adults.

And that, my friends, is a Tribes Learning Community!

Learning Strategies

Learning Strategies

OVERVIEW

BY CAROL RANKIN

*Carol Rankin, M.Ed.,
MFCC, oversees program
development for Center-
Source Systems. As a former
school counselor and mar-
riage, family and child counselor, Carol has worked with
families and children of all
ages. Her strong commitment
to quality education stems
from years of involvement in
her own children's schools.
She is appreciative of the
skills, expertise and dedication of exceptional teachers
and administrators who
enrich children's lives
everyday.*

Many learning strategies in this section have been adapted from other sources, some familiar to you. We are indebted to innumerable creative teachers who have contributed learning strategies over the years, and we invite contributions of your favorite strategies and energizers for future printings of this book.

Strategies are ways to achieve learning objectives, whereas "activities" too often are considered time-fillers. The majority of Tribes strategies provide formats to incorporate academic subject content. See Chapter 10—Creating Cooperative Learning Experiences—for discussion of designing learning experiences through Tribes. Strategies can be used again and again, and in combination with many other cooperative learning structures from other sources.

The Learning Strategy Matrix that follows these introductory pages is alphabetized and coded so that you can select appropriate strategies and energizers. Each strategy contains the following notations:
- Approximate time required
- Grouping: community circle, tribes, sub groups
- Materials needed
- Relevant developmental tasks of early adolescence
- Objectives
- Instructions
- Suggested reflection questions
- Appreciation

Each learning strategy contains a notation of the developmental task it will support. The selected strategies assist students in the development of the four competencies that 10–15 year olds are so determined to accomplish! See Chapter 3—Meeting Them Where They Are—for a full discussion of the tasks of early adolescence.

Following the objectives and instructions are three kinds of suggested reflection questions:
- content (cognitive learning),
- collaborative (social learning), and
- discovering gifts (personal learning).

You do not need to ask all three types of reflection questions after a learning experience, but do use at least two of the different types. Base your choice on what you believe will make the content meaningful and the social or personal learning significant for the majority of students in your class.

Many of the collaborative reflection questions are based on the concept of "appreciative inquiry," a process that elicits reflection on what the group did well together to make their learning successful. The personal reflection questions are designed to help students discover their strengths, skills, gifts, and preferred ways of learning and knowing (including multiple intelligences)—all so crucial for achieving the developmental competencies to assure futures of promise. Last, but every bit as important, are invitations for appreciation and recognition of skills and gifts in others. For a full discussion of reflection, appreciative inquiry, and appreciation, see Chapter 10—Creating Cooperative Learning Experiences.

The follow-up reflection questions and statements of appreciation serve several important purposes. They…

- enhance learning and the retention of concepts for academic achievement,
- encourage the community to reflect upon and develop collaborative skills,
- allow students the opportunity to discover personal strengths and gifts, and
- help sustain the positive learning environment.

Strategies need to be selected carefully and intentionally to follow the stages of group development. As outlined in Chapter 8—Initiating Responsive Education—inclusion activities should be used initially to create the caring learning environment. Later, the Tribes will indicate when they are ready to move into the influence stage and, finally, they will be ready to undertake more complex projects during the stage of community. The Learning Strategy Matrix that follows will help you to select strategies that are appropriate to the stage that your classroom is experiencing.

Strategies also need to be carefully tailored to fit the ethnicity, culture, age level, interests, language, and socio-economic status of the students in your class. A strategy that is not sensitive to the community culture undermines the teaching process. Following are some examples of this:

- Using the names of Christian holidays but not those of other religions;
- Urging Native Americans, Latinos, and indigenous populations to make personal statements during the inclusion stage. The opportunity to share first about their culture, family, or group is traditional for them, and therefore more comfortable and inclusive;
- Ignoring the economic realities of a community (i.e., using examples of luxury items in a low-income area);
- Urging Cambodian, Thai and some of the other Asian students to demonstrate eye contact during attentive listening (when in their own culture averting one's eyes denotes respect).

It is very important to plan and implement strategies well. The following chart will give you a quick summary for implementing Tribes strategies.

SUMMARY: FACILITATING TRIBES STRATEGIES

Remind students about the Tribes agreements:
- Whenever appropriate, ask the class or tribe to review the agreements.
- Have the agreements posted at all times.
- Respect and model the agreements congruently yourself.

Give the instructions:
- Select and tailor an appropriate strategy or series of them to achieve your learning objectives.
- Tell your students what the objectives are (what they will learn).
- Give instructions simply and concisely; do not get off the track or use too many words.
- Tell students how much time they will have to complete the task.

If students are in a community circle:
- Initiate the sharing yourself.
- Let the students know who will be next—which way you'll go around the circle.
- Ask people to speak directly to one another.
- Withhold your own comments on what students share.
- Encourage people to use first names.
- Make it okay to pass.
- Deal with put-downs or a lack of attentive listening.
- Give people a second opportunity to share if they pass the first time.
- Ask appropriate cognitive, collaborative, and/or personal reflection questions.
- Wind things up when people feel bored or restless.

If students are working in tribes or small groups:
- Follow suggestions noted above.
- If using roles, discuss them, assign them, or have students choose them.
- Describe the task to be accomplished (materials, resources, and time for completion).
- Ask students to clarify the task to you or each other.
- Observe their interaction and assist only as needed.
- Ask reflection questions.
- Assess (or have students assess) and evaluate outcomes.

Invite statements of appreciation and recognition of gifts:
- Suggest sentence starters.
- Be a good role model.

Celebrate class, tribe, or individual contributions and achievements!

ENERGIZERS

In the midst of any time together groups of people periodically will experience lower energy within an environment. Concentration becomes more difficult; boredom and sleepiness can set in and will be counterproductive to accomplishing the task at hand.

Adolescent students, especially, become restless. They are likely to withdraw or even create a disturbance. The remedy? A quick five-minute physical activity to revitalize the group with an "energizer."

Energizers are satisfying because they engage many of the multiple intelligences, primarily: body/kinesthetic, musical/rhythmic, interpersonal and visual/spatial.

Six outcomes can be achieved through the use of energizers:

- The energy of the classroom or group is revitalized.
- People's attention can be drawn back to the classroom after a time away (recess, lunch break, or some other interruption).
- Different types of academic learning activities can be bridged, renewing energy and concentration.
- People can feel connected again with one another and the whole community.
- Multiple intelligences can be reached and are engaged.
- They add to the fun of learning and being together!

At the end of the Learning Strategy section you will find a sampling of some favorite Tribes energizers. Some are more physical than others and, as with other activities in this book, it is up to you to select the most appropriate ones for your students. Much depends upon the level of trust within the class at any one time. A larger collection of 101 tried and true energizers contained in a desktop card file or "Energizer Box" is also available from CenterSource Systems.

LEARNING STRATEGIES MATRIX

STRATEGY TITLE	Page	INCLUSION	Presenting Self	Social Skills	Agreements	INFLUENCE	Decisions/Problem Solving	Resolving Conflict	Goal Setting	COMMUNITY	Energizer	Celebration	ACADEMICS
Active Ignoring	236	●		●		●		●					
A Funeral for Put-Downs	237		●			●	●	●					
All In the Family	238	●	●	●									
"Am I Napoleon?"	239	●	●			●				●			●
A Poem by Our Tribe	240	●	●			●	●			●		●	●
Appreciating Others	242	●		●						●		●	
Architects and Builders	244	●				●	●						●
A Special Friend I Know	245	●	●	●									
Boasters	246	●	●	●	●								
Brainstorming	248	●	●			●	●	●		●		●	●
Bubble Gum	384									●	●		
Building a Time Machine	249	●		●		●	●	●					
Bumper Sticker	250	●	●	●						●		●	
Bumpety-Bump-Bump	384									●	●		
Campaign Manager	251	●	●							●		●	●
Career Choices	252	●	●			●	●						●
Cares—Concerns—Compliments	253	●	●	●		●				●			
Celebrity Sign-In	254		●			●	●						●
Chain Reaction	255	●	●	●						●		●	●
Changes	384									●	●		
Clap-Slap	384									●	●		
Client-Consultants	256	●		●		●	●						●
Community Circle	257	●	●	●	●					●		●	●

Format:

Inclusion

clear statements of purpose and objectives
strategies to accomplish tasks
reflection + appreciation
- content (cognitive) learning
- collaborative (social) "   - what did the group do? well together
· discovering gifts (personal) "

use 2
at a time

STRATEGY TITLE	Page	INCLUSION	Presenting Self	Social Skills	Agreements	INFLUENCE	Decisions/Problem Solving	Resolving Conflict	Goal Setting	COMMUNITY	Energizer	Celebration	ACADEMICS
Community Circle Metaphor	259	●	●	●						●		●	
Confrontation	260	●		●		●		●	●				
Consensus-Building	261	●		●		●	●	●	●				
Cooperation Squares	262	●		●		●	●	●					
Cruising Careers	264	●								●			●
Current Events Debate Circle	265	●			●	●	●						●
Dear Abby	266	●	●			●	●						
Do After Me	385									●	●		
Dream Quilt	267	●	●	●		●			●	●			●
Electricity	385									●	●		
Extended Nametags	268	●	●	●									
Family Changes—Comparing/Contrasting	269	●	●	●									●
Final Countdown	270									●		●	
Find the Word	271	●		●		●							●
Finding All We Have In Common	272	●	●	●									
Flies On the Ceiling	273	●		●		●		●	●	●			
Fold the Line Reading	274	●		●		●		●					●
Fork and Spoon	385									●	●		
Gallery Walks	275	●	●	●		●				●		●	●
Give Me a Clue	276	●		●		●	●						●
Goal-Storming	278	●		●		●	●						●
Graphing Who We Are	279	●		●		●	●						●
Group Inquiry	280	●		●		●	●	●		●			●

LEARNING STRATEGIES MATRIX

STRATEGY TITLE	Page	INCLUSION	Presenting Self	Social Skills	Agreements	INFLUENCE	Decisions/Problem Solving	Resolving Conflict	Goal Setting	COMMUNITY	Energizer	Celebration	ACADEMICS
Group Problem-Solving	283	●		●		●	●						●
Hagoo	386									●	●		
I Like My Neighbors	386									●	●		
"I'm Proud" Appreciation Circle	284	●	●	●									
Interview Circle	285	●	●	●		●	●						
I Used to Be; We Used to Be	286	●	●	●	●	●							
Jigsaw	287	●		●		●	●						●
Joy	288	●	●	●									
Kitchen Kapers	289	●	●			●	●	●					
Life Map	290	●	●	●									
Lineup	386									●	●		
Live Wire	291	●	●	●									
Making a Choice	292			●		●	●						●
Meet Someone Special	294	●	●	●									
Milling to Music	295	●	●	●									●
Multiple Intelligence Exploration	296	●	●						●				
Name Wave	386									●	●		
Newspaper Scavenger Hunt	303	●		●		●	●						●
Now I Am	305	●		●									
Observe the Put-Downs	306				●	●			●				
On My Back	307	●	●										●
One-Minute History	308	●	●	●									
One Special Thing About Me	309	●	●	●									●

STRATEGY TITLE	Page	INCLUSION	Presenting Self	Social Skills	Agreements	INFLUENCE	Decisions/Problem Solving	Resolving Conflict	Goal Setting	COMMUNITY	Energizer	Celebration	ACADEMICS
One, Two, Three	310	●		●		●	●						
Open Forum	311	●	●	●		●	●						
Our Treasury	312	●		●		●	●						
Our World Is Changing	313	●		●		●			●				
Outlines	314	●	●	●									●
Pantomime	316	●	●										
Paraphrase Passport	317	●		●	●								●
Paraphrasing	318	●		●	●								●
Partner Introduction	319	●	●	●									
Path-Maze	320					●	●			●			●
Peer-Response Huddle	322	●		●		●	●						●
Peer-Response Tic-Tac-Toe	323			●		●	●						●
Pen Pals	387									●	●		
People Hunt	324	●	●	●									
People Patterns	387									●	●		
People Puzzles	328	●		●									●
Perception and Transmission...Information	329	●		●		●		●					
Personal Contract	331	●		●		●	●	●	●				●
Personal Journal	332	●	●										●
Problem Solving...Appreciative Inquiry	333					●	●						●
Put Down the Put-Downs	335	●	●		●	●		●					
Put Yourself on the Line	336	●		●		●	●						
Rain	387									●	●		

LEARNING STRATEGIES MATRIX

STRATEGY TITLE	Page	INCLUSION	Presenting Self	Social Skills	Agreements	INFLUENCE	Decisions/Problem Solving	Resolving Conflict	Goal Setting	COMMUNITY	Energizer	Celebration	ACADEMICS
Reasons and Alternatives	337	●		●									
Reflecting Feelings	338	●		●		●		●					
Reporting Information...Intelligences	340					●	●		●				●
Roles People Play	341	●		●		●		●					
Self-Esteem Cards	344	●	●	●									
Shoe 'n Tell	345	●	●	●									
Shuffle Your Buns	388									●	●		
Singing the Blues	346	●	●	●									
Slip Game	347	●	●	●									
Snowball	388									●	●		
Snowball I-Messages	349	●		●									●
Something Good	350	●	●	●									
Something I Cherish	351	●	●	●									
Space Pioneers	352	●		●		●	●						
Spider Web	354	●	●	●						●		●	●
Student-Developed Lesson Plans	355	●		●		●	●						●
Study Buddies	356					●	●						●
Suggestion Circle	357	●		●		●	●	●					
Taking a Closer Look	358	●		●		●							
Teaching Agreements	360	●		●	●	●	●						
Teaching I-Messages	361	●		●		●		●					
Teaching Listening	362	●		●									
Teaching Paraphras'g/Reflect'g Feelings	363	●		●									●

LEARNING STRATEGIES MATRIX

STRATEGY TITLE	Page	INCLUSION	Presenting Self	Social Skills	Agreements	INFLUENCE	Decisions/Problem Solving	Resolving Conflict	Goal Setting	COMMUNITY	Energizer	Celebration	ACADEMICS
That's Me—That's Us!	364	●	●							●		●	
The Ideal Classroom	365	●	●	●		●	●	●	●				
The Week in Perspective	366	●	●	●									
Third-Party Mediation	367	●		●		●	●	●					
Three Ball Pass	388									●	●		
Thumbs Up, Thumbs Down	368					●	●						
Tower Building	369	●		●		●	●						
Tribal Peer Coaching	370	●		●		●	●						●
Tribe Graffiti	371	●		●									
Tribe Mimes/Role-Play	372	●	●			●		●					●
Tribe Portrait	373	●	●	●									
Tribes Team Together	374	●	●	●						●			●
Two For Tuesday	375	●	●	●	●					●		●	
Two Truths and a Lie	389									●	●		
Urgent!	376	●		●		●	●						
What We Need from Each Other	377	●			●	●			●	●			
What's In Your Wallet?	378	●	●	●									
What's On Your Mind?	379	●	●	●		●	●	●		●			
What's the Tint of Your Glasses?	380	●		●		●		●					
Where Do I Stand?	381	●	●	●		●	●						
Wishful Thinking	382	●	●	●									
Zap	389									●	●		
Zoom, Zoom, Brake!	389									●	●		

Learning Strategies

Active Ignoring

TIME: 30 minutes

GROUPING: tribes

MATERIALS: none

DEVELOPMENTAL TASKS:
Independence/Autonomy
Social Competency
Sense of Purpose
Problem Solving

OBJECTIVES

1. To realize the importance of attentive listening in relationships
2. To be aware of nonverbal behavior as part of communication
3. To promote awareness of the pain experienced by one who is excluded from a group
4. To experience influence

INSTRUCTIONS

1. Have the community sit in tribes.
2. Discuss the importance of inclusion within groups, families, communities, and the class. Tell the students they will conduct a little experiment to learn how people feel when they are excluded.
3. Ask for one volunteer from each tribe. Have the volunteers step out of the room, and wait to be asked to return.
4. Tell the remaining students that they are to talk among themselves in their tribes, and when the volunteers return, to go on talking but to ignore, turn their positions away from, and not listen to the volunteers.
5. While the tribes are choosing what to talk about, tell the volunteers that they are to go back to their tribes and attempt to tell their tribes something special.
6. Allow one minute only for the "ignoring" experience, then stop the activity, and begin with personal reflection questions.
7. If other tribe members want to volunteer, repeat the activity.

SUGGESTED REFLECTION QUESTIONS

PERSONAL REFLECTION

- How did you feel when everyone ignored you and went on talking?
- How did your feelings change by the end of the minute?

CONTENT (COGNITIVE LEARNING)

- How were the other students sitting as they ignored you?
- What kinds of gestures did they use while they were talking?
- Why is it important to learn what it feels like to be ignored?
- What do you think happens to people who are ignored all the time?

COLLABORATIVE (SOCIAL LEARNING)

- What social skills were you not using when you were ignoring?
- How did you feel ignoring another member?
- What can your tribe do to make sure that everyone feels included?

DISCOVERING GIFTS (PERSONAL LEARNING)

- How did you help your group during this activity?
- What special strengths did you discover about yourself?

APPRECIATION

Invite statements of appreciation (and recognition of gifts):

- "I appreciated…"
- "I liked it when…"

A Funeral For Put-Downs

OBJECTIVES

1. To promote awareness and sensitize the students to the hurt of put-downs
2. To involve the students in eliminating put-downs
3. To create a positive community climate and inclusion

INSTRUCTIONS

1. Give each student a slip of paper.
2. Have each student write a hurtful put-down remark or behavior he or she never wants to hear or see again.
3. Have each tribe put their slips in a community box and ask three to four students to take turns reading the slips to the class.
4. Invite several students to share how they felt when put down by another person in the school.
5. Take the class outside and light a fire within a metal wastebasket or trashcan. Throw the box of slips into the fire. (Other options are to bury the slips or put them into a dumpster.)
6. Invite statements of good-bye to the put-downs.
7. Ask the students what they could do to help each other keep the painful statements dead.

TIME:	35 minutes
GROUPING:	community, tribes
MATERIALS:	2-inch paper slips, pencils

DEVELOPMENTAL TASKS:
Independence/Autonomy
Sense of Purpose

SUGGESTED REFLECTION QUESTIONS

CONTENT (COGNITIVE LEARNING)

- What did you do?
- Why is it important to "burn, bury, or trash" the put-downs?
- What can the community do to keep the put-downs buried?

COLLABORATIVE (SOCIAL LEARNING)

- What can your tribe do to keep those put-downs buried?
- What did the community or your tribe do to make this activity successful?

DISCOVERING GIFTS (PERSONAL LEARNING)

- How did it feel to burn or bury the put-downs?
- What personal strengths will help you to keep those put-downs buried? What can you do?

APPRECIATION

Invite statements of appreciation (and recognition of gifts):

- "I appreciated…"
- "It was great when…"

All In The Family

TIME: 20 minutes

GROUPING: subgroups

MATERIALS: none

DEVELOPMENTAL TASKS:
Independence/Autonomy
Social Competency
Sense of Purpose

OBJECTIVES

1. To build inclusion
2. To promote awareness of how other family members feel

INSTRUCTIONS

1. Ask the students to form groups in different parts of the room according to their birth positions in their families (eldest, youngest, in-betweens, only child).
2. Have each student share with the other members of his or her group:
   - How does it feel to be (firstborn, etc.)?
   - What are the responsibilities he or she has?
   - What are the advantages he or she has?
3. Merge the groups so that the eldest are with the in-betweens, and the only children are with youngest (or mix the groups together whichever way you want).
4. Now ask these groups to share:
   - Who do you think has the most power in your family?
   - How do you feel toward other siblings?
5. Who gets attention in your family and how do they get it?

SUGGESTED REFLECTION QUESTIONS

CONTENT (COGNITIVE LEARNING)

- What did you learn about birth order and power in a family?
- What generalizations can you make about birth order?

COLLABORATIVE (SOCIAL LEARNING)

- What skills did your group use to make this activity successful?
- How did your group make sure that everyone had a chance to participate fully?

DISCOVERING GIFTS (PERSONAL LEARNING)

- How did you feel when you were with others in the same birth position as you?
- What did you feel about others in the same birth position/different birth position?
- What did you learn about yourself?
- How do you contribute to your family in a special way?
- How can knowing this help you to get along with your sisters and brothers?

APPRECIATION

Invite statements of appreciation (and recognition of gifts):
- "I'm a lot like you when…"
- "I felt good when…"

"Am I Napoleon?"

OBJECTIVES

1. To build inclusion
2. To identify and learn about famous people in history, politics, science, or some other academic content

INSTRUCTIONS

1. Give each person a 3 x 5-inch index card, a pin, and a pencil.
2. Ask each student to print on the card in large block letters the name of some famous person, living or dead.
3. Ask each student to pin his or her "famous person" card onto the back of another student, without letting that student know the name on the card.
4. Tell the students to find out who they are by milling around and asking other students questions that can be answered "yes" or "no." Students may ask only one question each time they talk to another student. Continue the process until everyone has identified his or her famous name. Simple hints from other students or the teacher may be given to help those having a difficult time.

SUGGESTED REFLECTION QUESTIONS

CONTENT (COGNITIVE LEARNING)

- Who were some of the famous people?
- What kinds of questions did you ask?
- What do you know about the person whose name was pinned onto your back?

COLLABORATIVE (SOCIAL LEARNING)

- How did you help each other successfully identify your famous people?
- What effect did this activity have on the community?

DISCOVERING GIFTS (PERSONAL LEARNING)

- In what ways do you identity with your famous person?
- What special qualities do you have in common with any of the famous people?
- What skills did you use to discover who your famous person was?

APPRECIATION

Invite statements of appreciation (and recognition of gifts):

- "I liked it when…"
- "I'm a lot like you when…"

TIME:	20 minutes
GROUPING:	community
MATERIALS:	3 x 5-inch cards, pins, colored pencils or felt pens

DEVELOPMENTAL TASKS:
Social Competency
Problem Solving

A Poem By Our Tribe

TIME: 50 minutes

GROUPING: tribes

MATERIALS: scratch paper, 3 x 5-inch cards, felt pens

DEVELOPMENTAL TASKS:
Independence/Autonomy
Sense of Purpose

OBJECTIVES

1. To write a tribe poem using individual member contributions
2. To demonstrate synergism and inclusion within the tribe
3. To develop an appreciation of individual contributions to a tribe effort and to experience influence

INSTRUCTIONS

1. Have the community meet in tribes. Tell the students they will be writing a tribe poem.
2. Assign roles for each tribe member:
   • Taskmaster: gets materials and monitors the time
   • Recorder: makes a final copy of the poem
   • Facilitator: ensures that each tribe member's ideas are heard and respected
   • Reader: reads the final version of the poem to the community
3. Have the taskmasters obtain three cards for each tribe member and a different colored felt pen for each.
4. Write on the chalkboard the following sentence starters for use in the tribal poem:
   • I wish...I dreamed...
   • I used to be...but now I am...
   • I seem to be...but really I am...
5. Tell your students: "Here are a number of ways to start a tribe poem. Put your heads together in your tribes. Choose the sentence starter you like best or make up your own."
6. Ask each tribe member to take a piece of scratch paper and write as many versions of the completed sentence as possible during the time available (five to ten minutes).
7. Ask each tribe member to choose his or her two best lines and write one line on each of two cards.
8. Explain that each tribe will put together its poem as follows (steps may be written on the chalkboard):
   • each tribe member reads his or her two cards to the tribe
   • the tribe gives positive feedback (feelings, words, etc. that they liked) after each tribe member shares
   When all the tribe members have shared, the tribe cooperates to:
   • pick at least one card from each tribe member
   • decide in what order the lines should go in the tribe poem (the tribe may decide to modify lines only with the consent of the author)
   • decide on a one- or two-word title
9. When the tribe members have agreed on the order of the lines and the title, have the Recorder make a final copy and have all the tribe members sign the poem.
10. Ask the tribes to post their poems, and have each tribe's Reader take turns reading their poem to the class.

SUGGESTED REFLECTION QUESTIONS

CONTENT (COGNITIVE LEARNING)

- What did you learn about writing poetry?
- Why would you like to express your feelings using poetry?

COLLABORATIVE (SOCIAL LEARNING)

- How were your ideas encouraged and honored by your tribe?
- Which agreement is the most important for your tribe to honor in a strategy like this?

DISCOVERING GIFTS (PERSONAL LEARNING)

- How did you help your tribe? What special strengths or talents did you use?
- How did you encourage other tribe members to contribute?

APPRECIATION

Invite statements of appreciation (and recognition of gifts):

- "Thank you, (name), for…"
- "It was great when…"

Adapted from "Writing a Group Poem," by Nan & Ted Graves, Cooperative Learning, Vol. 11, No. 4, July, 1991

Appreciating Others

TIME: 45 minutes

GROUPING: community, tribes

MATERIALS: "Appreciating Others" worksheets, pencils, large paper, felt pens

DEVELOPMENTAL TASKS:

Independence/Autonomy
Social Competency

OBJECTIVES

1. To increase awareness of the importance of stating appreciation
2. To practice the Tribes agreements
3. To provide for initial inclusion
4. To discover personal gifts

INSTRUCTIONS

1. Pass out the "Appreciating Others" worksheet to all class members.
2. In the front of the room post a large visual of the worksheet from which you can use as a model.
3. Ask each student to fill in the boxes with positive statements—one to self, best friend, Mom and/or Dad, and a classmate.
4. Ask the students to meet in tribes to share their positive statements.
5. Have one member of each tribe record all the core ideas that are included on the tribe members' worksheets.
6. Ask the recorder from each tribe to report the summaries to the community.
7. Suggest that students tell one of their statements to the person to whom it was written.

SUGGESTED REFLECTION QUESTIONS

CONTENT (COGNITIVE LEARNING)

- Why did you learn to give statements of appreciation?
- What were three statements shared by your tribe members?

COLLABORATIVE (SOCIAL LEARNING)

- How can making statements of appreciation help a tribe work together better?
- Why is it important to make statements of appreciation to friends, family, and to others?
- What do you appreciate about the community or your tribe?

DISCOVERING GIFTS (PERSONAL LEARNING)

- How do you feel when you receive a statement of appreciation from someone else?
- What special qualities do you appreciate about yourself?
- What did you learn about yourself from this activity?

APPRECIATION

Invite statements of appreciation (and recognition of gifts):
- "I liked it when…"
- "Thank you for…"

OPTION

Ask how many students would commit to using at least one appreciation statement every day. Have tribes write contracts to do so. Post the contracts and review them regularly.

APPRECIATING OTHERS

SELF	BEST FRIEND
MOM/DAD	CLASSMATE

Suggested positive statement forms:

_____, I liked it when you…

_____, I appreciate it when…

_____, I'm glad you…

_____, thanks for…

This page may be duplicated for classroom use.

Architects and Builders

TIME: 40 minutes

GROUPING: tribes

MATERIALS: pre-cut shapes, scissors, glue, colored paper

DEVELOPMENTAL TASKS:
Independence/Autonomy
Social Competency
Problem Solving

OBJECTIVES

1. To promote inclusion and influence
2. To work cooperatively on tasks
3. To practice subject-related vocabulary

INSTRUCTIONS

1. Prepare a drawing, picture or collage of items that are familiar to the students. (*Note:* You may include subject-related material in the collage such as geometric shapes, representations of concepts, vocabulary, geographical locations, etc.)
2. Have the tribes designate one person from each tribe to be the "architect." All others are "builders." (*Note:* The method for choosing the "architect" can be a strategy all by itself.)
3. Have the architects leave the room or move to a separate area of the room to study the "plans" (collage).
4. Ask the architects to return to their tribes. Architects must direct the builders to construct a duplicate of the prepared collage using verbal directions *only*. Architects may study the plans as often as they wish during the building process. (*Note:* It is helpful to have architects clasp hands behind their backs to avoid gestures while giving instructions. No pointing allowed!)
5. Allow 15–20 minutes for construction.
6. Call time, and allow 5 minutes for the community to circulate and admire each tribe's creation. If you chose, have an impartial judge choose the most accurate/most creative/most unusual replica.

SUGGESTED REFLECTION QUESTIONS

CONTENT (COGNITIVE LEARNING)

- What did you discover about a community member during this activity?
- What do you think about the roles and rules in this activity?
- What improvements could you make for future "architects and builders?"

COLLABORATIVE (SOCIAL LEARNING)

- What was easy/difficult for your tribe about this task?
- How were the agreements honored and practiced by your tribe?

DISCOVERING GIFTS (PERSONAL LEARNING)

- How much did you participate?
- What strengths or skills did you contribute?
- What did you enjoy most about this activity?
- Would you rather be an "architect" or a "builder?" Why?

APPRECIATION

Invite statements of appreciation (and recognition of gifts):

- "I appreciated it when…"
- "(Name), you were really helpful when…"
- "(Name), thank you for…"

A Special Friend I Know

OBJECTIVES

1. To build community inclusion
2. To share feelings about an aspect of school
3. To experience the "Think—Pair—Share" structure★
4. To discover gifts

INSTRUCTIONS

1. Have the community meet in tribes. Ask the students to think silently for a moment about the following questions:
   - When were you a special friend to someone?
   - What made you a special friend?
   - What did you do or say?
2. Invite each student to turn to a tribe member and share his or her special qualities by speaking in the present tense. Example:
   - "Marie, I would like you as my special friend because (two or three of her special qualities)."

SUGGESTED REFLECTION QUESTIONS

CONTENT (COGNITIVE LEARNING)

- What qualities did you share that were similar?
- Why is friendship important?

COLLABORATIVE (SOCIAL LEARNING)

- Why is being a good listener important in being a good friend?
- How did this strategy help you as a tribe/community?
- How did the community or your tribe make this activity successful?

DISCOVERING GIFTS (PERSONAL LEARNING)

- How did you help your tribe during this strategy?
- What special qualities do you have that make you a good friend to others?
- What qualities would you like to develop more of?

APPRECIATION

Invite statements of appreciation (and recognition of gifts):
- "I liked it when…"
- "It helped me when…"
- "I admired you when…"

★ *This is a structure from* Cooperative Learning Resources, *by Spencer Kagan.*

TIME: 30 minutes

GROUPING: community, tribes

MATERIALS: none

DEVELOPMENTAL TASKS:
Independence/Autonomy
Sense of Purpose

Boasters

TIME: 30–45 minutes

GROUPING: tribes, subgroups

MATERIALS: 12-inch-high cutouts of student profiles

DEVELOPMENTAL TASKS:
Independence/Autonomy
Social Competency
Sense of Purpose

OBJECTIVES

1. To make statements of appreciation to self and others
2. To build self-esteem
3. To build inclusion
4. To discover gifts

INSTRUCTIONS

1. Prepare posterboard or construction paper cutouts similar to the one on the next page for each student, or have each student prepare one for him or herself.
2. Ask the community to meet in tribes.
3. Have each student write his or her name in large, colorful letters on the head area of his or her cutout.
4. Instruct the tribe members to pass the cutouts around the tribe so that each tribe member can write a positive statement on each other tribe member's cutout.
5. Have a discussion about complimenting yourself and how it is different than bragging. Then ask each student to write a positive statement about him or herself on his or her own card.

SUGGESTED REFLECTION QUESTIONS

CONTENT (COGNITIVE LEARNING)

- Why is it important to be able to make positive statements about others?
- What are two positive statements that you made to others/they made to you?

COLLABORATIVE (SOCIAL LEARNING)

- How can making positive statements to each other help us work together better?
- What did you appreciate about your group or tribe during this activity?

DISCOVERING GIFTS (PERSONAL LEARNING)

- How did you feel when you knew someone else was writing on your card?
- How did you feel when you read the comments on your card?
- What special gifts do you appreciate about yourself?
- Do you ever compliment yourself?
- Make a plan for complimenting yourself at least once every day.

APPRECIATION

Invite statements of appreciation (and recognition of gifts):
- "I'm glad you notice that I…"
- "I felt good when…"

BOASTERS

Brainstorming

TIME: 20 minutes

GROUPING: tribes

MATERIALS: markers, large paper

DEVELOPMENTAL TASKS:
Independence/Autonomy
Social Competency
Problem Solving

OBJECTIVES

1. To energize a tribe
2. To promote inclusion and influence
3. To experience the fun and creative power of brainstorming as a decision-making or problem-solving technique

INSTRUCTIONS

1. Ask each tribe to appoint a recorder to jot down all the ideas on paper, chalkboard, or newsprint as fast as ideas are called out.
2. Instruct the tribes on the "DOVE" rules that they need to follow in order to "brainstorm."
   - D defer judgment
   - O off beat, original
   - V vast number
   - E expand, elaborate
3. Have the community meet in tribes. Explain that each tribe will have five minutes to call out and write down as many ideas as possible on a subject. Examples:
   - "How could we design a better bathtub—one for more enjoyment, efficiency, and comfort than ordinary tubs?"
   - Other possible subjects: better bicycle, bedroom, car, school cafeteria, school
4. Stop the brainstorming after five minutes. Ask each recorder to read his or her tribe's list. Lead applause after each tribe's creative ideas.
5. If time allows, have the tribes draw their creations. Find a way to include everyone in the tribe.

SUGGESTED REFLECTION QUESTIONS

CONTENT (COGNITIVE LEARNING)

- Why is brainstorming fun?
- How do the "DOVE" rules help you to brainstorm?

COLLABORATIVE (SOCIAL LEARNING)

- What would have happened if we had judged, commented, or discussed ideas as they were offered?
- How could you tell that your tribe members were enjoying themselves?
- What did your tribe members do well as they followed the "DOVE" rules?

DISCOVERING GIFTS (PERSONAL LEARNING)

- How much did you participate?
- How did you contribute to your tribe?
- What special qualities did you bring to this activity?

APPRECIATION

Invite statements of appreciation (and recognition of gifts):
- "I liked it when you said…"
- "I felt good when…"
- "Your suggestions helped me to…"

Building A Time Machine

OBJECTIVES

1. To encourage tribe members to create something together
2. To have tribes present their creations to the community
3. To experience influence

INSTRUCTIONS

1. Ask the students if they have ever read any books or seen any movies about time machines.
2. Call on a few students to share what they know about time machines.
3. Let the students know that their tribes will have an opportunity to build a time machine.
4. Have the community meet in tribes. Give each group equal amounts of "junk" to build their time machines.
5. Give the tribes the next twenty minutes to construct their time machines.
6. Have the tribes take turns presenting their time machines to the class.
7. Have each student write a letter to someone in another time that could be delivered by his or her tribe's time machine.

SUGGESTED REFLECTION QUESTIONS

CONTENT (COGNITIVE LEARNING)

- What decisions did your tribe have to make?
- Why is it important to use your imagination?
- What did you learn by doing this strategy?

COLLABORATIVE (SOCIAL LEARNING)

- How did your tribe make its machine?
- What really helped your tribe to be creative and innovative?
- What special strengths do you want to continue to develop as a tribe?

DISCOVERING GIFTS (PERSONAL LEARNING)

- How did you help your tribe build the time machine?
- How did you feel while you were working?
- What special talents did you use/discover about yourself?

APPRECIATION

Invite statements of appreciation (and recognition of gifts):

- "(Name), you helped when…"
- "I liked it when…"

TIME:	45 minutes
GROUPING:	tribes
MATERIALS:	assorted junk

DEVELOPMENTAL TASKS:
Independence/Autonomy
Problem Solving

Bumper Sticker

TIME: 30 minutes

GROUPING: community, tribes

MATERIALS: colored paper strips, colored pencils or markers

DEVELOPMENTAL TASKS:
Independence/Autonomy
Social Competency
Sense of Purpose

OBJECTIVES

1. To present something special about oneself
2. To build inclusion
3. To encourage attentive listening

INSTRUCTIONS

1. Review agreements.
2. Give each student a long strip of paper and a marker or colored pencil with which to create a "bumper sticker" that he or she would enjoy displaying on his or her automobile bumper.
3. Have each student in turn share his or her bumper sticker with the community. Remind everyone to give his or her full attention to the speaker.
4. Tell the students they may ask questions, and express mutual feelings and concerns after everyone has shared.

SUGGESTED REFLECTION QUESTIONS

CONTENT (COGNITIVE LEARNING)

• What similar kinds of things did you put on your bumper stickers?
• What is one special thing you learned about another student?

COLLABORATIVE (SOCIAL LEARNING)

• How well did everyone listen when you shared your bumper sticker?
• What did the group do to help others feel more comfortable when they shared?

DISCOVERING GIFTS (PERSONAL LEARNING)

• How did you feel as you shared?
• How does your bumper sticker express your unique qualities as a person in this community?
• Would you want to put your bumper sticker on your car or your bicycle? Why or why not?

APPRECIATION

Invite statements of appreciation (and recognition of gifts):
• "I liked it when…"
• "I admired you for…"

Campaign Manager

OBJECTIVES

1. To build inclusion
2. To foster positive feelings in the community
3. To build self-esteem

INSTRUCTIONS

1. Have students meet in their tribes.
2. Pass out paper circles, cards, and a small bag to each tribe.
3. Instruct each tribe member to write his or her name on a slip of paper and drop it into a bag. Then have each member draw a name out of the bag (making sure he or she doesn't draw his or her own).
4. Tell the students that each is to be the "campaign manager" for the person whose name he or she drew, a person who has been nominated for "Wonderful Person of the Year."
5. Explain that each student will design a campaign button on the circle of paper, and list three good campaign statements on the card to promote his or her nominee. The campaign managers may interview their candidates if they need more information on special qualities.
6. Have the campaign managers deliver the campaign speeches (using the cards) and present their nominees with their campaign buttons. Lead applause and cheering.

SUGGESTED REFLECTION QUESTIONS

CONTENT (COGNITIVE LEARNING)

- What similarities did you notice between the campaign buttons and the presentations?
- Why is it important to make a good campaign speech?

COLLABORATIVE (SOCIAL LEARNING)

- What social skills did your tribe need to make this activity successful?
- What do you value most about being a member of your tribe?

DISCOVERING GIFTS (PERSONAL LEARNING)

- What special qualities did your campaign manager present about you? How did you feel?
- What skills did you use to present your candidate's campaign?
- What strengths would you bring to the job if you were a campaign manager?

APPRECIATION

Invite statements of appreciation (and recognition of gifts):
- "I liked it when…"
- "I felt good when…"

TIME: 60 minutes

GROUPING: tribes

MATERIALS: small circles with 6-inch diameter, 3 x 5-inch cards, pencils, small bags

DEVELOPMENTAL TASKS:
Independence/Autonomy
Social Competency
Sense of Purpose

Career Choices

TIME: 40 minutes

GROUPING: community

MATERIALS: career signs

DEVELOPMENTAL TASKS:
Independence/Autonomy
Sense of Purpose

OBJECTIVES

1. To help the students make choices and honor each other's choices
2. To give the students an opportunity to share some of their career views
3. To experience influence

INSTRUCTIONS

1. Make two signs with a career choice such as "chemist" and "marine biologist" (or use two other occupations) written on each of them and put them up on different sides of the room.
2. Tell your students that they are going to be asked to make a choice about occupations related to the field of science or health.
3. They will make their choice by moving to one side of the room or the other, to stand under the sign of the occupation of their choice. Example: Point out the sign "chemist" on one side of the room and "marine biologist" on the other side of the room.
4. Have students discuss in groups of 3 or 4 why they chose the occupation.

SUGGESTED REFLECTION QUESTIONS

CONTENT (COGNITIVE LEARNING)

- Why is it important to make choices?
- What other occupations did you consider?

COLLABORATIVE (SOCIAL LEARNING)

- In what ways did the community honor the agreements?
- Which agreement might be the most important in a strategy like this?
- What do you appreciate the most about this community?

DISCOVERING GIFTS (PERSONAL LEARNING)

- Why did you make the choice you did?
- How did you feel about making your choice public?
- How do your special talents or strengths relate to the choice you made?

APPRECIATION

Invite statements of appreciation (and recognition of gifts):

- "I appreciated it when…"
- "It was great when…"

Cares—Concerns—Compliments

OBJECTIVES

1. To build inclusion and influence
2. To gather and appreciate different points of view

INSTRUCTIONS

1. Have the students sit in a community circle, or in their tribes.
2. Review the tribes agreements.
3. Ask the students, "Before we begin our day, who has a care, concern, or compliment to share?"
4. Allow the students to share briefly one at a time with the community or in their tribes.
5. After all students who want to have shared, allow the students to open topics for extended discussion.

SUGGESTED REFLECTION QUESTIONS

CONTENT (COGNITIVE LEARNING)

- What did you find out about your community/tribe members?
- What thoughts or feelings do you share in common with others?

COLLABORATIVE (SOCIAL LEARNING)

- How were the agreements honored and practiced?
- In what way(s) did this activity help the community or your tribe?
- What makes you proud to be a member of this community/your tribe?

DISCOVERING GIFTS (PERSONAL LEARNING)

- How do you usually express your cares, concerns and compliments?
- How much did you participate?
- How did you help the community or your tribe in a special way?

APPRECIATION

Invite statements of appreciation (and recognition of gifts):
- "I appreciate…"
- "(Name), thank you for…"
- "(Name), you were really helpful when…"

TIME: 20 minutes

GROUPING: community, tribes

MATERIALS: none

DEVELOPMENTAL TASKS:
Independence/Autonomy
Social Competency
Sense of Purpose

OPTION

This activity can also be used on Monday mornings, to review the weekend, or to share "something interesting, positive, or exciting."

Celebrity Sign-In

TIME:	varies
GROUPING:	community, tribes
MATERIALS:	row of chairs in front of room
SUBJECT:	history

DEVELOPMENTAL TASKS:

Independence/Autonomy
Social Competency

OBJECTIVES

1. To structure a cooperative learning experience for a history topic
2. To enhance communication skills
3. To experience influence

INSTRUCTIONS

1. Give each tribe the name of a celebrity or historical character, and allow time for each tribe to learn as much as they can about the person.
2. Set up a row of chairs in front of the room facing the class.
3. Ask each tribe to select a tribe member to "be" their celebrity.
4. Have each celebrity sign in on the chalkboard and then take a seat in the row of chairs ("interview panel").
5. Ask each character to tell the other panel members about his or her prominence in history. After they have all done so, call time out and let tribe members huddle with their character to remind them of more data to present. After several huddles, invite the audience to ask questions of the "celebrity." Allow tribe members to help answer.
6. Lead rounds of applause after each character's performance.

SUGGESTED REFLECTION QUESTIONS

CONTENT (COGNITIVE LEARNING)

- What did you learn about the different celebrities?
- Why is this an interesting way to learn new information?
- What values were reflected by the characters?
- In what other ways can you use this activity?

COLLABORATIVE (SOCIAL LEARNING)

- What did tribe members do to support their celebrity?
- In what ways did your tribe work well together to make this activity successful?

DISCOVERING GIFTS (PERSONAL LEARNING)

- How did you feel while you were portraying your character?
- What strengths or skills did you use while you were portraying your character?
- How did you help your tribe or the community in a special way?

APPRECIATION

Invite statements of appreciation (and recognition of gifts):

- "(Name), I respect you for…"
- "(Name), I liked the way you portrayed…"

Chain Reaction

TIME: 15–30 minutes

GROUPING: community, tribes

MATERIALS: none

DEVELOPMENTAL TASKS:
Independence/Autonomy
Social Competency
Sense of Purpose

OBJECTIVES

1. To build inclusion and influence
2. To increase communication skills
3. To share personal interests, opinions and ideas
4. To ask each other questions about subject matter

INSTRUCTIONS

Note: This is a good activity for students to help each other prepare for a test.

1. Have the community meet in tribes.
2. Remind the students of their right to pass and to honor the other agreements. Remind tribe members to give full, caring attention.
3. Have one tribe member begin by asking a question of a second tribe member. Have the second tribe member answer the question and then ask another question of a third tribe member. Instruct the tribes to continue the chain until each tribe member has answered and then asked a question. In large tribes have students ask the persons directly across from them. This helps the students to speak loudly enough.
4. Explain that questions may be autobiographical or deal with curriculum or a number of issues (politics, hobbies, education, friendship, family interests).

SUGGESTED REFLECTION QUESTIONS

CONTENT (COGNITIVE LEARNING)

- What did you learn about your tribe members?
- Why is this a good way to find out information about each other?

COLLABORATIVE (SOCIAL LEARNING)

- In what ways did your tribe honor the tribal agreements?
- How do the agreements protect you?
- How well did the group give full, caring attention?
- What do you feel about your tribe members now?

DISCOVERING GIFTS (PERSONAL LEARNING)

- How did you feel when it was your turn?
- What skills did you use to help your tribe make this activity successful?
- What unique qualities did you discover about yourself?

APPRECIATION

Invite statements of appreciation (and recognition of gifts):

- "I liked it when…"
- "I admired your honesty when…"

Client-Consultants

TIME: 30 minutes

GROUPING: tribes

MATERIALS: none

DEVELOPMENTAL TASKS:
Independence/Autonomy
Social Competency
Sense of Purpose
Problem Solving

OBJECTIVES

1. To encourage active listening
2. To experience group support for a concern
3. To assist a peer, colleague, or friend to resolve a problem
4. To promote influence

INSTRUCTIONS

1. Have the class sit in their tribes.
2. Tell the students that each will have a turn expressing a concern or a problem that he or she may be experiencing at school. Each person will have a turn at being a "client" while the other tribe members are listening as "consultants." Explain that the consultants:
   • are to be non-judgmental
   • are not to tell the client what to do
   • are to offer alternative suggestions to the client for solving the problem
   • and may ask for additional information if it seems helpful or necessary.
3. Review or remind the students about their caring listening skills (especially paraphrasing).
4. Allow approximately 10 minutes for each client's turn.

SUGGESTED REFLECTION QUESTIONS

CONTENT (COGNITIVE LEARNING)

• What solutions did the consultants suggest for your problem?
• Why is having a consultant helpful to you sometimes?

COLLABORATIVE (SOCIAL LEARNING)

• What social skills did your tribe members need to be good consultants?
• How could you tell when the consultants were really listening well?
• How does this activity affect the feeling tone in your tribe?

DISCOVERING GIFTS (PERSONAL LEARNING)

• How does it feel to share your own concern with others?
• What did you learn about yourself that you can be proud of?
• How did you help others in your group during this activity?

APPRECIATION

Invite statements of appreciation (and recognition of gifts):
   • "I felt (feeling) when you…"
   • "I cared a lot when you said…"
   • "I feel I would like to help you…"
   • "I admired you for…"

Community Circle

OBJECTIVES

1. To build inclusion and community
2. To teach social skills

INSTRUCTIONS

1. Have the community sit in a large circle.
2. Review the Tribes agreements.
3. Ask a "Question-of-the-Day."
   Example: "I feel excited when…"
   (*Note:* The best questions are those most relevant to the participants' experiences, interests and cultures. See more suggested questions below.)
4. Have everyone respond in turn to the question. Allow time at the end for those who passed to respond if they desire.

TIME:	20 minutes
GROUPING:	community
MATERIALS:	none

DEVELOPMENTAL TASKS:
Social Competency
Sense of Purpose

SUGGESTED REFLECTION QUESTIONS

CONTENT (COGNITIVE LEARNING)

- What is one new thing you learned in the community?
- Why is it sometimes difficult to find something to say in a large group?

COLLABORATIVE (SOCIAL LEARNING)

- In what ways did the community listen to what you shared?
- How does sharing this way help our class or community?

DISCOVERING GIFTS (PERSONAL LEARNING)

- What new things did you notice about yourself during this activity?
- How did you contribute to the community today?

APPRECIATION

Invite statements of appreciation (and recognition of gifts):
- "I liked it when…"
- "I feel like you when…"

SUGGESTED QUESTIONS-OF-THE-DAY

1. I feel happy when…
2. I feel sad when…
3. I feel angry when…
4. I feel scared when…
5. I feel excited when…
6. I feel annoyed when…
7. I feel stressed when…
8. I feel alone when…
9. The scariest thing is…
10. My favorite hobby is…
11. My favorite pet is…
12. My favorite food/junk food is…

13. My favorite T.V. show is…
14. My favorite weekend activity is…
15. My favorite song is…
16. My favorite type of music is…
17. My favorite book is…
18. My favorite sport is…
19. My favorite color is…
20. My favorite weather is…
21. Rain makes me feel…
22. Wind makes me feel…
23. Sunshine makes me feel…
24. Snow makes me feel…
25. Fog makes me feel…
26. Today I feel…
27. When I think of blue, I think of…
28. When I think of red, I think of…
29. When I think of green, I think of…
30. When I think of yellow, I think of…
31. When I think of orange, I think of…
32. When I think of black, I think of…
33. When I think of brown, I think of…
34. If I were an animal, I would be…
35. If I were a building, I would be…
36. If I were a famous actor/actress, I would be…
37. If I were a famous athlete, I would be…
38. When I think of starting high school, I…
39. When I graduate from high school, I want to…
40. When I become an adult, I want to…
41. When I start my career, I want to…
42. When I daydream, I usually think about…
43. Someday I want to…
44. I can't wait until…
45. Friends are…
46. Families are…
47. Put downs make me feel…
48. Appreciations make me feel…
49. When I am doing math, I am most like what animal?
50. Relate to the curriculum:

        The best/worst thing about this science project is…

        The main character in the book we are reading is like/not like me when…

        These math problems make me feel…

Community Circle Metaphor

OBJECTIVES

1. To build community inclusion
2. To share feelings about an aspect of school

INSTRUCTIONS

1. Begin with everyone in a community circle. Explain that the students will be completing the following sentence:

   "When I am working on (name a subject such as math, writing, reading, art, music) I am most like a (name an animal) because I (name a behavior or quality)."

2. After brief thinking time, have the students form pairs. Ask the partners to face each other and discuss their answers to the question. Give the partners two to five minutes to share.
3. Ask several pairs to share their answers with the community.

SUGGESTED REFLECTION QUESTIONS

CONTENT (COGNITIVE LEARNING)

• What did your answers have in common?

COLLABORATIVE (SOCIAL LEARNING)

• Why is sharing with a partner easier than sharing with the community?
• What did the community do to make this activity successful?

DISCOVERING GIFTS (PERSONAL LEARNING)

• Did you share as fully as you could? Why or why not?
• How did you feel about sharing with your partner?
• How did you help your partner?

APPRECIATION

Invite statements of appreciation (and recognition of gifts):
• "It felt good when…"
• "One thing I liked about what you said was…"

TIME:	40 minutes
GROUPING:	community, pairs
MATERIALS:	sentence strips

DEVELOPMENTAL TASKS:
Independence/Autonomy
Sense of Purpose

Confrontation

TIME: 15–40 minutes

GROUPING: full group

MATERIALS: none

DEVELOPMENTAL TASKS:
Independence/Autonomy
Social Competency
Problem Solving

OBJECTIVES

1. To provide a way to work out problems
2. To enhance self-awareness
3. To teach communication skills
4. To encourage influence

INSTRUCTIONS

1. One day when a problem between two students comes to your attention, invite the community to sit in one community circle. Ask the two students for permission to share the problem with the community.
2. State the problem or have the two students involved describe it. Example:
    Tanya: "Dawn keeps moving ahead of me when we are supposed to take turns."
    Dawn: "No, I don't. Tanya is always bossing people around."
3. Review the agreements carefully, and ask everyone to listen attentively without comment.
4. Have the two students involved sit facing each other in the center of the circle.
5. Ask each to tell the other what he or she is feeling about the problem by using "I-Messages;" help them phrase the "I-Messages" if you need to.
6. Ask each to repeat exactly what the other has stated.
7. Then ask each what he or she could do to help solve the problem.
8. If they have difficulty, turn to the rest of the community for suggestions. Tell the students not to judge who is right or wrong.
9. If the discussion wanders, ask questions to redirect the students to the problem. If the problem cannot be solved, set a time to work with the pair privately.
10. When a solution is reached, have the students write a contract with each other.

SUGGESTED REFLECTION QUESTIONS

CONTENT (COGNITIVE LEARNING)

• Why is it important to tell someone that you are upset with him or her?
• What do you think will happen now?

COLLABORATIVE (SOCIAL LEARNING)

• What kind of listeners were you?
• Why is listening important when you're involved in a conflict?
• How did the community help the students work out the problem?

DISCOVERING GIFTS (PERSONAL LEARNING)

• How do you feel right now?
• What feelings did you have as the discussion was going on?
• How did you help the two students or the community in a special way?

APPRECIATION

Invite statements of appreciation (and recognition of gifts):
• "I admire you for…"
• "I learned that…"

Consensus-Building

OBJECTIVES

1. To reach a consensus or agreement on shared concerns, ideas, or priorities
2. To build tribe cohesiveness
3. To experience influence

INSTRUCTIONS

1. Have the students meet in tribes, and distribute 5 x 7-inch cards to each person.
2. Discuss the importance of groups having a way to make decisions together in a way that gives every member a way to contribute his or her ideas.
3. State a question that students will try to come to an agreement on through discussion. Example: What field trip sites would be most interesting for our class?
4. Ask each student to write down five answers to the question.
5. Have two tribe members get together, compare lists and agree on four ideas eliminating all others.
6. Have two pairs get together, compare lists, agree on 4 out of their 8 combined ideas and eliminate the others.
7. Have the tribes report their four final ideas to the class. Keep a list on the chalkboard of all ideas. Have the class discuss all of the ideas and eliminate those that seem unworkable or less possible. Then use "sticker voting" to give each student an opportunity to choose his or her three preferred ideas. (See "Group Problem Solving.")
8. Add up the value of the stickers to determine the final choice of the class. The value of the stickers are: Blue=15 points, Red=10 points and Yellow=5 points.

TIME:	25–40 minutes
GROUPING:	tribes, pairs
MATERIALS:	5 x 7-inch file cards

DEVELOPMENTAL TASKS:
Independence/Autonomy
Problem Solving

SUGGESTED REFLECTION QUESTIONS

CONTENT (COGNITIVE LEARNING)

• What four ideas did your group come up with?

COLLABORATIVE (SOCIAL LEARNING)

• Why might making decisions this way be easier/difficult sometimes?
• How did your group come to a consensus?
• In what ways did your group work together really well?

DISCOVERING GIFTS (PERSONAL LEARNING)

• How did you feel when your tribe made their final choices?
• How did you influence your tribe's decision?
• What special strengths or skills did you bring to your tribe?

APPRECIATION

Invite statements of appreciation (and recognition of gifts):
• "I like our choices because…"
• "I appreciated it when…"
• "Our tribe is cool because…"

Cooperation Squares

TIME: 30 minutes

GROUPING: tribes

MATERIALS: puzzle sets (see next page for directions)

DEVELOPMENTAL TASKS:
Social Competency
Problem Solving

OBJECTIVES

1. To encourage cooperation
2. To help students become aware of their own behaviors that may help or hinder community effort
3. To build inclusion and influence

INSTRUCTIONS

1. Begin the strategy with a community circle discussion of the meaning of cooperation. List on the chalkboard the requirements for cooperation as generated by the community.
2. Ask the community to meet in tribes. Describe the activity as a puzzle that only can be solved through cooperation.
3. Hand out one puzzle set (see next page for instructions) to each tribe.
4. Read or state the following instructions aloud:
   "Each tribe should have an envelope containing pieces for forming five squares of equal size. Each square contains three puzzle pieces. Each tribe needs to select five students who each get three puzzle pieces; the other tribe members can be observers. The strategy is complete when each of the five tribe members has formed a perfect square. While doing this, the five tribe members may not speak or signal for puzzle pieces, but they may give puzzle parts to others in the tribe if they think they might help them complete their squares."
5. Now ask each tribe to distribute the puzzle pieces equally among its five chosen members.
6. Have the observers share their observations after the puzzles are completed.

SUGGESTED REFLECTION QUESTIONS

CONTENT (COGNITIVE LEARNING)

• What did you learn about nonverbal cooperation?
• Why did you do this strategy without talking?

COLLABORATIVE (SOCIAL LEARNING)

• What social skills did your tribe need to make this activity successful?
• Why is "giving" a social skill?

DISCOVERING GIFTS (PERSONAL LEARNING)

• How did you feel when someone helped your tribe in a special way? When someone did not notice how to help?
• In what ways did you help your tribe during this activity?
• What special strengths or gifts did you discover about yourself?

APPRECIATION

Invite statements of appreciation (and recognition of gifts):
• "I liked it when…"
• "I felt good when…"

DIRECTIONS FOR MAKING A PUZZLE SET

A puzzle set consists of one envelope containing fifteen cardboard pieces that are cut in the design below. When properly arranged they form five separate squares of equal size. Each square contains three pieces. Prepare one puzzle set for each group of five persons.

To prepare a puzzle set:
1. Cut out five six by six-inch cardboard squares.
2. Line them up in a row and mark them as illustrated below, penciling the letters a, b, c, etc. lightly, so that they can be easily erased later.
3. Cut each square as marked.

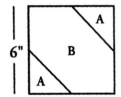 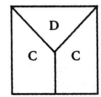 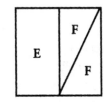 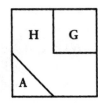 

4. Mark 5 envelopes A, B, C, D and E.
5. Place the 15 cardboard pieces, a-j on top of five envelopes as follows:

   A: pieces i, h, e
   B: pieces a, a, a, c
   C: pieces a, j
   D: pieces d, f
   E: pieces g, b, f, c

6. Before inserting the pieces into the envelopes, erase penciled letters and write the appropriate envelope letter on each piece. This will make it easy to return the pieces to the envelopes so that the activity may be used again.

Cruising Careers

TIME: 15 minutes

GROUPING: community

MATERIALS: name slips

DEVELOPMENTAL TASKS:
Social Competency

OBJECTIVES

1. To build community inclusion
2. To divide people into tribes or learning groups
3. To explore career options

INSTRUCTIONS

1. Prepare a small slip of paper for each student. Depending on the number of tribes that the community will divide into, select names of that many different types of jobs or careers. Examples: professional athletes, artists, politicians, engineers, scientists, lawyers, cowboys/girls, teachers, doctors, carpenters, construction workers.
2. Write the name of a career (or use a picture) on each slip so that the students who will be in the "athletes" tribe all have slips marked "athletes," and so on.
3. If you are assigning students to specific tribes, write the name of the student on one side of the slip and the name of the career on the other side.
4. Before distributing the slips, tell the students that they are not to let anyone else know what career names are on their slips.
5. Ask the students to circulate silently while acting out typical activities of the careers named on their slips. Tell them that they need to find the other students who are acting out the same career as themselves.
6. When all the students with the same career names find each other, have the "career tribes" sit together and discuss and reflect.

SUGGESTED REFLECTION QUESTIONS

CONTENT (COGNITIVE LEARNING)

- What do you think about this way of finding tribe members?
- What made this a fun way to divide into tribes?

COLLABORATIVE (SOCIAL LEARNING)

- How did you identify who was in your tribe?
- How did your tribe respond when you found each other?
- What did the community members do to make this activity successful?

DISCOVERING GIFTS (PERSONAL LEARNING)

- What senses or skills were most helpful to you as you tried to find your tribe members?
- Did you discover anything new about yourself while doing this activity?

APPRECIATION

Invite statements of appreciation (and recognition of gifts):

- "I was (feeling) when…"
- "Thank you, (name), for…"
- "I liked it when…"

OPTION

Have the community divide into tribes by humming, or singing familiar tunes. Multicultural and adult groups (teachers and parents) may enjoy using different dance steps. Reinforce curriculum by using historical or literary characters.

Current Events Debate Circle

OBJECTIVES

1. To enable students to express their views
2. To encourage discussion of current events
3. To enhance the student's ability to see different sides of an issue
4. To provide a structure for learning or reviewing the curriculum
5. To experience influence

TIME:	30 minutes
GROUPING:	community
MATERIALS:	none
SUBJECT:	history, social studies, politics, science

DEVELOPMENTAL TASKS:
Independence/Autonomy
Sense of Purpose

INSTRUCTIONS

1. Arrange six chairs in a circle.
2. Tell the community that you would like to have five volunteers sit in the circle to express their views on (topic). Explain that the extra chair is for anyone who wants to come in briefly and add information to the debate (facts, dates, etc.), after which he or she must go back to his or her seat. Examples:
   • Should skateboards be allowed at school?
   • How important is it for people to learn to use computers?
   • How can people resist peer pressure to use cigarettes, alcohol, or other drugs?
3. Say that the remaining community members are to be silent until all the students in the circle have been heard.
4. After the circle members have debated the topic, invite the community to direct questions to the circle members.

SUGGESTED REFLECTION QUESTIONS

CONTENT (COGNITIVE LEARNING)

• What did you learn about the topic?
• Why is the debate circle a good way to learn about a topic?

COLLABORATIVE (SOCIAL LEARNING)

• What social skills did the community members need to be good debaters?
• How did it help to have the "open" chair in the circle?
• How did the group members show that they were listening to each other?

DISCOVERING GIFTS (PERSONAL LEARNING)

• How did you feel being inside/outside the circle?
• What part of this activity did you enjoy the most? What does this say about your special strengths or skills?
• How did you contribute to the community in a special way?

APPRECIATION

Invite statements of appreciation (and recognition of gifts):
   • "I liked it when…"
   • "I am glad you said…"
   • "I appreciated you for…"

Dear Abby

TIME: 30–45 minutes

GROUPING: tribes

MATERIALS: 5 x 8-inch cards

DEVELOPMENTAL TASKS:
Independence/Autonomy
Social Competency
Sense of Purpose
Problem Solving

OBJECTIVES

1. To encourage active decision-making
2. To build appreciation for another's point of view
3. To share a concern or problem anonymously, and have peers suggest solutions
4. To promote influence

INSTRUCTIONS

1. Have the community meet in tribes, and give each tribe a pile of cards on which you have previously written a concern or problem (real issues) appropriate to your students' age level.
2. Ask tribe members to each take a turn at reading a problem out loud from a card to the rest of the tribe. Then have them say, "If I were Dear Abby I would suggest that this person (advice)."
3. Later (that day or a different one), distribute blank cards to the tribes and ask each tribe member to write one real concern or problem on the card, addressing it to the fictitious new columnist, "Dear Abby."
4. Collect the cards and redistribute the cards back to tribe members to suggest what they, as Dear Abby," would advise the person to do.

SUGGESTED REFLECTION QUESTIONS

CONTENT (COGNITIVE LEARNING)

- What type of problems seemed to be the most frequent?
- Why is being able to solve problems an important skill?

COLLABORATIVE (SOCIAL LEARNING)

- How could you tell when your tribe members were listening well?
- What is the link between good listening and good solutions to problems?

DISCOVERING GIFTS (PERSONAL LEARNING)

- What did you feel when you listened to other students' concerns?
- How did you feel when you were giving a solution?
- What expertise did you discover about yourself?
- How did you contribute to your group in a special way?

APPRECIATION

Invite statements of appreciation (and recognition of gifts):
- "(Name), you were a good listener…"
- "(Name), I liked it when you said…"

Dream Quilt

TIME:	40 minutes
GROUPING:	community, pairs
MATERIALS:	squares of paper: a size that works for your room

DEVELOPMENTAL TASKS:
Independence/Autonomy
Sense of Purpose

OBJECTIVES

1. To build community inclusion
2. To share a personal goal for the year

INSTRUCTIONS

Note: This is an excellent strategy to start the year or the semester.

1. Have the community sit in a circle.
2. Ask each student to think of a goal for the year, something he or she wants to accomplish.
3. Ask students to choose a partner and take turns sharing their goals.
4. Now pass out squares of paper to the students and ask them to write or illustrate their goals.
5. In a community circle, ask the students to share their goals with the class.
6. After all the students have shared their goals, have them decorate their square, sign their name, and post all the squares together on a bulletin board in the form of a quilt.

SUGGESTED REFLECTION QUESTIONS

CONTENT (COGNITIVE LEARNING)

- What did you learn?
- What type of goals did most of you have?
- Why are goals important?

COLLABORATIVE (SOCIAL LEARNING)

- What skills did the community use to make this strategy successful?
- What could the community do to improve this strategy?

DISCOVERING GIFTS (PERSONAL LEARNING)

- How did you feel about putting your goals down on paper?
- What other goals didn't you put down that you might want to share?
- What personal strengths will you use to reach your goals?

APPRECIATION

Invite statements of appreciation (and recognition of gifts):

- "Thanks, (name), for…"
- "I appreciated your sharing…"

Extended Nametags

TIME: 15–25 minutes

GROUPING: community, triads

MATERIALS: 5 x 8-inch cards, pencils, clock

DEVELOPMENTAL TASKS:
Independence/Autonomy
Social Competency
Sense of Purpose

OBJECTIVES

1. To promote inclusion by sharing personal history, interests, beliefs, etc.
2. To enhance communication skills

INSTRUCTIONS

1. Distribute 5 x 8-inch cards.
2. Ask each student to print his or her first name or nickname in the center of the card, and directly under it the quality he or she most values in people.
3. Then have each student write the following in the corners:
   - upper left—a place where he or she spent his or her happiest summer
     option: his or her favorite place on earth
   - lower left—the name of a person who taught him or her something important
     option: the name of his or her best friend
   - lower right—the year he or she last spent three great days in a row
     option: the year he or she went on a big trip
   - upper right—three things he or she does well
     option: a goal that he or she has for the future
4. Have the students meet in triads. Explain that the triad will talk about the upper left corner of their cards for three minutes, which means each person has one minute to talk. Ask them to keep track of their time and to share equally.
5. After three minutes, have the triads give statements of appreciation. Allow two minutes for the statements. Examples:
   - "I liked it when…"   • "You're a lot like me when…"
6. Have the students form new triads three more times, sharing the other three corners and giving statements of appreciation after each round.
7. Form a community circle and invite each student to share something special he or she learned about a class member.

SUGGESTED REFLECTION QUESTIONS

CONTENT (COGNITIVE LEARNING)

- Why is it important for the members of a community to have opportunities to share information about themselves?
- Are there other good questions we could ask?

COLLABORATIVE (SOCIAL LEARNING)

- How did you know that others were listening well when you spoke?
- How did this activity help our class community get better acquainted?

DISCOVERING GIFTS (PERSONAL LEARNING)

- What were you feeling when you were speaking/listening?
- What unique qualities did you discover about yourself?

APPRECIATION

Invite statements of appreciation (and recognition of gifts):
   - "I liked hearing…"
   - "I admire your…"

Family Changes—Comparing/Contrasting

OBJECTIVES

1. To give students an opportunity to share something about their parents
2. To have students compare and contrast the differences between their parents when they were younger and now

INSTRUCTIONS

1. Ask each student to find two pictures of one of their parents—one as a child and one current. (*Note:* If you have a student in your class who lives with a relative or guardian, please modify the instructions by asking all students to bring, or draw, two photos of a parent, relative, guardian, mentor, or friend.) Ask the students to mount the photos together on cardboard and bring them to school. Give the students a few days to gather the photos.
2. Have the community meet. Have each student share his or her parents' photos with the community.
3. When everyone has shared, explain the meaning of compare and contrast (compare is to look for the similarities, contrast is to look for the differences). Then ask for a volunteer to compare and contrast his or her parents' photos.

TIME:	two class periods
GROUPING:	community
MATERIALS:	photos of a parent—mounted on cardboard

DEVELOPMENTAL TASKS:
Independence/Autonomy
Sense of Purpose

SUGGESTED REFLECTION QUESTIONS

CONTENT (COGNITIVE LEARNING)

• What did you learn about comparing and contrasting?
• What did you learn about your parents or someone else's parents?
• Why is this strategy difficult?

COLLABORATIVE (SOCIAL LEARNING)

• What social skills were important during this strategy?
• How can the community improve this strategy?
• What do you appreciate about this community?

DISCOVERING GIFTS (PERSONAL LEARNING)

• How did you feel sharing your parents' pictures?
• How did you feel listening to others as they shared?
• What "people skills" did you use during this activity?

APPRECIATION

Invite statements of appreciation (and recognition of gifts):
• "It helped me when…"
• "I liked it when…"
• "Thank you for…"

Final Countdown

TIME: 5 minutes

GROUPING: full group

MATERIALS: none

DEVELOPMENTAL TASKS:
Independence/Autonomy
Social Competency
Sense of Purpose

OBJECTIVES

1. To bring closure to a class or a day
2. To provide opportunities for sharing and recognition

INSTRUCTIONS

1. Just before the last five minutes of class, have students prepare to leave and then sit in a community circle for the "Final Countdown."
2. Say, "I need to hear four things before we say goodbye for today." "I need to hear…
   - a statement of appreciation for someone here,
   - something or someone you are thankful for,
   - something good about your day, and
   - a clean, funny joke."
3. Choose volunteers until the "Final Countdown" is completed. Make sure the same people are not chosen each time.

SUGGESTED REFLECTION QUESTIONS

Note: Keep reflection questions very brief, as this is a closure activity.

CONTENT (COGNITIVE LEARNING)

- Who heard something you know or agree with?

COLLABORATIVE (SOCIAL LEARNING)

- Who will share tomorrow?

DISCOVERING GIFTS (PERSONAL LEARNING)

- Who discovered something new about yourself today?

APPRECIATION

Invite statements of appreciation (and recognition of gifts):
- "Thank you, (name), for sharing!"

Find The Word

OBJECTIVES

1. To introduce a unit's vocabulary words and their meanings
2. To build inclusion and influence

INSTRUCTIONS

1. Give each student a card with a word printed on it from the social studies, history, science, or language unit. (If the words have been only recently introduced, write a word list on the chalkboard.)
2. Have each student pin his or her card on the back of another student without that student seeing it.
3. Tell the students to move around the room and ask each other questions that can be answered "yes" or "no" until each student determines what is written on the card on his or her back. Explain that they may ask each student only one question and then must move along to the next student.

SUGGESTED REFLECTION QUESTIONS

CONTENT (COGNITIVE LEARNING)

- What kind of questions did you ask?
- Why might this be a fun way to learn new vocabulary words?

COLLABORATIVE (SOCIAL LEARNING)

- What social skills did the community need to make this activity work well?
- In what ways did you, as a community, help to make this activity successful?

DISCOVERING GIFTS (PERSONAL LEARNING)

- How did you feel when you found out what or who you were?
- What did you enjoy most about this activity?
- Did you find any hidden gifts or talents about yourself that you were not aware of?

APPRECIATION

Invite statements of appreciation (and recognition of gifts):

- "I enjoyed it when…"
- "I liked it when…"
- "I'm similar to (name) because…"

TIME:	20–30 minutes
GROUPING:	community
MATERIALS:	3 x 5-inch index cards, safety pins, markers
SUBJECT:	social studies, history, reading or vocabulary

DEVELOPMENTAL TASKS:
Independence/Autonomy
Problem Solving

Finding All We Have In Common

TIME: 35–45 minutes

GROUPING: community, pairs

MATERIALS: none

DEVELOPMENTAL TASKS:
Independence/Autonomy
Social Competency
Sense of Purpose

OBJECTIVES

1. To give students an opportunity to introduce themselves
2. To give students an opportunity to work in pairs and find commonalties
3. To build inclusion

INSTRUCTIONS

1. State that we are a unique group about to start an exciting journey together, and that, like any people coming together, we need to learn about each other.
2. Have each student find a partner he or she does not know at all or does not know very well. Say, "In the next five minutes find out all the things that you have in common with your partner (likes, dislikes, qualities, skills, goals or whatever)."
3. Have the community sit in a circle. Have each partner introduce him or herself and tell what he or she discovered.

SUGGESTED REFLECTION QUESTIONS

CONTENT (COGNITIVE LEARNING)

- What are things many of you have in common?
- Why is finding out what you have in common a good way to get to know somebody?

COLLABORATIVE (SOCIAL LEARNING)

- Why is attentive listening so important for this strategy?
- How did you and your partner make this activity successful?
- What do you appreciate about this community?

DISCOVERING GIFTS (PERSONAL LEARNING)

- How did you feel about finding out/sharing what you and your partner have in common?
- What strengths or personal qualities do you and your partner have in common?

APPRECIATION

Invite statements of appreciation (and recognition of gifts):
- "I really liked…"
- "It was great when…"

Flies On The Ceiling

OBJECTIVES

1. To identify the dynamics of group interaction
2. To process a sequence of learning activities and behaviors
3. To practice reflecting on systems and situations
4. To experience influence

INSTRUCTIONS

1. After students have been working together on a task, have them set aside their books and papers.
2. Ask the students to close their eyes and imagine they had been flies on the ceiling watching their tribe work together during the last few minutes or hours. Tell them to "run the movie backwards now" and think about what the flies saw happening.
    • Who did what to get you started?
    • What did you do while your tribe was working together?
    • What did other tribe members do?
    • What helpful things happened?
    • Who did them?
    • Did everyone participate?
    • How did you help each other?
3. After a few minutes, have the tribe members share what they as flies saw happening. It is helpful to have each tribe choose a recorder to make a list of behaviors, positions, acts, interactions, etc.
4. Have the tribes give their report to the community.
5. Then ask each tribe to make a list of: "things that we did to help our tribe work well together" and/or "things that we could do to help our tribe work together better next time."

SUGGESTED REFLECTION QUESTIONS

CONTENT (COGNITIVE LEARNING)

• These questions were handled in #2 above.

COLLABORATIVE (SOCIAL LEARNING)

• Why is it important to look at how groups are working together?
• What do you appreciate most about your tribe?

DISCOVERING GIFTS (PERSONAL LEARNING)

• How could you use this strategy in other groups and relationships?
• How did you help your tribe work together?
• How did you contribute in a special way?

APPRECIATION

Invite statements of appreciation (and recognition of gifts):
    • "Thanks for…"
    • "It helped me when…"

TIME: 35 minutes

GROUPING: tribes

MATERIALS: paper, pencils

DEVELOPMENTAL TASKS:
   Social Competency
   Sense of Purpose
   Problem Solving

Fold The Line Reading

TIME: 30 minutes

GROUPING: community line-up, and pairs

MATERIALS: textbook or handout reading material

DEVELOPMENTAL TASKS:
Independence/Autonomy
Social Competency

OBJECTIVES

1. To build interdependence
2. To practice reading with a partner
3. To experience influence

INSTRUCTIONS

1. Have the students get some identical reading (history, social studies, or other).
2. Ask the students to line up (without talking) across the room according to their birth dates, beginning with January on one side of the room.
3. Starting on one side, have each student in turn state his or her birth month and date.
4. Create two lines by leading the last person, so that each student is facing a partner. Have the partners stand an arm's length apart.
5. Have one partner read the first paragraph of the text. The other partner paraphrases what was read.
6. Next have the other partner read the next paragraph. Partners alternate reading and paraphrasing until they finish reading the selection you assigned.

SUGGESTED REFLECTION QUESTIONS

CONTENT (COGNITIVE LEARNING)

• What did you learn from the material you just read?

COLLABORATIVE (SOCIAL LEARNING)

• Why is reading together helpful?
• Why is a choosing partner using a lineup fun?
• What did you and your partner do to make this activity successful?

DISCOVERING GIFTS (PERSONAL LEARNING)

• How do you feel reading to another person?
• How did you help make this strategy successful?
• What special strengths or skills did you discover about yourself?

APPRECIATION

Invite statements of appreciation (and recognition of gifts):
• "I liked your reading because…"
• "Thanks for helping me…"

Gallery Walks

OBJECTIVES

1. To build communication skills
2. To build self-esteem and pride in work
3. To build inclusion and influence

INSTRUCTIONS

1. Invite several students to stand next to projects on which they have been working. Refer to them as "Artists of the Day."
2. Have the remaining students form triads.
3. Invite the triads to take a "gallery walk" around the room to view articles on display, projects-in-making, etc.
4. Have each student artist stand by his or her work and share the origin of his or her ideas, materials used, personal objectives, feelings about finished work, etc.

SUGGESTED REFLECTION QUESTIONS

CONTENT (COGNITIVE LEARNING)

- What kind of things did the artists mention?
- What different talents do people have?
- How did the artists seem to feel about their work?

COLLABORATIVE (SOCIAL LEARNING)

- What social skills did "gallery walkers" and artists need to use to make this activity successful?
- In what ways could the community make this activity even more successful?

DISCOVERING GIFTS (PERSONAL LEARNING)

- What did you do best when you presented your work?
- How did you help to keep the focus on the other artists?
- What special talents do you feel proud of?

APPRECIATION

Invite statements of appreciation (and recognition of gifts):
- "I liked it when you said…"
- "Some of your talents are…"
- "I like your masterpiece because…"

TIME: 30 minutes

GROUPING: community and triads

MATERIALS: student art work or lesson topic

DEVELOPMENTAL TASKS:
Independence/Autonomy
Social Competency
Sense of Purpose

Give Me A Clue

TIME: 20–30 minutes

GROUPING: tribes, subgroups

MATERIALS: clue cards, colored cubes, colored pencils

DEVELOPMENTAL TASKS:

Independence/Autonomy
Problem Solving

OBJECTIVES

1. To demonstrate understanding of geometric vocabulary terms
2. To use spatial reasoning to think in three dimensions
3. To learn that accomplishing a group task depends upon each member contributing skills and knowledge

INSTRUCTIONS

1. Have students meet in tribes or small groups of four to six members.
2. State the objectives and the task: to build a three-dimensional figure with colored cubes, using the information on the "Build It" clue cards.
3. Distribute eight colored cubes (two blue, two green, two red, and two yellow) to each tribe. Have each tribe member draw one clue card.
4. State the rules:
   - the clue card is his or hers alone and no one else may touch it
   - the blocks may be touched only when it is a member's turn
   - students share their clue by reading its information aloud
   - help may be asked in reading the information
   - if a question arises, ask tribe members before asking the teacher
5. Tell students to:
   - read the clues on their cards to their tribe
   - share their thinking to help the tribe come to an understanding of each vocabulary term
   - analyze the clues until a solution seems to have been found
6. Tell the students that they will recognize the correct solution when everyone agrees that the three-dimensional figure matches with the clues.
7. Have the tribes record their solution by drawing it.

SUGGESTED REFLECTION QUESTIONS

CONTENT (COGNITIVE LEARNING)

- Which vocabulary words needed to be clarified by your tribe? What do they mean?

COLLABORATIVE (SOCIAL LEARNING)

- What did tribe members do to help your tribe be successful?
- What did tribe members say or do that opened up your thinking?
- Describe the benefits of working as a tribe rather than alone.

DISCOVERING GIFTS (PERSONAL LEARNING)

- What did you do that was helpful?
- Did you discover any clues about hidden strengths or abilities you may have? What are they?

APPRECIATION

Invite statements of appreciation (and recognition of gifts):
- "It was helpful when…"
- "I liked it when…"

○ **BUILD IT #1**

There are six blocks in all.
One of the blocks is yellow.

○ **BUILD IT #1**

The green block shares
one face with each of the
other five blocks.

○ **BUILD IT #1**

The two red blocks do not
touch each other.

○ **BUILD IT #1**

The two blue blocks do not
touch each other.

○ **BUILD IT #1**

Each red block shares
an edge with the
yellow block.

○ **BUILD IT #1**

Each blue block shares
one edge with each of
the red blocks.

This strategy is adapted from Get It Together—Math Problems for Groups 4–12. *Lawrence Hall of Science, Berkeley, 1989. (See "Resources" for additional information.) Permission to use granted. © 1989 The Regents of the University of California, from* Get It Together—EQUALS, *Lawrence Hall of Science.*

This page may be duplicated for classroom use.

Goal-Storming

TIME: 60 minutes

GROUPING: community, tribes

MATERIALS: large paper, markers, tape

DEVELOPMENTAL TASKS:
Independence/Autonomy
Sense of Purpose
Problem Solving

OBJECTIVES

1. To enable a large group to identify shared goals and concerns
2. To structure interest-related work groups
3. To experience influence

INSTRUCTIONS

Note: "Goal-Storming" is a variation of "Brainstorming." The group should be familiar with the Brainstorming process.

1. Decide upon a relevant question for the full community to address:
    Example: "Where would we like to go on a field trip?"
2. Ask the community to form small groups or meet in tribes.
3. Review the rules for "Brainstorming:"
    D defer judgment
    O offbeat, original
    V vast number
    E expand, elaborate
4. Ask each tribe to choose a recorder and then brainstorm for five minutes, listing all ideas.
5. Ask the recorders to read all the ideas to the community. Discuss consensus and how to form a consensus. (See "Consensus-Building.")
6. Instruct each tribe to form a consensus on three ideas.
7. Record the three ideas from each tribe on the chalkboard.
8. Discuss the ideas as a full community. Combine ideas that are repetitive.
9. At this point choose one of these options:
    • Form task or interest groups around listed concerns.
    • Sticker vote as individuals to determine highest priority.

SUGGESTED REFLECTION QUESTIONS

CONTENT (COGNITIVE LEARNING)

• Why is this a good way to find out what a group wants?
• What makes goal-storming difficult?
• Why are the DOVE brainstorming guidelines important?

COLLABORATIVE (SOCIAL LEARNING)

• What social skills did the community use to make brainstorming successful?
• What skills and strengths did your tribe use that helped you work well together?

DISCOVERING GIFTS (PERSONAL LEARNING)

• How do you feel about the group's priority?
• How did you contribute to your group in a special way?

APPRECIATION

Invite statements of appreciation (and recognition of gifts):
• "I liked it when you…"
• "I felt good when…"

Graphing Who We Are

OBJECTIVES

1. To graph and review information gathered by tribes
2. To develop an appreciation of differences
3. To develop a sense of community
4. To experience influence

INSTRUCTIONS

1. Prior to initiating this strategy, select some different types of graphs (Venn diagram, bar graph, line graph and/or picture graphs) to teach the recording of statistical information. Sketch the graph models on newsprint or the blackboard. Set aside large sheets of paper, one for each tribe.
2. Have the students meet in their tribes, and explain that each tribe will graph information on the large sheets of paper about the members of their tribes (heights, eye colors, numbers of siblings, distance from school, shoe sizes, head circumferences, etc.).
3. Have tribe members choose roles: recorder, reader, measurer, taskmaster. Review the responsibilities of each role.
4. Ask each tribe to discuss and choose which graph model they will use.
5. Invite a tribe to use you as an example, measuring your height and recording the information.
6. Have the tribes present their graphs when completed to the community.

TIME: 30–60 minutes

GROUPING: tribes

MATERIALS: wall graph formats, large paper, tape measures, rulers, maps

DEVELOPMENTAL TASKS:
Independence/Autonomy
Sense of Purpose
Problem Solving

SUGGESTED REFLECTION QUESTIONS

CONTENT (COGNITIVE LEARNING)

- Why is it important to be able to read graphs?
- What did you learn about graphing in this strategy?

COLLABORATIVE (SOCIAL LEARNING)

- What social skills did you need, as a tribe, to be successful in this strategy?
- What cooperative skills do you think your tribe needs to practice?

DISCOVERING GIFTS (PERSONAL LEARNING)

- How did you help your tribe?
- What did you discover that you appreciate about yourself?
- What did your tribe appreciate about you?

APPRECIATION

Invite statements of appreciation (and recognition of gifts):
- "I appreciated..."
- "It was great when..."

Adapted from All About Us, *by Nan and Ted Graves, Cooperative Learning, Vol. 11, No. 2, December, 1990*

Group Inquiry

TIME: varies

GROUPING: tribes

MATERIALS: dependent upon content resources and extent of research

DEVELOPMENTAL TASKS:
Independence/Autonomy
Sense of Purpose
Problem Solving

OBJECTIVES

1. To practice constructive thinking skills (accessing information, interpreting, synthesizing and applying)
2. To practice collaborative team skills
3. To transfer responsibility to students

INSTRUCTIONS

1. Inclusion: Build inclusion within the tribes by using the structure, write/pair/share. Ask people to take 5–10 minutes to write down the skills, talents and abilities that they bring to the group. You may want to list and discuss the various collaborative skills. (See chapter 6 for Tribes collaborative skills.) Have people share their lists first in pairs. Then share with the tribe.
2. Content and Objectives: Discuss the general subject content and sub-content areas to be researched by the tribes. It is optional whether the class or teacher defines the sub-content areas. List the objectives to be learned from the experience. Have the tribes choose or randomly draw slips of content areas. (See option.)
3. Resources: Detail resources they can use for their inquiry or research (books, articles, computer info, library, interviews, films, etc.).
4. Task: Describe the task to be accomplished (group report, presentation, role play, article, etc.) within a specific time; inquiry projects can run from one hour to several weeks or months.
5. Roles: You may want to use roles within the tribes (facilitator, encourager, materials manager, recorder, etc.). If so, have people choose their roles according to the skills and resources they believe they bring to the group.
6. Accountability:
   - For presentations to the whole class, a peer evaluation sheet may be used. (See "Peer Evaluation of Group Presentation" on the page following this strategy.)
   - Your own observations of individual performance can be made by taking notes.
   - Group and individual reports can be made and graded.

SUGGESTED REFLECTION QUESTIONS

CONTENT (COGNITIVE LEARNING)

- What was the most important content (theory, information, etc.) that can be applied to the topic today? (Discuss, share or write about this question.)
- Help people to understand the topic.
- What would you like to know more about?

COLLABORATIVE (SOCIAL LEARNING)

- What was the value for our community in using this teaching method?
- What collaborative skills were demonstrated by your tribe?

OPTION

Instead of using subtopics within tribes, use the "Jigsaw" method and have individual tribe members research the subject in expert groups and then return to teach content to their tribe.

DISCOVERING GIFTS (PERSONAL LEARNING)

• What skills did you use to contribute to your tribe in a special way?

• What skills did you notice in others that you would also like to learn?

• What skills, talents and abilities are you particularly proud of?

APPRECIATION

Invite oral or written statements of appreciation (and recognition of gifts) to individuals or whole tribes:

• "Thank you for…"

• "I liked it when…"

PEER EVALUATION OF GROUP PRESENTATION

GROUP NAME:

EVALUATION CRITERIA	OUTSTANDING	GOOD	IMPROVEMENT NEEDED	POOR
1. Content				
2. Organization				
3. Cooperation of tribe members				
4. Use of aids: handouts, video, etc.				
5. Involvement/Interest for class				

Specific Suggestions for Improvement:

I Appreciated Learning:

This chart is an adaptation of one in the article "Using Jigsaw Groups for Research and Writing in High School," by Glory-Ann Drazinakis, Cooperative Learning, Vol. 13, No. 2. Winter 1993.

This page may be duplicated for classroom use.

Group Problem-Solving

OBJECTIVES

1. To teach a group problem-solving process
2. To analyze alternatives
3. To experience influence

INSTRUCTIONS

1. Have the class community meet in tribes.
2. Give each tribe five minutes to come up with three typical problems that a student might have with another student—or that a student might have with someone else at the school.
3. Have each tribe read their problem to the class. Make sure that the problems are well defined.
4. Explain that each tribe will have ten minutes to brainstorm and list possible solutions. Review the "Brainstorming" strategy and post the brainstorming rules. Give each tribe a large sheet of paper, a felt pen and three colored stickers (red, blue and yellow).
5. Write the "Group Problem-Solving" process on the board.
   - Brainstorm for ten minutes. Have one person record all ideas.
   - Each person selects three top choices with colored stickers (1st choice blue=25 points; 2nd choice red=15 points; 3rd choice yellow=5 points).
   - Add up the total points for each idea.
   - Present your top solutions to the community.

Note: If this strategy is used for real-time problems, you may want to teach the tribes how to make a "Tribe Action Plan" that will identify tasks, responsibilities and completion dates. See chapter 7 for the plan format.

SUGGESTED REFLECTION QUESTIONS

CONTENT (COGNITIVE LEARNING)

- What is the value of this process?
- What other ways can decisions be made in the tribe?

COLLABORATIVE (SOCIAL LEARNING)

- In what ways did your tribe honor our tribe agreements?
- What social skills did your tribe use when doing this strategy?
- What did you like best about how your tribe worked together?

DISCOVERING GIFTS (PERSONAL LEARNING)

- How do you feel about your action plan?
- How do you feel about your participation?
- What did you do to help your tribe be successful?
- What new strengths or skills did you discover in yourself?

APPRECIATION

Invite statements of appreciation (and recognition of gifts):
- "Thanks for your help…"
- "You made a positive difference when…"

TIME:	40 minutes
GROUPING:	tribes
MATERIALS:	large paper, markers, colored stickers

DEVELOPMENTAL TASKS:
Independence/Autonomy
Sense of Purpose
Problem Solving

"I'm Proud" Appreciation Circle

TIME: 30 minutes

GROUPING: community, or tribes

MATERIALS: none

DEVELOPMENTAL TASKS:
Independence/Autonomy
Social Competency
Sense of Purpose

OBJECTIVES

1. To encourage sharing good feelings about oneself
2. To encourage acceptance and appreciation of others
3. To build inclusion

INSTRUCTIONS

1. Discuss the difference between stating appreciation of oneself and bragging.
2. Invite one person of the community or one person in each tribe to sit in the middle as the focus person.
3. Have the focus person make an "I'm proud" statement. Examples:
   - "I'm proud that I am…"
   - "I'm proud that I am able to…"
   - "I'm proud that I…"
4. Have the other tribe members give positive feedback or make statements of appreciation to the focus person.
5. Continue the process until each person takes a turn being the focus person.

SUGGESTED REFLECTION QUESTIONS

CONTENT (COGNITIVE LEARNING)

- How did you choose your "I'm proud" statement?
- What did you learn about your tribe members?

COLLABORATIVE (SOCIAL LEARNING)

- Why is it important to be able to acknowledge what we are proud of?
- What did your tribe do to show their support when you made your "I'm proud" statements?
- What about your tribe makes you feel proud?

DISCOVERING GIFTS (PERSONAL LEARNING)

- How did you feel when you made your "I'm proud statements?"
- How did you feel when you gave/received statements of appreciation?
- What skills did you use to help the group?
- What strengths did the group recognize in you?

APPRECIATION

Invite statements of appreciation (and recognition of gifts):
   - Is there anyone who would like to make a statement to anyone else in the class?

OPTION

Use the strategy in a community circle.

Interview Circle

OBJECTIVES

1. To build inclusion and influence
2. To enhance communication skills
3. To share personal beliefs, feelings, and interests

INSTRUCTIONS

1. Ask the community to sit in a large circle.
2. Explain that we will interview one student who will sit in the center of the circle and answer three questions. The person will choose the questions from people who raise their hands. He or she has the right to "pass" on any questions that she or he chooses not to answer.
3. Model the activity first by being in the center and responding to three questions yourself.
4. Suggest that questions may be autobiographical or may relate to issues, curriculum, politics, hobbies, friendship, sports, etc.
5. Have the community interview a few students each day until everyone has had a turn.

SUGGESTED REFLECTION QUESTIONS

CONTENT (COGNITIVE LEARNING)

- What did you discover about a community member?
- Why is it difficult to answer some of the questions?

COLLABORATIVE (SOCIAL LEARNING)

- Which social skills did you, as a community, use to make this activity successful?
- How could you tell when the community was using good listening skills?

DISCOVERING GIFTS (PERSONAL LEARNING)

- How did you feel about being interviewed?
- What did you learn about yourself from this activity?
- What unique qualities are you proud of as a result of this activity?★

APPRECIATION

Invite statements of appreciation (and recognition of gifts):
- "I liked it when…"
- "I admired your honesty when…"

TIME: 15–30 minutes

GROUPING: community, tribes

MATERIALS: none

DEVELOPMENTAL TASKS:
Independence/Autonomy
Social Competency
Sense of Purpose

★OPTION

Suggest that students record their discovered qualities in their journals.

I Used to Be; We Used To Be

TIME: 45 minutes

GROUPING: tribes

MATERIALS: paper, pencils

DEVELOPMENTAL TASKS:
Independence/Autonomy
Sense of Purpose

OBJECTIVES

1. To give the students an opportunity to look at personal changes
2. To give tribes an opportunity to look at how they have changed
3. To share personal and tribal changes
4. To experience influence

INSTRUCTIONS

1. Have the community meet in tribes.
2. Ask each student to (silently) compare the following things about himself or herself today, and his or her old self in the past: physical appearance, favorite things to do, behavior, hobbies, beliefs, fears, friends, etc.
3. Have each tribe member write a poem, using the following format:
   > I used to be…
   > But now I am…
   > I used to be…
   > But now I am…
4. Ask the tribe members to share their finished poems.
5. While students are still in their tribes ask each tribe member to create a poem about his or her tribe, using the following format:
   > We used to be…
   > But now we are…
   > We used to be…
   > But now we are…
6. Ask the tribe members to share their finished poems.
7. Ask each tribe to share one or two of its "we" poems with the community.

*OPTION

Suggest that students record their discovered qualities in their journals.

SUGGESTED REFLECTION QUESTIONS

CONTENT (COGNITIVE LEARNING)

- What did you find out about your tribe members?
- What changes have your tribe members made?

COLLABORATIVE (SOCIAL LEARNING)

- How well did your tribe honor the agreements during this strategy?
- How do your tribe members feel about each other now?
- What do you appreciate about your tribe?

DISCOVERING GIFTS (PERSONAL LEARNING)*

- How do you feel about how you have changed?
- What other changes do you want to make?
- What changes or special qualities make you feel especially proud?

APPRECIATION

Invite statements of appreciation (and recognition of gifts):
- "I appreciated it when…"
- "Thank you, (name), for…"

Jigsaw

TIME: varies depending on lesson task

GROUPING: tribes

MATERIALS: vary

SUBJECT: any lesson topic

DEVELOPMENTAL TASKS:
Independence/Autonomy
Social Competency
Sense of Purpose

OBJECTIVES

1. To structure team learning/team teaching in tribes
2. To build the academic self-image of students
3. To develop tribe spirit and pride
4. To help each student feel valuable to others
5. To experience inclusion and influence

INSTRUCTIONS

1. Select a lesson that you consider appropriate for the following process.
2. Divide it into equal parts (or the number of members per tribe) and define study questions. Prepare sufficient materials for the study groups.
3. Explain the Jigsaw process to your class. Then ask the students to meet in tribes.
4. If you have not already done so, engage them with an activity on the personal feeling level to awaken interest about a topic.
5. Give each tribe one set of lesson materials. Ask each tribe to decide who will become an "expert" for each part of the lesson.
6. Ask people responsible for Part I to move to a jigsaw study group; do the same for the other parts.
7. Tell the groups what their specific task is and the amount of time that will be allowed. Move from group to group, helping only as needed.
8. When all have finished, ask people to return to their own tribes.
9. Beginning with Part I, ask the "experts" to share the materials that they prepared in their Jigsaw group; prepare a format for sharing if you think it will help them.
10. After each segment has been shared, take time for a full group discussion, and then meet in tribes to reflect on the experience.

SUGGESTED REFLECTION QUESTIONS

CONTENT (COGNITIVE LEARNING)

- What did you learn?
- Why is this a good way to learn a lot in a short time?

COLLABORATIVE (SOCIAL LEARNING)

- What skills did you, as a tribe, use to make this activity successful?
- What strengths do you see your tribe using more of in the future?

DISCOVERING GIFTS (PERSONAL LEARNING)

- How did you feel to have other students teaching you?
- How did you feel teaching others what you had learned? Why?
- What special gifts or talents did you discover about yourself?

APPRECIATION

Invite statements of appreciation (and recognition of gifts):
- "I liked it when..."
- "I want to thank, (name), for..."

Acknowledgement is made to Elliot Aronson's work. (See Bibliography.)

Joy

TIME: 20 minutes

GROUPING: community or tribes

MATERIALS: none

DEVELOPMENTAL TASKS:
Social Competency
Sense of Purpose

OBJECTIVES

1. To give each person an opportunity to share something special with others
2. To practice listening skills
3. To build inclusion

INSTRUCTIONS

1. Ask each student to think of three things that he or she would like to share. Use the letters of the word "joy" to structure what is to be shared:

   J: something in your life that just happened

   O: one thing you would like to do for yourself

   Y: a part of you that makes you a very special person

   Point out that the key letters stand for, "**J**ust **O**ne **Y**ou!"
2. Urge the students to listen attentively as each student takes a turn sharing.

SUGGESTED REFLECTION QUESTIONS

CONTENT (COGNITIVE LEARNING)

- Why is it helpful to share information about yourself?

COLLABORATIVE (SOCIAL LEARNING)

- How could you tell when people were really listening well?
- What can we do to help each other to be good listeners?
- What did the community or your tribe do to make this activity successful?

DISCOVERING GIFTS (PERSONAL LEARNING)

- What did you discover about yourself?
- How often do you give yourself a pat on the back for your special qualities?

APPRECIATION

Invite statements of appreciation (and recognition of gifts):
- "It helped me when…"
- "I appreciated…"
- "Thank you for…"

Kitchen Kapers

OBJECTIVES

1. To build inclusion and influence
2. To experience the creative power of brainstorming as a problem-solving technique
3. To promote creativity and fun

INSTRUCTIONS

1. Prepare packets containing two 3 x 5-inch cards, two paper clips, four tooth-picks, and one pencil in a sealed business-sized envelope.
2. Have the community meet in tribes or form subgroups. Review the agreements.
3. Give each tribe a packet. State that they will have twelve minutes to invent and build "one kitchen utensil every household simply must have." Encourage bizarre, zany, and unique ideas. State that all tribe members need to participate.
4. Stop the "inventors" at twelve minutes.
5. Ask each tribe to then prepare a short, three minute commercial advertising its product. All members need to take part in the commercial.
6. Have each tribe present their commercial to the community.

SUGGESTED REFLECTION QUESTIONS

CONTENT (COGNITIVE LEARNING)

- What inventions did the tribes create?
- How did the purpose of the utensil change as you built it?
- What did you learn from this activity?

COLLABORATIVE (SOCIAL LEARNING)

- How did leadership in your tribe evolve?
- How can a building project like this help build tribe spirit?
- What allowed your tribe to be creative and innovative?

DISCOVERING GIFTS (PERSONAL LEARNING)

- How did you feel before your tribe knew what it would build?
- How did you feel when you completed the invention?
- How did you help your tribe in a special way?
- What personal skills or strengths did you discover about yourself?

APPRECIATION

Invite statements of appreciation (and recognition of gifts):
- "I felt good when…"
- "I liked it when…"

TIME: 25–30 minutes

GROUPING: tribes, subgroups

MATERIALS: 3 x 5-inch cards, paper clips, tooth picks, pencils, envelopes

DEVELOPMENTAL TASKS:
Independence/Autonomy
Problem Solving

Life Map

TIME: 30 minutes

GROUPING: tribes

MATERIALS: large paper, colored pencils or markers

DEVELOPMENTAL TASKS:
Independence/Autonomy
Social Competency
Sense of Purpose

OBJECTIVES

1. To build inclusion
2. To create a visual illustration of one's life
3. To encourage attentive listening

INSTRUCTIONS

1. Ask the community to meet in tribes.
2. Give each student a piece of paper and crayons or markers and have him or her draw a visual illustration of "my life to date," the significant trends and patterns in the form of a map.
3. Invite each student to share his or her "Life Map" with his or her tribe members, explaining the rationale for "road signs," "place names," ups and downs, and so on.
4. Ask the students to give their full, undivided, caring attention to the speakers; after each student's presentation ask his or her tribe members to draw out more details, ask questions, and express their mutual feelings or concerns.

SUGGESTED REFLECTION QUESTIONS

CONTENT (COGNITIVE LEARNING)

• Why is it important to be able to draw a "Life Map?"
• How were the maps in your tribe the same?

COLLABORATIVE (SOCIAL LEARNING)

• How could you tell that your tribe members were being good listeners when others shared their "Life Maps?"
• How did tribe members help each other during this activity?

DISCOVERING GIFTS (PERSONAL LEARNING)

• How did you feel as you made your life map/as you shared with your tribe?
• What did you learn about yourself?
• How are you a unique and special individual?

APPRECIATION

Invite statements of appreciation (and recognition of gifts):
• "I felt good when…"
• "I like it when…"

Live Wire

TIME:	15 minutes
GROUPING:	community, tribes, triads
MATERIALS:	wire

DEVELOPMENTAL TASKS:
Independence/Autonomy
Social Competency
Sense of Purpose

OBJECTIVES

1. To create a visual illustration of one's life
2. To encourage attentive listening
3. To promote inclusion

INSTRUCTIONS

1. Have the community form tribes or triads.
2. Give each student a 30 inch long piece of light, bendable wire with which to construct a visual illustration of his or her "life to date:" the significant trends, patterns, and events of his or her years thus far.
3. Invite each student to share his or her "Live Wire" with other tribe members, explaining the rationale for its design.
4. Review the agreements. After one student shares, the others may ask questions, and express their mutual feelings or concerns.

SUGGESTED REFLECTION QUESTIONS

CONTENT (COGNITIVE LEARNING)

- What did you learn in this activity?
- What similarities/differences were there among your experiences?

COLLABORATIVE (SOCIAL LEARNING)

- Why is the right to pass important for this activity?
- In what ways did your group members listen to or help each other?
- How can you, as a group, continue to improve your listening skills?

DISCOVERING GIFTS (PERSONAL LEARNING)

- How did you feel as you made/shared your lifeline?
- What did you learn about yourself from making or sharing your lifeline?
- What special qualities did others appreciate about you?

APPRECIATION

Invite statements of appreciation (and recognition of gifts):
- "I felt good when…"
- "(Name), thank you for…"

Making A Choice

TIME: 45 minutes

GROUPING: tribes

MATERIALS: "Making A Choice" hand-outs

DEVELOPMENTAL TASKS:
Independence/Autonomy
Problem Solving

OBJECTIVES

1. To learn how to use a point system for evaluating choices
2. To involve students in evaluating choices
3. To create a positive decision-making process
4. To experience influence

INSTRUCTIONS

1. Have the students meet in tribes, and give each tribe the handout "Making A Choice."
2. Have tribe members read the problem aloud, discuss the advantages and disadvantages of the alternatives and make a choice.
3. Tell them to rate the criteria for each alternative by writing one, two or three in the appropriate boxes. Then add up the totals in each column. The tribe choice is the alternative with the highest rating.
4. After the tribes have made their choices, have them present their choice to the class. Point out how often people can have the same information and come up with different solutions.

SUGGESTED REFLECTION QUESTIONS

CONTENT (COGNITIVE LEARNING)

- What have you learned about making choices?
- How could a "weighted" point system help you or your tribe make a choice?

COLLABORATIVE (SOCIAL LEARNING)

- How did your tribe members help each other?
- What social skills did you, as a tribe, need to make a choice this way?

DISCOVERING GIFTS (PERSONAL LEARNING)

- How did you feel when your tribe came up with your solution?
- How did you help your tribe?
- What new skills or strengths did you discover about yourself?

APPRECIATION

Invite statements of appreciation (and recognition of gifts):
- "I appreciated it when…"
- "You helped when…"

MAKING A CHOICE HANDOUT

INTRODUCTION

When we have a problem, we have a choice between alternative ways to solve it. One aspect of making a choice is to identify and compare the advantages and disadvantages of the alternatives. A systematic approach can be used to make the comparison. Study and complete the model chart below so that you can learn to use it to make good choices.

PROBLEM

You are a playground equipment committee for a brand new elementary school, grades K–6. You have been given the task of deciding which piece of playground equipment you will put in first. Your total budget for this year is $500. The money must be spent within the next two months. You want good quality and something that will have the widest possible use. It must also be attractive and you want students to be able to use it as soon as possible. There is no chance of more money this year.

ALTERNATIVES	ADVANTAGES	DISADVANTAGES
Three tetherball poles	Cost would be within budget	Contractor can't do it for seven weeks
Two basketball poles, backboards, and hoops	Several students can play at a time	It might cost a bit more than $500
Large sandbox	Younger students have been asking for one; it would cost $400	Uncertain if older children would use it
Two swings	Everybody likes swings and contractor could install within two weeks	Only two students at a time could use them

Rate the criteria for each: 3=good or high, 2=medium, 1=low or poor

CRITERIA	TETHERBALL	BASKETBALL	SANDBOX	SWINGS
Low cost to install				
Low maintenance				
In use soon				
Attractive				
Appeals to all ages				
TOTAL				

This page may be duplicated for classroom use.

Meet Someone Special

TIME: 20–30 minutes

GROUPING: community, pairs

MATERIALS: none

DEVELOPMENTAL TASKS:
Independence/Autonomy
Social Competency
Sense of Purpose

OBJECTIVES

1. To introduce individuals to a community
2. To build community inclusion
3. To build self-esteem and appreciation for uniqueness

INSTRUCTIONS

Note: This is a good activity to help new students introduce themselves to each other.

1. Have the community sit in a circle while you give directions.
2. Review the Tribes agreements.
3. Ask each student to stand up, look about for someone he or she does not know well, invite that person to be his or her partner.
4. Have one partner interview the other one for five to ten minutes, listening attentively so he or she will remember important unique qualities and details about the person; at the end of five to ten minutes, have the partners switch roles.
5. After the stated time, call the pairs back to the community circle and ask each student to introduce his or her partner and share the special things he or she learned.

SUGGESTED REFLECTION QUESTIONS

CONTENT (COGNITIVE LEARNING)

- What new things did you learn from your partner?
- Why did you do this activity?

COLLABORATIVE (SOCIAL LEARNING)

- Why don't people take this type of time to get to know each other in other settings? In business and social organizations? In community meetings?
- What important social skills were used in this activity?
- What did community members do to make this activity successful?

DISCOVERING GIFTS (PERSONAL LEARNING)

- How well did you listen to your partner?
- How did you feel to have this much time to share about yourself?
- What did you learn about yourself that surprised you?
- What important social skills did you use during this activity?

APPRECIATION

Invite statements of appreciation (and recognition of gifts):

- "I appreciated it when…"
- "I liked it when…"

Milling to Music

OBJECTIVES

1. To build community inclusion
2. To review curriculum topic

INSTRUCTIONS

1. Prepare for each student a slip on which there are four numbered questions. Example:
   - Describe three cities, towns or houses in which you have lived.
   - Share your favorite way to relax or spend vacation time.
   - Describe what your house, apartment, or living space is like.
   - If you were given $100,000 tomorrow, what would you do with it?
2. Give the students their slips with the four topics and ask them to stand up.
3. Explain that when the music starts they are to begin milling around silently but greeting each other as they pass by.
4. Explain that when the music stops (or when you give the hand signal), each student is to stop and discuss question #1 with a student standing close by for 1 minute. Explain that when the music begins again, they are to repeat the process until they have discussed all four questions.

SUGGESTED REFLECTION QUESTIONS

CONTENT (COGNITIVE LEARNING)

- What kind of greetings did you use?
- What similar things did you share?

COLLABORATIVE (SOCIAL LEARNING)

- What skills did you, as community members, use to make this activity successful? (Suggest some: listening, speaking clearly, sharing time, respecting differences.)
- How has the atmosphere changed in the room?
- How do you feel about the community now?

DISCOVERING GIFTS (PERSONAL LEARNING)

- What did you learn about yourself?
- How are you a unique individual in the community?
- What special strengths are you proud of?

APPRECIATION

Invite statements of appreciation (and recognition of gifts):
- "I liked it when…"
- "I appreciated the sharing that (name) did."

TIME: 15–25 minutes

GROUPING: community

MATERIALS: slips with numbered topics, cassette tape player and lively music

DEVELOPMENTAL TASKS:
Social Competency
Sense of Purpose

Multiple Intelligence Exploration

TIME: varies

GROUPING: tribes

MATERIALS: multiple intelligence checklists, pencils

DEVELOPMENTAL TASKS:
Independence/Autonomy
Social Competency
Sense of Purpose

OBJECTIVES

1. To explore the concept of multiple intelligence as it relates to one's personal experiences and preferences
2. To identify one's learning preferences and ways of knowing (i.e., multiple intelligences)
3. To appreciate others' learning preferences, natural abilities, and differences

INSTRUCTIONS

1. Have the students meet in their tribes.
2. Ask, "Do you notice how you are each special in certain ways? Take a moment to think about how you are different from each other, different from your sisters or brothers, different from your friends in special ways."
3. Say, "See if you can identify and write down three unique qualities that you appreciate about yourself or that others appreciate about you."
4. Say, "Now share one of those qualities with your tribe members."
5. State, "Learning about your natural abilities and valuing your unique gifts can be very helpful. Today we will begin to explore your preferences—your special ways of learning and knowing."
6. Pass out the Multiple Intelligence Checklists and read the directions at the top. (*Note:* It is important to give students unlimited time to complete the checklist. You may want to divide the checklist up and allow time during several different days.)
7. After students have completed the checklists, review the characteristics of each of the nine multiple intelligences (see chapter 10). (*Note:* As recommended by Dr. Thomas Armstrong, this checklist does not contain elements from the Existential intelligence, as it is an area that is best identified through personal reflection.)
8. Have students tally their checklists according to the directions on the Multiple Intelligences Tally Sheet that follows the checklist.
9. Give the students an opportunity to share their preferred ways of learning and knowing with their tribe members.
10. State, "The results of this checklist are 'not cast in concrete.' Your preferred ways of learning may change with time as you develop new interests and experience new things. Share with your tribe members which area(s) you might be interested in developing a bit more." (*Note:* The checklist may be given at other times during the school year. Students may want to develop personal goals about exploring new MI areas through a variety of classroom projects.)

SUGGESTED REFLECTION QUESTIONS

CONTENT (COGNITIVE LEARNING)

- What did you learn from this activity?
- Which multiple intelligence is the easiest to understand? The hardest to understand?

COLLABORATIVE (SOCIAL LEARNING)

- How did you help each other during this activity?
- What different abilities did tribe members demonstrate to help make this activity successful?
- What special abilities do you appreciate about your tribe members?

DISCOVERING GIFTS (PERSONAL LEARNING)

- What did you discover about yourself?
- Did the results of your checklist "fit" or make sense for you?
- Which multiple intelligences are the most fun/most comfortable for you?
- Through which multiple intelligence(s) do you prefer to learn new material?

APPRECIATION

Invite statements of appreciation (and recognition of gifts):

- "You really helped out with..."
- "You are really good at..."
- "Thank you for..."

Reference:

"Multiple Intelligences Checklist," adapted from 7 Kinds of Smart *by Thomas Armstrong, ©1993 by Thomas Armstrong. Used by permission of Plume, a division of Penguin Putnam Inc. Educators and human development professionals worldwide appreciate the work that Dr. Armstrong has done to bring the concepts of multiple intelligence to life through enjoyable and meaningful application.*

MULTIPLE INTELLIGENCES CHECKLIST

INSTRUCTIONS:

It is hoped that this checklist will be fun to do and will help you discover your many gifts. This is not a test—it's just for your own information—but it is based on wonderful studies done by many wise people about how we learn and why it is really great to know our own preferences; each one of us is unique and our preferences help us understand our special ways of learning and knowing.

Check any items that seem to apply to you. You may check as many as you like.
Please have a good time and enjoy yourself!

1. _____ I enjoy reading books.

2. _____ I have always liked math and science classes best and I do well in them.

3. _____ I enjoy drawing, painting and doodling.

4. _____ I love being outdoors and enjoy spending my free time outside.

5. _____ I have a pleasant singing voice and I like to sing.

6. _____ I'm the kind of person others come to for advice.

7. _____ I have some important goals for my life that I think about often.

8. _____ I love animals and I spend a lot of time with them.

9. _____ I like English, social studies and history better than math and science.

10. _____ I try to look for patterns and regularities in things, such as every third stair on the staircase has a notch in it.

11. _____ I like to figure out how to take apart and put back together things like toys and puzzles.

12. _____ I am an active person and if I can't move around I get bored.

13. _____ I frequently listen to music because I enjoy it so much.

14. _____ I like going to parties and social events.

15. _____ I think I am a very independent person.

16. _____ I enjoy watching nature shows on television like the Discovery Channel, National Geographic and Nova.

17. _____ I am good at using words to get others to change their mind.

18. _____ I enjoy playing around with a chemistry set and am interested in new discoveries in science.

19. _____ When I watch a movie or video, I am more interested in what I see than what I hear.

20. _____ I think I am well coordinated.

21. _____ I can play a musical instrument.

22. _____ I don't like to argue with people.

23. _____ Sometimes I talk to myself.

24. _____ It's fun to watch birds or other animals, to watch their habits, and to learn more about them.

25. _____ I'm good at Scrabble and other word games.

26. _____ I believe that almost everything has a logical explanation.

27. _____ When I close my eyes, sometimes I can see clear images in my head that seem real.

28. _____ I have good skills in one or more sports and learn new sports quickly.

29. _____ I can easily keep time to a piece of music.

30. _____ I enjoy getting other people to work together.

31. _____ I like to spend time alone thinking about things that are important to me.

32. _____ I'm very good at telling the difference between different kinds of birds, dogs, trees and stuff like that.

33. _____ I like to learn new words and know their meanings.

34. _____ I like to play games and solve brainteasers that require tactics and strategy.

35. _____ I am good at reading maps and finding my way around unfamiliar places.

36. _____ I don't like organized team sports as much as individual sports activities, such as tennis, swimming, skiing, golf or ballet.

37. _____ I know the tunes and titles of many songs and musical pieces.

38. _____ I consider myself a leader (and others call me that).

39. _____ I would rather spend a vacation in a cabin in the woods than at a fancy resort.

40. _____ I enjoy visiting zoos, natural history museums or other places where the world is studied.

41. _____ It's easy for me to memorize things at school.

42. _____ It is fun for me to work with numbers and data.

43. _____ I like some colors better than others.

44. _____ I don't mind getting my hands dirty from activities like painting, clay, or fixing and building things.

45. _____ Sometimes I catch myself walking along with a television jingle or song in my mind.

46. _____ When I have a problem, I'll probably ask a friend for help.

47. _____ I think I know what I am good at and what I'm not so good at doing.

48. _____ I like being outside whenever possible; I feel confident and comfortable there.

49. _____ I like to look things up in the dictionary or an encyclopedia.

50. _____ I like to ask people questions about how things work or why nature is the way it is.

51. _____ I sketch or draw when I think.

52. _____ Sometimes when I talk with people, I gesture with my hands.

53. _____ I like to make up my own tunes and melodies.

54. _____ I have at least three close friends.

55. _____ I have hobbies and interests that I prefer to do on my own.

56. _____ I like camping and hiking.

57. _____ I like to talk to friends and family better than watching TV.

58. _____ I have an easy time understanding new math concepts in school.

59. _____ I enjoy reading things more when they have lots of pictures and drawings.

60. _____ I would rather play a sport than watch it.

61. _____ Often I keep time to music by tapping to the beat or humming the tune when I am studying or talking on the phone.

62. _____ I am easy to get to know.

63. _____ I want to be self-employed or maybe start my own business.

64. _____ I want to become a volunteer in an ecological organization (such as Greenpeace or Sierra Club) to help save nature from further destruction.

65. _____ I like to write things like stories, poems and reports.

66. _____ I like things better when they are organized, categorized or measured.

67. _____ I am good at playing Pictionary, doing jigsaw puzzles, and solving mazes.

68. _____ I like to "ham it up" in skits, plays, speeches, sports or other types of activities.

69. _____ I can tell when notes are off-key.

70. _____ I feel comfortable most of the time, even in the midst of a crowd.

71. _____ I like to spend time by myself thinking about things that I value.

72. _____ When I was younger I used to dislodge big rocks from the ground to discover the living things underneath.

73. _____ I'm really good at describing things in words.

74. _____ I think I am good at working with numbers and data.

75. _____ I am better at remembering faces than names.

76. _____ I like working with my hands in activities such as sewing, carving, or model-building.

77. _____ I know what I like and don't like in music.

78. _____ I am good at making new friends.

79. _____ I like to think about things before I take any action.

80. _____ I have a green thumb and I am really good at keeping plants alive and healthy.

Note: As recommended by Dr. Armstrong, this checklist does not contain elements from the Existential intelligence, as it is an area that is best identified through personal reflection.

Reference:
"Multiple Intelligences Checklist," adapted from 7 *Kinds of Smart,* by Thomas Armstrong, copyright ©1993 by Thomas Armstrong. Used by permission of Plume a division of Penguin Putnam Inc. The adaptation was done by Jeanne Mancour, who oversees Training Services for CenterSource Systems and who is a former high school teacher.

MULTIPLE INTELLIGENCES TALLY SHEET

Circle the numbers below that you checked on your Multiple Intelligence checklist.

Then count how many **circles** you have in each **column,** and write that number at the bottom of each column.

	1	2	3	4	5	6	7	8
	9	10	11	12	13	14	15	16
	17	18	19	20	21	22	23	24
	25	26	27	28	29	30	31	32
	33	34	35	36	37	38	39	40
	41	42	43	44	45	46	47	48
	49	50	51	52	53	54	55	56
	57	58	59	60	61	62	63	64
	65	66	67	68	69	70	71	72
	73	74	75	76	77	78	79	80
How many *circles* in each column?								
	LIN	L–M	SP	B–K	MU	NTER	NTRA	NAT

Look at the columns where you counted the most circles. You may have one, two or three areas that stand out. It doesn't really matter how many, but rather what "fits" and seems right for you. See the key below to discover your natural preferences!

LIN = Linguistic

L-M = Logical-Mathematical

SP = Spatial

B-K = Bodily-Kinesthetic

MU = Musical

NTER = Interpersonal

NTRA = Intrapersonal

NAT = Naturalist

Congratulations! You are a unique and special individual with many wonderful abilities, gifts and talents!

Newspaper Scavenger Hunt

OBJECTIVES

1. To learn how to find information in a newspaper
2. To work together to find the needed information
3. To experience influence

INSTRUCTIONS

1. Explain to the students that they will have ten to twenty minutes to find all the items in the paper described on the "Newspaper Scavenger Hunt" sheet, circle them in the newspaper with their colored pencil, and write the page numbers next to the items on the sheet. Say that everybody in the tribe is expected to participate and locate items.
2. Have the community meet in tribes. Assign roles in each tribe:
   - Taskmaster: gets the materials and monitors the time
   - Facilitator: ensures that each tribe member works his or her section of the paper
   - Spokesperson: reads the page numbers to the community when called upon
3. Have each taskmaster pick up one copy of the newspaper, one worksheet for his or her tribe, and a different colored pencil or pen for each tribe member.
4. Have each tribe divide the newspaper up between tribe members.
5. When time is up, ask the spokesperson from each tribe to share how many items his or her tribe was able to find. Randomly ask tribes to share what they found for various items on the worksheet.

TIME:	45 minutes
GROUPING:	tribes
MATERIALS:	one complete newspaper for each tribe, "Newspaper Scavenger Hunt" worksheets, colored pencils

DEVELOPMENTAL TASKS:
Independence/Autonomy
Problem Solving

SUGGESTED REFLECTION QUESTIONS

CONTENT (COGNITIVE LEARNING)

- What did you learn about using a newspaper?
- What are the sections of a newspaper?

COLLABORATIVE (SOCIAL LEARNING)

- Which agreement is the most important in a strategy like this?
- How did your tribe help each other to participate in this activity?

DISCOVERING GIFTS (PERSONAL LEARNING)

- How did you feel when you found your items in the newspaper?
- What special strengths or skills did you use in your role to help your tribe members?
- Which role suits you the best?

APPRECIATION

Invite statements of appreciation (and recognition of gifts):
- "I liked it when…"
- "Thanks, (name), for…"

Adapted from Lesson Plan: Scavenger Hunts, *by John Myers, Cooperative Learning, Spring, 1992*

NEWSPAPER SCAVENGER HUNT WORKSHEET

Look through your newspaper and locate the information asked for below. Circle the item in the paper with a colored pencil. Write in the page number where you found the information. When you are finished, fold the newspaper back into its original condition.

1. a comic where two people are arguing_____
2. an ad for a job in local or state government_____
3. a map_____
4. a picture of a famous person_____
5. the word "business"_____
6. an editorial article criticizing local, state, or federal government_____
7. an article about an environmental problem_____
8. the word "conflict"_____
9. an article about conflict in sports_____
10. an advertisement for a used car made in 1987_____
11. news about some aspect of education_____
12. a cartoon making a political statement_____
13. a letter to the editor about local government_____
14. an ad for a movie related to law enforcement_____
15. an article about a foreign country_____
16. a story which has to do with children_____
17. the word "defense"_____
18. an article relating to guns_____
19. a birth or death notice_____
20. the circulation (number of papers sold daily)_____

What strategy did your tribe use?

_____

_____

Make up four more questions:

_____

Adapted from Lesson Plan: Scavenger Hunts, *by John Myers, Cooperative Learning, Spring, 1992*

This page may be duplicated for classroom use.

NOW I AM

TIME: 20 minutes

GROUPING: community

MATERIALS: none

DEVELOPMENTAL TASKS:
Social Competency

OBJECTIVES

1. To recognize and identify feelings
2. To develop observation skills
3. To build inclusion

INSTRUCTIONS

1. Have the community sit in a circle; review the agreements.
2. Whisper a different feeling or emotion in each students' ear one at a time:
   Examples:

fear	frustration	surprise	rage
nervousness	hope	soreness	love
dreaminess	anger	uncomfortable	wild
unhappiness	tired	embarrassed	weird
itchiness	stubborn	excitement	sleepy

3. Ask the students to act out their words nonverbally.
4. Have the community guess what each student is acting out.

SUGGESTED REFLECTION QUESTIONS

CONTENT (COGNITIVE LEARNING)

- Which feelings were the easiest/most difficult to act out?
- How did you figure out what feeling was being represented?

COLLABORATIVE (SOCIAL LEARNING)

- How can you help each other discover the feelings you have at different times?
- Why is it sometimes difficult to act or speak in front of a group? What did the community do to help make it easier and fun?

DISCOVERING GIFTS (PERSONAL LEARNING)

- What did you enjoy about this activity?
- What did you learn about yourself by participating in this activity?

APPRECIATION

Invite statements of appreciation (and recognition of gifts):

- "I liked the way you acted it out because…"
- "I feel a lot like you when…"

FOLLOW-UP ACTIVITIES

Have each student:

1. Draw feelings using colors that match the feelings.
2. Make a face of how you feel this minute.
3. Write a story about a person who always acts the same.
4. Print feeling words on cards, and have people act them out.

Observe The Put-Downs

TIME: 40 minutes

GROUPING: community

MATERIALS: taped ½ hour sitcom, age appropriate

DEVELOPMENTAL TASKS:
Independence/Autonomy
Social Competency
Sense of Purpose

OBJECTIVES

1. To promote awareness of put-downs and their effects
2. To practice reflecting on systems and situations

INSTRUCTIONS

1. Have a ½ hour, age appropriate sitcom videotaped and ready to view.
2. Ask the students to predict how many put-downs are present in a typical ½ hour comedy.
3. Tell the students to watch closely, and write down a tally mark each time they hear a put-down.
4. After five minutes, stop the tape and have the students share statements from the show that they marked as put-downs.
5. Continue watching/tallying until the end of the show. (*Note:* Do not be surprised if the totals for a ½ hour show are over 50!)

SUGGESTED REFLECTION QUESTIONS

CONTENT (COGNITIVE LEARNING)

- Why do people laugh at put-downs on TV?
- Who is never laughing at the put-downs?
- How many of this type of shows do people watch per week?

COLLABORATIVE (SOCIAL LEARNING)

- Why is the tribes agreement of "no put-downs" so important?
- How can you tell the difference between humor and put-downs?
- How can you help others to see the difference between humor and put-downs?

DISCOVERING GIFTS (PERSONAL LEARNING)

- What did you feel as your tally grew larger?
- How can you effect a change in put-downs/humor in your own life?
- What personal strengths will help you to help others not put people down?

APPRECIATION

Invite statements of appreciation (and recognition of gifts):
- "I appreciate…"
- "You were really good at…"
- "Thanks for…"

On My Back

OBJECTIVES

1. To build self-esteem
2. To encourage giving statements of appreciation
3. To build inclusion

INSTRUCTIONS

1. Give each student a large piece of paper, a felt marker, and two pieces of masking tape.
2. Ask each student to print his or her name at the top of the paper.
3. Have the students attach the papers to each other's shoulders so that they hang down like capes on their backs.
4. Have the students stand and circulate so that each person in the group can write statements of appreciation on other people's paper capes. Emphasize that the statements need to be positive.
5. When each student has several written statements on his or her cape, ask the community to sit in a circle or have them form tribes. Have the students read their statements aloud or have them exchange papers and read to each other.
6. Encourage people to save their papers, perhaps to use as posters for their bedroom walls.

SUGGESTED REFLECTION QUESTIONS

CONTENT (COGNITIVE LEARNING)

- What were some of the neat things people wrote?
- What similarities did you see in what people wrote?
- How did the fact that this activity was anonymous help you to be honest?

COLLABORATIVE (SOCIAL LEARNING)

- How did you take care of each other?
- How did you take turns?
- What can you do to offer positive statements to others more often?

DISCOVERING GIFTS (PERSONAL LEARNING)

- What feelings did you have while people were writing on your back?
- What feelings did you have while your statements were being read aloud or while you were reading your statements?
- What statements felt very special to you?
- What new gifts did you discover after hearing the statements that were written about you?

APPRECIATION

Invite statements of appreciation (and recognition of gifts):
- "I like it when…"
- "I felt good when…"

TIME:	20 minutes
GROUPING:	community, tribes
MATERIALS:	large paper, tape, markers

DEVELOPMENTAL TASKS:
Independence/Autonomy
Social Competency
Sense of Purpose

OPTION

Use as a learning strategy for well known characters in history, politics, current events, literature, etc.

One-Minute History

TIME: 20–30 minutes

GROUPING: community, tribes, triads

MATERIALS: none

DEVELOPMENTAL TASKS:
Independence/Autonomy
Social Competency
Sense of Purpose

OBJECTIVES

1. To give each student an opportunity to share his or her background
2. To build inclusion

INSTRUCTIONS

1. Have the community sit in a circle or meet in tribes or triads.
2. Instruct the students that each student will have one minute in turn to tell his or her personal history. Remind the listeners to give full attention without interrupting.

SUGGESTED REFLECTION QUESTIONS

CONTENT (COGNITIVE LEARNING)

- What did you learn about someone else?
- Why is it important to be able to summarize your life?

COLLABORATIVE (SOCIAL LEARNING)

- How could you tell that others were using good listening skills?
- Why was a minute enough/not enough time to share?
- Did the students who shared later in the activity share more or less? Why?
- How did you help each other during this activity?

DISCOVERING GIFTS (PERSONAL LEARNING)

- How did you feel about sharing?
- What special skills did you use to help your group during this activity?
- How are you a unique individual in the group?

APPRECIATION

Invite statements of appreciation (and recognition of gifts):
- "I liked it when you said…"
- "I felt good when…"
- "I was particularly interested when you…"

One Special Thing About Me

OBJECTIVES

1. To give students an opportunity to introduce themselves
2. To give students an opportunity to work in pairs before sharing
3. To promote inclusion

INSTRUCTIONS

1. Have the community sit in a circle. Say that we are a unique group about to start an exciting journey together and, like any people coming together, we need to learn about each other.
2. Say: "Think about yourself and something about you that people would remember. Think about something that makes you special. It doesn't have to be something big, but it needs to say something about you. It can be silly, fun, sentimental, or kind."
3. State that there will be one minute of quiet time before sharing with a partner.
4. After the minute, ask each student to share with a partner for two to three minutes.
5. After the students have shared with their partners, ask them to re-form the community circle.
6. Then go around the circle, inviting each student to state his or her name and what makes him or her special. Start with yourself to provide good modeling.

SUGGESTED REFLECTION QUESTIONS

CONTENT (COGNITIVE LEARNING)

- Why is it difficult to think of something that makes you special?
- What types of things make you feel special?

COLLABORATIVE (SOCIAL LEARNING)

- Why is it easier to share with a partner?
- What social skills did community members use to make this activity successful?

DISCOVERING GIFTS (PERSONAL LEARNING)

- How did you feel sharing with one other person?
- How did you feel sharing in the community circle?
- What did you discover about yourself?
- What is something special that you are proud of?

APPRECIATION

Invite statements of appreciation (and recognition of gifts):

- "I liked it when you said…"
- "Thank you for sharing…"

TIME: 35–45 minutes

GROUPING: community, pairs

MATERIALS: none

DEVELOPMENTAL TASKS:
Independence/Autonomy
Social Competency
Sense of Purpose

One, Two, Three

TIME: 10–15 minutes

GROUPING: community, tribes, subgroups

MATERIALS: pencils, paper

DEVELOPMENTAL TASKS:
Independence/Autonomy
Social Competency
Sense of Purpose

OBJECTIVES

1. To make choices between competing alternatives
2. To allow students to affirm and explain their choices
3. To practice decision-making
4. To promote influence

INSTRUCTIONS

1. Ask the students to meet in tribes, form groups of four to six, or meet as a community.
2. State that you will ask a question and then offer three alternative answers. Tell the students that you will be asking them to make some choices by ranking the three alternatives in the order of their importance or preference. Tell each student to write down the three alternatives and then put a number 1, number 2 or number 3 after each item according to his or her first, second and third choice. Examples:
    • Where would you rather be on a Saturday afternoon?
      at the beach?
      in the woods?
      window shopping downtown?
    • Which do you consider most important in a friendship?
      honesty?
      loyalty?
      generosity?
3. Have the students share their choices with each other and explain why they made the selections.

SUGGESTED REFLECTION QUESTIONS

CONTENT (COGNITIVE LEARNING)

• How did your choices compare to choices made by others?
• Why are some choices harder to make than others?
• What choices might be more difficult/easier to make?

COLLABORATIVE (SOCIAL LEARNING)

• Why is being able to make a choice an important skill?
• What did you, as a community, do to make this activity successful?

DISCOVERING GIFTS (PERSONAL LEARNING)

• What feelings did you have when you had difficulty choosing?
• What have you learned about yourself?
• What personal strengths or skills helped you make your choices?
• In what special way did you contribute to the group?

APPRECIATION

Invite statements of appreciation (and recognition of gifts):
    • "I liked it when…"
    • "I appreciated your dilemma when…"

Open Forum

TIME: 30 minutes

GROUPING: tribes, subgroups

MATERIALS: none

DEVELOPMENTAL TASKS:
Independence/Autonomy
Sense of Purpose

OBJECTIVES

1. To encourage acceptance of diverse feelings, beliefs, and cultures
2. To build inclusion

INSTRUCTIONS

1. Have the community meet in tribes or subgroups.
2. Tell the students that you will write a discussion question on the chalkboard, and each tribe member is to take a turn responding to the question. Discussion is not allowed until each tribe member has had an opportunity to respond to the question. After all tribe members have had a chance to speak, students may ask one another follow-up questions and ask for clarification of what was said.
3. Remind the groups about the tribe agreements, especially "attentive listening."
4. Examples of inclusion questions:
    • What is the best book you ever read? Why did you like it?
    • How did you select your friends?
    • What guides your life?
    • If you could be an animal for a day, what would you be? Why?
    • What goal do you have for your future?

SUGGESTED REFLECTION QUESTIONS

CONTENT (COGNITIVE LEARNING)

• What was something you learned from your discussion?

COLLABORATIVE (SOCIAL LEARNING)

• What social skills did your group use to make this activity successful?
• How could you tell that your tribe members were being good listeners when you shared?

DISCOVERING GIFTS (PERSONAL LEARNING)

• How did you feel answering the questions?
• How did you participate? Are you happy with the way you participated? Why?
• How did you help the group in a special way?
• What did you learn about yourself from participating in this activity?

APPRECIATION

Invite statements of appreciation (and recognition of gifts):
    • "I liked it when…"
    • "I'm a lot like you when…"
    • "You're a lot like me when…"

OPTION

Use the strategy for academic questions.

Our Treasury

TIME: 60 minutes

GROUPING: tribes

MATERIALS: none

DEVELOPMENTAL TASKS:
Independence/Autonomy
Problem Solving

OBJECTIVES

1. To allow for individual influence
2. To practice group decision-making

INSTRUCTIONS

1. Ask the community to meet in tribes.
2. Give each group a fictitious sum of money (or paper money), which is to be its tribe treasury.
3. Tell each tribe to brainstorm about the best uses of this money. (Review the brainstorming process if necessary.) Have the tribes make a list of their ideas.
4. Have each tribe decide what four things on its list it would spend its treasury on.
5. Ask each tribe to report its decision to the community.

SUGGESTED REFLECTION QUESTIONS

CONTENT (COGNITIVE LEARNING)

- What were some of the things you listed?
- What did you learn about making choices?
- Why is deciding how to spend money often difficult?

COLLABORATIVE (SOCIAL LEARNING)

- How did you resolve differences of opinion among tribe members?
- What are the most important social skills you need when making decisions as a tribe?

DISCOVERING GIFTS (PERSONAL LEARNING)

- How do you feel about the decisions you made?
- What have you learned about yourself?
- How did you contribute to your tribe in a positive way?

APPRECIATION

Invite statements of appreciation (and recognition of gifts):
- "I appreciated it when…"
- "I knew what you meant when you said…"
- "I liked it when…"

Our World Is Changing

OBJECTIVES

1. To create a tribe list of changes in the world
2. To give individuals an appreciation of change
3. To practice brainstorming

INSTRUCTIONS

1. Have the community meet in tribes and have the tribe members greet each other.
2. Review the rules for brainstorming (see "Brainstorming" strategy).
3. Have each tribe select a recorder. Have the recorders raise their hands so you can be certain each recorder is ready.
4. Have the tribes brainstorm and write lists of how the world has changed since their parents (or grandparents) were born. Give the tribes five minutes to brainstorm.
5. Have the community meet. Have tribes report one or two changes that have made an impact on their lives. (*Suggestion:* Ask the student with the shortest hair in each tribe, or some other characteristic, to report.)

SUGGESTED REFLECTION QUESTIONS

CONTENT (COGNITIVE LEARNING)

- What do you feel are the most important changes that have happened?
- Why is it important to know how the world has changed?

COLLABORATIVE (SOCIAL LEARNING)

- Why is brainstorming a good strategy to use?
- What social skills did your group need or use to be successful at this strategy?

DISCOVERING GIFTS (PERSONAL LEARNING)

- How did you feel sharing the changes you recognized?
- What did you do to help your tribe?
- What special strengths or skills do you bring to your tribe??

APPRECIATION

Invite statements of appreciation (and recognition of gifts):

- "I liked it when you said…"
- "Thank you for…"

TIME: 45 minutes

GROUPING: community, tribes

MATERIALS: paper, pencils

DEVELOPMENTAL TASKS:
Independence/Autonomy
Problem Solving

OPTION

Have the tribes conduct research, interviews, or make graphs, drawings or collages that show how the world has changed since their parents were born.

Outlines

TIME: 30–40 minutes

GROUPING: community, tribes

MATERIALS: "T-Shirt Outline" worksheet, colored pens or pencils

DEVELOPMENTAL TASKS:
Independence/Autonomy
Social Competency
Sense of Purpose

NOTE

There are endless other fine questions for this activity: someone you admire, a quality you like in a friend, something you want to learn, favorite subject or book, academic material. Select those most appropriate for the group's age and culture.

OBJECTIVES

1. To build inclusion
2. To practice communication and listening skills
3. To discuss academic topics

INSTRUCTIONS

1. Have the students meet either in their tribes or the community circle.
2. Explain the objectives, and pass out "T-Shirt Outline" worksheets.
3. Tell students how to fill in the outline:
   - in area #1 write an alliterative adjective that goes with your first name. Example: "Vivacious Vicki"
   - in area #2 write or draw two to three things you enjoy doing
   - in area #3 name a real or pretend place you would like to visit
   - in area #4 write a word you'd like people to say when they describe you
   - in area #5 write a wish you have for yourself
4. Sharing: First review the Tribes agreements, and ask the students to share the time equally so that each student has an opportunity to speak during each round.
   - Round 1: each student shares his or her name and alliterative adjective with another student, telling why he or she chose the adjective (three minutes).
   - Round 2: each student finds two other people and shares the information he or she wrote in area #2 (four minutes).
   - Round 3: each student finds two other people and shares the information of area #3 (four minutes).
   - Round 4: each finds three to four others and shares area #4 (four minutes).
   - Round 5: each Round 4 group combines with another Round 4 group. Names and alliterative adjectives are shared again with students telling why they chose their particular adjectives.

SUGGESTED REFLECTION QUESTIONS

CONTENT (COGNITIVE LEARNING)
- What did you learn about your tribe members?
- What were the similarities among your tribe members' wishes?

COLLABORATIVE (SOCIAL LEARNING)
- How could you tell when people were listening well to each other?
- How many students do you feel you know better now?

DISCOVERING GIFTS (PERSONAL LEARNING)
- What did you enjoy most about this activity?
- What did you learn about yourself from this activity?
- What unique qualities do you bring to your group?

APPRECIATION

Invite statements of appreciation (and recognition of gifts):
- "I like it when…"
- "I'm glad you're…"

T-SHIRT OUTLINE

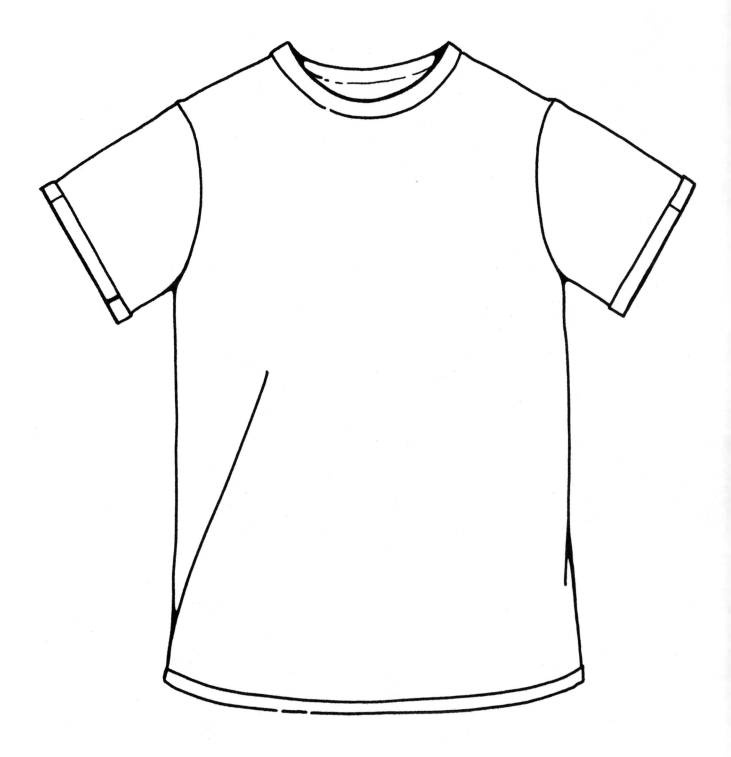

Pantomime

TIME: 20 minutes

GROUPING: community

MATERIALS: none

DEVELOPMENTAL TASKS:
Independence/Autonomy
Social Competency

OBJECTIVES

1. To build self-esteem
2. To build inclusion
3. To experience communication without words

INSTRUCTIONS

1. Have the students form two groups. Have each group take a turn doing expressions and movements.
2. There is no discussion until both groups have finished.
3. The following are suggestions of expressions and movement:
    - facial expressions: funny, scared, sad
    - feeling walks: walk angrily, walk sadly
    - weather walks: walk in the rain
    - people walks: robber, clown
    - animal walks: dog, cat, duck
    - characters and situations: an acrobat on a tightrope
    - exploring senses: taste a lemon, smell a skunk
    - handling imaginary objects: play with a yo-yo
    - experiencing different environments: you are on the moon

SUGGESTED REFLECTION QUESTIONS

CONTENT (COGNITIVE LEARNING)

- Why was it easy/difficult to demonstrate your feelings?
- What did you find out about others in your group?

COLLABORATIVE (SOCIAL LEARNING)

- What did we have to do to make this activity successful?
- How could you tell that others were being good watchers and listeners?

DISCOVERING GIFTS (PERSONAL LEARNING)

- What did you find out about yourself? How are you a unique individual?
- What special skills did you use during this activity?

APPRECIATION

Invite statements of appreciation (and recognition of gifts):
- "I liked it when…"
- "I'm like you when…"
- "I felt good when…"

Paraphrase Passport*

OBJECTIVES

1. To follow up on the "Reflective Feeling" strategy
2. To practice listening
3. To practice paraphrasing while discussing a topic

INSTRUCTIONS

1. Review the strategy "Reflecting Feelings" with the community. Have the students discuss how they felt when they played the roles of speaker, feeling reflector, and observer.
2. Tell students they will be discussing topics by using "paraphrasing passports," which is a way to learn how to be a good listener. In "Paraphrase Passport" no one has permission to speak until he or she correctly restates (paraphrases) the idea of the previous speaker. Example:

   John: "I am concerned that violence is increasing in many cities, and believe that unemployment is a major cause."

   Sarah: "John, you are concerned about the increase in violence and attribute it to unemployment."

3. Have students again form the triads they were in for "Reflecting Feelings" and choose who will be the first speaker. Explain that the first student contributes an idea and the second student must restate it correctly before contributing his or her idea.

   Topic to discuss:

   "How does good listening help to develop caring and learning in a community?"

SUGGESTED REFLECTION QUESTIONS

CONTENT (COGNITIVE LEARNING)

- What did you learn from your discussion about listening?
- Why is listening an important social skill?

COLLABORATIVE (SOCIAL LEARNING)

- How well did you paraphrase what the person before you said?
- How did your group help each other during this activity?

DISCOVERING GIFTS (PERSONAL LEARNING)

- How might "Paraphrase Passport" help you to listen to others?
- How could good listening help you to be a better friend?
- What communication skills do feel particularly good at?

APPRECIATION

Invite statements of appreciation (and recognition of gifts):

- "I liked it when you said…"
- "It felt good when…"

---

* This structure is from Cooperative Learning, Resources for Teachers, by Spencer Kagan

TIME:	20 minutes
GROUPING:	community, triads, tribes
MATERIALS:	none
DEVELOPMENTAL TASKS:	Independence/Autonomy Social Competency

Paraphrasing

TIME: 30–45 minutes

GROUPING: community, tribes

MATERIALS: colored paper strips

SUBJECT: language therapy or bilingual education

DEVELOPMENTAL TASKS:

Independence/Autonomy
Social Competency
Sense of Purpose

OBJECTIVES

1. To build inclusion and influence
2. To teach and practice paraphrasing

INSTRUCTIONS

VERSION A:

1. Have the community stand or sit in a large circle.
2. Turn to the student on your left and ask a question. Examples:
   - "What is your favorite color?"
   - "What is your favorite holiday?"
   - "What is your favorite fruit?"
3. The next student answers and the first student who asked the question repeats back the answer. Example:
   Student #1: "What's your favorite color?"
   Student #2: "Red."
   Student #1: "Shawn's favorite color is red."
4. Have students continue the sequence around the circle.

VERSION B:

1. Give all the students colored paper strips prepared as follows:
   "_____'s favorite _____ is _____."
2. Have tribe members pair up and decide who is #1 and who is #2.
3. Have partner #1 ask a question and partner #2 give the answer.
4. Then have partner #1 fill in the blanks on his or her strip.
5. Have partners switch so that partner #2 now asks the question.
6. After all the students fill in the blanks on their colored strips have the tribes staple the strips together and display them.

SUGGESTED REFLECTION QUESTIONS

CONTENT (COGNITIVE LEARNING)

- What similarities did you notice in people's answers?
- Why are we learning about paraphrasing?

COLLABORATIVE (SOCIAL LEARNING)

- Why is it important to take turns in this strategy?
- How could you tell people were cooperating during this activity?

DISCOVERING GIFTS (PERSONAL LEARNING)

- How did you like working with a partner?
- What did you contribute during this activity?
- What "people skills" do you feel most comfortable using?

APPRECIATION

Invite statements of appreciation (and recognition of gifts):
- "I liked working with you, (name), because…"
- "Thank you for..."

OPTION

The activity can be used for various combinations of curriculum materials. A variation on Version A is to have students ask each other across the circle or to integrate it with the "Spider Web" activity. In Version B, older students work in groups of three or four, asking and recording things they have learned on any lesson topic.

Partner Introduction

OBJECTIVES

1. To give students an opportunity to introduce themselves
2. To give students an opportunity to work in pairs before sharing
3. To experience inclusion

INSTRUCTIONS

1. State that we are a unique group about to start an exciting journey together, and, like any people coming together, we need to learn about each other.
2. Have each student find a partner he or she does not know very well. Have the partners decide who will be the interviewer and who will be the interviewed. For one minute the interviewer will tell his partner all the things that he does not know about him. The interviewee is only to listen and not respond. For example, an interviewer might say, "I don't know your name," "I don't know how many people are in your family," etc.
3. The partner being interviewed then responds for two minutes giving information that they would be willing to have shared with the whole community.
4. Have the partners switch roles and repeat the strategy.
5. Have the community form a circle and have each student introduce his or her partner to the community, and share one thing they learned about their partner.

SUGGESTED REFLECTION QUESTIONS

CONTENT (COGNITIVE LEARNING)

- What did you learn about your partner?
- What are the most common things you shared?

COLLABORATIVE (SOCIAL LEARNING)

- Why might interviewing be a good way to get to know somebody?
- Why is attentive listening so important for this strategy?
- What special strengths or skills did community members use to make this activity successful?

DISCOVERING GIFTS (PERSONAL LEARNING)

- How did you feel to interview your partner?
- How did you feel to have your partner share what you said?
- What communication or "people skills" do you feel particularly good using?

APPRECIATION

Invite statements of appreciation (and recognition of gifts):

- "One thing I liked was…"
- "Thank you for…"

TIME: 35–45 minutes

GROUPING: community, pairs

MATERIALS: none

DEVELOPMENTAL TASKS:
Independence/Autonomy
Social Competency
Sense of Purpose

Path-Maze

TIME: 30 minutes

GROUPING: pairs, community

MATERIALS: masking tape

DEVELOPMENTAL TASKS:
Social Competency
Problem Solving

OPTION

This activity may be used to reinforce subject related content material. Students enjoy making the path more difficult by having "language of the discipline" vocabulary words written in the grid squares. The students must define the words in order to proceed. With subject related material, allow team members to discuss the answers before they make a decision.

OBJECTIVES

1. To help pairs begin to experience the stage of influence
2. To develop non-verbal problem solving skills
3. To energize students and build community
4. To reinforce subject related content material

INSTRUCTIONS

1. Use masking tape to draw a giant grid on the floor. Make the grid approximately 10 feet wide by 12½ feet long. Use the tape to make 4 squares across and 5 squares long. Each square is approximately 2½ feet by 2½ feet in size.
2. On a piece of scratch paper, draw the grid and trace an imaginary path through the grid.
3. Have the students line up on one side of the grid and tell them that you have traced an imaginary pathway through the grid from one end to the other. However, let them know that you are the only one who knows the secret pathway. It is their job to find out for themselves the secret path. The students can work individually (intrapersonally) or with a partner (interpersonally) to see if they can find the secret path, however, they cannot talk to each other. If they step on a square that is on the secret path, they will hear (teacher will say) a "ding," which means they are correct. If they step in a square that is not on the secret path, they will hear an "errrrr," which means they are incorrect. If they hear the ding, they can proceed on. If they hear the "errrr," they must go to the end of the line and start over.
4. The next pair in the line must remember the path from the previous pairs' trials and errors as they attempt to find the path through the maze.
5. When an individual or team has found the secret path, the group may talk about the experience.

SUGGESTED REFLECTION QUESTIONS

CONTENT (COGNITIVE LEARNING)

- How is this grid like being a new student in a classroom or school?
- What multiple intelligences might be useful to solve this puzzle?
- How is this activity like "life?"

COLLABORATIVE (SOCIAL LEARNING)

- How did you learn to negotiate with your partner when you weren't allowed to use words?
- How did you and your partner help each other?

DISCOVERING GIFTS (PERSONAL LEARNING)

- How would you change your approach to solving the puzzle?
- What skills did you use to solve the puzzle?
- What new gifts did you discover about yourself?

APPRECIATION

Invite statements of appreciation (and recognition of gifts):

"I appreciated…"

"I liked it when…"

"You were really good at…"

Peer-Response Huddle

TIME: 15 minutes

GROUPING: tribes

MATERIALS: none, or 5 x 7–inch cards

DEVELOPMENTAL TASKS:
Independence/Autonomy
Sense of Purpose
Problem Solving

OBJECTIVES

1. To structure a cooperative learning experience
2. To develop energy and interest in curricula
3. To build pride
4. To promote influence

INSTRUCTIONS

1. Have the community meet in tribes.
2. Have the tribe members count off, beginning with the number one, or pass out numbered cards so that each tribe member has a number.
3. Tell the students that you will call out a question, and that each tribe has thirty seconds to huddle and decide upon one answer. Say you will then call out a number, and that each tribe member with that number will quickly stand up. Say you will ask one of the students standing to give the answer.
4. Keep the questions, huddle time, and responses going as rapidly as possible so that the energy takes on a "popcorn" effect. Don't call on the first person that pops up unless you intend to promote competition. After an answer is given, lead the applause.

SUGGESTED REFLECTION QUESTIONS

CONTENT (COGNITIVE LEARNING)

• What did you learn that you didn't know before?
• Why is this a good way to review information?

COLLABORATIVE (SOCIAL LEARNING)

• What social skills did your tribe need to be successful?
• How can your tribe improve the way it worked together?

DISCOVERING GIFTS (PERSONAL LEARNING)

• How did you feel when your number was called?
• How did you help your tribe in a special way?
• What personal strengths did you discover about yourself?
• How do you feel about your tribe now?

APPRECIATION

Invite statements of appreciation (and recognition of gifts):
• "I liked it when…"
• "I want to thank you, (name), for…"

Acknowledgement to Spencer Kagan's structure, "Numbered Heads Together"

Peer-Response Tic-Tac-Toe

OBJECTIVES

1. To promote decision-making
2. To review content-related vocabulary

INSTRUCTIONS

Note: This is played similar to "bingo" but on a Tic-Tac-Toe format.

1. Write a list of ten vocabulary words on the board, numbered 1–10. (*Note:* You may also use ten words relating to subject material, such as state capitals.)
2. Have students meet in tribes or groups of 4–5.
3. Have each student draw his/her own Tic-Tac-Toe board and randomly write down one number in each square, using nine out of ten numbers from 1-10.
4. Say the definition or clue related to a word on the list. Example: This state capital hosts the Aloha Bowl each January.
5. Have the students, in tribes, discuss which numbered answer is correct, and have them mark an "X" on the numbered square on their individual tic-tac-toe boards.
6. When a winner is declared in each tribe, simply start a new game.
7. After 5–10 minutes, ask various students to come up with the definitions or clues for each word.

SUGGESTED REFLECTION QUESTIONS

CONTENT (COGNITIVE LEARNING)

- What did you learn?
- How did you improve your knowledge of this subject?

COLLABORATIVE (SOCIAL LEARNING)

- How did you know that your group members were listening well to each other?
- What were some things that your group members did to help each other?
- Why is learning in a group more valuable than learning individually?

DISCOVERING GIFTS (PERSONAL LEARNING)

- How did you contribute to your tribe?
- What personal strengths or skills helped you during this activity?
- How do you usually prefer to learn information like this?

APPRECIATION

Invite statements of appreciation (and recognition of gifts):

- "I liked how…"
- "One thing I like about this group is…"
- "Thank you for…"

TIME: 20–30 minutes

GROUPING: community, tribes

MATERIALS: paper, pencils

DEVELOPMENTAL TASKS:
Independence/Autonomy
Problem Solving

People Hunt

TIME: 40 minutes

GROUPING: community

MATERIALS: "People Hunt" worksheets, pencils

DEVELOPMENTAL TASKS:
Independence/Autonomy
Social Competency
Sense of Purpose

OPTIONS

Personalize the "People Hunt" by looking at students' permanent folders and making up relevant questions.

Use the strategy to review academic subjects by writing appropriate questions.

OBJECTIVES

1. To promote community inclusion
2. To introduce oneself to others
3. To encourage sharing information

INSTRUCTIONS

1. Give one-third of the students worksheet I, one-third worksheet II, and one-third worksheet III.
2. Have the students circulate around the room, stopping to introduce him or herself, and asking different students the questions listed on his or her worksheet. Tell them to write down the names of those who fit the descriptions.
3. After ten to fifteen minutes, ask the community to meet in tribes or form groups of five for reflection questions.

SUGGESTED REFLECTION QUESTIONS

CONTENT (COGNITIVE LEARNING)

• What did you learn that impressed or surprised you?

COLLABORATIVE (SOCIAL LEARNING)

• How could you tell when group members were participating fully in this task?
• What social skills were used to be successful with this task?

DISCOVERING GIFTS (PERSONAL LEARNING)

• How did you approach this task, did you go to people or did you wait for people to come to you?
• What strengths or skills did you use?
• What did you learn about yourself from this activity?
• Do you feel any different now than when you first walked into the room?

APPRECIATION

Invite statements of appreciation (and recognition of gifts):
• "I liked it when you…"
• "I felt good when…"
• "I'm like you when…"

PEOPLE HUNT WORKSHEET I

FIND:

1. A person who does not own a TV

   His or her name is_____

2. A person whose birthday is within a month of yours

   His or her name is_____

3. A person who can cross his or her eyes

   His or her name is_____

4. A person who traveled over 2,000 miles last summer

   His or her name is_____

5. A person who lives in a house where no one smokes

   His or her name is_____

6. A person who owns a horse

   His or her name is_____

7. A person who is new to this school

   His or her name is_____

8. A person who likes brussels sprouts

   His or her name is_____

9. A person who is an artist

   His or her name is_____

10. A person who has more than six brothers and sisters

    His or her name is_____

This page may be duplicated for classroom use.

PEOPLE HUNT WORKSHEET II

FIND:

1. A person who can speak two languages

   His or her name is_____

2. A person who has been to a concert

   His or her name is_____

3. A person who has two different colored eyes

   His or her name is_____

4. A person with a new baby in his or her home

   His or her name is_____

5. A person whose birthday is the same month as yours

   His or her name is_____

6. A person who can roll his or her tongue

   His or her name is_____

7. A person who has been ice skating this past year

   His or her name is_____

8. A person not born in this country

   His or her name is_____

9. A person who has more than four animals in his or her home

   His or her name is_____

10. A person who woke up with a smile this morning

    His or her name is_____

This page may be duplicated for classroom use.

PEOPLE HUNT WORKSHEET III

FIND:

1. A person not born in California (New York, Texas, etc.)

   His or her name is_____

2. A person who stayed home last summer

   His or her name is_____

3. A person whose birthday is one month before yours

   His or her name is_____

4. A person who is the oldest child in his or her family

   His or her name is_____

5. A person who can touch his or her nose with his or her tongue

   His or her name is_____

6. A person who likes to invent things

   His or her name is_____

7. A person who jogs for exercise

   His or her name is_____

8. A person who has four dogs in his or her home

   His or her name is_____

9. A person who has been horseback riding in the past three months

   His or her name is_____

10. A person who has planted a tree

    His or her name is_____

This page may be duplicated for classroom use.

People Puzzles

TIME: 20 minutes

GROUPING: tribes

MATERIALS: picture, puzzles

DEVELOPMENTAL TASKS:
Social Competency
Problem Solving

OBJECTIVES

1. To build inclusion
2. To form or assign membership in tribes

INSTRUCTIONS

1. Before using the strategy, prepare one puzzle for each group or tribe. Cut each puzzle so that the number of pieces matches the number of people in each group or tribe.
2. To build random groups, put all the pieces of all the puzzles in a box and have each person take a piece. To assign tribes put the name of one person on each piece of puzzle.
3. Before having the students form their tribes, have a discussion about what possible put-downs could occur and how to avoid them.
4. Ask the students to circulate and find the puzzle pieces that match the ones they are carrying. Tell them they are not to talk while doing this. Tell them they may talk when their group's puzzle has been completed.
5. Once all of the puzzles have been completed, you may choose to have each tribe make up a story relating to the picture its puzzle has formed. Have each tribe select one member to be a storyteller and tell the tribe's story to the community.

SUGGESTED REFLECTION QUESTIONS

CONTENT (COGNITIVE LEARNING)

- What made this task difficult/easy?
- Was this a fun way to find students who would be in your tribe?

COLLABORATIVE (SOCIAL LEARNING)

- How did you help students whose puzzle pieces didn't fit yours?
- What did you talk about when your puzzle was completed?
- How did you help each other during this activity?

DISCOVERING GIFTS (PERSONAL LEARNING)

- How did you feel when you first started this activity? At the end?
- How were you able to help your tribe?
- What did you discover about yourself from participating in this activity?

APPRECIATION

Invite statements of appreciation (and recognition of gifts):
- "I liked it when…"
- "I'm a lot like you when…"
- "I admire you for…"

Perception And Transmission Of Information

OBJECTIVES

1. To promote inclusion and influence
2. To promote an understanding of different points of view
3. To demonstrate how perceptual limitations can affect communications

INSTRUCTIONS

1. Have the community meet in tribes.
2. After an inclusion activity, hand out copies of the young girl/old woman drawing to each tribe. Instruct the tribe members to glance at the drawings briefly, without discussion. Then collect all copies immediately.
3. Ask people to share what they saw in the drawing. Emphasize the concept that people perceive differently; ask questions such as, "Would you talk to this person on the bus?" or, "Does this person remind you of someone you may have met or know?"
4. Give copies of the drawing to each tribe member and have the tribes continue the discussion.
5. Assist students who have difficulty identifying both aspects of the drawing.
6. Have the tribe members expand their discussions to other areas in which their points of view might be limited by their perception of information.

SUGGESTED REFLECTION QUESTIONS

CONTENT (COGNITIVE LEARNING)

- Why do some of you see a young girl while others see an old woman? Is there a correct way to see the picture?
- Why is this an important activity to do?

COLLABORATIVE (SOCIAL LEARNING)

- Why do conflicts arise between individuals who perceive information differently?
- How can you resolve conflicts based on different perceptions?
- How did community members show their appreciation of different perceptions during this activity?

DISCOVERING GIFTS (PERSONAL LEARNING)

- What did you feel towards the students who saw the drawing the same way you did/differently than you did?
- How did you feel when you "discovered" the other aspect of the drawing?
- Did you discover any hidden gifts or talents in yourself that you were not aware of?

APPRECIATION

Invite statements of appreciation (and recognition of gifts):

- "I am a lot like you when…"
- "I felt good when you said…"

TIME: 40 minutes

GROUPING: community

MATERIALS: copies of young girl/old woman drawing

SUBJECT: perception

DEVELOPMENTAL TASKS:
Independence/Autonomy
Social Competency

OPTION

Use prior to history curricula concerning warfare, debates, constitutional rights, different political views, viewpoint of parents versus teenager, etc.

PERCEPTION AND TRANSMISSION OF INFORMATION

This page may be duplicated for classroom use.

Personal Contract

TIME: 15 minutes

GROUPING: tribes

MATERIALS: 5 x 8-inch index cards, pencils

DEVELOPMENTAL TASKS:
Independence/Autonomy
Sense of Purpose

OBJECTIVES

1. To reflect upon personal situations
2. To commit to new attitudes, behaviors or achievements
3. To experience support from peers
4. To build influence

INSTRUCTIONS

1. Have the community meet in tribes. Ask each tribe member to identify a personal behavior, attitude or achievement they would like to accomplish.
2. Explain how writing a "personal contract" makes change easier. Explain that a contract is a commitment that is specific, believable, and attainable in a certain period of time.
3. Give students time to consider, then have each write a personal contract as follows:

   "I, (name), will (describe specific commitment or action) by (specific date)."
   Signed:_____
   Witnessed:_____
   Witnessed:_____

4. Have each student ask two tribe members to sign as witnesses and be supportive of the change to be made.
5. Suggest each student ask tribe members to check on progress of the contract's completion.
6. Keep contracts in tribe envelopes for periodic review.

SUGGESTED REFLECTION QUESTIONS

CONTENT (COGNITIVE LEARNING)

- For what personal behavior, attitude, or achievement did you write a contract?
- Why is developing a personal contract difficult?
- How can a personal contract help you make the change you want to make?

COLLABORATIVE (SOCIAL LEARNING)

- What role did the witnesses play in this contract?
- What support did you get from your tribe members?

DISCOVERING GIFTS (PERSONAL LEARNING)

- How does having a contract make you feel?
- How did you feel as a witness?
- How will this help you change?
- What personal strengths will help you complete your contract?

APPRECIATION

Invite statements of appreciation (and recognition of gifts):

- "I appreciated…"
- "I like my contract because…"

Personal Journal

TIME: ongoing

GROUPING: tribes, individuals

MATERIALS: notebooks*

DEVELOPMENTAL TASKS:
Independence/Autonomy
Sense of Purpose

OBJECTIVES

1. To allow time and privacy for reflecting on personal learning
2. To provide a method for noting personal goals, commitments, hopes, and growth
3. To facilitate sharing of personal observations
4. To build inclusion

INSTRUCTIONS

1. Plan regular time throughout the week for students to write about personal learning, school experiences, and discovered interests and gifts. Tell the class that personal journals are a way to reflect on their own progress, hopes and goals, and that no one has access to another's journal without permission.
2. Urge the students to periodically review and compare their recent entries with former ones, and to congratulate themselves for signs of growth or learning. Suggest that they write "I Learned" statements.
3. Have tribe members share things from their personal journals when they choose to do so.

SUGGESTED REFLECTION QUESTIONS

CONTENT (COGNITIVE LEARNING)

- What sort of information do you imagine most of you are writing in your journals?
- Why is keeping a personal journal a helpful thing to do?
- How can keeping a journal show you your personal growth?

COLLABORATIVE (SOCIAL LEARNING

- What communication skills were helpful when your tribe members shared from their personal journals?
- How does your tribe show support for each other?

DISCOVERING GIFTS (PERSONAL LEARNING)

- How does it feel to have a personal data bank?
- What are you learning about yourself through your journal?
- What special gifts or qualities do you appreciate about yourself?
- In what special ways do you notice yourself changing or growing?

APPRECIATION

Invite statements of appreciation (and recognition of gifts):
- "I appreciate your need for privacy because…"
- "I liked it when you…"
- "I value who you are because…"

*Note: Discovering Gifts student journals for classroom use are available from CenterSource Systems.

Problem Solving Through Appreciative Inquiry

OBJECTIVES

1. To improve group effectiveness and pride by looking for what the group is doing well and what the group values rather than identifying a problem to correct
2. To empower and give groups a sense of competency and pride
3. To encourage positive approaches to innovation and creativity

INSTRUCTIONS

1. Ask community groups or tribes to discuss and report back their conclusions on the question: "What do people usually do to solve a problem when a group of people (a team or organization) is not working well together?" Ask for a report back in 5 minutes.
2. Acknowledge their reported solutions (such as, people analyze what is wrong, blame others, make new rules, or somehow fix the problem). Continue by saying that a very positive way for groups to improve is to look at what they are doing well (or what is working well) instead of what is wrong. "Let's try this different way of problem solving."
3. Give the tribes 5-10 minutes to discuss one of the following questions:
   • Describe a time when you felt your group performed really well. What were people doing?
   • Describe a time when you felt proud to be a member of your tribe. What was happening?
   • What do people in your group do that you value and that contributes to success?
4. You may want to have the tribes list their responses before reporting to the class community.
5. Group members can also summarize their learning from the strategy and/or possible use of the approach to problem solving by writing in their journals.

SUGGESTED REFLECTION QUESTIONS

CONTENT (COGNITIVE LEARNING)

• Why is it helpful to look at the positive side of a situation or problem?
• How could appreciative inquiry be used to study or research a topic in history or literature? What would you anticipate learning?

COLLABORATIVE (SOCIAL LEARNING)

• How did this approach help your tribe or the community?
• What do you intend to do differently together?
• What hopes do you have for your group now?

DISCOVERING GIFTS (PERSONAL LEARNING)

• What did you learn about yourself?
• What creative or positive contributions are you making to your tribe?
• How can appreciative inquiry be helpful to you in other groups?

TIME: varies

GROUPING: community or tribes

MATERIALS: none

DEVELOPMENTAL TASKS:
Social Competency
Sense of Purpose
Problem Solving

OPTION

Use appreciative inquiry as an active learning curriculum strategy by having students design role-plays using history or literature content to show how history or literature characters might have handled a situation in a different way to solve a people problem. Initiate thinking on the task by having students brainstorm or pose "what if…" questions.

APPRECIATION

Invite statements of appreciation (and recognition of gifts):

- "I felt (feeling) when you…"
- "It's so helpful when you…"
- "I appreciate how you…"
- "I admire you for the way you…"

Put Down the Put-Downs

OBJECTIVES

1. To build community inclusion
2. To list put-downs and the feelings they cause
3. To share the personal experience of receiving a put-down
4. To practice brainstorming

INSTRUCTIONS

1. Have students meet in tribes.
2. Lead a brief discussion about put-downs (hurtful names and behaviors).
3. After reviewing the rules for brainstorming, have each tribe select a recorder.
4. Ask the tribes to brainstorm put-downs that people use in the class or school.
5. Then have each tribe make a list of the feelings they have when they receive a put-down. Give each student time to share a time when a put-down really was hurtful.
6. Ask the tribes to brainstorm: "What could we do to help each other put-down the put-downs?"
7. Have each tribe present their list to the class, and ask reflection questions.

SUGGESTED REFLECTION QUESTIONS

CONTENT (COGNITIVE LEARNING)

- What were some of the "feeling words" you shared?
- What were some of your solutions for dealing with people who use put-downs?

COLLABORATIVE (SOCIAL LEARNING)

- Why do put-downs hurt your feelings?
- What are some important social skills to use when you brainstorm?
- How did your tribe members help each other to brainstorm or problem-solve during this activity?

DISCOVERING GIFTS (PERSONAL LEARNING)

- How did you feel when you remembered getting put-down?
- How do you feel when you put-down another person?
- How did you help your tribe reach a solution?
- What personal qualities can you use to carry out the solution?

APPRECIATION

Invite statements of appreciation (and recognition of gifts):
- "Thanks for…"
- "One thing I liked about what you said was…"

TIME: 40 minutes

GROUPING: tribes

MATERIALS: paper, pencils

DEVELOPMENTAL TASKS:
Independence/Autonomy
Social Competency
Sense of Purpose
Problem Solving

OPTION

Have the community select two or three ideas for ending put-downs. Use sticker voting (Group Problem-Solving) to do so.

Put Yourself On The Line

TIME: 15 minutes

GROUPING: community, tribes

MATERIALS: none

DEVELOPMENTAL TASKS:
Independence/Autonomy
Sense of Purpose

OBJECTIVES

1. To practice taking a stand among peers
2. To build appreciation for different opinions
3. To use a structure to promote critical thinking on curriculum topics and issues
4. To experience influence

INSTRUCTIONS

1. Ask the community to stand up.
2. Describe an imaginary line down the center of the room. Say the imaginary line represents a "continuum." Identify positions at either end of the line as "strongly agree" and "strongly disagree." State that the middle position is for those who have no opinion, choose to pass, are non-risk-takers, or are "moderates."
3. Tell the students to move to places on the line that express their feelings or opinions when you call out statements. Examples:
    • It's okay to talk to strangers on the street.
    • It's important to always please the teacher.
    • One should never climb dangerous mountains.
    • Always do what your friends do so you won't be left out.
    • Select lesson topics or current events; or have students suggest topics.
4. When the students take their place on the line have the ones near each other discuss why they are there. Pick one representative from each area of the line to report to the community.
5. Have the tribes meet to share feelings on a particularly controversial topic.

SUGGESTED REFLECTION QUESTIONS

CONTENT (COGNITIVE LEARNING)

• What did you learn?
• What did you see happen?
• Why is making your opinion public sometimes important?
• Why is recognizing individual opinions important?

COLLABORATIVE (SOCIAL LEARNING)

• Why is it important not to put down other people's opinions?
• Why might you not want to "take a stand" on a topic?
• What did the community do to help you feel comfortable about taking a stand?

DISCOVERING GIFTS (PERSONAL LEARNING)

• How did you feel about publicly taking a stand?
• Why might you have been tempted to change your position?
• What personal strengths kept you from changing your position?
• How are you a unique individual in this community?

APPRECIATION

Invite statements of appreciation (and recognition of gifts):
    • "I appreciated it when…"
    • "One thing I like about this group is…"

Reasons and Alternatives

OBJECTIVES

1. To explore motives and alternatives concerning the use of cigarettes, alcohol, or drugs
2. To develop peer support for non-use of alcohol and other drugs
3. To build inclusion and influence in tribes

INSTRUCTIONS

1. Have the community meet in tribes. Ask each tribe to appoint a recorder. Pass out two large sheets of paper and a marker to each tribe.
2. Tell the students that they will be brainstorming; review the rules of brainstorming.
3. Ask the tribes to brainstorm for five minutes on the subject: "Why do people smoke, drink alcohol, or use drugs?" Ask each recorder to jot down all ideas as quickly as they are called out.
4. After five minutes, stop the brainstorming and have the recorders take new sheets of paper. Ask the tribes now to brainstorm about another subject: "What are some alternatives to using cigarettes, alcohol, or other drugs?"
5. Stop the brainstorming after five minutes. Have the recorders report back to the tribe or community.
6. Ask the students to write in their personal journals what they intend to do about using chemical substances and how they would like to live their lives. Have them share their commitments with their tribe members.
7. Next ask the tribes to discuss what they are willing to do to help friends say "no" to the use of cigarettes, alcohol, or other drugs. Have each tribe make a list and report back to the community.

TIME: 45–60 minutes

GROUPING: tribes

MATERIALS: large paper, markers

DEVELOPMENTAL TASKS:
Independence/Autonomy
Sense of Purpose
Problem Solving

SUGGESTED REFLECTION QUESTIONS

CONTENT (COGNITIVE LEARNING)

- What did you learn about substance abuse?
- Why was this an important activity to do today?
- How can this knowledge change your behavior?

COLLABORATIVE (SOCIAL LEARNING)

- Why is brainstorming a good structure for this lesson?
- What skills did your tribe use during the brainstorming process?
- What would your tribe like to do more of the next time you use a brainstorming strategy?

DISCOVERING GIFTS (PERSONAL LEARNING)

- How do you feel about your tribe members?
- What did you learn about yourself from this activity?
- What personal strengths will help you to live the commitment you have made?

APPRECIATION

Invite statements of appreciation (and recognition of gifts):
- "It helped me when…"
- "I appreciated…"

Reflecting Feelings

TIME: 40 minutes

GROUPING: tribes

MATERIALS: "Feeling Statements" worksheets

DEVELOPMENTAL TASKS:
Independence/Autonomy
Social Competency
Sense of Purpose

OBJECTIVES

1. To build community inclusion
2. To teach and practice listening skills
3. To share ideas and feelings about a given topic

INSTRUCTIONS

1. Discuss with the community how a person's feelings can be identified by the tone of his or her voice (harsh, friendly, concerned), body language (leaning forward, withdrawn), or words.
2. Ask the students to form triads and decide which triad members will be A, B, or C. Ask for a show of hands of all A's, all B's, and all C's to avoid confusion.
3. Explain that the triad members will play the following roles in each round (post a chart, if necessary):

	A	B	C
Round 1	Speaker	Feeling Reflector	Observer
Round 2	Feeling Reflector	Observer	Speaker
Round 3	Observer	Speaker	Feeling Reflector

4. Distribute a set of three feeling statements to each triad, and have each member draw one slip.
5. First, have the speaker tell the reflector who is speaking the statement, and then they are to role-play their statements with much feeling. The "reflectors" will rephrase the feeling back to the speaker. Example:
   > Speaker: "A father is speaking to his son. He says, 'I am delighted that we can go fishing together on Saturday.'"
   > Reflector: "You feel excited and very happy that we will be able to fish together all day on Saturday."
6. The Observer then tells the Speaker and Reflector what he or she heard and saw.
7. Rotate the roles so that everyone has a turn in each of the three roles.

SUGGESTED REFLECTION QUESTIONS

CONTENT (COGNITIVE LEARNING)

• What did you learn about reflecting feelings?

COLLABORATIVE (SOCIAL LEARNING)

• Why is listening such an important skill?
• Why is the observer's role important?
• How did your group help each other with your roles?

DISCOVERING GIFTS (PERSONAL LEARNING)

• What strengths or skills did you use to play the different roles?
• How are you going to use this information tomorrow?

APPRECIATION

Invite statements of appreciation (and recognition of gifts):
• "Thanks for…"
• "I liked it when…"

FEELING STATEMENTS

Friend: Just because I don't wear name brand clothes, the other kids treat me like I don't exist!

Friend:

Student: I don't get this assignment. I don't see how this is going to help me.

Teacher:

Mom: Your room is a mess! This is driving me crazy!

Son/Daughter:

FEELING STATEMENTS

Friend: My mother won't let me talk on the phone for more than five minutes. She's even making me pay part of the phone bills.

Friend:

Student: I never say anything in class because it doesn't come out right.

Friend:

Friend: My mother dragged me to a discount store and made me buy three outfits! I'm not going to wear them anyway!

Friend:

FEELING STATEMENTS

Student: I wish you wouldn't make me wait when I want your help. You are always helping somebody else.

Teacher:

Friend: My parents always complain about what I don't do, but they never notice when I do something right!

Friend:

Friend: I wanted to go to the movies with all of you Friday night, but my parents just told me I'm grounded.

Friend:

This page may be duplicated for classroom use.

Reporting Information Through Multiple Intelligences

TIME: varies

GROUPING: tribes

MATERIALS: content-related subject material

DEVELOPMENTAL TASKS:
Independence/Autonomy
Problem Solving

OBJECTIVES

1. To practice constructive thinking skills
2. To practice collaborative team skills
3. To transfer responsibility to students
4. To promote retention of content-related material

INSTRUCTIONS

Note: Students should already be familiar with the "brainstorming" strategy.

1. Review the characteristics of each of the nine multiple intelligences (see chapter 10).
2. Tell the students that as a tribe they will have time during the next several weeks to demonstrate each of he intelligences by presenting content-related material to the community in different ways. Give an example from a topic they have been learning or have already researched.
3. Have the tribes choose a recorder and list the nine multiple intelligences.
4. Give the tribes time to brainstorm how they plan to present the content-related material to the community through the use of the nine multiple intelligences.
5. Review the plans that the tribes have made.
6. Tell the students that they will have _____ (hours, days, or weeks) to prepare for their class presentation.
7. Prior to the presentations, prepare a peer evaluation sheet that lists the multiple intelligences. Have students evaluate how effective each presentation was at conveying the content-related material through the nine multiple intelligences.

SUGGESTED REFLECTION QUESTIONS

CONTENT (COGNITIVE LEARNING)

• What did you learn from this activity?
• Which multiple intelligence was the easiest to prepare for? The hardest?

COLLABORATIVE (SOCIAL LEARNING)

• What did you do to make sure that everyone had a role?
• What collaborative skills were demonstrated?

DISCOVERING GIFTS (PERSONAL LEARNING)

• What did you notice about yourself during the preparation? The presentation?
• Through which multiple intelligence(s) do you prefer to learn new material?

APPRECIATION

Invite oral or written statements of appreciation (and recognition of gifts) to individuals or to whole tribes:

• "You really helped out with…"
• "You are really good at…"

Roles People Play

OBJECTIVES

1. To promote an awareness of helpful group roles
2. To learn how the accomplishment of group tasks depends upon helpful behaviors
3. To learn collaborative skills

INSTRUCTIONS

1. Discuss the objectives and ask students to review the Tribes agreements.
2. Distribute the handout on "Roles That People Play In Groups."
3. Ask the students to study the cartoon and decide which role (or roles) they usually play when working with others in their tribe.
4. Ask the students to write answers to the questions on the bottom of the handout. Allow five to ten minutes time.
5. Have them share their responses with a partner.
6. Ask the students to share with their tribe a new role that he or she will try for the day (or week).

OPTION #1: A ROLE PLAY

- Have each tribe plan and present a brief role-play in which one person is playing an unhelpful role.
- Ask the class to guess which role is being demonstrated.

OPTION #2: FOR ADULT AND/OR MULTICULTURAL GROUPS

- Delete the "What People Say" right hand column on the role description handout before distributing it to the tribes.
- Have the groups brainstorm and list all the things that people of their own peer group culture may say.
- Then proceed with steps three to six in the instructions above, or use role-play option #1.

SUGGESTED REFLECTION QUESTIONS

CONTENT (COGNITIVE LEARNING)

- What happens in a group when even one person is acting in an unhelpful role?

COLLABORATIVE (SOCIAL LEARNING)

- What helpful roles do people play in your tribe?
- How do those roles make working together easier?
- Are people in your tribe able to play different roles? How is that helpful?

DISCOVERING GIFTS (PERSONAL LEARNING)

- What feelings did you have during this strategy?
- What did you learn about yourself?
- What helpful role(s) do you often use in groups?

APPRECIATION

Invite statements of appreciation (and recognition of gifts):

- "I appreciated it when…"
- "Thank you for…"

TIME: 20 minutes

GROUPING: community, tribes

MATERIALS: handout on roles

DEVELOPMENTAL TASKS:
Independence/Autonomy
Social Competency
Sense of Purpose
Problem Solving

DESCRIPTIONS OF HELPFUL ROLES	WHAT PEOPLE SAY
Encourager: Tells group positive things and keeps energy going well.	Right on! Good job! Yes! Let's do it. Keep going. Brilliant!
Organizer: Helps group stay on task and time; encourages management of materials and resources.	File the papers. We have one bottle of glue. First we should…
Peace Keeper: Helps members to solve problems, make decisions, express feelings and understand each other.	Time out. Let's talk about this! You both have a good point.
Idea Person: Gives and seeks helpful ideas. Initiates action and clarifies.	What if we looked at it this way? Another idea would be to… What ideas do you have? Let's brainstorm more ideas.
Helper: Is supportive and friendly, willing to listen and help others.	We need to hear from everyone. I'll help you. Let's work on it together.

UNHELPFUL ROLE DESCRIPTIONS	WHAT PEOPLE SAY
Joker: Claims attention by interrupting, goofing off, distracting and trying to be funny.	There's a spider on your head. At recess I'm going to… Look at this! Want some gum?
Boss: Takes charge. Knows it all. Tells people what and how to do things. Usually doesn't listen well.	Do it my way! That's not right. The best way is to…
Sitter: Doesn't participate. Sits on the side. Always claims the right to pass. Will not help others. Can seem judgmental.	I pass. Don't count me in.
Put-Downer: Ridicules others and their ideas.	That's stupid. You're so dumb. We tried that once. How can you be so oblivious?
Talker: Goes on and on talking. Ignores others also wanting time. Controls by not pausing between sentences.	Blah, blah, blah. And then he said to me… I also know that… Stop interrupting me.

This page may be duplicated for classroom use.

ROLES PEOPLE PLAY IN GROUPS

Encourager • Joker • Organizer • Boss • Peace Keeper • Talker • Idea Person • Sitter • Helper • Put-Downer

QUESTIONS

Why do you think that it's the easiest role for you to play?

What other role or roles would you like to play to help your group?

Which role do you usually play in a group?

How willing are you to try out a new helpful role today?

Self-Esteem Cards

TIME: 15 minutes

GROUPING: tribes

MATERIALS: 3 x 5-inch cards

DEVELOPMENTAL TASKS:
Independence/Autonomy
Social Competency
Sense of Purpose

OBJECTIVES

1. To build self-esteem
2. To reinforce the concept of appreciation
3. To foster positive feelings among tribe members
4. To build inclusion

INSTRUCTIONS

Note: This strategy should not be used until tribe members know one another fairly well.

1. Have the community meet in tribes; pass out cards.
2. Instruct each tribe member to write his or her first name in an upper corner of the card.
3. Tell the tribe members to place all their cards in a center pile. Have each tribe member draw a card (not divulging whose card he or she has), and write a thoughtful, warm statement on the card about the student whose name is on the card.
4. Have the students return all of the cards to the central pile when done writing and repeat the process of drawing and writing four or five additional times. If anyone draws his own card, begin the drawing again or have the students exchange cards.
5. After the final writing, return all cards and draw again. This time have each tribe member read the remarks on the card to the student whose name is on the card, delivering the tribe's message as warmly and sincerely as possible while the rest of the tribe listens.

SUGGESTED REFLECTION QUESTIONS

CONTENT (COGNITIVE LEARNING)

- What did you learn by doing this activity?
- How did you choose the statements you wrote for your tribe members?

COLLABORATIVE (SOCIAL LEARNING)

- How does making thoughtful, warm statements to each other bring your tribe closer together?
- Why is it important to receive positive statements from others?

DISCOVERING GIFTS (PERSONAL LEARNING)

- How did you feel while your card was being read to you?
- How did you contribute to your tribe during this activity?
- What unique qualities does your tribe appreciate about you?
- How do you feel about your tribe now?

APPRECIATION

Invite statements of appreciation (and recognition of gifts):
- "I felt good when…"
- "Thank you for…"

Shoe 'n Tell

OBJECTIVES

1. To build inclusion
2. To practice active listening
3. To have fun

INSTRUCTIONS

1. Ask each student to bring a pair of his or her shoes from home in a paper sack. (Allow a few days.)
2. Have the full group (or tribes) sit in a circle(s).
3. Explain that sharing from the sack could take on any of these forms:
   - how these shoes help me to do things that I like to do
   - sharing from the point of view of the shoe (what it's like being the shoe that belongs to the person sharing)
   - sharing from the point of view of the shoe (how I'd like to be taken care of if I could have it my way).

SUGGESTED REFLECTION QUESTIONS

CONTENT (COGNITIVE LEARNING)

- How did the shoes tell you about the students who shared?
- How did you go about choosing the shoes you shared?

COLLABORATIVE (SOCIAL LEARNING)

- How did tribe members show they were interested?
- How does your tribe show appreciation for each other's uniqueness?

DISCOVERING GIFTS (PERSONAL LEARNING)

- How did you feel sharing your shoes?
- What unique qualities do you bring to the group?
- What do others appreciate about you?

APPRECIATION

Invite statements of appreciation (and recognition of gifts):
- Going around the circle, ask each student to give a statement of appreciation to the student on the left.
- "(Name), I liked it when…"

TIME:	50 minutes
GROUPING:	community, tribes
MATERIALS:	each student brings a pair of shoes in a paper sack

DEVELOPMENTAL TASKS:
  Social Competency
  Sense of Purpose

Singing the Blues

TIME: 20–30 minutes

GROUPING: full group

MATERIALS: none or a guitar

DEVELOPMENTAL TASKS:
Independence/Autonomy
Social Competency

OBJECTIVES

1. To promote commonality and inclusion
2. To introduce sharing of concerns in a non-threatening, enjoyable way
3. To channel community energy

INSTRUCTIONS

1. Ask the community if they know what "the blues" are. State that in this activity, having "the blues" means feeling badly about something.
2. Ask if anyone has the blues and why.
3. Sing or strum a melody that is simple and fun. Example:
   A seven-year-old boy says his dog was hurt. Words could be "I've got the blues, I've got the blues, I've got the my-dog-was-hurt-blues."
4. Ask everyone to join in singing.
5. Share one of your own blues first. Lead the singing on it.
6. Invite the students to tell their blues and lead the singing.
7. Discourage the students from making fun of another's blues. Help them to understand it's a put-down to do so.

SUGGESTED REFLECTION QUESTIONS

CONTENT (COGNITIVE LEARNING)

- What did you learn about "the blues" today?
- How were your "blues" similar?

COLLABORATIVE (SOCIAL LEARNING)

- How did the singing make it easier to share?
- How did sharing each other's "blues" in this way affect the community in a positive way?

DISCOVERING GIFTS (PERSONAL LEARNING)

- Do you feel different after "singing the blues" than you did before?
- How would it feel to sing about "good times?"
- What skills did you use to help each other with this activity?
- What special strengths did you discover about yourself?

APPRECIATION

Invite statements of appreciation (and recognition of gifts):
- "I enjoyed singing because…"
- "I feel like you do when…"

Slip Game

OBJECTIVES

1. To build inclusion
2. To promote personal sharing

INSTRUCTIONS

1. Prepare a bag for each tribe containing slips of paper with questions on them. Make sure each bag contains the same number of question slips as the number of tribe members, plus a few extra. Examples:
   - "When are you really happy?"
   - "What is the most special positive quality about you?"
   - "When have you felt very proud?"
   - See more sample questions on next page.
2. Instruct the community to meet in tribes. Review the agreements. Pass out bags.
3. Everyone has the "right to pass" if they do not like the question that they draw and may select an alternative one from those that remain in the bag. They must put the original slip back after taking an alternative one. Ask tribe members to each draw a slip with their eyes closed; tell them about the right to pass and the option for drawing alternative questions.
4. Have tribe members take turns reading and answering their questions.

SUGGESTED REFLECTION QUESTIONS

CONTENT (COGNITIVE LEARNING)

- What's one thing someone shared that you found interesting?

COLLABORATIVE (SOCIAL LEARNING)

- Why is the "right to pass" such an important agreement for this activity?
- How did having the opportunity to choose another question slip help you and your tribe be successful?
- How did your tribe help each other feel more comfortable about sharing as the activity progressed?

DISCOVERING GIFTS (PERSONAL LEARNING)

- Why could it be difficult/easy for you to share?
- How did you feel when you were answering the question you drew?
- What did you learn about yourself? What unique qualities are you proud of?
- How did you help your tribe in a special way?

APPRECIATION

Invite statements of appreciation (and recognition of gifts):
- "I'm a lot like you when…"
- "I admired you for…"

TIME: varies

GROUPING: community, tribes

MATERIALS: question slips, paper bags

DEVELOPMENTAL TASKS:
Independence/Autonomy
Social Competency
Sense of Purpose

OPTION

Use the strategy for discussion on lesson topic questions.

SLIP GAME: SAMPLE QUESTIONS

What makes you angry?

What makes you happy?

What makes you sad?

What do you do for fun?

Do you have any pets?

What is your favorite food?

What is your favorite place?

What is your favorite animal?

What is your favorite sport?

What is your favorite song?

What is your favorite TV program?

What do you and your friends do for fun?

If you could have one wish, what would it be?

What famous person would you like to be?

In what period of time, past or future, would you choose to live in?

What foreign country would you like to visit?

What would you like to be really good at?

What is your favorite story?

What is one food you don't like?

What do you do when you feel lonely?

What would you do with one million dollars?

Would you rather be rich, famous or happy?

What would you do if you were the president?

What would you do to improve school?

What qualities do you look for in a friend?

Who is the best person in the world?

What do you do when you get really angry?

Snowball I—Messages

OBJECTIVES

1. To create community inclusion and energize the class
2. To give individuals practice in writing I-Messages

INSTRUCTIONS

Note: Use the strategy "Teaching I-Messages" prior to using this one.

1. Ask each student to bring one piece of paper, a pencil and something firm to write on and sit in a community circle.
2. Review the elements of an "I-Message" and the difference between an "I-Message" and a "You-Message."
3. Give examples of an "I-Message" and a "You-Message" and ask the students to think of an example of each.
4. Ask several students to model an "I-Message" and then a "You-Message."
5. Ask each student to draw two lines that divide the paper into four squares, and to write a "You-Message" in one square.
6. After the students have done so, tell them you will give them two commands: "crumple" and "toss." Explain that when you say "crumple," they will crumple their papers into "snowballs," and when you say "toss," they will toss the "snowballs" into the center of the circle.
7. Then have the students pick up a "snowball," read the "You-Message," and change it into an "I-Message." Have the students write the "I-Message" in another square.
8. Repeat the process one more time.
9. Have each student take a snowball back to his or her tribe, and have the tribes critique the messages.

SUGGESTED REFLECTION QUESTIONS

CONTENT (COGNITIVE LEARNING)

- Why is it important to know the difference between a "You-Message" and an "I-Message?"
- What kinds of messages do you get/give in "You-Messages?"

COLLABORATIVE (SOCIAL LEARNING)

- Why is this strategy a good way to learn about "I-Messages?"
- How can you use "I-Messages" in your life with others?
- How can you encourage the community or your tribe to use "I-Messages" with each other?

DISCOVERING GIFTS (PERSONAL LEARNING)

- How did it feel to change a "You-Message" into an "I-Message?"
- What communication or "people" skills do you feel particularly comfortable with?
- What "people" skills or personal strengths do others recognize in you?

APPRECIATION

Invite statements of appreciation (and recognition of gifts):

- "I liked…"
- "I enjoyed it when…"

TIME: 45 minutes

GROUPING: community, tribes

MATERIALS: paper and pencils

DEVELOPMENTAL TASKS:
Independence/Autonomy
Social Competency

Something Good

TIME: varies

GROUPING: community

MATERIALS: none

DEVELOPMENTAL TASKS:
Social Competency
Sense of Purpose

OBJECTIVES

1. To build inclusion
2. To encourage sharing of positive feelings

INSTRUCTIONS

1. Have the community sit in a large circle.
2. Ask each student to share one positive experience that happened during the previous week or recent past. Say that there will be no discussion until all have shared.

SUGGESTED REFLECTION QUESTIONS

CONTENT (COGNITIVE LEARNING)

- Were there any similarities about the "good things" you shared?
- When was the last time you told someone about a positive experience?

COLLABORATIVE (SOCIAL LEARNING)

- How can you tell that others are using good listening skills?
- Did you share more freely as the activity progressed? Why?
- How did this activity help the community?

DISCOVERING GIFTS (PERSONAL LEARNING)

- How did you feel while sharing with the community?
- What communication or "people skills" did you use during this activity?
- What did you learn about yourself?

APPRECIATION

Invite statements of appreciation (and recognition of gifts):
- "I liked it when…"
- "I'm like you when…"
- "I felt good when…"

Something I Cherish

TIME: 20 minutes

GROUPING: community, tribes

MATERIALS: none

DEVELOPMENTAL TASKS:
Independence/Autonomy
Social Competency
Sense of Purpose

OBJECTIVES

1. To increase communication skills
2. To build inclusion

INSTRUCTIONS

1. Ask the community to meet in tribes.
2. Ask each tribe member to take a turn sharing "one thing that I cherish," explaining why it is so special or why she or he wants others to know, etc.
3. To draw the tribes back into the community, have each tribe member share with the community one item that another member of his or her tribe cherishes. Make sure each tribe member speaks of and is spoken about by another member of his or her tribe.

SUGGESTED REFLECTION QUESTIONS

CONTENT (COGNITIVE LEARNING)

• What types of things do your tribe members cherish?
• Why is it important to share what you cherish with each other?

COLLABORATIVE (SOCIAL LEARNING)

• How could you tell that your tribe members were listening when others shared?
• How can this type of sharing help families, friendships, your tribe, this community?
• How did people show that they valued your contribution?

DISCOVERING GIFTS (PERSONAL LEARNING)

• How did you feel about sharing something you cherished?
• How were you able to help your tribe or the community during this activity?
• What did you discover about yourself?

APPRECIATION

Invite statements of appreciation (and recognition of gifts):
• "I liked it when…"
• "I felt good when…"
• "I was interested when…"

Space Pioneers

TIME: 35 minutes

GROUPING: tribes

MATERIALS: pencils, paper

DEVELOPMENTAL TASKS:
Independence/Autonomy
Problem Solving

OBJECTIVES

1. To give practice in assessing different qualities and opinions
2. To encourage sharing
3. To encourage understanding and acceptance of others' perspectives
4. To provide an opportunity to look at evolving styles of communication and leader-behavior within the group
5. To encourage influence

INSTRUCTIONS

Note: Use the strategy "Consensus Building" prior to having the class community do this strategy.

1. Read the "Space Pioneers" scenario (on next page) while students are seated in tribes.
2. Write the list of "Advisors" (or a similar list of your own selection) on the blackboard for all to see.
3. Ask each participant to identify the five advisors they would want to help settle the newly discovered planet.
4. Discuss the difference between a group of people making a decision by consensus in contrast to voting.
5. Announce that the tribes have fifteen minutes to reach a consensus on which five advisors to take into space.
6. Ask the tribes to appoint a recorder to take notes.
7. After fifteen minutes have the recorders report the final consensus lists to the community.

OPTIONS

Have the students...
- agree on a name for the new planet;
- share one personal possession each would take on the trip; or
- brainstorm and agree on what supplies and equipment they would need.

Use the strategy to explore academic topics such as...
- people to design a model city; or
- people to work on a national policy for children.

SUGGESTED REFLECTION QUESTIONS

CONTENT (COGNITIVE LEARNING)
- What do you see as the main purpose of Space Pioneers?
- Why would you want to, or not want to, go on this trip?

COLLABORATIVE (SOCIAL LEARNING)
- What did you have to do to reach consensus on who you would take?
- What was most effective about how your group came to an agreement?
- How did different group members provide leadership for this activity?

DISCOVERING GIFTS (PERSONAL LEARNING)
- How did you feel about your tribe's choice?
- What did you contribute to help your group make the selection?
- What unique strengths or skills did you discover about yourself?

APPRECIATION

Invite statements of appreciation (and recognition of gifts):
- "I liked it when..."
- "I admired you for saying..."
- "I'm much like you when..."

SPACE PIONEERS

A new planet has been discovered in our solar system. This planet resembles Earth in every way, except that there are no human beings living there. Our government wants the students of this class to be the first pioneers to settle on the newly discovered planet. They want you to select five adult advisors who you think would be valuable on the new planet. Select from the following list of ten people:

1. Zelda Learner, age 45, middle school teacher
2. Oroville Oates, age 41, farmer
3. Clara Kettle, age 34, cook
4. Dr. Margarita Flowers, age 27, botanist
5. Woodrow Hammer, age 56, carpenter
6. Flo Nightengale, age 37, registered nurse
7. Irma Intel, age 32, engineer
8. Melvin Melody, age 24, musician
9. Reverend Adam Goodfellow, age 51, minister
10. Tiger Forest, age 24, golf pro

Spider Web

TIME: varies depending on group size

GROUPING: community

MATERIALS: ball of colored yarn

DEVELOPMENTAL TASKS:
Independence/Autonomy
Social Competency
Sense of Purpose

OBJECTIVES

1. To build inclusion and a sense of community
2. To practice attentive listening

INSTRUCTIONS

1. Ask the community to sit in one large circle.
2. Explain that during this activity each student will have an opportunity to share his or her name and something special about himself or herself. Give the students a minute to think of something special.
3. Have one student begin the activity by stating his or her name and something about himself or herself. Example:
   "My name is Sue, and I am wonderful at organizing things."
4. Then, have the student hold onto the end of the yarn and roll the yarn ball to someone across from him or her in the circle. Have the students continue this process until everyone has either shared or passed and a "spider web" pattern has been created.
5. It is fun to "play" with the web before rolling it up. Have everyone pick up the web, stand, and hold it up overhead. Have them hold it waist high and shake it.
6. If time permits, have the students reroll the web one by one in reverse order.

SUGGESTED REFLECTION QUESTIONS

CONTENT (COGNITIVE LEARNING)
- How can you symbolically interpret this "spider web?" Note symbolism, design, community involvement, etc.
- Why is this a good community-building activity?

COLLABORATIVE (SOCIAL LEARNING)
- What did you learn about each other as a result of this activity?
- How does "Spider Web" bring you closer together as a community?

DISCOVERING GIFTS (PERSONAL LEARNING)
- What did you learn about yourself as a result of this activity?
- How do you feel after participating in this activity?

APPRECIATION

Invite statements of appreciation (and recognition of gifts):
- "I liked it when you said…"
- "I admire you for…"

OTHER WAYS TO DO SPIDER WEB

1. Make a statement of appreciation to someone in the circle; continue until each student has received a statement.
2. Toss the yarn up and into the center, see where it goes, and then give that person a statement of appreciation.
3. Paraphrase what the previous person said, then give an appreciation.
4. Answer a question asked of the community.

Student-Developed Lesson Plans

OBJECTIVES

1. To promote tribal influence
2. To have students develop their own lesson plans

INSTRUCTIONS

1. Have tribes meet for two or three minutes and create their own inclusion.
2. Give each tribe a copy of the "A Tribes Learning Experience."
3. Discuss the elements that make up the plan:
   - an inclusion activity to awaken interest or connect to previous experiences
   - an academic learning goal
   - a social learning goal
   - a tribal strategy or cooperative learning structure (or a sequence of the same)
   - instructions
   - reflection questions
   - time for statements of appreciation.
4. Have each tribe plan a twenty-minute lesson on a theme or academic topic for younger students or the community.
5. When finished, the lessons can be presented or taught to the class by the tribes.

TIME: 90 minutes

GROUPING: tribes

MATERIALS: copies of "Tribes Lesson Plan"

DEVELOPMENTAL TASKS:
Independence/Autonomy
Problem Solving

SUGGESTED REFLECTION QUESTIONS

CONTENT (COGNITIVE LEARNING)

- What was the most difficult thing about this strategy?
- What did you learn by doing this strategy?

COLLABORATIVE (SOCIAL LEARNING)

- What did your tribe do to work well together?
- What does your tribe want to do more of to work together even better next time?

DISCOVERING GIFTS (PERSONAL LEARNING)

- How do you feel about developing lesson plans now?
- What did you do to help your tribe be successful?
- What strengths or skills did you discover about yourself?

APPRECIATION

Invite statements of appreciation (and recognition of gifts):
- "I liked it when…"
- "I appreciated…"

Study Buddies

TIME: 20–30 minutes

GROUPING: pairs

MATERIALS: study materials

DEVELOPMENTAL TASKS:
Independence/Autonomy
Problem Solving

OBJECTIVES

1. To build interdependence
2. To practice study materials before a test
3. To experience influence

INSTRUCTIONS

1. Have the students choose some identical study material to be reviewed such as spelling words, vocabulary words, or other subject-related material. (Examples: elements in Periodic table, Bloom's taxonomy of classification, Chinese dynasties, etc.).
2. Ask the students to get into pairs. (You may use strategies such as birthday line-up, fold-the-line, random buddies or numbered slips to form pairs.)
3. Ask the students to decide on a study strategy they will use. (Strategies might include quizzing each other, explaining concepts, reviewing difficult words, etc.)
4. Have the students use the strategy they have chosen to review the study material.

SUGGESTED REFLECTION QUESTIONS

CONTENT (COGNITIVE LEARNING)

• What did you learn today?
• Why is studying together helpful?

COLLABORATIVE (SOCIAL LEARNING)

• How did you help each other make this strategy successful?
• What special qualities did you discover about your partner?

DISCOVERING GIFTS (PERSONAL LEARNING)

• How do you feel studying with another person?
• How do you usually prefer to study?
• What special strengths or skills did you use to make this activity successful?

APPRECIATION

Invite statements of appreciation (and recognition of gifts):
• "I liked studying with you because…"
• "Thanks for helping me."

Suggestion Circle

TIME:	30 minutes
GROUPING:	community
MATERIALS:	none

DEVELOPMENTAL TASKS:
Independence/Autonomy
Social Competency
Sense of Purpose
Problem Solving

OBJECTIVES

1. To encourage attentive listening
2. To experience group support for a concern
3. To assist a peer, colleague, or friend to resolve a problem
4. To experience individual problem-solving in the influence stage

INSTRUCTIONS

1. Have the community form a circle.
2. Review the agreements. Choose a recorder who will write down the suggestions made by the community.
3. Ask for a volunteer to share a concern or problem that he or she is experiencing and for which he or she would like some suggestions for resolving.
4. Tell the community that they are to listen without judgment or comment while the problem is being shared, but they may ask for additional information, if necessary, when the student has finished sharing.
5. Invite the students to make a suggestion, one at a time, to the person who shared. Encourage them not to repeat what someone else has already suggested.
6. Have the recorder give the list of possible solutions to the person who shared the problem.

SUGGESTED REFLECTION QUESTIONS

CONTENT (COGNITIVE LEARNING)

- Why did we do this strategy?
- What types of suggestions were offered?

COLLABORATIVE (SOCIAL LEARNING)

- Why is it important to get ideas for solving problems from others?
- Which social skills did you, as a community, use during this strategy?
- Where else could this strategy be used?

DISCOVERING GIFTS (PERSONAL LEARNING)

- How did you feel to give suggestions?
- How could this type of a process help you?
- How did you contribute in a special way?

APPRECIATION

Invite statements of appreciation (and recognition of gifts):
- "Thanks for…"
- "What made a difference for me was…"

Taking A Closer Look

TIME: 30 minutes

GROUPING: tribes, pairs

MATERIALS: question slips

DEVELOPMENTAL TASKS:
Independence/Autonomy
Social Competency
Sense of Purpose

OBJECTIVES

1. To explore individual attitudes about the use of alcohol or other drugs
2. To practice attentive listening
3. To build peer support and influence

INSTRUCTIONS

1. Have the community divide up into pairs, and have each partner decide whether he or she will be an "A" or a "B." Pass out prepared question slips (see following page), or generate your own questions appropriate for the culture and age level of your students.
2. Suggest that the partners move to a comfortable place where they can hear each other well. Explain that partner A will begin by answering the questions while B listens, and that at the end of five minutes, the partners will switch roles.
3. Review the agreements, particularly attentive listening.
4. Give the signal to switch after five minutes, and call the partners back to the community circle after the additional five minutes.
5. Have the community discuss and reflect on the experience.

SUGGESTED REFLECTION QUESTIONS

CONTENT (COGNITIVE LEARNING)

- What kind of messages did you get about using substances?
- How did this activity stretch your own thinking about drugs?

COLLABORATIVE (SOCIAL LEARNING)

- Why did we work in pairs rather than as a community?
- How did you and your partner help each other during this activity?

DISCOVERING GIFTS (PERSONAL LEARNING)

- Did you make any new decisions as a result of this experience? What were they?
- What did you discover about yourself from this activity?
- What is one thing that you felt proud of as you participated in this activity?

APPRECIATION

Invite statements of appreciation (and recognition of gifts):
- "I really appreciated it when…"
- "(Name), you are special because…"
- "Thank you, (name), for…"

QUESTION SLIP
TAKING A CLOSER LOOK

1. What kinds of messages did you get about cigarettes, alcohol, or drugs when you were younger (right or wrong to use/okay for men, but not for women/beer and wine don't hurt you)?

2. Where did these messages come from (school/family/media/church/friends)?

3. What was the first decision you ever made about choosing to use or not use cigarettes, alcohol or drugs? How old were you? What happened? What process did you use to make a decision?

4. Describe what your life would be like if you did not use any of these substances. Option: What might it be like if you did use? Ask people to think about over-the-counter or prescription drugs they may use. Coffee?

5. What have you learned about chemical substances that you would want your brother, sister or child to know?

6. Would you feel comfortable with your child using cigarettes, drugs, or alcohol as much as you do?

Teaching Agreements

TIME: two class periods

GROUPING: tribes

MATERIALS: large paper, felt pens, poster paint

DEVELOPMENTAL TASKS:
Independence/Autonomy
Sense of Purpose
Problem Solving

OBJECTIVES

1. To have each tribe create a lesson to help teach an agreement to the community
2. To transfer responsibility to tribes for lesson development
3. To experience influence

INSTRUCTIONS

1. Review the agreements of attentive listening, right to pass, no put-downs, and mutual respect (and any others you've created for your class).
2. Explain to the students that you are looking for new and creative ways to teach these agreements and would like their help.
3. Have each tribe choose (or assign) one of the agreements. Explain that each tribe will create a lesson to teach that agreement to the community. Explain that they can use butcher paper, felt pens, and paint (or other art media you have available) to make any posters or signs needed to teach the lesson. Emphasize that you want them to be creative. Let them know they will have the rest of the period and one other period to create their lessons and share them with the community.
4. When the tribes are finished, have them present their lessons to the community.

SUGGESTED REFLECTION QUESTIONS

CONTENT (COGNITIVE LEARNING)

- What did you learn about creating a lesson?
- Which agreement do you think is the most important? Why?

COLLABORATIVE (SOCIAL LEARNING)

- What social skills did your tribe need to be successful at this strategy?
- What allowed your tribe to be creative and innovative?

DISCOVERING GIFTS (PERSONAL LEARNING)

- How did you feel when your tribe presented its lesson?
- What did you contribute to help your tribe be successful?
- In what ways are you a creative person?
- What special skills did you discover about yourself?

APPRECIATION

Invite statements of appreciation (and recognition of gifts):
- "You helped a lot when..."
- "I liked..."

Teaching I-Messages

OBJECTIVES

1. To give tribes practice in brainstorming and to introduce words to express feelings
2. To show the link between "feeling words" and "I-Messages"
3. To practice giving "I-Messages"

TIME:	50 minutes
GROUPING:	tribes
MATERIALS:	large paper and felt pens

DEVELOPMENTAL TASKS:
Independence/Autonomy
Social Competency
Sense of Purpose

INSTRUCTIONS

Note: Teach this strategy before using "Snowball I-Messages."

1. Ask the community to sit in tribes, and have each tribe select a recorder. Explain that they will be brainstorming (see "Brainstorming" strategy).
2. Discuss various "feeling words" (happiness, anger, upset, love). Ask the tribes to brainstorm and write down as many "feeling words" as they can in five minutes.
3. After five minutes, ask the tribes to take turns calling out the "feeling words" they wrote down. Have a student record the words on the blackboard. Lead a discussion on why sharing feelings is important for clear communication.
4. Ask, "Why is it important to have a way to let people know how their behavior affects us?" Explain that "I-Messages" are a way to share feelings but not blame.
5. Use the formats in chapter 9 to write examples of "I-Messages" and "You-Messages" on the board. Explain the difference between the two types of messages, and ask the class to contrast the impact they each have.
6. Have each tribe member write four "I-Messages" using the feeling words they listed earlier. Each person should write to a friend, a relative, a classmate and a teacher. Allow ten minutes work time.
7. Have the tribes review the "I-Messages" written by their tribe members. Have them help each other change statements that are "You-Messages" to "I-Messages."
8. Ask the students to practice using "I-Messages" during the next few days, and to report back to their tribe on what happened.

SUGGESTED REFLECTION QUESTIONS

CONTENT (COGNITIVE LEARNING)

• Why is it important to use "I-Messages?"

COLLABORATIVE (SOCIAL LEARNING)

• How can "I-Messages" help you to lessen conflict with friends?
• How did your tribe support each other while learning to use "I-Messages?"

DISCOVERING GIFTS (PERSONAL LEARNING)

• How does it feel to receive a "You-Message?"/an "I-Message?"
• What did you discover about yourself?

APPRECIATION

Invite statements of appreciation (and recognition of gifts):

• "It helped me when…"
• "I liked it when…"

Teaching Listening

TIME: 30 minutes

GROUPING: tribes

MATERIALS: none

DEVELOPMENTAL TASKS:
Independence/Autonomy
Social Competency

OBJECTIVES

1. To practice components of attentive listening:
   Attending, Paraphrasing, Reflecting Feelings
2. To share ideas and feelings about any given topic
3. To build inclusion

INSTRUCTIONS

1. Discuss and demonstrate attentive listening skills (refer to chapter 8). Write components on chalkboard.
2. Ask the students to form triads, and designate each triad member as an A, B, or C. Ask for a show of hands of all A's, all B's and all C's to avoid confusion.
3. Explain that each person will have an opportunity to play each role; in round 1, A will observe, B will be speaker, and C will be listener. Post this chart:

	A	B	C
Round 1	Observer	Speaker	Listener
Round 2	Speaker	Listener	Observer
Round 3	Listener	Observer	Speaker

4. Give the speakers a topic of your choice to speak on for two to five minutes. Example: Should students be allowed to vote?
5. Ask the listeners to practice one or two components of attentive listening.
6. Ask the observers to pay attention to the interaction and after two to five minutes give feedback to the listeners. Ask them to include what they saw the listener doing both verbally and nonverbally, and their observations of how the speakers responded.
7. Have the triads repeat the process until all three members have had an opportunity to be observers, speakers, and listeners.

SUGGESTED REFLECTION QUESTIONS

CONTENT (COGNITIVE LEARNING)

- Why was it important to have an observer?
- How can you be a good listener, speaker, or observer?

COLLABORATIVE (SOCIAL LEARNING)

- How can you tell if someone is being a good listener?
- Why is listening such a good skill?
- How did your tribe use listening skills to make this activity successful?

DISCOVERING GIFTS (PERSONAL LEARNING)

- How did it feel to be listened to in that way?
- How well did you attend, paraphrase, and reflect feelings?
- What special skills did you bring to your group?

APPRECIATION

Invite statements of appreciation (and recognition of gifts):
- "I felt good when…"
- "I liked it when…"

Teaching Paraphrasing/Reflecting Feelings

OBJECTIVES

1. To build community inclusion
2. To teach and practice the listening skills of paraphrasing and reflecting feelings
3. To share ideas and feelings about a given topic

INSTRUCTIONS

1. Have the students form pairs and decide who is partner #1 and who is #2.
2. Have the partners sit "knees to knees" and "eyes to eyes."
3. Demonstrate how to paraphrase a statement. Example:
   Heidi says, "Sometimes I think I'd like to be an airline pilot."
   Paraphrase response: "Now and then you wonder about becoming a pilot."
4. Ask the #1 partners to speak briefly on the topic: "A time when I listened carefully." Partners #2 are to listen and then paraphrase the statement they heard. After three minutes have the partners switch roles.
5. Ask the community, "What is the importance of paraphrasing?"
6. Demonstrate how to reflect feelings along with paraphrasing. Example:
   Heidi says, "Becoming an airline pilot would be exciting because there still are not many women pilots."
   Paraphrase: "You feel excited whenever you imagine being one of the few women pilots."
7. Ask the #2 partners to speak briefly on the topic: "A time that I found my work a challenge." Partners #1 are to listen and then paraphrase the key statement and feelings. After three minutes have the partners switch roles.
8. Have the partners share what each felt during the activity.

TIME:	30 minutes
GROUPING:	pairs
MATERIALS:	none

DEVELOPMENTAL TASKS:
Independence/Autonomy
Social Competency
Sense of Purpose

SUGGESTED REFLECTION QUESTIONS

CONTENT (COGNITIVE LEARNING)

- What listening skills did you use during this strategy?
- How does good listening help to build community?

COLLABORATIVE (SOCIAL LEARNING)

- How does reflecting feelings help you communicate better?
- In what ways did you and your partner help each other during this activity?

DISCOVERING GIFTS (PERSONAL LEARNING)

- How would you feel if someone listened to you like this?
- How can you use these skills in your everyday life?
- How did you help your partner during this activity?

APPRECIATION

Invite statements of appreciation (and recognition of gifts):
- "I could tell you were listening when…"
- "I appreciated your…"

That's Me—That's Us!

TIME: 40 minutes

GROUPING: community, tribes

MATERIALS: none

DEVELOPMENTAL TASKS:
Independence/Autonomy
Sense of Purpose

OBJECTIVES

1. To build community inclusion
2. To help the students identify personal or community skills, interests, or achievements

INSTRUCTIONS

1. Tell the students that you will call out a series of questions, and those who identify or agree are to jump up and say, "That's me!"
2. Start with a few simple topics that are appropriate to the students' age level and interest. Examples:
   - How many people have moved in the last two years?
   - How many people have green eyes?
   - How many people like broccoli?
3. Use this strategy to learn how the tribes are working together. Ask the tribes to stand and say, "That's us!" Examples:
   - Which tribes had no put-downs today?
   - In which tribe did everyone participate on the task?
   - Which tribe figured out why the rain forest in the Amazon is threatened?

SUGGESTED REFLECTION QUESTIONS

CONTENT (COGNITIVE LEARNING)

- What did you find out about your tribe members/community members?
- What's one more question you might add?

COLLABORATIVE (SOCIAL LEARNING)

- Why was listening important?
- How could you tell that your entire tribe would stand up?
- What did the community or your tribe members do to make this activity fun for each other?

DISCOVERING GIFTS (PERSONAL LEARNING)

- How did you feel about jumping up?
- What did you discover about yourself?

APPRECIATION

Invite statements of appreciation (and recognition of gifts):
- "It helped me when…"
- "Thanks for…"

The Ideal Classroom

OBJECTIVES

1. To involve students in defining class agreements
2. To alter the climate from negative to positive
3. To transfer responsibility to students
4. To experience influence

INSTRUCTIONS

1. Draw a large circle on the board and label it "The Ideal Classroom."
2. Ask the students to think about the following question: How would people act and interact in an ideal classroom?
3. Have students divide up into pairs.
4. Ask the partners to discuss and make a list of what an ideal classroom would be like. After ten minutes have them share their ideas with their tribe.
5. Have the tribes save the lists. Ask everyone to think about the question until the next day.
6. On the following day, use the strategy "One, Two, Three" or "Group Problem-Solving" to have the community select one to three ideas that they consider most important for their classroom.
7. Post the ideas in a prominent place.
8. Ask, "How many of you want to make these agreements that the whole community respects for the next (week, month or year)?" Invite students to stand and say, "That's me!"
9. Ask, "Who will help to remind others to respect our agreements?"

SUGGESTED REFLECTION QUESTIONS

CONTENT (COGNITIVE LEARNING)

- What is the ideal classroom like?
- What would have to change to make this classroom an ideal classroom?

COLLABORATIVE (SOCIAL LEARNING)

- What social skills would be needed in your ideal classroom?
- How can these rules apply to other areas of life?
- How did working together in pairs help during this activity?
- What did you, as a tribe, do well together to make this activity successful?

DISCOVERING GIFTS (PERSONAL LEARNING)

- What personal skills did you use during this activity?
- What usually works best for you when you tackle a problem?

APPRECIATION

Invite statements of appreciation (and recognition of gifts):
- "It felt good when…"
- "One thing I liked about what you said was…"

TIME: 40 minutes

GROUPING: tribes, pairs

MATERIALS: paper, pencils

DEVELOPMENTAL TASKS:
Social Competency
Problem Solving

The Week In Perspective

TIME: 10–15 minutes

GROUPING: triads, pairs

MATERIALS: none

DEVELOPMENTAL TASKS:
Independence/Autonomy
Social Competency
Sense of Purpose

OBJECTIVES

1. To give each student an opportunity to reflect on recent experiences
2. To increase communication skills and sharing
3. To build inclusion and influence

INSTRUCTIONS

1. Ask the community to form triads or pairs.
2. Tell the students that they will take turns interviewing each other. Ask them to decide who will be the first person to be interviewed, the second, and the third (if using triads).
3. Urge the students to listen attentively to the person being interviewed and not discuss anything he or she is saying.
4. Provide the students with questions to ask. Examples:
   • "What new and good thing happened to you this past week?"
   • "What was hard about your week?"
   • "Is there something you meant to do this week but put off?"
   • "What one thing did you do that you enjoyed?"

SUGGESTED REFLECTION QUESTIONS

CONTENT (COGNITIVE LEARNING)

• What did you learn by doing this activity?
• Why is answering questions about your week easy/difficult?

COLLABORATIVE (SOCIAL LEARNING)

• What makes interviewing a challenging skill to master?
• Why are being the interviewer and the interviewee both important skills?
• How did your group help each other during this activity?
• How do you feel as a community now?

DISCOVERING GIFTS (PERSONAL LEARNING)

• How did you feel while you were being interviewed?
• What did you learn about yourself during this activity?
• How did you contribute to your group in a special way?
• What special "people skills" did you use during this activity?

APPRECIATION

Invite statements of appreciation (and recognition of gifts):
   • "I liked it when you said…"
   • "I appreciate you for…"

Third-Party Mediation

TIME: varies

GROUPING: community, tribes

MATERIALS: none

DEVELOPMENTAL TASKS:
Independence/Autonomy
Sense of Purpose
Problem Solving

OBJECTIVES

1. To provide a process for conflict resolution and a mutually agreeable solution
2. To model that a third-party-mediator does not make judgments or take sides
3. To develop trust and acceptance of individual differences
4. To build inclusion yet allow influence (a sense of value)

INSTRUCTIONS

Note: This method can be used with groups as well as individuals.

1. Call together two students who are in conflict and tell them that it is likely a mutually agreeable solution can be worked out. Ask if they would like that to happen. Make it clear that you will not take sides or set yourself up as a judge.
2. Ask each student, one at a time, to describe the conflict; say the other is not to interrupt. Encourage each student to focus on what is going on now rather than list past grievances. If they try to interrupt each other or are not listening, ask each to summarize the other's position.
3. Ask each student in turn to state how the situation makes him or her feel. Encourage use of "I-Messages." Reflect back their feelings. Have each person rephrase the other's feelings.
4. Have both students state what they would like as an outcome to the conflict. As mediator, encourage both to modify their "ideal states," look at alternatives, and decide what they would be willing to give up and work toward.
5. Have both students acknowledge what changes they each are willing to make in a specific period of time.
6. Have the students draw up a list of the steps each agrees to take and have them make an appointment to check back with the mediator.

SUGGESTED REFLECTION QUESTIONS

CONTENT (COGNITIVE LEARNING)

- What steps did the mediator use to help the two students resolve their conflict?
- Why is having a third-party mediator helpful in some conflicts?

COLLABORATIVE (SOCIAL LEARNING)

- What social skills did you and the community use as you observed the conflict?
- How did this activity help the community in a special way?

DISCOVERING GIFTS (PERSONAL LEARNING)

- Volunteers: What did you feel as we worked through your conflict? What personal strengths or special skills did you use to help resolve the conflict?
- Observers: What were you feeling for the students in conflict? How did you help the two students and the community as a whole while you observed this activity?
- How can this help you in the future? At home?

APPRECIATION

Invite statements of appreciation (and recognition of gifts):
- "It was helpful when you…"
- "I appreciated…"

Thumbs Up, Thumbs Down

TIME: 5–10 minutes

GROUPING: community

MATERIALS: none

DEVELOPMENTAL TASKS:
Independence/Autonomy
Sense of Purpose

OBJECTIVES

1. To encourage active decision-making
2. To encourage the expression of opinions
3. To accept individual differences
4. To encourage influence

INSTRUCTIONS

1. Have the community sit in a circle.
2. Demonstrate three different ways the students can vote or express their opinions on an issue:
   - thumbs up—agree
   - thumbs down—disagree
   - thumbs sideways—no opinion or pass
3. Then, in rapid-fire sequence, ask controversial questions appropriate to the age level and interests of the community and have students vote. Examples:
   - "How do you feel about eating at McDonalds?"
   - "Playing soccer? Football? Skateboards?"
   - "People helping each other in tribe learning groups?"

SUGGESTED REFLECTION QUESTIONS

CONTENT (COGNITIVE LEARNING)

- What other issues could you vote on?
- How did this type of voting differ from other voting you've done?
- Why is discovering different ways to vote important?

COLLABORATIVE (SOCIAL LEARNING)

- How is this type of voting helpful to our community?
- How did community members show their acceptance of different votes?

DISCOVERING GIFTS (PERSONAL LEARNING)

- How did you feel about making your opinions known in public like this?
- Why might you have been tempted to change your vote as you looked around?
- What special strengths kept you from changing your vote?
- How are you a unique individual in this community?

APPRECIATION

Invite statements of appreciation (and recognition of gifts):
- "I felt good when…"
- "One thing I like about this group is…"

OPTION

This activity can be related to lesson topics by having the students vote on decisions made by characters in books or history, or by having the students express their opinions on lessons, activities, etc.

Tower Building

TIME:	20–30 minutes
GROUPING:	tribes, subgroups
MATERIALS:	8½ x 11-inch paper, masking tape

DEVELOPMENTAL TASKS:
Independence/Autonomy
Problem Solving

OBJECTIVES

1. To promote an awareness of influence issues
2. To explore nonverbal communication
3. To build tribe cohesiveness

INSTRUCTIONS

1. Have the community meet in tribes. Pass out fifteen to twenty pieces of paper and one roll of masking tape to each tribe.
2. Tell the tribes that they are to nonverbally construct a tower or castle using only the given supplies, and that they will have ten minutes to complete the task.
3. At the end of ten minutes, stop the action.
4. Have all the tribes view each other's buildings.
5. Ask tribe members to return to their tribes for discussion and reflection.

SUGGESTED REFLECTION QUESTIONS

CONTENT (COGNITIVE LEARNING)

- What was the purpose of this activity beyond building a tower?
- Why might nonverbal communication be as important as verbal communication?

COLLABORATIVE (SOCIAL LEARNING)

- What social skills did you, as a group, need to successfully build your tower?
- How did leadership in your group develop while you were building your castle?
- How did your group make sure that all members got to participate?

DISCOVERING GIFTS (PERSONAL LEARNING)

- What did you learn about yourself?
- Is this your usual style of working with others?
- What special strengths did you use while working with others in your group?
- How would you change the way you work in a group?

APPRECIATION

Invite statements of appreciation (and recognition of gifts):

- "I appreciated it when…"
- "I thought that (name) was very…"
- "Our tribe is…"

Tribal Peer Coaching

TIME: varies

GROUPING: tribes, triads, pairs

MATERIALS: vary

DEVELOPMENTAL TASKS:
Independence/Autonomy
Social Competency
Sense of Purpose

OBJECTIVES

1. To help slower learners understand or learn subject matter
2. To provide peer support for learning
3. To structure a cooperative learning experience
4. To build inclusion and encourage kindness
5. To experience influence

INSTRUCTIONS

1. Have the community meet in tribes. Ask tribe members to share which members are very sure that they understand the concept or material from a lesson topic or unit.
2. Ask if those tribe members would be willing to be "coaches" for a short time to the other tribe members who may not be quite as sure.
3. Have tribe members form pairs or triads, with one coach in each subgroup.
4. Tell the coaches that their goal is to have their students be able to repeat back or explain to them the information or concept being learned. Suggest some ways that the coaches can be helpful.
5. Tell the students how much time will be allowed, and remind them of their attentive listening skills.
6. When time is up, ask those who were "students" to explain to their whole tribes what they learned from their coaches.

SUGGESTED REFLECTION QUESTIONS

CONTENT (COGNITIVE LEARNING)

- What did you learn about coaching/being coached?
- Why is peer coaching a powerful way to help you learn?

COLLABORATIVE (SOCIAL LEARNING)

- What social skills does a peer coach need?
- What recommendations do you have for a peer coach?
- In what ways did your tribe or group work together well to make this activity successful?

DISCOVERING GIFTS (PERSONAL LEARNING)

- How did you feel as a coach/being coached?
- How did you help others during this activity?
- What special strengths or skills did you discover about yourself?

APPRECIATION

Invite statements of appreciation (and recognition of gifts):
- "I appreciated it when…"
- "(Name), you really helped me when…"
- "Thank you, (name), I think you are…"

Tribe Graffiti

TIME:	60 minutes
GROUPING:	tribes
MATERIALS:	large paper, colored pencils or felt pens

DEVELOPMENTAL TASKS:
Independence/Autonomy
Social Competency
Sense of Purpose

OBJECTIVES

1. To encourage the sharing of feelings and beliefs
2. To gather and appreciate many points of view
3. To review subject matter in cooperative learning groups
4. To build inclusion and promote influence

INSTRUCTIONS

1. Ask the community to meet in tribes.
2. To each tribe, distribute pens and a large piece of paper (at least 2 x 6-feet long) labeled with one of the following subjects (or an academic topic) on each:

   - pet peeves
   - what I wonder about
   - ambitions
   - favorite moments
   - things that scare me a lot
   - things that excite me

3. Invite the tribes to write "graffiti" on their paper for three to five minutes, all tribe members writing at once.
4. At the end of three to five minutes, ask the tribes to stop writing and exchange papers. Have the tribes now write on their new graffiti papers for the next three to five minutes. Repeat this procedure until all the tribes have had a chance to write graffiti on all the papers.
5. Return original papers to tribes and allow the members time to read the graffiti and discuss similarities in what people wrote.
6. Have each tribe report its findings back to the community.

SUGGESTED REFLECTION QUESTIONS

CONTENT (COGNITIVE LEARNING)

- What general things did the community write?
- Why did you exchange papers?

COLLABORATIVE (SOCIAL LEARNING)

- How did your tribe members cooperate?
- In what special ways did your tribe members help each other?

DISCOVERING GIFTS (PERSONAL LEARNING)

- What did you write that told something about yourself?
- Which graffiti topic meant the most to you?
- What unique qualities did you bring to this activity?

APPRECIATION

Invite statements of appreciation (and recognition of gifts):
- "It was helpful when you…"
- "I liked it when you wrote…"

Tribe Mimes/Role-Play

TIME: 45 minutes

GROUPING: tribes

MATERIALS: none

DEVELOPMENTAL TASKS:
Independence/Autonomy
Social Competency
Problem Solving

OBJECTIVES

1. To build self-esteem
2. To promote inclusion and influence
3. To act out or role-play dilemmas or problem situations

INSTRUCTIONS

Note: This strategy can be used very effectively with lesson topics.

1. Have the students meet in their tribes. Ask if anyone knows what a "mime" is or how circus clowns communicate with an audience. Explain that "mime" means acting out a message or image without speaking any words.

2. Give each tribe a written message or image to act out. Examples:
   - harnessing a horse
   - baking a cake
   - fixing a bicycle tire
   - washing a window

3. Have each tribe decide how to portray the message without speaking.

4. Have each tribe present its mime to the class, and have the other students guess what is being portrayed.

5. Then explain "role play" which means adding speech to what is being acted out. Give the tribes prepared cards that contain problem situations that may be confronting students. Example: Terry and Aaron are approached by two friends who ask them to go with them after school to smoke cigarettes they just found. Act out how Terry and Aaron could handle the situation so that they feel proud of themselves.

6. Give the tribes time to plan how to role-play the problem cards, and invite them to present their role-plays.

7. Be sure to follow all presentations with reflection questions.

SUGGESTED REFLECTION QUESTIONS

CONTENT (COGNITIVE LEARNING)

- What did you learn from the mime presentations?
- Why is acting out a situation using mime a good way to learn?

COLLABORATIVE (SOCIAL LEARNING)

- What social skills did people in your tribe need to do mime?
- How did leadership in your tribe develop during this activity?

DISCOVERING GIFTS (PERSONAL LEARNING)

- How did you feel while you were acting your part? Observing others?
- What strengths or skills did you use while you were acting your part?
- How did you help your tribe in a special way?

APPRECIATION

Invite statements of appreciation (and recognition of gifts):
- "I really liked it when…"
- "I enjoyed most seeing…"

OPTION

Rather than defining the problem situations yourself, have the tribes define them. They can write their situations on cards and exchange them with other tribes to act out.

Tribe Portrait

TIME: varies (see note)

GROUPING: tribes

MATERIALS: paper, felt pens, pencils, erasers

DEVELOPMENTAL TASKS:
Independence/Autonomy
Sense of Purpose

OBJECTIVES

1. To develop self-awareness
2. To develop awareness of spatial relationships
3. To develop cooperative skills
4. To practice observation skills
5. To build inclusion and influence

INSTRUCTIONS

1. Explain to the community that each tribe will draw a self-portrait and that the portrait will include individual drawings of each tribe member.
2. Ask the community to meet in tribes, get their materials, and find a space to work.
3. Discuss possible put-downs that could occur and how to avoid them.
4. Each tribe member asks one other member to do a sketch of him or her.
5. "Artists" draw their subjects using pencils.
6. After completing portraits, have the artists check with subjects for additions or corrections.
7. After corrections and additions have been made, have the artists use marking pens on portrait.
8. When the portraits of all the tribe members are finished, the tribe decides how to present their portraits to the rest of the class.

Note: This project can best be done over a period of two to five days. Also, the teacher may move from tribe to tribe giving some instruction. Excellent opportunity to bring in outside art resource person to work with small groups.

SUGGESTED REFLECTION QUESTIONS

CONTENT (COGNITIVE LEARNING)

- Why did you draw a tribal portrait?
- Why was it easy/difficult to draw a tribal portrait?

COLLABORATIVE (SOCIAL LEARNING)

- How did this task require you to work together?
- How well did you work together?
- How did you make sure that every member of your tribe participated?

DISCOVERING GIFTS (PERSONAL LEARNING)

- How did you feel when your portrait was being done?
- How did you feel when you saw your portrait?
- How did you help your tribe during this activity?
- What talents or gifts did you discover in yourself?

APPRECIATION

Invite statements of appreciation (and recognition of gifts):

- "I like what you drew because…"
- "When I look at our tribal portrait I feel…"

Tribes Team Together

TIME: 20–40 minutes

GROUPING: tribes

MATERIALS: paper, pencil, poster paper

DEVELOPMENTAL TASKS:
Independence/Autonomy
Social Competency
Sense of Purpose

OBJECTIVES

1. To build inclusion and community in tribes or small groups
2. To review material learned (curriculum specific)
3. To develop critical thinking

INSTRUCTIONS

1. Have students meet in tribes or small groups of 4–5.
2. Ask students to share as much information as they can about themselves in two minutes (i.e., interests, hobbies, birth date, brother's name, etc.).
3. Have one student from each tribe leave the room.
4. Have each tribe, in turn, answer a question about the person that is missing (or about the subject-related material). Examples:
   • Has (person missing) ever broken a bone?
   • What is (missing person)'s favorite flavor of ice cream?
5. Have the tribe members from outside return to the room. (*Note:* It is very helpful to have the returning students line up at the back of the room with all of the other students in tribes facing forward, so there is no "helping.")
6. Ask the set of four questions again, to those students who have just returned to the room. Score points for matched answers.
7. Repeat steps 3-7 until all group members have had a chance to be the person who leaves the room.

OPTION

Have students tell as much as they can about a specific subject, i.e., the Civil War, Shakespeare, geometric shapes.

SUGGESTED REFLECTION QUESTIONS

CONTENT (COGNITIVE LEARNING)

• What did you learn by doing this activity?
• What questions were the hardest/the easiest? Why?
• Why did we do this activity in tribes instead of just pairs?

COLLABORATIVE (SOCIAL LEARNING)

• How did you make sure that everyone participated?
• How did your tribe cope with questions that were difficult to answer?
• How did your tribe members help each other?
• How do you feel as a tribe now?

DISCOVERING GIFTS (PERSONAL LEARNING)

• Which role did you like best? Why?
• How did you help your tribe in a special way?

APPRECIATION

Invite statements of appreciation (and recognition of gifts):
• "You were really good at…"
• "That was fun when you…"

Two For Tuesday

TIME: 20 minutes

GROUPING: community

MATERIALS: none

DEVELOPMENTAL TASKS:
Independence/Autonomy
Social Competency
Sense of Purpose

OBJECTIVES

1. To build inclusion and community
2. To increase awareness of the importance of stating appreciations

INSTRUCTIONS

1. Have the community sit in a large circle.
2. Review the tribes agreements.
3. Ask the students to think of two statements of appreciation or two positive comments about themselves or others.
4. Have everyone respond in turn. Allow time at the end for those who passed to respond if they desire.

SUGGESTED REFLECTION QUESTIONS

CONTENT (COGNITIVE LEARNING)

• What are some thoughts that people shared?
• Were there any similarities in things that people shared?

COLLABORATIVE (SOCIAL LEARNING)

• How did the community members show that they were listening to each other?
• How does sharing positive thoughts help communities?

DISCOVERING GIFTS (PERSONAL LEARNING)

• How did you feel about sharing with the community today?
• How did you contribute to the community in a special way?
• What do you appreciate about yourself today?

APPRECIATION

Invite statements of appreciation (and recognition of gifts):

• "I appreciated it when…"
• "Thank you, (name), for…"

Urgent!

TIME: varies

GROUPING: community, tribes

MATERIALS: none

DEVELOPMENTAL TASKS:
Independence/Autonomy
Social Competency
Sense of Purpose

OBJECTIVES

1. To build inclusion and influence
2. To provide students an opportunity to think of significant other persons in their lives
3. To encourage communicating with a special person
4. To promote caring and acceptance for the concerns of others

INSTRUCTIONS

1. Have the community sit in a circle. Review the agreements.
2. Invite each student who cares to participate to send a verbal message to a person in his or her life with whom he or she feels an urgent need to communicate. Messages can involve suggestions for change in a person's life, reaffirmation of caring and friendship, or messages to well known people (i.e., a President, character from literature, scientist, historical figure, etc.).
3. Explain that the format for a message is: "Dear (name), I urge you to…" Have each student end his or her message by saying: "Your (adjective) friend, (name)." Model a message yourself.
4. There is no follow-up discussion after this activity. All messages are sent in an atmosphere of total acceptance.

APPRECIATION

Invite statements of appreciation (and recognition of gifts):
- "I liked it when…"
- "I felt good when…"
- "I appreciated it when…"

What We Need From Each Other

OBJECTIVES

1. To promote inclusion and mutual respect for a substitute teacher, student teacher, or volunteer
2. To identify needs and expectations
3. To promote transfer of responsibility for practicing collaborative skills

TIME: 20 minutes

GROUPING: community

MATERIALS: easel, large paper, markers

DEVELOPMENTAL TASKS:
Social Competency
Sense of Purpose
Problem Solving

INSTRUCTIONS

1. Prepare the following chart with examples prior to the community circle:

What does (substitute's name) need from you?	What do you need from (substitute's name)?
Respect	Energizer break
Attentive Listening	Slow down

2. Prior to the arrival of the substitute, student teacher or volunteer, invite the community to respond to the questions on the chart. Record their responses in the appropriate columns. (*Note:* When student teachers or volunteers are in the classroom with the teacher, prepare the chart together as a community.)
3. Leave instructions for the substitute to review the chart with the students, and to initiate a discussion about what the community needs from each other for the day. Have the substitute encourage the community to add information to the chart.
4. Encourage the substitute to make a verbal statement of what she has heard that the students need for the day. Have the substitute ask the students to turn to a neighbor and make a verbal statement about what the community has agreed on.
5. Suggest that the substitute leave the chart up for the day so students can remind themselves and each other of the agreements.

SUGGESTED REFLECTION QUESTIONS

CONTENT (COGNITIVE LEARNING)

- Why is it important to take the time to fill out this chart?
- What will the outcome for the community be after taking the time to do this?

COLLABORATIVE (SOCIAL LEARNING)

- Why is it important for the class to follow agreements when a new person joins our community?
- How will this chart help the community to follow the agreements?

DISCOVERING GIFTS (PERSONAL LEARNING)

- In what way did you help the community during this activity?
- What strengths and skills will you use to help the community follow through with what you have agreed upon?

APPRECIATION

Invite statements of appreciation (and recognition of gifts):
- "I liked your suggestion…"
- "Thank you for including…"
- "You are really good at noticing…"

What's In Your Wallet?

TIME: 30 minutes

GROUPING: tribes

MATERIALS: personal items

DEVELOPMENTAL TASKS:
Independence/Autonomy
Sense of Purpose

OBJECTIVES

1. To create tribal inclusion
2. To give the students an opportunity to share something of themselves

INSTRUCTIONS

1. Remind the students of the agreements.
2. Ask each student to select something from his or her desk, wallet, purse, or backpack that is special and symbolic of him or her.
3. Ask the students to meet in their tribes to share their special items.

SUGGESTED REFLECTION QUESTIONS

CONTENT (COGNITIVE LEARNING)

- What was the value of this strategy?
- What did you learn?

COLLABORATIVE (SOCIAL LEARNING)

- How could you tell when your tribe members were listening to each other?
- What would you, as a tribe, like to do more of to help each other listen even better?

DISCOVERING GIFTS (PERSONAL LEARNING)

- Was it hard for you to select something special to share? Why?
- How did you feel after sharing your special object?
- How does your special object relate to your special gifts or talents?

APPRECIATION

Invite statements of appreciation (and recognition of gifts):
- "I liked it when…"
- "I appreciated you, (name), for…"

What's On Your Mind?

TIME: 20–30 minutes

GROUPING: community

MATERIALS: none

DEVELOPMENTAL TASKS:
Independence/Autonomy
Social Competency
Sense of Purpose
Problem Solving

OBJECTIVES

1. To promote group support for a concern
2. To assist a peer, colleague or friend to resolve a problem
3. To promote influence

INSTRUCTIONS

1. Have the community members sit in a large circle.
2. Review the tribes agreements.
3. Ask the students to share, "What's currently on your mind?"
4. Have everyone respond in turn to the question. Allow time at the end for those who passed to respond if they desire.
5. List any concerns that require further exploration on a chart.
6. Take time to explore concerns listed on the chart. (Use the "Suggestion Circle" or "Client-Consultants" strategies to explore concerns, if needed.)

SUGGESTED REFLECTION QUESTIONS

CONTENT (COGNITIVE LEARNING)

- What kinds of things were shared?
- What similarities did you notice?
- Why is it important to share?

COLLABORATIVE (SOCIAL LEARNING)

- How did the community members help each other?
- How can we continue to help others in our community?

DISCOVERING GIFTS (PERSONAL LEARNING)

- How does it feel to share what's on your mind?
- What personal strengths or skills did you use to help make this activity successful?
- What communication skills or "people" skills do you feel most comfortable using?

APPRECIATION

Invite statements of appreciation (and recognition of gifts):
- "I liked it when…"
- "Thank you for…"
- "You were really helpful when…"

What's The Tint of Your Glasses?

TIME: 45 minutes

GROUPING: tribes

MATERIALS: poster paper and colored pencils/pens for each tribe

DEVELOPMENTAL TASKS:
Independence/Autonomy
Sense of Purpose

OBJECTIVES

1. To build understanding that our different backgrounds give us different perspectives
2. To show that seeing things differently is okay.
3. To experience how different viewpoints help us to see the whole picture
4. To promote multicultural awareness, acceptance and understanding
5. To experience influence

INSTRUCTIONS

1. Have the community meet in tribes.
2. Have each student draw a pair of eyeglasses on a sheet of paper.
3. Ask each student to draw small designs or symbols on his or her glasses in response to the questions you will read. Examples:
   - What is your country of birth?
   - How many sisters and brothers do you have?
   - What language do your parents speak other than or in addition to English?
   - Have you ever lived on a farm or ranch? In a big city?
4. Have the tribe members compare glasses. Ask, "Do any look the same?"
5. Discuss how different experiences give people different perspectives and opinions. Example:
   - How a city person versus a country person might look at pigs in a pen (pigs are dirty/pigs are great).
6. Ask each tribe to make a list of three other examples.
7. Have each tribe report their list to the community. Ask, "What can happen when people believe everyone sees things the same way?" Discuss perceptions, assumptions, conflict, or respect for differences.

SUGGESTED REFLECTION QUESTIONS

CONTENT (COGNITIVE LEARNING)

- What did you learn about how different people see the same thing?

COLLABORATIVE (SOCIAL LEARNING)

- In what ways did your tribe work together well during this activity?
- How did your tribe show support for each other's differences?

DISCOVERING GIFTS (PERSONAL LEARNING)

- How did you feel when someone had a different point of view?
- How can you help others see your point of view?
- What personal strengths did you use to communicate your point of view?

APPRECIATION

Invite statements of appreciation (and recognition of gifts):
- "Thanks, (name), for…"
- "I appreciate your…"

Where Do I Stand?

TIME: 15–40 minutes

GROUPING: community, tribes

MATERIALS: animal signs, string, tape

DEVELOPMENTAL TASKS:
Independence/Autonomy
Social Competency

OBJECTIVES

1. To encourage sharing
2. To encourage respect for individual differences
3. To experience inclusion and influence

INSTRUCTIONS

1. On large cards, print four animal names: lion, deer, fox, dove. (*Note:* Alternate signs could include: mountain, river, ocean, meadow; piano, trumpet, drum, flute; have students suggest signs.)
2. Suspend the animal signs from the ceiling in four areas of the classroom.
3. Ask each student to stand under the sign for the animal that they are most like when in their tribe. Encourage people to talk among themselves while they are deciding where to stand.
4. When all the students have chosen animals and have taken their places under the signs, ask them to share why they placed themselves where they did.
5. Continue the activity by repeating steps 3 and 4 with other situations. Examples:
   • How are you with your friends?
   • How are you with your family?
   • How are you by yourself?
   • How are you in a social situation with people you don't know?
6. Ask the students to meet in tribes and talk about their choices—why they stood where they did.
7. Have all write in their Personal Journals what they learned.

SUGGESTED REFLECTION QUESTIONS

CONTENT (COGNITIVE LEARNING)

• What are the qualities of a lion/fox/dove/deer?
• What did you learn about other students in the community/about yourself?

COLLABORATIVE (SOCIAL LEARNING)

• Why would you find it difficult to take a stand?
• How is taking a stand an important skill for all of us?
• How did the community and your tribe help you feel comfortable taking a stand?

DISCOVERING GIFTS (PERSONAL LEARNING)

• How did you feel when you took your stand?
• How did you feel sharing your reasons with the community?
• What did you learn about yourself?
• In what special ways did you contribute to the group?

APPRECIATION

Invite statements of appreciation (and recognition of gifts):
• "I was interested when…"
• "I appreciated it when you said…"

Wishful Thinking

TIME: varies

GROUPING: tribes, community

MATERIALS: none

DEVELOPMENTAL TASKS:
Independence/Autonomy
Social Competency

OBJECTIVES

1. To provide the opportunity to express a wish
2. To build inclusion

INSTRUCTIONS

1. Have the students sit or stand in a community circle or in tribes. Instruct them that no discussion is allowed during this activity.
2. Ask each student in turn to make a brief statement beginning with, "I wish..." related to personal life, feelings about politics, school, the community, etc.
3. If possible, take turns around the circle more than once.

SUGGESTED REFLECTION QUESTIONS

CONTENT (COGNITIVE LEARNING)

- How easy/difficult was it for you to think of wishes to share?
- Why are wishes important?
- What wishes do you have in common?

COLLABORATIVE (SOCIAL LEARNING)

- How did your tribe members show that they were listening to each other's wishes?
- How did tribe members help each other share?

DISCOVERING GIFTS (PERSONAL LEARNING)

- How did you feel while you were sharing your wish/listening to others share?
- What skills did you use while participating in this activity?
- What did you learn about yourself?

APPRECIATION

Invite statements of appreciation (and recognition of gifts):
- "I liked it when..."
- "I felt good when..."
- "I admired your honesty when..."

Energizers

Energizers

BUBBLE GUM

Each group has a pair of mittens and a pack of bubble gum. From the pack, each member must open a piece of gum with the mittens on and then pass the gum and mittens to the next member to do the same. To incorporate curriculum, discuss how bubble gum often has pictures of famous people in it (sports figures, musicians, etc.). Each group should choose a famous person from the unit being studied and prepare a report or project to present to the class.

BUMPETY-BUMP-BUMP

Form a circle standing up, with a chosen "it" in the center. The "it" walks up to you and stands in front of you and says one of the following:

"Center, bumpety-bump-bump"

"Self, bumpety-bump-bump"

"Right, bumpety-bump-bump"

"Left, bumpety-bump-bump"

You must say his or her name, your name, or the person's name to the right or left of you before "it" completes saying "bumpety-bump-bump;" otherwise you become "it."

CHANGES

Have students get in pairs (or do in a full group by having five volunteers come and stand in the front of the room). Instructions are to look at your partner (or class volunteers) and notice and remember as much as you can about his or her appearance. Partners turn back to back (volunteers leave the room) and change three noticeable things about their appearance. Students must guess what changes have been made. This energizer is easy to repeat, because as time goes on, the changes can be more subtle, specific, even scientific (i.e., change three things involving color, quantity, your torso, etc.).

CLAP-SLAP

Get a rhythm going: two claps, two slaps on lap. Go around the circle filling the blanks to the following chant: My name is (Karen), I come from (Kuwait) and I sell (Kleenex). The first sound must match the beginning sound in your name.

DO AFTER ME

Sit in a large circle. One person begins by entering the circle and making a gesture, sound, or movement (the more ridiculous, the more fun), and then points to someone else in the circle to succeed him. This person makes the same gesture, sound, or movement as the preceding person made, and then adds her own performance. She then chooses the next person, and this person need only repeat the preceding action and add one before choosing someone new. The game is over when everyone has had a chance in the circle.

ELECTRICITY

Have everyone sit down in one large circle. Hold hands. One person starts a squeeze on one side and the next person quietly passes it on around the circle. Variation: send an "ooh" or an "aah" the other way.

FORK AND SPOON

This is a hilariously confusing exercise in communication. Have everyone seated in a circle. The leader has a fork in the right hand and a spoon in the left hand. The leader turns to the person on the right and, holding up the fork, says, "This is a fork." The person being spoken to says, "A what?" The leader repeats, "A fork," and hands the fork over. The person with the fork says, "Oh, a fork!" Now, the person with the fork turns to the person on his/her right and says, "This is a fork." The person being spoken to says, "A what?" The person with the fork turns to the leader and asks, "A what?" The leader says, "A fork." Then the person turns to his/her right and says, "A fork," and hands over the fork to the next person. That person says, "Oh, a fork," turns to the person on the right and begins again with, "This is a fork." When the person replies, "A What?" each person must go back up the line, one at a time, asking, "A what?" until the leader tells them, "A fork." Then, "Oh, a fork," is said down the line until it reaches the person holding and then handing over the fork, beginning again with, "This is a fork." Now that the fork is flowing smoothly to the right, start the process to the left with the spoon! The leader must now be alert for responding in both directions to the "A what?" questions, saying "A fork" to the right and "A spoon" to the left. Watch the fun when both the fork and the spoon reach the same person at once, usually midway around the circle.

HAGOO

Divide into two teams and form two lines. Have people stand shoulder to shoulder facing a person on the other team. Stand a yard apart. One person from each team will volunteer to walk past each person in the row of the opposite team. The people on the team try to make the volunteer from the other team smile as he/she walks by. No touching is allowed. If the volunteer cracks up he/she must join the opposite team. If he/she makes it to the end straight faced, he/she goes back in the row with his/her original team.

I LIKE MY NEIGHBORS

Have all members seated on chairs in a circle, with one person standing in the middle as "it." The person in the middle makes a statement such as, "I like my neighbors, especially those who are wearing running shoes (wearing glasses, are over thirteen, have a birthday in September, etc.)." All those people who are wearing running shoes must jump up from their seats and scramble to find a chair; the person in the middle also scrambles for an empty chair. The one person left standing becomes the new "it."

Extension: Two or more people seated away from each other may make eye contact and nonverbally "plot" to change places. When they make the dash to each others' seats, the "leader" may try to beat them to it.

LINEUP

Have students line up in order of birth date, height, number of family members, number of the bus they ride to school, alphabetical order of middle name, etc. Have them do this without talking. This is a good energizer for getting your group focused, settled, and silent. The lineup is also a handy way to get your class into random cooperative groups.

NAME WAVE

All stand in a circle. One person says his/her name and at the same time makes a motion or gesture. (Example: "Beth," as she waves her hand.) The person to the right says, "Beth," and waves her hand as Beth did. The name and motion spread around the circle in a "wave." When the circle is complete, the next person says his/her name and a different motion and that "waves" around the circle. Continue until all names are said and activated.

PEN PALS

Give each participant a 3 x 5 index card and tell them to write a little known fact about themselves on the card, something they won't mind the group eventually knowing. State that they are not to write their name on the card. Collect all cards, shuffle and redistribute. If someone gets his/her own card back, it is exchanged for another. When everyone has an unfamiliar card, have all stand and circulate, asking one another questions about the information on the card. For example, "Did you barrel race horses as a child?" When the person answering the description is found, he/she signs the card and puts it on a designated wall space. When you are finished, the community has an instant bulletin board of people and their accomplishments. This is a good full group inclusion energizer—good for parents on back-to-school night, too!

PEOPLE PATTERNS

Discuss types of patterns (A B A B, A B C A B C, A B B A B B). Have the members of a tribe or small group establish themselves in a pattern and stand in front of the class in that order. For example, an A B A B pattern might be "stripes on shirt, no stripes on shirt" or "earrings, no earrings." The people pattern should tell the audience what type of pattern they are demonstrating (A B A B, etc.). Members of the class must try to guess who can go next in the pattern; they may not guess the pattern until they have named a person to stand next in the people pattern. The person to correctly identify the pattern will join his or her tribe or small group to establish the next pattern. Pattern criteria should be clearly visible to all.

RAIN

Have everyone sit in a circle, facing the center. Ask all to close their eyes, pausing for a moment or two to become quiet while each person gets ready to hear the sound the person on the right will be making. Keep eyes closed as the rainstorm begins with the leader rubbing her palms together, back and forth. The person to the left joins her, and then the person to her left, and so on, around the circle. When the leader hears the drizzle sound being made by the person on the right, she starts snapping her fingers. When the snapping action has been picked up by everyone around the circle, the leader switches to hand clapping, then to thigh slapping, and finally to foot stomping. After foot stomping, the leader reverses the order of sounds, introducing thigh slapping, hand clapping, finger snapping and finally palm rubbing. For the last round, the leader stops rubbing her palms and takes the hand of the person on her left. Each person follows suit around the circle until there is silence once again.

SHUFFLE YOUR BUNS

Have all participants seated in a circle with chairs pushed in tight. (All chairs should be of equal height.) The leader stands and moves to the center of the circle, leaving one empty chair. Model the directions by saying, "Shuffle to the right." Only the person with the empty chair to his or her right may "shuffle their buns" into the chair to the right. As each person moves, he/she vacates his/her chair for the next person to "shuffle their buns." This begins to move around the circle quite rapidly. Now the leader may say, "Shuffle to the left." At this command, the person that just completed a shuffle to the right must reverse and "shuffle their buns" into the empty chair to the left. The procession then follows; each time a chair is vacated, someone is shuffling into it. It must be understood that one cannot "shuffle their buns" unless s/he is moving into an empty/vacated seat. Once the group has mastered shuffling their buns, the leader speeds up the process by reversing commands frequently enough so as to confuse the action. The object now is for the leader to shuffle his or her buns into an empty seat. Having interrupted the flow, the person now in the middle giving the "shuffle" commands is the person who failed to shuffle fast enough and lost his or her seat to the leader. To really get things rolling, give each person in the group a one-time-only opportunity to automatically reverse the shuffle by slapping the empty chair next to them instead of shuffling into it. This "confusion" allows the person in the middle a better opportunity to find a seat, and keeps anyone from having to be the middle person for too long.

SNOWBALL

Each student places his/her name on a piece of paper and wads it up. Students line up, half on either side of the room. At a signal they begin a snowball fight. At the end, each gets a snowball, learns new information about the person whose snowball they found, and shares it with the class.

THREE BALL PASS

This is a mini "group juggle." Using something that is easy to catch, establish a pattern around the room as follows: leader says someone's name and tosses him/her the ball; s/he chooses another person, says that person's name, and tosses him/her the ball; continue in this manner until each person has caught and tossed the ball once. The ball will end the pattern in the hands of the leader. Repeat the pattern until it can be done quickly. Begin again, and after several people have caught and tossed the ball, throw in the second ball, using the same pattern sequence; then throw in the third ball. This is a great energizer for learning names. After the group has mastered "Three Ball Pass," have them reverse the pattern! For a real challenge, have your group try it silently (after the pattern is established).

TWO TRUTHS AND A LIE

This energizer is great for building inclusion and re-entry after a school vacation. Have each person write down three things about themselves, what they did over vacation, etc. Of these three statements, two must be true and one must be a lie. Suggest that the lie should not be very obvious; it can even be a small detail. The rest of the class (or small group) must guess which one is the lie.

ZAP

Have all participants stand in a circle. The leader has everyone "create some energy" by rubbing their hands together quickly, back and forth. Next the leader has everyone take a deep breath in, hold for two to three seconds, and breathe out. Do two more deep breaths, while continuously rubbing hands. Now the leader instructs (while all are still rubbing hands) that on the count of three, everyone will make a sweeping point with their right arm to the center of the circle and yell, "Zzzzzzaaaappp!" This energizer really creates some energy, while at the same time allowing for the expenditure of energy. Try zapping a person (only if they want to be zapped), or even social issues such as classroom put-downs.

ZOOM, ZOOM, BRAKE!

Have everyone stand in a community circle, facing in, shoulder to shoulder. Introduce the sound "zoom" and say that the sound goes zooming around the circle whenever you say it. When you say it, look to your right. That person immediately says, "zoom," while looking to his or her right and this continues quickly around the circle. After going around the circle once, say that the car was only in first gear. Shift up into second and then third gear, the "zoom" going faster each time with more power. Now introduce the "brake" by demonstrating a screeching noise along with a hand signal of pulling back the brake. Have everyone try it with his or her own screeching brake sound. Now the group is ready to play. The rules are that you only get to brake once. When someone "brakes," the zoom reverses direction and goes the opposite way around the circle. Eventually everyone will get a chance to "brake" or the facilitator can call an end to the noise.

R*esources*

Resources

The History of Tribes and Tribes TLC®

The initial version of the Tribes process began to evolve in the early seventies, a time when concerned educators and parents again began groping for ways to motivate children's learning, to bring up test scores, to manage school behavior problems, and to stem the tide upon which many good teachers were leaving the teaching profession. National surveys were alerting the general public, industry leaders and the U.S. Congress that the majority of high school students did not have the knowledge or skills to do well in the world of work and social complexities that they would face in life. Twenty years ago? Or is it today?

At the same time, Jeanne Gibbs realized that her own children's achievements and behavior in school seemed to be influenced by the quality of the classroom and school environment. Being a student at heart, Jeanne began exploring studies on school climate, human development, child development, and the dynamics of organization systems. In 1973 she was challenged by her employer, the Medical Services of Contra Costa County, California, to consult with the County Department of Education towards the prevention of substance abuse related problems within eighteen county school districts. There was little research at that time on prevention other than studies which confirmed that informational curricula alone did not deter problems. The author reasoned that since environment influences human behavior, building positive environments within schools and families not only would be preventive, but could be significant in promoting academic learning and social development. This was a pretty far out idea when scary films, talk by former addicts and information on the perils of drug use were the favored strategies.

Nevertheless, the concept made enough sense to some other visionaries at the California Department of Education who in 1974 funded a small grant that would enable twenty six elementary school teachers to meet one day a month for eight months to pilot a group development process that Jeanne had been using for many years within community settings. As the teachers began to experience the caring environment within their own work groups, they began to use the term, "tribe." Repeatedly they said, "We feel like a family… we feel like a tribe."

From 1975 through 1985 numerous applications of the group development process were made through a non-profit corporation which Jeanne organized. The "people process" proved to be valuable in alcohol recovery centers, juvenile facilities, convalescent homes, daycare centers, peer assistance and recreational programs. It was used to facilitate planning committees, conferences and university classes. California schools began to request training when they learned that the Tribes small group process decreased student behavior problems, increased self-esteem and improved teachers' energy and morale. The Research Triangle Institute, under a U.S. Department of Education contract, identified Tribes TLC® as a program to teach Kindergarten to 12th grade students social skills.[1] The Council of the Great City Schools has cited Tribes as a model schools are using to prevent violence.[2]

By 1986 educators recognized the value of using small groups for the teaching of academic curricula. Some teachers who had training in cooperative learning methods discovered that the Tribes group process improved the capacity of students to work together. Based on the extensive research of the cooperative learning field and teachers' experience with the process, the book, *Tribes, A Process for Social Development and Cooperative Learning,* was published in 1987. The demand for training accelerated throughout the country, and in 1991 quality materials incorporating new research, concepts and methods were designed by the author and her colleagues. The more comprehensive version of the Tribes process became known as "Tribes TLC®," and resulted in the writing and publication of, *Tribes, A New Way of Learning and Being Together,* 1994, and the new 2001 edition.

The primary mission of Tribes TLC® as now defined is "to assure the healthy development of every child in the school community so that each has the knowledge, skills and resiliency to be successful in our rapidly changing world."

Indeed, this can happen when schools engage all teachers, administrators, students and families in working together as a learning community—a community dedicated to caring and support, active participation, and positive expectations for all of the young people in the circle of concern.

REFERENCES

1. Alberg, J., Eller, S., and Petry, C. A Resource Guide for Social Skills Instruction, Center for Research in Education, Research Triangle Institute (U.S. Department of Education, Office of Special Education Programs), Longmount, Colorado: Sopers Publishers, 1994.

2. Newkumet, M.B. and Casserly, M. Urban School Safety: Strategies of the Great City Schools. Washington, DC: Council of the Great City Schools, 1994.

A Fact Sheet on Tribes TLC®

THERE ARE CERTIFIED TRIBES TLC® TRAINERS SERVING:

All U.S. States and Canada, as well as distant lands such as Australia, Guam, American Samoa, the People's Republic of China, the Dominican Republic, the Northern Marianas, Micronesia, the Marshall Islands, and South America.

DEMOGRAPHICS OF TRAINERS

Certified Tribes TLC® Trainers include individuals of almost all races and ethnic groups. Over one fourth of the 550 trainers are bilingual or multilingual. Approximately one-third are administrators (Assistant Superintendents, Principals, Coordinators, State Department Officials and Program Managers). There are also Psychologists, Private Consultants, Deacons, University Instructors and, of course, public and private school classroom teachers, including National Board Certified teachers. The Certified Tribes Trainers have degrees ranging from Bachelors to PhD's. Ages of the trainers range from age 22 to 76. There are trainers living in 32 U.S. states, as well as many other countries.

THE TRIBES PROCESS CAN BE FOUND IN:

- Public Schools
- Private Schools
- Parochial Schools
- Native American and First Nation Schools
- International Schools
- University Programs
- State Departments of Education
- After School Programs
- Recreation Programs
- Family Resource Centers
- Church groups
- Drug and Alcohol Treatment Centers
- Regional Educational Centers

FUNDING:

Funding sources for training in the Tribes process come from Federal, State and local resources as well as Foundations. Call CenterSource for more information.

CenterSource Systems, LLC   7975 Cameron Drive, #500   Windsor, California 95492
800 810 1701   Fax: 707 838 1062   e-mail: tribes@tribes.com   www.tribes.com

Results Reported by Tribes Schools

SPRING BRANCH ISD, TEXAS In the spring of 1999, 55 classroom teachers and their students participated in a Tribes evaluation survey. Among the results found in their study were the following:

- Teachers who have implemented Tribes indicated that they spent less time managing student behavior.
- Students in Tribes classes reported that they got along better with others.
- Mutual respect was evidenced through behaviors in Tribes classrooms.
- Teachers indicated that they had more time for creative teaching, and students saw new learning as "fun."
- Group behaviors changed even at bus stops as students began accepting more responsibility for their behavior.

Tribes has been selected as a Promising Practice in the President's Initiative on Race.

REGION VII ESC IN KILGORE, TEXAS found that discipline referrals reduced in some cases by over 50%.

BELOIT CITY SCHOOLS, WISCONSIN, completed a three-year longitudinal study on Tribes and found that thorough and consistent classroom implementation of the Tribes process and higher CTBS reading scores were significantly associated with higher performance on WRCT for this sample. The year 3 evaluation came to the following conclusions: Tribes has indirect impact on student achievement by improving the classroom environment. The highly effective Tribes classrooms produce significant achievement benefits. Teachers spend less time managing and disciplining students, freeing more time for instruction. The Tribes environment made it easier for students to proactively engage in the learning process, take academic risks, and accept responsibility for outcomes.

OKLAHOMA MIDDLE SCHOOL In a recent study of discipline referrals made by teachers in an Oklahoma middle school, 73% of the referrals (disruptive behavior, fighting, refusal to work) were made by teachers not yet trained in Tribes. An equal number of Tribes trained teachers made 27% of referrals during the same period of time.

WATERLOO, IOWA Suspensions in a large Waterloo, Iowa, elementary school decreased 21% in one year. Suspensions for special education students decreased 82%. All teachers in the school had been trained in the process of Tribes.

THE STATE OF HAWAII study of 17 elementary schools using the process of Tribes found that mutual respect was the common denominator for all students and faculty.

CenterSource Systems, LLC 7975 Cameron Drive, #500 Windsor, California 95492
800 810 1701 Fax: 707 838 1062 e-mail: tribes@tribes.com www.tribes.com

The Research Triangle Institute's In-Depth Study of Tribes as a Social Skills Program

We are proud that the respected Research Triangle (RTI) chose to study the Tribes process as a social skills instructional program. Their book, *A Resource Guide for Social Skills Instruction,* by Joni Alberg, Christene Petry, and Susan Eller, contains a seven-page description of Tribes based upon site visits conducted around the country over a two year period, material submitted to them by CenterSource Systems, and a review of the book *Tribes, A Process for Social Development and Cooperative Learning.* Although the original intent of the RTI contract with the U.S. Department of Education was to identify programs for teaching social skills to students with disabilities, Dr. Alberg's staff and advisory committee quickly learned that educators were every bit as interested in knowing about programs that could teach social skills to all students.

Resource Guide for Social Skills Instruction describes the need for social skills instruction, how to select a program, and how to teach social skills. Their instructions on teaching social skills concur with concepts incorporated into this book and TLC® teacher training. Chapter 2 of the Research Triangle Institute's book is on social skills instruction and begins with concrete advice:

If social skills are to be learned they must be taught just as academic subjects are taught. You can apply the same effective teaching principles to social skills instruction as you apply to your teaching of academic content. Thus, no matter what the content, effective teachers:

- are clear about their instructional goals;
- are knowledgeable about their content and strategies for teaching it;
- communicate to their students what is expected of them and why;
- are knowledgeable about their students, adapting instructions to their needs and anticipating misconceptions in their existing knowledge;
- prepare students to share responsibility with the teacher for their own learning by providing students with the skills to learn independently;
- monitor students' understanding by providing regular feedback;
- integrate their instruction with that in other subject areas;
- understand that students are more likely to remember and use what they learn if they see a purpose beyond meeting school requirements; and
- accept responsibility for student outcomes.

RTI's site observations in schools using the Tribes process included both self-contained and mainstreamed settings with children who had learning disabilities, emotional/behavioral disabilities, communication disorders, hearing impairments, and severe mental and physical disabilities. Some of their observations and conclusions were:

1. Few program modifications were required for students with disabilities except for the use of sign language by a teacher with hearing impaired students, and adaptation of some activities to accommodate students with orthopedic disabilities.

2. Tribes appeared less successful with students who had severe disabilities and those who are completely nonverbal and cannot participate in groups.

3. The five elements of cooperative learning were noted in Tribes classrooms: positive interdependence, face-to-face interaction, interpersonal and small group skills, individual accountability, and group processing.

4. Observers noticed situations where students demonstrated internalization of the norms (agreements) when they called their peer's attention to inappropriate behavior and related it to the norms. "For example, in one class, student X overheard student Y make a derogatory comment to student Z. Student X told student Y that the comment was a put-down and the student should apologize (and did)."

5. The administrators, teachers, and support personnel that were interviewed expressed their beliefs that "teacher tribes" are important for successful implementation and providing necessary peer support.

6. The practice in Tribes of transferring some of the responsibility for behavior management from teachers to students was observed. A 5th grade teacher is reported as saying, "Tribes is my classroom management because it sets the stage for learning and builds a basis for support among the kids."

In addition to being selected as one of eight social skills programs studied in depth, the Research Triangle Institute *Resource Guide* includes annotations for the use of Tribes in elementary, middle/junior high, and senior high/postsecondary grade levels.

REFERENCES

1. Alberg, J., Eller, S., Petry, C., Nero, B. *Resource Guide for Social Skills Instruction.* Researched and compiled under the contract: Approaches and Choices to Developing Social Competence in Students with Disabilities, U.S. Department of Education, 1991–3.

2. Newkumet, M.B. and Casserly, M. *Urban School Safety: Strategies of the Great City Schools.* Washington, D.C.: Council of the Great City Schools, 1994.

The Impact of Group Processing

Tribes has always emphasized the importance of using reflection or process questions after each group strategy or learning experience. The motto shared among Tribes teachers has been, "The activity alone is not enough!" Throughout the years, CenterSource Systems trainers have been helping teachers define three types of reflection questions: (1) about the content [facts and concepts] of a lesson; (2) about the collaborative social and constructive thinking skills used by students within their tribes; and (3) about the personal learning and meaning that a lesson had for the students. Reflection questions were emphasized as a way to develop metacognition (learning about our learning) and responsibility among students to improve their learning groups (tribes). Empirical studies confirm that the time spent with students on "group processing" also leads to the greater retention of subject matter and academic achievement.

The study, "The Impact of Group Processing on Achievement in Cooperative Learning Groups," by Stuart Yager, Roger Johnson, David Johnson, and Bill Snider describes three learning conditions assessed in three classes composed of 84 third graders. An intensive five-week unit on transportation was taught in all three classrooms but in different processes.

Classroom A used the conventional individualistic learning method whereby students study alone and fill daily worksheets. Classrooms B and C used cooperative learning groups (four students to a group) with students working together and each group completing the worksheets together. In addition, classroom C spent 5 minutes processing their work as a group and setting goals for improvement. A 50-item factual knowledge multiple-choice test on the subject was given to all children prior to the unit and three weeks after the unit. A 25-item test was given after twelve instructional days and another 25-item test as soon as the unit was completed.

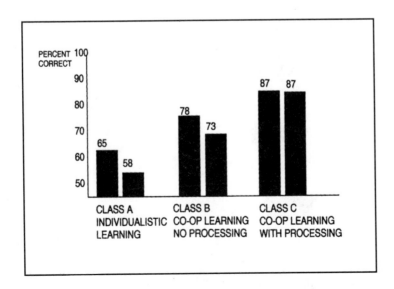

The graph was constructed from the research data. The first bar graph for each class shows achievement and the second bar graph indicates retention of knowledge after three weeks. Pretest scores for all students had averaged about 50%. In classroom A, using the individualistic approach, marginal gains moved from 50 to 65% in achievement, with retention dropping to 58% three weeks after the unit was completed. In classroom B, using cooperative learning groups and no processing, gains moved from 50 to 78%, with 73% retention. Results in classroom C, using cooperative learning groups with processing are impressive, with higher achievement (87%) and no loss in the retention of knowledge after three weeks.

Other studies by the same researchers show comparably dramatic results from the contribution of group processing to learning and individual achievement. Interested readers can learn more by accessing these research articles: Stuart Yager, Roger Johnson and David Johnson, "Oral Discussion, Group-to-Individual Transfer, and Achievement in Cooperative Learning Groups," Journal of Educational Psychology, 77: 60-66, 1985. Stuart Yager, Roger Johnson, David Johnson, and Bill Snider, "The Impact of Group Processing Achievement in Cooperative Learning Groups," The Journal of Social Psychology, 126:389-397, 1986.

From: Discovering Gifts in Middle School: Learning in a Caring Culture Called Tribes *(2001).*

Initiating Classroom Parent Tribes

OBJECTIVES

1. To develop participation and mutual support among the parents of the classroom.
2. To provide parents with a satisfying initial experience in the Tribes process.
3. To motivate parents to continue meeting throughout the year as a classroom learning community.
4. To provide information on the goals of Tribes, its process, and collaborative agreements.
5. To help parents learn how to foster resiliency in their children.

TIME:	60 minutes
FACILITATORS:	Two classroom parents trained by teachers
MATERIALS:	Tribes agreements posted on wall, 3 x 5-inch cards, pencils, large pieces of paper, felt tip pens

INSTRUCTIONS

8 min.
1. As parents arrive the teacher and parent facilitators (PFs) invite the parents to sit in small groups of prearranged chairs or desks (four to seven in a group).

2. The teacher welcomes all, gives overview of the hour and tells why the Tribes process is being used within the class or school. He or she introduces the PFs, and briefly, describes their roll.

4 min.
3. The PFs share their names, students' names, and their commitment to having the parents of the class become a supportive learning community.

4. The PFs then describe the Tribes agreements and ask the parents to honor them during their time together. They demonstrate the Tribes hand signal as a way to call attention.

5 min.
5. The parent facilitators discuss the importance of the Tribes agreements and attentive listening, and they demonstrate the skills.

1 min.
6. After asking each group to select a timekeeper, the PFs each ask the parents to share their name and one great quality about their students. Ask the timekeepers in each group to monitor the sharing time.

5 min.
7. The PFs ask the parents to think about, then share with one other person in the group, two things they hope for their children during the year. As one parent shares, the other notes down in one to three words the parent's hopes on a card. When the time is up, the PFs collect the cards.

5 min.

5 min.
8. The teacher responds to some of the hopes listed, tying them to goals for the year.

5 min.
9. The PFs ask the following reflection questions:
   • How many people enjoyed being able to talk with other parents tonight?
5 min.
   • How many would like to get together this way again?

5 min.
10. The PFs demonstrate and invite statements of appreciation in tribes.

11. They invite everyone to close in a community circle, sharing, "I learned" statements.

This material may be duplicated for classroom use.

A TRIBES TLC® LEARNING EXPERIENCE

1. PROVIDE FOR INCLUSION—A YOU QUESTION, ENERGIZER OR STRATEGY:

2. IDENTIFY THE OBJECTIVES:

Content Objective:

Collaborative Objective:

To have all members: (check 1–3)

❑ Participate fully
❑ Listen attentively
❑ Express appreciation of others' ideas
❑ Reflect often on group interaction
❑ Other:

❑ Think constructively
❑ Make group decisions
❑ Work cooperatively on tasks
❑ Respect and value different skills and opinions

3. IDENTIFY THE STRATEGY(IES):

4. ASK REFLECTION QUESTIONS BASED ON THE OBJECTIVES:

Content:

Collaborative:

Discovering Gifts:

5. PROVIDE AN OPPORTUNITY FOR APPRECIATION:

This material may be duplicated for classroom use.

FORM A: STUDENT ASSESSMENT

OUR TRIBE'S WORK TOGETHER

Tribe Name _____   Date _____

Using the numbers 1 (poorly), 2 (okay), and 3 (great!), rate how well your tribe did the following:

RATING   SOCIAL SKILL OR GROUP INTERACTION

_____   1. We listened to each other.

_____   2. We checked our understanding of the task.

_____   3. We shared ideas and information.

_____   4. We encouraged and helped each other.

_____   5. We stayed on the task and used our time well.

_____   6. Other:

Total Score: _____

This form may be duplicated for classroom use.

FORM A: STUDENT ASSESSMENT

OUR TRIBE'S WORK TOGETHER

Tribe Name _____   Date _____

Using the numbers 1 (poorly), 2 (okay), and 3 (great!), rate how well your tribe did the following:

RATING   SOCIAL SKILL OR GROUP INTERACTION

_____   1. We listened to each other.

_____   2. We checked our understanding of the task.

_____   3. We shared ideas and information.

_____   4. We encouraged and helped each other.

_____   5. We stayed on the task and used our time well.

_____   6. Other:

Total Score: _____

This form may be duplicated for classroom use.

FORM B: STUDENT ASSESSMENT

PARTICIPATION IN MY GROUP

Date _____

Name _____ Tribe _____

	NEVER	SOMETIMES	MOSTLY	ALWAYS
1. I listened to people in my tribe.				
2. I helped other people.				
3. I contributed ideas and information.				
4. I helped to clarify and summarize ideas and information.				
5. I encouraged others.				
6. I participated in making decisions.				
7. I expressed appreciation to others.				
8. I helped us to reflect on what we learned.				

NOTES

FORM C: STUDENT ASSESSMENT

MY CONSTRUCTIVE THINKING SKILLS

Date _____

Name _____   Tribe _____

INSTRUCTIONS:

Read the descriptions of constructive thinking skills below and estimate how well you do each skill. You can use a different colored pencil or pen each week to evaluate your own progress in using these skills.

	NEVER	SOMETIMES	MOSTLY	ALWAYS
1. I am able to **access information** (using the library, computer, articles, interviewing, and working with others).				
2. I can **organize information** (using graphics, charts, note cards, computer data entry).				
3. I am able to **compare and summarize** facts and ideas.				
4. I can **plan and use** what I learn to solve problems and be creative.				
5. I am able to **reflect and evaluate** how well something is working and make improvements.				

OTHER COMMENTS

Appendix

Appendix

Notes and References

INTRODUCTION—HERE WE ARE

1. The popularized phrase is from the title of the book, *Caught in the Middle: Educational Reform for Young Adolescents in California Public Schools*. (1987). Sacramento, CA: California Department of Education.

2. The expression is from the title of the book, *Boxed in and Bored: How Middle Schools Continue to Fail Young Adolescents—And What Good Middle Schools Do Right*. (1990). Peter C. Scales. Minneapolis, MN: Search Institute.

VIEWPOINT

1. From *Delicious Laughter: Rambunctious Teaching Stories*. (1990). Mathnawi of Jelahuddin Rumi. (Coleman Barks, translation). Athens, GA: Maypop Books, p. 65.

2. Comer, James. *Maintaining A Focus on Child Development,* Phi Delta Kappan, March 1997, p. 559.

3. *Turning Points: Preparing American Youth for the 21st Century*. (1989). New York, NY: Carnegie Council on Adolescent Development, Carnegie Corporation of New York, pp. 8–9.

4. Piaget, Jean. (1950). *The Psychology of Intelligence*. New York, NY: Harcourt Brace.

5. Wheelock, Anne. (1998). *Safe To Be Smart: Building a Culture for Standards-Based Reform in Middle Grades*. Columbus, OH: National Middle Schools Association, p. 101.

6. Thompson, Scott. *The Authentic Standards Movement and Its Evil Twin,* Phi Delta Kappan, January 2001, pp. 358–362.

7. Lipsitz, Joan. (1994). *Successful Schools For Young Adolescents*. New Brunswick, NJ: Transaction Books, p. 15.

CHAPTER ONE: CAUGHT IN THE MIDDLE

1. From *95 Poems* by e.e. cummings. (1923–1954). New York, NY: Harcourt Brace Company.

2. Linda Darling-Hammond is a William F. Russell Professor of Education, Columbia University and co-director of the National Center for Restructuring Education. The quote is from her 1977 book, *The Right To Learn: A Blueprint for Creating Schools That Work*. San Francisco, CA: Jossey-Bass, p. 47.

3. *Promoting Social and Educational Learning: Guidelines for Educators, Study Guide,* Association for Supervision and Curriculum Development, 1998.

4. Gardner, Howard. (1993). *Multiple Intelligences: The Theory in Practice*. New York, NY: Basic Books.

5. *Caught in the Middle: Educational Reform for Young Adolescents in California Public Schools*. (1997). Sacramento, CA: California Department of Education, p. v.

6. Goodlad, John. (1997). *In Praise of Education*. New York: Teachers College Press, Columbia University, p. 130.

7. Kohn, Alfie. (1998). *How Not to Teach Values: What to Look For in a Classroom*. San Francisco, CA: Jossey-Bass, pp. 16–43.

8. Benard, Bonnie. (1991). *Fostering Resiliency in Kids: Protective Factors in Families, Schools and Community*. Portland, OR: Northwest Regional Educational Laboratory.

9. Gibbs, Jeanne. (2000). *Tribes: A New Way of Learning and Being Together*. Windsor, CA: CenterSource Systems, p. 22.

10. Piaget, Jean. (1970). *Science of Education and Psychology of the Child*. New York, NY: Orion.

11. Comer, James. (1999). *Child by Child: The Comer Process for Change in Education*. New York, NY: Teachers College Press, p. xx.

12. Comer, James. *Maintaining A Focus on Child Development*, Phi Delta Kappan, March 1997, p. 559.

13. *Turning Points: Preparing American Youth for the 21st Century*. (1989). New York, NY: Carnegie Council on Adolescent Development, Carnegie Corporation of New York, pp. 8–9.

14. Benson, Peter. (1990). *The Troubled Journey*. Minneapolis: Search Institute. Peter Benson's remark is cited in Hersch, Patricia. (1998). *A Tribe Apart: Journey into the Heart of American Adolescence*. New York, NY: Ballentine Books, p. 12.

15. John Gardner was the architect of the ESEA, Elementary and Secondary Education Act in 1965, and Secretary of Health, Education and Welfare under President Lyndon Johnson. Massive appropriations for school reform were authorized, and the primary continuing result (as reported by John Goodlad) was that "schooling took on the business and political trappings that go with the control and distribution of billions of dollars." Goodlad, John. (1997). *In Praise of Education*. p. 88.

16. The quote is from Urie Bronfenbrenner's book, *Two Worlds of Childhood*. (1970). New York, NY: Sage Foundation, p. 1. The work of Dr. Bronfenbrenner, Professor of Psychology and Human Development, provided the central philosophy for the process of Tribes—that human development depends upon the ecology of the systems impacting the person. The mission and goal of Tribes articulates this fundamental theory to foster children's human development in school communities.

17. Peter Scales. *Boxed in and Bored*. p. 13.

18. Lipsitz, Joan. (1984). *Successful Schools for Young Adolescents*. New Brunswick, NJ: Transaction Books, p. 15.

CHAPTER TWO: GETTING TO KNOW YOU

1. The quote reportedly first was made by Marcel Proust. This author appreciated discovering it in a report written by Caroline Wong, Principal of the Moanalua Middle School (Honolulu), in the *Focus on Learning—Self-Study for Accreditation Report,* 1998. Building on research studies resulted in the school being cited as a Blue Ribbon School (1998) by the U.S. Department of Education. The school uses the process of Tribes to involve the staff of 55 in 18 collegial planning groups, and to reach and teach 900 students. Caroline Wong tells the story in Chapter 5.

2. Lipsitz, Joan. (1977). *Growing Up Forgotten: A Review of Research and Programs Concerning Early Adolescence*. Lexington, Mass: DC: Heath.

3. Scales, Peter. (1996). *Boxed in and Bored: How Middle Schools Continue to Fail Young Adolescents—And What Good Middle Schools Do Right*. Minneapolis, MN: Search Institute, p. 25.

4. Hersch, Patricia. (1998). *A Tribe Apart: Journey into the Heart of American Adolescence*. New York, NY: Ballantine Books, p. 14.

5. Bronfenbrenner, Urie. (1979). *The Ecology of Human Development: Experiments by Nature and Design*. Cambridge, MA: Harvard Press, p.9.

6. Bronfenbrenner. (1979). p. 9.

7. Dewey, John. (1956). *The Child and the Curriculum and the Child and Society*. Chicago, IL: University of Chicago Press.

8. Bronfenbrenner. (1979). p. 9.

9. Miller, Ron. (1990). *What Are Schools For? Holistic Education in American Culture*. Brandon, VT: Holistic Education Press.

10. Benard, Bonnie. (1991). *Fostering Resiliency in Kids: Protective Factors in the Family, School and Community*. Portland, OR: Western Regional Center for Drug-Free Schools and Communities, Northwest Regional Educational Laboratory, pp. 1–20.

11. *This We Believe: Developmentally Responsive Middle Level Schools*. (1995). Columbus, OH: National Middle School Association, p. 5.

12. *This We Believe*. (1995). p. 6.

13. The developmental profiles were summarized from:

    • Elkind, David. *The Social Determination of Childhood and Adolescence,* Education Week, Feb. 24, 1999.

    • *This We Believe*. (1995). Columbus, OH: National Middle School Association.

    • *Turning Points: Preparing American Youth for the 21st Century*. (1989). Washington, DC: Carnegie Council on Adolescent Development, Carnegie Task Force on Education of Young Adolescents.

    • Erickson, Erik. H. (1996). *Identity, Youth and Crisis*. New York, NY: W.W. Norton.

    • Scales, Peter. (1996). *Boxed in and Bored: How Middle Schools Continue to Fail Young Adolescents —And What Good Middle Schools Do Right*. Minneapolis, MN: Search Institute.

14. Bronfenbrenner, Urie. *What Do Families Do?* Family Affair, Institute for American Values, 1991, v. 4, no. 1–2, p. 3.

15. Corbin, Joanne. *Development-Prerequisite for Learning,* in *Child by Child: The Comer Process for Change in Education*. (1999). Comer, James. New York, NY: Teachers College Press, p. 247.

16. Mizell, Hayes. *Six Steps to an Achieving Middle School,* keynote speech at the Charlotte-Mecklenburg Schools (NC) First Annual Middle Schools Institute, June 14, 1999.

17. *This We Believe: Developmentally Responsive Middle Level Schools*. (1995). Columbus, OH: National Middle School Association, p. 5.

CHAPTER THREE: MEETING THEM WHERE THEY ARE

1. Leon Botstein, at the age of 23, became the youngest college President in American history upon his appointment as President of Bard College in 1975. He is the author of *Jefferson's Children: Education and the Promise of American Culture*. (1997). New York, NY: Doubleday. The book is an exciting exploration of the promise of American culture, education and democracy—and how schools can be restructured to reflect the realities of modern childhood. The quote is from page 85.

2. Dobson, Terry and Miller, Victor. (1993). *Aikido in Everyday Life: Giving in to Get Your Way*. Berkeley, CA: North Atlantic Books, p. 99.

3. Dobson. (1993). p. 107.

4. *Secondary Schools and Cooperative Learning: Theories, Models and Strategies*. (1995). Pedersen, Jon E. and Digby, Annette D. (Eds.). New York, NY: Garland Publishing.

5. Readers may secure a copy of the paper, *Rather Than Fixing Kids, Transform the Environment with Tribes Learning Communities,* by Jeanne Gibbs, as published in Research/Practice. Minneapolis, MN: Center for Applied Research and Educational Improvement, Fall 1998. Phone CenterSource Systems at 1-800-810-1702 or download the paper from www.tribes.com.

6. Erickson, Eric. (1963). *Childhood and Society.* New York, NY: W.W. Norton, p. 306.

7. *What Work Requires of Schools: SCANS Report for America 2000, Secretary's Commission on Achieving Necessary Skills.* (1991–98). Washington, DC: U.S. Department of Labor.

8. The statement by Margaret Mead was shared by her daughter, Mary Catherine Bateson, at the conference, *In Praise of Education,* Bellevue, WA: June 18, 1999.

9. Goodlad, John. (1994). *Educational Renewal: Better Teachers, Better Schools.* San Francisco, CA: Jossey-Bass, pp. 199–200.

CHAPTER FOUR: ASSURING FUTURES OF PROMISE

1. Werner, Emily and Smith, Ruth. (1989). *Vulnerable But Invincible: A Longitudinal Study of Resilient Children and Youth.* New York, NY: Adams, Bannister and Cox.

2. A key objective of Tribes is to bring knowledge of resiliency studies to educators and parents. The articulate papers of our friend, Bonnie Benard, are to be credited with summarizing more than forty years of research studies. Her initial work was supported by the Western Regional Center for Drug Free Schools and Communities, Northwest Regional Educational Laboratory, Portland, OR. It is a great honor to have Bonnie Benard write this article for this book.

3. Benard, Bonnie. (1991). *Fostering Resiliency in Kids: Protective Factors In the Family, School, and Community.* Portland, OR: Northwest Regional Educational Laboratory.

4. Benard. (1991).

5. Resnick, M., Bearman, P., Blum, R., Bauman, K., Harris, K., Jones, J., Tabor, J., Beuring, T., Sieving, R., Shew, M., Ireland, M., Bearinger, L., and Udry, J. *Protecting Adolescents from Harm: Findings from the National Longitudinal Study on Adolescent Health,* Journal of the American Medical Association, 1997, pp. 278, 823–832.

6. Werner, E. and Smith, R. (1992). *Overcoming the Odds: High-Risk Children from Birth to Adulthood.* New York, NY: Cornell University Press.

7. Noddings, N. *Schools Face Crisis in Caring,* Education Week, December 1988, p. 32.

8. Meier. D. (1995). *The Power of Their Idea: Lessons for America from a Small School in Harlem.* Boston, MA: Beacon Press.

9. Hattie, J., Marsh, H., Neill, J., and Richards, G. *Adventure Education and Outward Bound: Out-of-Class Experiences That Make a Lasting Difference.* Review of Educational Research, 1997, pp. 67, 43–87.

10. Muller, W. (1996). *How, Then, Shall We Live? Four Simple Questions That Reveal the Beauty and Meaning of Our Lives.* New York, NY: Bantam Books.

11. Kessler, R. (2000). *The Soul of Education: Helping Students Find Connection, Compassion, and Character at School.* Alexandria, VA: Association for Supervision and Curriculum Development.

12. Catterall, J. *Involvement in the Arts and Success in Secondary School,* Americans for the Arts Monographs, 1997, v.1, no. 9.

13. Melchior, A. *National Evaluation of Learn and Serve America: Interim and Final Evaluation,* National Corporation for Community Service, 1996–1998.

14. Sergiovanni, T. (1994). *Building Community In Schools*. San Francisco, CA: Jossey-Bass.

15. Permission to use has been granted by Red Grammer of Red Note Records. "See Me Beautiful" is from his Teaching Peace CD or audiotape, available from CenterSource Systems. An order form is contained in the back of this book.

CHAPTER FIVE: *A CULTURE FOR GROWING EARLY ADOLESCENTS*

1. S.B. Sarason. (1972). *The Creation of Settings and the Future Societies*. San Francisco, CA: Jossey-Bass.

2. The colorful phrase was made by Dr. Stanley Katz, Professor at Princeton University, in a plenary session at the conference, *In Praise of Education*, Seattle, WA, June 18, 1999.

3. Darling-Hammond, Linda. *Creating Standards Without Standardization*, in *The Right To Learn: A Blueprint for Creating Schools That Work*. (1997). Darling-Hammond, Linda. San Francisco, CA: Jossey-Bass, p. 233.

4. Comer, James. *Maintaining a Focus on Child Development*, Phi Delta Kappan, Mar 1997, p. 560.

5. Noddings, Nel. *A Morally Defensible Mission for Schools in the 21st Century*, Phi Delta Kappan, Jan 1995, p. 366.

6. Wheelock, Anne. (1998). *Safe To Be Smart: Building A Culture for Standards-Based Reform in the Middle Grades*. National Middle School Association. Also see excellent articles in the Phi Delta Kappan magazine, December 2000, special section: Leadership for Effective Middle School Practice: Randy Elmore, Leadership for Effective Middle School Practice, p.269; Camille McElroy, Middle School Programs That Work, p.277; Elmore and Wisenbaker, The Crabapple Experience—Program Evaluations.

7. Fullan, Michael. *Turning Systemic Thinking On Its Head*, a paper prepared for the U.S. Department of Education, 1994.

8. Caine, Geoffrey and Renate. (1991). *Making Connections: Teaching and the Human Brain*. Alexandria, Virginia: Association for Supervision and Curriculum Development.

9. John Goodlad. (1997). *In Praise of Education*. New York, NY: Teachers College Press, Columbia University, p. 103.

10. Bruner, Jerome. (1996) *The Culture of Education*. Cambridge, MA: Harvard University.

CHAPTER SIX: *CREATING THE LEARNING COMMUNITY*

1. Meier, Deborah. *Reinventing Teaching*, Teachers College Record, 1992–1993, v. 4, pp. 594–609.

2. Johnson, David W. and Johnson, Roger T. *Cooperative Learning and Nonacademic Outcomes of Schooling*, in *Secondary Schools and Cooperative Learning: Theories, Models and Strategies*. (1995). Pedersen, J. and Digby, A. (Eds.). New York, NY: Garland Publishing, pp. 81–150.

3. Werner, E.E. and Smith, R.S. (1982). *Vulnerable But Invincible: A Study on Resilient Children*. New York, NY: McGraw Hill.

4. Sergiovanni, Thomas. (1996). *Leadership for the Schoolhouse*. San Francisco, CA: Jossey-Bass, p. 97.

5. McKnight, John. *Are Social Service Agencies the Enemy of the People?* Utne Reader, July-August 1992, pp. 89–90.

6. Lickona, Thomas. (1991). *Education for Character: How Our Schools Can Teach Respect and Responsibility*. New York, NY: Bantam Books, p. 95.

7. Jensen, Eric. (1998). *Teaching With the Brain in Mind.* Alexandria, VA: Association for Supervision and Curriculum Development.

8. See comments of Laura Horton, Fort-Francis River Board of Education, Ontario, and Anne Wilson, Ojibwe elder, First Nation, Manitou Rapids, Ontario, pp. 72 and 88, respectively, in *Tribes: A New Way of Learning and Being Together.* (2000). Windsor, CA: CenterSource Systems.

9. Johnson, David and Johnson, Roger. *Cooperative Learning and Non-Academic Outcomes of Schooling,* in *Secondary Schools and Cooperative Learning: Theory, Models and Strategies.* (1995). Pedersen, J. and Digby, A. (Eds.). New York, NY: Garland Publishing, p. 83.

10. Years ago research reports led to the practice in Tribes of using long-term membership groups rather than rotating people in and out of random task groups. Two of the published articles are:

    • Lott, Albert and Lott, Bernice. *Group Cohesiveness and Individual Learning,* Journal of Educational Psychology, April 1966, v. 57, pp. 61-72.

    • Fox, Robert, Luszki, Margaret and Schmuck, Richard. (1966). *Social Relations in the Classroom: Diagnosing Learning Environments.* Chicago, IL: SRA, Inc.

11. Sarason, Seymour. (1990). *The Predictable Failure of School Reform.* San Francisco, CA: Jossey-Bass.

12. McKnight, John. (1992). p. 90.

13. Houston, Paul. *The School Administrator,* 1998, v. 55, no. 5.

14. Starhawk. (1997). *Dreaming the Dark.* New York, NY: Beacon Press, p. 92.

CHAPTER SEVEN: LEARNING ABOUT LEARNING

1. *Turning Points: Preparing American Young for the 21st Century.* (1989). Washington, DC: Carnegie Council on Adolescent Development, p. 8.

2. *Turning Points.* (1989). p. 9.

3. The author is appreciative of the comprehensive review made by Caroline Wong. *A Comprehensive Review of the Research Literature on Middle Level Education Provides Compelling Support for the Implementation of the Middle School Concept,* Hawaii Department of Education, Spring/Summer 1997, p. 7. References supporting conclusions in this paragraph are:

    • Lounsbury, J. and Clark, D. (1990). *Inside Grade 8: From Apathy to Excitement.* Reston, VA: National Association of Secondary School Principals.

    • Lounsbury, J. and Johnston, H. (1988). *Life in the Three Sixth Grades.* Reston, VA, National Association of Secondary School Principals.

    • MacIver, D. and Epstein, J. *Middle Grades Research: Not Yet Mature, But No Longer a Child,* Elementary School Journal, 1993, v. 93, no. 5, pp. 519–533.

4. Csikszentmihalyi, Mihaly. *Education for the 21st Century,* Education Week, April 19, 2000.

5. An article, *Teaching to the Test,* reports that when a 4th grade teacher in Texas took all of her test preparation materials for the Texas Student Assessment and stacked them atop one another, they stood about as tall as she is – close to 6 feet. The same article refers to a 10-State study by researchers from the University of Wisconsin finding little overlap between what state assessments test and what teachers teach. In one of the 10 states, the overlap in one subject was

found to be just 5 percent. "It's a very sloppy system right now," said John F. Jennings, the director of the Center on Education Policy, a Washington research group. The article is by Ulrich Boser, Education Week, June 7, 2000, p. 1.

6. Scott Thompson's article, *The Authentic Standards Movement and Its Evil Twin,* in Phi Delta Kappan, January 2001, helps readers to understand the impact of high stakes testing as the sole indicator of student success, and the alternative of moving to "authentic standards" to improve learning. The same issue has articles by Susan Ohanian, *News From the Resistance Trail,* and Alfie Kohn, *Fighting the Tests: A Practical Guide to Rescuing Our Schools.*

7. The statement by Margaret Mead was shared by her daughter, Mary Catherine Bateson, at the conference, *In Praise of Education,* Bellevue, WA, June 18, 1999.

8. Caine, Geoffrey and Renate. (1991). *Making Connections: Teaching and the Human Brain.* Alexandria, VA: Association for Supervision and Curriculum Development.

9. Pert, Candace, B. (1997). *Molecules of Emotion: The Science Behind Mind-Body Medicine.* New York, NY: Simon and Schuster.

10. Pert. (1997).

11. Hannaford, Carla. (1995). *Smart Moves—Why Learning is Not All in Your Head.* Arlington, VA: Great Ocean Publishers.

12. Jensen, Eric. (1998). *Teaching with the Brain in Mind.* Arlington, VA: Association for Supervision and Curriculum Development.

13 Prescott, James and Heath, Robert, in Jensen, Eric (1998).

14. Freire, Paulo. (1970). *Pedagogy of the Oppressed.* New York, NY: Herder and Herder.

15. Franklin, Ursula. Introduction to the symposium, *Towards an Ecology of Knowledge,* at the University of Toronto, as reported by Gordon Wells in *Dialogic Inquiry in Education: Building on the Legacy of Vygotsky.* (1996). Toronto: Ontario Institute for Studies in Education, University of Toronto, p. 16.

16. Toffler, Alvin. (1980). *Third Wave.* New York, NY: Wm. Morrow, New York, NY.

17. The nine principles for active learning are based on:

    *   Barbara L. McCombs' original work, *Twelve Learner-Centered Psychological Principles,* Midwest Center Educational Laboratory. (www.mcrel.org).

    *   *Learner-Centered Principles: A Framework for School Redesign and Reform,* American Psychological Association. (www.apa.org).

    *   Duffy, Thomas and Jonassen, David (Eds.). (1992). *Constructivism and the Technology of Instruction.* Hillsdale, NJ: Lawrence Erlbaum Associates.

18. Anderson, Keisha-Gaye. *U.S. Fails Math,* Psychology Today, Jan–Feb 2000.

19. The Russian cognitive theorist, L.S. Vygotsky, stated that learning from social experience is the process whereby human development occurs, in Johnson, David and Johnson, Frank. (2000). *Joining Together: Group Theory and Group Skills.* Boston, MA: Allyn and Bacon, p. 50.

20. Hertz-Lazarowitz, Rachel and Shachar, H. *Changes in Teachers' Verbal Behavior in Cooperative Classrooms,* Cooperative Learning, 1990, v. 11, no. 2, pp. 13–14.

21. Reich, Robert. (1991). *The Work of Nations.* New York, NY: Alfred A. Knopf.

22. The chart is a synthesis of ideas from two documents:

- Brooks, M. and Brooks, J. (1993). *The Case for Constructivist Classrooms*. Association for Supervision and Curriculum Development, p.17.

- Gibbs, Jeanne. (2000). *Tribes: A New Way of Learning and Being Together*. Windsor, CA: CenterSource Systems, p. 19.

23. Gardner, Howard. (1993). *Frames of Mind: Theory of Multiple Intelligences*. New York, NY: Basic Books.

24. Stoddard, Lynn. (1992). *Redesigning Education: A Guide for Developing Human Greatness*. Tucson, AZ: Zephyr Press.

25. Botstein, Leon. (1997). *Jefferson's Children: Education and the Promise of American Culture*. New York, NY: Doubleday, p. 111.

26. Lazear, David. (1989). *Seven Ways of Teaching: The Artistry of Teaching With Multiple Intelligences*. Palatine, IL: Skylight Publishing, p. 9.

27. The poem written by Andrew Whyte and contributed to this book is deeply appreciated. It demonstrates one of many of this young man's "discovered gifts"—nurtured in his Tribes 5th grade class. His teacher is Jim Strachan who is also a Tribes TLC ® certified trainer in Toronto.

CHAPTER EIGHT: INITIATING RESPONSIVE EDUCATION—THE COMMUNITY CIRCLE

1. Campbell, Joseph. (1970). *The Masks of God: Creative Mythology*. New York, NY: Viking Press, p. 52.

2. Cohen, Jonathan (Ed.). (1999). *Educating Minds and Hearts: Social and Emotional Learning and the Passage Into Adolescence*. New York, NY: Teachers College Press, p. 3.

3. Valliant, G.E. (1977). *Adaptation to Life*. Boston, MA: Little, Brown.

4. Naisbitt, John. (1999). *High Tech—High Touch: Technology and Our Search For Meaning*. New York, NY: Bantam Books.

5. Goleman, Daniel. (1995). *Emotional Intelligence*. New York, NY: Bantam Books.

6. Cohen. (1999). p. 7

7. Johnson, David and Johnson, Roger. (1989). *Cooperation and Competition: Theory and Research*. Edina, MN: Interaction Book Company, pp. 169–179.

8. Cotton, Kathleen. (1997). *Educating for Citizenship: School Improvement Research Series, Close-up #19*. Portland, OR: Northwest Regional Educational Laboratory.

9. Brooks, Jacquelyn and Martin. (1993). *In Search of Understanding: The Case for Constructivist Classrooms*. Alexandria, VA: ASCD.

10. Bybee, Roger. (1997). *Constructivism and the Five E's: The Biological Science Curriculum Study*. Miami, FL: Miami Museum of Science. www.miamisci.org. Internet document.

11. Yager, Stuart, Johnson, Roger, Johnson, David and Snider, Bill. *The Impact of Group Processing on Achievement in Cooperative Learning Groups,* The Journal of Social Psychology, 1986, v. 126, pp. 389–397.

12. Kafka, Franz. (1946). *The Advocates: The Complete Stories*. New York, NY: Schocken Books, p. 449.

13. The statement of Julia Lewis is from Robert Coles' 1998 article, *In School,* Boston Globe Magazine, p. 15.

CHAPTER NINE: BUILDING SMALL GROUPS FOR GROWTH AND LEARNING

1. The quotes are from students of Dr. Teri Ushijima's 5th grade class at the Mililani Mauka School in Honolulu, Hawaii and Denise White's 6th grade class at the Thoreau Demonstration Academy, Tulsa, Oklahoma.

2. Kohn, Alfie. (1996). *Beyond Discipline: From Compliance to Community*. Alexandria, VA: Association for Supervision and Curriculum Development, pp. 76–77.

3. It is amusing to have learned that one school trained all of their students to be conflict managers and every person wears a "Conflict Manager" shirt. The *1998 Conflict Resolution: A Secondary School Curriculum* is available from the San Francisco Community Board Program.

4. Frankl, Viktor. (2000). *Man's Ultimate Search for Meaning*. New York, NY: Perseus Book Group.

CHAPTER TEN: CREATING COOPERATIVE LEARNING EXPERIENCES

1. Hochman, Jere. (1997). *Thinking About Middle School*. Columbus, OH: National Middle School Association, p. 59

2. Guild, Pat Burke. *Where Do the Learning Theories Overlap?* Educational Leadership, Sept 1997, p. 30.

3. The statement was made by Dr. Mark Chasen in an address to the Commonwealth Club of San Francisco, August 2000.

4. Sizer, Ted. (1984). *Horace's Compromise: The Dilemma of the American High School*. Boston, MA: Houghton-Mifflin.

5. Lieberman, Ann and Miller, Lynne. *Teaching and Teacher Development: A New Synthesis for a New Century,* in *Education in a New Era*. (2000). Brandt, Ron S. (Ed.). Alexandria, VA: Association for Supervision and Curriculum Development, p. 56.

6. Johnson, David W., Johnson, Roger T. and Smith, Karl. *Cooperative Learning and Individual Student Achievement,* in *Secondary Schools and Cooperative Learning: Theories, Models and Strategies*. (1995). Pedersen, Jon E. and Digby, Annette (Eds.). New York, NY: Garland Publishing, p. 4.

7. Johnson, David W., Johnson, Roger, T. and Holubec, Edythe Johnson. (1994). *New Circles of Learning: Cooperation in the Classroom and School*. Alexandria, VA: ASCD, p. 15

8. Johnson. (1994). p. 16.

9. Johnson. (1994). p. 23.

10. Johnson. (1994). p. 24

11. Johnson. (1994). p. 25.

12. Johnson, David W., Johnson, Roger, T. and Smith, Karl. *Cooperative Learning and Individual Student Achievement,* in *Secondary Schools and Cooperative Learning: Theories, Models and Strategies*. (1995). Pedersen, Jon E. and Digby, Annette. New York, NY: Garland Publishing, p. 5.

13. Johnson, David W. and Johnson, Roger, T. (1989). *Cooperation and Competition: Theory and Research*. Edina, MN: Interaction Book Company.

14. Johnson. (1989).

15. Brady, Marion. (1989). *What's Worth Teaching? Selecting, Organizing and Integrating Knowledge*. New York State University Press.

16. Kovalik, Susan. (1999). *ITI: The Model, Integrated Thematic Instruction*. Kent, WA: Books for Educators.

17. Smilovitz, R. (1996). *If Not Now, When? Education Not Schooling*. Kearney, NE: Morris.

18. *What Work Requires of Schools, SCANS Report for America 2000, Secretary's Commission on Achieving Necessary Skills*. Washington, DC: U.S. Department of Labor, 1991–1998.

19. Johnson, David W. and Johnson, Roger, T. (1989). *Cooperation and Competition,* Theory and Research. Edina, MN: Interaction Book Company, p. 25.

20. Kagan, Spencer and Kagan, Miguel. (1998). *Staff Development and the Structure Approach to Cooperative Learning,* in *Professional Development for Cooperative Learning: Issues and Approaches*. Brody, Celeste and Davidson, Neil (Eds.). Albany, NY: State University of New York Press, pp. 106–7.

21. Kagan, Spencer. (1999). *Cooperative Learning*. San Clemente, CA: Resources for Teachers.

22. Johnson, David and Johnson, Roger. (1998). *Circles of Learning*. Edina, MN: Interaction Book Company, and Johnson, David and Johnson, Frank. (2000). *Joining Together: Group Theory and Group Skills*. (7th edition). Allyn and Bacon: Boston, MA.

23. Gardner, Howard. (1999). *Intelligence Reframed: Multiple Intelligences for the 21st Century*. Basic Books.

24. Educators and human development professionals worldwide appreciate the work that Dr. Armstrong has done to bring the concepts of multiple intelligence to life through enjoyable and meaningful application. The multiple intelligences checklist was adapted from *7 Kinds of Smart,* ©1993 by Thomas Armstrong. Used by permission of Plume, a division of Penguin Putnam Inc. For additional information about Tom Armstrong's work regarding multiple intelligences (including information on books, videos, presentations, weblinks and other resources) visit www.thomasarmstrong.com or write him at P.O. Box 548, Cloverdale, CA 95425.

25. Yager, Stuart; Johnson, Robert; Johnson, Roger and Snider, Bill. *The Impact of Group Processing on Academic Achievement in Cooperative Learning Groups,* The Journal of Social Psychology, 1986, v. 126, pp. 389–397.

26. Appreciative Inquiry is now being used in the organizational development field. It emerged in the mid-seventies when David Cooperrider and his associates at Case Western Reserve University felt a need to challenge the traditional Change Management problem based theory being used throughout corporate organizations. Sue Annis Hammond's 1996 book, *Appreciative Inquiry,* provides a brief overview of the process. The book is available from The Thin Book Company, P.O. Box 260608, Plano, TX 75026-0608. Phone: 888-316-9544.

CHAPTER ELEVEN: LEARNING THROUGH DISCOVERY

1. Adler, Mortimer. (1982). *The Padideia Proposal: An Educational Manifesto*. New York, NY: Macmillan, p. 50.

2. Fosnot, Catherine Twomey. (1996). *Constructivism: Theory, Perspectives and Practice*. New York, NY: Teachers College Press.

3. Marlowe, Bruce and Page, Marilyn. (1998). *Creating and Sustaining the Constructivist Classroom*. Thousand Oaks, CA: Corwin Press, p. 27.

4. Darling-Hammond, Linda. (1997). *The Right To Learn: A Blueprint for Creating Schools That Work*. San Francisco, CA: Jossey-Bass, p. 96.

5. Fosnot. (1996). p. 27.

6. Goodlad, John. (1984). *A Place Called School*. New York: McGraw Hill, and Flanders, M. *Basic Teaching Skills Derived from a Model of Speaking and Listening,* Journal of Teacher Education, Spring 1973, v. 24, pp. 24–37.

7. Summarized from M. David Merrill's article, *Constructivism and Instructional Design,* in *Constructivism and the Technology of Instruction.* (1992). Duffy, T. and Jonassen, D. (Eds.). Hillsdale, NJ: Erlbaum Associates, pp. 102–3.

8. Windschitl, Mark. *The Challenges of Sustaining a Constructivist Classroom Culture,* Phi Delta Kappan magazine, June 1999, p. 754.

9. Readers who wish to become more familiar with the exhaustive wealth of research and literature on constructivism may begin to do so by obtaining the following books and checking an abundance of articles on Internet:

   • Fosnot, Catherine Twomey. (1996). *Constructivism: Theory, Perspectives and Practice.* New York, NY: Teachers College Press.

   • Marlowe, Bruce and Page, Marilyn. (1998). *Creating and Sustaining the Constructivist Classroom.* Thousand Oaks, CA: Corwin Press.

   • Duffey, T.M. and Jonassen, D.H. (Eds.). (1992). *Constructivism and the Technology of Instruction.* Hillsdale, NJ: Erlbaum Associates.

   • Brooks, Martin G. and Brooks, Jacqueline. (1993). *In Search for Understanding: The Case for Constructivist Classrooms.* Alexandria, VA: ASCD.

10. The concepts of Russian cognitive theorist, Lev Vygotsky, are discussed well by Gordon Wells in his 1996 paper, *Dialogic Inquiry in Education: Building on the Legacy of Vygotsky.* Toronto: Ontario Institute for Studies in Education, University of Toronto.

11. The "Five E's" were developed as an instructional model for constructivism by Roger Bybee, a Principal Investigator for the *Biological Science Curriculum Study* at the Miami Museum of Science. Source: www.miamisci.org.

12. Brooks and Brooks attribute the list to Roger Bybee's article, from the National Center for Improving Science Education, *The Sisyphean Question in Science Education,* in Classroom Compass, Southwest Educational Development Laboratory, 1999, v. 1, no. 2. The first and second lists used in this chapter are from Brooks and Brooks, (1993), p. 48.

13. Ohanian, Susan. *There's Only One True Technique for Good Discipline,* in *Who's In Charge? A Teacher Speaks Her Mind.* (1994). Ohanian, Susan. Heinemann. Available through Amazon.com.

14. Susan Kovalik and Associates train teachers nation-wide to organize curriculum into year long themes that integrate subject disciplines. The model is based on brain research, hands-on teaching strategies and curriculum development. Susan's lively book is available from CenterSource Systems. *ITI: The Model, Integrated Thematic Instruction.* Kent, WA: Books for Educators. The quotation used is from 3rd edition, p. 145.

15. Postman, Neil and Weingartner, Charles. (1969). *Teaching as a Subversive Activity.* New York: Dell Publishing.

16. The author wants to acknowledge that the purpose of this example is to emphasize that it is important for the teacher guide not to seek polished action plan language but the creative ideas and commitment of group members to the content learning task. The guide is always in control by approving or not, and arranging activities that support the discovery.

17. Asp, Elliott. *Assessment in Education: Where Have We Been? Where Are We Headed?* In *Education in a New Era.* (2000). Brandt, Ron (Ed.). Alexandria, VA: ASCD, pp. 124–5.

18. The material, *In a Discovery Learning Classroom...* , is adapted from a list contained in Classroom Compass, Southwest Educational Development Laboratory, 1999, v. 1, no. 2. The laboratory attributes the suggestions to an adaptation made from Brooks, M. and Brooks, J. (1993). *In Search for Understanding: The Case for Constructivist Classrooms.* Alexandria, VA: ASCD.

19. The statement was made by Walt Haney of the Center for the Study of Testing, Evaluation and Education Policy, Boston College, in Wheelock, Anne. (2000). *Safe To Be Smart, Building a Culture for Standards-Based Reform in the Middle Grades*. Alexandria, VA: ASCD, p. 164.

20. The Tribes Assessment Kit is available from CenterSource Systems. There is an order form in the Resource Section, or phone: 800-810-1701.

21. Nancy Atwell's poignant confession is from her 1987 book, *In the Middle: Writing, Reading and Learning with Adolescents*. Upper Montclair, NJ: Bynton/Cook, p. 127.

22. Postman, Neil and Weingartner, Charles. (1969). *Teaching as a Subversive Activity*. New York: Dell, p. 3.

CHAPTER TWELVE: DISCOVERING GIFTS THROUGHOUT THE RESPONSIVE MIDDLE SCHOOL

1. Gardner, John W. (1961). *Excellence—Can We Be Equal and Excellent Too?* New York, NY: Harper and Row.

2. Gardner, Howard. (2000). *The Disciplined Mind: Beyond Facts and Standardized Tests, The K-12 Education That Every Child Deserves*. New York, NY: Penguin Putnam, p. 232.

3. The statement was made by Dr. Ted Sizer, Director of the Coalition of Essential Schools, in a plenary session at the conference, *In Praise of Education*. Seattle, WA, June 18, 1999.

4. Dr. Keith Larick is the Superintendent of the Tracy Unified School District in the Bay Area of California. His statement opens the 15-minute videotape, *Learning for the 21st Century*, which is available from CenterSource Systems.

5. Gardner. (2000). pp. 19–20.

6. De Pree, Max. *Teacher Leader*, Phi Delta Kappan, Feb 2001, p. 434.

7. Sergiovanni, Thomas, J. (1999). *Rethinking Leadership: A Collection of Articles*. Arlington Heights, IL: Skylight Training and Publishing. pp. 97–9.

8. Barth, Roland. *Teacher Leader*, Phi Delta Kappan, Feb 2001, p. 444. One study reports ten areas of participation that principals use to transfer leadership to teachers:

   • choosing textbooks and instructional materials

   • shaping the curriculum

   • setting standards for student behavior

   • deciding whether students are tracked into special classes

   • designing staff development and in-service programs

   • setting promotion and retention policies

   • deciding school budgets

   • selecting new teachers; and

   • selecting new administration.

9. Sergiovanni. (1999). p. 87.

10. Schein, E. (1985). *Organization Cultures and Leadership: A Dynamic View*. San Francisco, CA: Jossey-Bass.

11. Barth, Roland. *The Leader as Learner,* Education Week, March 5, 1997.

12. *Learning to Lead, Leading to Learn: Improving School Quality Through Principal Professional Development.* (2000). Oxford, OH: National Staff Development Council.

13. Cohen, Jonathan. *Educating Minds and Hearts: Social Emotional Learning and the Passage into Adolescence.* New York, NY: Teachers College Press, Columbia University.

14. Joyce, B. and Showers, G. (1982). *Transfer of Training: The Contribution of Coaching.* Eugene, OR: Center for Educational Policy and Management, University of Oregon.

15. Gibbs, Jeanne. (1999). *Guiding Your School Community To Live a Culture of Caring and Learning.* Windsor, CA: CenterSource Systems, p. 52.

16. The report is from the National Commission on Teaching and America's Future and cited in the article, *High-quality Teachers Are Key to Student Success,* California School Board News, Dec. 31, 1998. Information on the National Commission on Teaching may be found at www.tc.columbia.edu/-teachcomm.

17. Kruse, Sharon. *Collaborate,* At Issue Designs, National Staff Development Council, 1999, Summer Issue, p. 15.

18. Darling-Hammond, Linda. *Reforming the School Reform Agenda,* Phi Delta Kappan, 1993, pp. 74–76.

19. Cooper, Carole and Boyd, Julie. *Creating Sustained Professional Growth Through Collaborative Reflection,* in *Professional Development for Collaborative Learning: Issues and Approaches.* (1998). Brody, Celeste and Davidson, Neil (Eds.). p. 50.

20. Cooper. (1998). p. 51.

21. We thank Dr. Armstrong and his publisher for permission to modify the adult multiple intelligences checklist for middle level students. The checklist was adapted from 7 *Kinds of Smart,* ©1993 by Thomas Armstrong. Used by permission of Plume, a division of penguin Putnam Inc., New York, NY.

22. Robert Samples' statement may be found on the preface page of the Armstrong book.

23. Wheelock, Anne. (1998). *Safe To Be Smart: Building a Culture for Standards-Based Reform in the Middle Grades.* Waterville, Ohio: National Middle School Association.

24. Coleman, Peter and Deutsche, Morton. (2000). *Cooperation, Conflict Resolution and School Violence—A Systems Approach,* Choices Brief #5. New York, NY: Institute for Urban and Minority Education, Teachers College Press, Columbia University.

25. Pipher, Mary. (1995). *Reviving Ophelia: Saving the Lives of Adolescent Girls.* New York, NY: Ballantine Books, p. 44.

26. Cohen, Judy & all. (1996). *Girls in the Middle—Working to Succeed in School.* Washington, DC: American Association of University Women Educational Foundation, pp. 14–15.

27. Pipher. (1995). p. 290.

28. The quote is from James Hillman's book, *The Soul's Code,* cited by Ron Taffel in *Nurturing Good Children Now,* New York, NY: Golden Books, 1999, p. 1.

29. Kagan, Spencer. (1999). *Cooperative Learning.* San Clemente, CA: Resources for Teachers, pp. 2, 7.

30. Gay, Geneva. (2000). *Culturally Responsive Teaching: Theory, Research and Practice.* New York, NY: Teachers College Press, Columbia University.

31. Brandt, Ron (Ed.). (2000). *Education in a New Era.* Alexandria, VA: Association for Supervision and Curriculum Development, p. 34.

32. Consultation and professional training can be arranged by contacting CenterSource Systems.

33. Gay. (2000). p. 29.

34. Christensen, Linda. (2000). *Reading, Writing and Rising Up—Teaching About Social Justice and the Power of the Written Word*. Milwaukee, WI: Rethinking Schools, p. 103.

35. Goodlad, John. (1997). *In Praise of Education*. New York, NY: Teachers College Press, Columbia University, p. 24.

36. The author expresses appreciation to Carroll Killingsworth for permission to use his lovely poem, *The Measure of a Child*. Carroll is a long-time teacher, principal and superintendent who cares deeply about the development of the whole child. He is the author of *The Gifts of Children* (in progress), and a developer of "The Gifts Project."

37. Madaus, G., West, Mary M., Harmon, M., Lomax, R. and Viator, K. (1992). *The Influence of Testing on Teaching Math and Science in Grades 4–12: Executive Summary*. Boston, MA: Center for the Study of Testing, Evaluation and Educational Policy, p. 2.

38. Gardner, Howard. (2000). p. 80.

39. Leonard Atkins is the Boston president of the National Association for the Advancement of Colored People. He made the statement after 80% of Black and 85% of Latino 10th graders failed the Massachusetts Comprehensive Assessment System (MCAS) math test in May 2000 compared to 45% of White students. Cited in *Failing Our Kids: Why the Testing Craze Won't Fix Our Schools*. (2000). Swope, Kathy and Miner, Barbara (Eds.). Milwaukee, WI: Rethinking Schools, LTD, p. 126.

40. Paris, Scott and Ayres, Linda. (1999). *Becoming Reflective Students and Teachers with Portfolios and Authentic Assessment*. Washington, DC: American Psychological Association, pp. 7–8.

41. Paris and Ayres. (1999). p. 28.

42. Paris and Ayres. (1999). p. 54.

43. Paris and Ayres. (1999). p. 58.

44. Paris and Ayres. (1999). p. 154.

45. Brown, Juanita and Isaacs, David. *Conversation as a Core Business Process,* The Systems Thinker, Pegasus Communications, Inc., Dec. 96/Jan. 97.

Bibliography

Adler, Mortimer. (1982). *The Padideia Proposal: An Educational Manifesto*. New York, NY: Macmillan

Alberg, J., Eller, S., and Petry, C. *A Resource Guide for Social Skills Instruction,* Center for Research in Education, Research Triangle Institute (U.S. Department of Education, Office of Special Education Programs), Longmount, Colorado: Sopers Publishers, 1994.

Anderson, Keisha-Gaye. *U.S. Fails Math,* Psychology Today, Jan–Feb 2000.

Armstrong, Thomas. (1999). *7 Kinds of Smart: Identifying and Developing Your Multiple Intelligences*. New York, NY: Penguin Putnam.

Aronson, Elliot. (1978). *The Jigsaw Classroom*. Beverly Hills, CA: SAGE Publications.

Asp, Elliott. *Assessment in Education: Where Have We Been? Where Are We Headed?* In *Education in a New Era*. (2000). Brandt, Ron (Ed.). Alexandria, VA: ASCD.

Atwell, Nancy. (1987). *In the Middle: Writing, Reading and Learning with Adolescents*. Upper Montclair, NJ: Bynton/Cook.

Barth, Roland. *Teacher Leader,* Phi Delta Kappan, Feb 2001.

Barth, Roland. *The Leader as Learner,* Education Week, March 5, 1997.

Benard, Bonnie. (1991). *Fostering Resiliency in Kids: Protective Factors in Families, Schools and Community*. Portland, OR: Western Regional Center for Drug Free Schools and Communities, Northwest Regional Educational Laboratory.

Benard, Bonnie. (1991). *Moving Toward a Just and Vital Culture: Multiculturalism in Our Schools*. Portland, OR: Western Regional Center for Drug Free Schools and Communities, Northwest Regional Educational Laboratory.

Benard, Bonnie. *Resiliency Paradigm Validates Craft Knowledge,* Western Center News, Northwest Regional Educational Laboratory, 1993.

Benard, Bonnie. *Resiliency Requires Changing Hearts and Minds,* Western Center News, Northwest Regional Educational Laboratory, 1993.

Benson, Peter. (1990). *The Troubled Journey*. Minneapolis, MN: Search Institute.

Boser, Ulrich. *Teaching to the Test,* Education Week, 2000.

Botstein, Leon. (1997). *Jefferson's Children, Education and the Promise Of American Culture*. New York, NY: Doubleday.

Brady, Marion. (1989). *What's Worth Teaching? Selecting, Organizing And Integrating Knowledge*. Albany, NY: State University of New York Press.

Brandt, Ron, Ed. (2000). *Education in a New Era*. Alexandria, VA: Association for Supervision and Curriculum Development.

Brody, Celeste and Davidson, Neil (Eds.). (1998). *Professional Development for Cooperative Learning: Issues and Approaches*. Albany, NY: State University of New York Press.

Bronfenbrenner, Urie. (1979). *The Ecology of Human Development: Experiments By Nature and Design*. Cambridge, MA: Harvard Press.

Bronfenbrenner, Urie. (1990). *Two Worlds of Childhood*. New York, NY: Sage Foundation.

Bronfenbrenner, Urie. *What Do Families Do?* Family Affair, Institute for American Values, 1991, v. 4, no. 1–2.

Brooks, Jacquelyn and Brooks, Martin. (1993). *In Search of Understanding: The Case for Constructivist Classrooms*. Alexandria, VA: ASCD.

Brown, Juanita and Isaacs, David. *Conversation as a Core Business Process,* The Systems Thinker, Pegasus Communications, Inc., Dec. 96/Jan. 97.

Bruner, Jerome. (1996). *The Culture of Education*. Cambridge, MA: Harvard University.

Bybee, Roger. (1997). *Constructivism and the Five E's: The Biological Science Curriculum Study*. Miami, FL: Miami Museum of Science.

Bybee, Roger. *The Sisyphean Question in Science Education,* Classroom Compass, Southwest Educational Development Laboratory, 1999, v. 1, No. 2.

Caine, Geoffrey and Renate. (1991). *Making Connections: Teaching And the Human Brain*. Alexandria, VA: Association for Supervision and Curriculum Development.

Campbell, Joseph. (1970). *The Masks of God: Creative Mythology*. New York, NY: Viking Press.

Catterall, J. *Involvement in the Arts and Success in Secondary School,* Americans for the Arts Monographs, 1997, v. 1, no. 9.

Caught in the Middle: Educational Reform for Young Adolescents in California Public Schools. (1987). Sacramento, CA: California Department of Education.

Christensen, Linda. (2000). *Reading, Writing and Rising Up—Teaching About Social Justice and the Power of the Written Word*. Milwaukee, WI: Rethinking Schools.

Cohen, Jonathan (Ed.). (1999). *Educating Minds and Hearts: Social and Emotional Learning and the Passage to Adolescence*. New York, NY: Teachers College Press.

Cohen, Judy & all. (1996). *Girls in the Middle—Working to Succeed in School*. Washington, DC: American Association of University Women Educational Foundation.

Coles, Robert. *In School,* Boston Globe Magazine, 1998.

Coleman, Peter and Deutsche, Morton. (2000). *Cooperation, Conflict Resolution And School Violence—A Systems Approach,* Choices Brief #5. New York, NY: Institute for Urban and Minority Education, Teachers College Press, Columbia University.

Comer, James. *Building Schools As Community,* Educational Leadership, 1997.

Comer, James. (1999). *Child By Child: The Comer Process for Change In Education*. New York, NY: Teachers College Press.

Comer, James. *Maintaining A Focus on Child Development,* Phi Delta Kappan, March 1997.

Conflict Resolution: A Secondary School Curriculum. (1990). San Francisco, CA: Community Board Program.

Conflict Resolution: An Elementary School Curriculum. (1990). San Francisco, CA: Community Board Program.

Cooper, Carole and Boyd, Julie. *Creating Sustained Professional Growth Through Collaborative Reflection,* In *Professional Development for Collaborative Learning: Issues and Approaches*. (1998). Brody, Celeste and Davidson, Neil (Eds.). Albany, NY: State University of New York Press.

Corbin, Joanne. *Development-Prerequisite for Learning,* In *Child By Child: The Comer Process for Change in Education.* (1999). Comer, James. New York, NY: Teachers College Press.

Cotton, Kathleen. (1997). *Educating for Citizenship: School Improvement Research Series,* Close-up #19. Portland, OR: Northwest Regional Educational Laboratory.

Csikszentmihalyi, Mihaly. *Education for the 21st Century,* Education Week, April 19, 2000.

cummings, e.e. (1923–1954). *95 Poems.* New York, NY: Harcourt Brace.

Darling-Hammond, Linda. *Reforming the School Reform Agenda,* Phi Delta Kappan, 1993.

Darling-Hammond, Linda. (1997). *The Right To Learn: A Blueprint For Creating Schools That Work.* San Francisco, CA: Jossey-Bass.

De Pree, Max. *Teacher Leader,* Phi Delta Kappan, Feb 2001.

Dewey, John. (1956). *The Child and the Curriculum and the Child and Society.* Chicago, IL: University of Chicago Press.

Dobson, Terry and Miller, Victor. (1993). *Aikido in Everyday Life: Giving In to Get Your Way.* Berkeley, CA: North Atlantic Books.

Duffy, Thomas and Jonassen, David (Eds.). (1992). *Constructivism and the Technology of Instruction.* Hillsdale, NJ: Lawrence Erlbaum Associates.

Elkind, David. *The Social Determination of Childhood and Adolescence,* Education Week, 1999.

Elmore, Randy. *Leadership for Effective Middle School Practice,* Phi Delta Kappan, December 2000.

Elmore, Randy and Wisenbaker. *The Crabapple Experience—Program Evaluations,* Phi Delta Kappan, December 2000.

Erickson, Erik H. (1963). *Childhood and Society.* New York, NY: W.W. Norton.

Erickson, Erik H. (1994). *Identity, Youth and Crisis.* New York, NY: W.W. Norton.

Flanders, M. *Basic Teaching Skills Derived from a Model of Speaking And Listening,* Journal of Teacher Education, Spring 1973, v. 24.

Fosnot, Catherine. *Constructivism: A Psychological Theory of Learning,* In *Constructivism: Theory, Perspectives and Practice.* (1996). Fosnot, Catherine Twomey (Ed.). New York, NY: Teachers College Press.

Fox, R., Luszki M. and Schmuck, R. (1966). *Social Relations in the Classroom: Diagnosing Learning Environments.* Chicago, IL: SRA, Inc.

Frankl, Victor. (2000). *Man's Ultimate Search for Meaning.* New York, NY: Perseus Book Group.

Franklin, Ursula. Introduction to the symposium, *Towards an Ecology of Knowledge,* University of Toronto, as reported by Gordon Wells. In *Dialogic Inquiry in Education: Building on the Legacy of Vygotsky.* (1996). Toronto, Ontario: Ontario Institute for Studies in Education, University of Toronto.

Freire, Paulo. (1970). *Pedagogy of the Oppressed.* New York, NY: Herder and Herder.

Fullan, Michael. *Coordinating Top-Down and Bottom-Up Strategies For Educational Reform, The Governance of Curriculum: The 1994 Yearbook,* Association for Supervision and Curriculum Development.

Fullan, Michael. *Turning Systemic Thinking On Its Head,* U.S. Department of Education, 1994.

Gardner, Howard. (2000). *The Disciplined Mind: Beyond Facts and Standardized Tests, The K–12 Education That Every Child Deserves*. New York, NY: Penguin Putnam.

Gardner, Howard. (1961). *Excellence—Can We Be Equal and Excellent, Too?* New York, NY: Harper and Row.

Gardner, Howard. (1993). *Frames of Mind: Theory of Multiple Intelligences*. New York, NY: Basic Books

Gardner, Howard. (1999). *Intelligence Reframed: Multiple Intelligences For the 21st Century*. New York, NY: Basic Books.

Gardner, Howard. (1993). *Multiple Intelligences: The Theory in Practice*. New York, NY: Basic Books.

Gay, Geneva. (2000). *Culturally Responsive Teaching: Theory, Research And Practice*. New York, NY: Teachers College Press, Columbia University.

Gibbs, Jeanne. (1999). *Guiding Your School Community To Live a Culture of Caring and Learning*. Windsor, CA: CenterSource Systems.

Gibbs, Jeanne. *Rather Than Fixing Kids, Transform the Environment with Tribes Learning Communities,* Research/Practice, Center for Applied Research and Educational Improvement, Fall 1998.

Gibbs, Jeanne. (2000). *Tribes: A New Way of Learning and Being Together*. Windsor, CA: CenterSource Systems.

Goleman, Daniel. (1995). *Emotional Intelligence*. New York, NY: Bantam Books.

Goodlad, John. (1984). *A Place Called School*. New York, NY: McGraw Hill.

Goodlad, John. (1994). *Educational Renewal: Better Teachers, Better Schools*. San Francisco, CA: Jossey–Bass.

Goodlad, John. (1997). *In Praise of Education*. New York, NY: Teachers College Press, Columbia University.

Guild, Pat Burke. *Where Do the Learning Theories Overlap?* Educational Leadership, ASCD, 1997.

Hammond, Sue Annis. (1996). *Appreciative Inquiry*. Plano, TX: The Thin Book Company.

Hanaford, Carla. (1995). *Smart Moves—Why Learning is Not All in Your Head*. Arlington, VA: Great Ocean Publishers.

Hattie, J., Marsh, H., Neill, J., and Richards, G. *Adventure Education And Outward Bound: Out-of-Class Experiences That Make a Lasting Difference,* Review of Educational Research, 1997.

Hersch, Patricia. (1998). *A Tribe Apart: Journey Into the Heart of American Adolescence*. New York, NY: Ballentine Books.

Hertz-Lazarowitz, Rachel and Shachar, H. *Changes in Teachers' Verbal Behavior in Cooperative Classrooms.* Cooperative Learning, 1990, v. 11, no. 2.

High-Quality Teachers Are Key to Student Success, California School Board News, Dec. 31, 1998.

Hochman, Jere. (1997). *Thinking About Middle School*. Columbus, OH: National Middle School Association.

Houston, Paul. *The School Administrator,* 1998, v. 55, no. 5.

Jensen, Eric. (1988). *Teaching With the Brain in Mind*. Alexandria, VA: Association for Supervision and Curriculum Development.

Johnson, David and Johnson, Frank. (2000). *Joining Together: Group Theory and Group Skills*. Boston, MA: Allyn and Bacon.

Johnson, David and Johnson, Roger. (1998). *Circles of Learning*. Edina, MN: Interaction Book Company.

Johnson, David and Johnson, Roger. (1989). *Cooperation and Competition: Theory and Research*. Edina, MN: Interaction Book Company.

Johnson, David, and Johnson, Roger. *Cooperative Learning and Nonacademic Outcomes of Schooling, In Secondary Schools and Cooperative Learning: Theories, Models and Strategies*. (1995). Pedersen, J. and Digby, A. (Eds.). New York, NY: Garland Publishing.

Johnson, David, Johnson, Roger and Holubec, Edythe Johnson. (1994). *New Circles of Learning: Cooperation in the Classroom and School*. Alexandria, VA: ASCD.

Johnson, David, Johnson, Roger and Smith, Karl. *Cooperative Learning and Individual Student Achievement, In Secondary Schools and Cooperative Learning: Theories, Models and Strategies*. (1995). Pedersen, J. and Digby, A. (Eds.). New York, NY: Garland Publishing.

Joyce, B., and Showers, G. (1982). *Transfer of Training: The Contribution of Coaching*. Eugene, OR: Center for Educational Policy and Management, University of Oregon.

Kafka, Franz. (1946). *The Advocates: The Complete Stories*. New York, NY: Schocken Books.

Kagan, Spencer. (1999). *Cooperative Learning*. San Clemente, CA: Resources For Teachers.

Kagan, Spencer and Kagan, Miguel. *Staff Development and the Structure Approach to Cooperative Learning, In Professional Development for Cooperative Learning: Issues and Approaches*. (1998). Brody, Celeste and Davidson, Neil (Eds.). Albany, NY: State University of New York Press.

Kessler, R. (2000). *The Soul of Education: Helping Students Find Connection, Compassion, and Character at School*. Alexandria, VA: Association for Supervision and Curriculum Development.

Kohn, Alfie. (1996). *Beyond Discipline: From Compliance to Community*. Alexandria, VA: Association for Supervision and Curriculum Development.

Kohn, Alfie. *Fighting the Tests: A Practical Guide to Rescuing Our Schools, Phi Delta Kappan*, January 2001.

Kohn, Alfie. (1998). *How Not To Teach Values: What To Look For In A Classroom*. San Francisco, CA: Jossey-Bass.

Kovalik, Susan. (1999). *ITI: The Model, Integrated Thematic Instruction*. Kent, WA: Books for Educators.

Kruse, Sharon. *Collaborate, At Issue Designs*, National Staff Development Council, Summer 1999.

Lazear, David. (1989). *Seven Ways of Teaching: The Artistry of Teaching With Multiple Intelligences*. Palatine, IL: Skylight Publishing.

Learner-Centered Principles: A Framework for School Redesign and Reform, American Psychological Association.

Learning to Lead, Leading to Learn: Improving School Quality Through Principal Professional Development, National Staff Development Council, 2000.

Lieberman, Ann and Miller, Lynne. *Teaching and Teacher Development: A New Synthesis for a New Century, In Education in a New Era*. (2000). Ron S. Brandt (Ed.). Alexandria, VA: Association for Supervision and Curriculum Development.

Likona, Thomas. (1991). *Education for Character, How Our Schools Can Teach Respect and Responsibility*. New York, NY: Bantam Books.

Lipsitz, Joan. (1977). *Growing Up Forgotten: A Review of Research And Programs Concerning Early Adolescence*. Lexington, MA: D.C. Heath.

Lipsitz, Joan. (1984). *Successful Schools for Young Adolescents*. New Brunswick, NJ: Transaction Books.

Lott, Albert and Lott, Bernice. *Group Cohesiveness and Individual Learning,* Journal of Educational Psychology, April 1966, v. 57.

Lounsbury, J. and Clark, D. (1990). *Inside Grade 8: From Apathy to Excitement*. Reston, VA: National Association of Secondary School Principals.

Lounsbury, J. and Johnston, H. (1988). *Life in the Three Sixth Grades*. Reston, VA: National Association of Secondary School Principals.

MacIver, D. and Epstein, J. *Middle Grades Research: Not Yet Mature, But No Longer a Child,* Elementary School Journal, 1993.

Madaus, G., West, M., Harmon, M., Lomax, R., and Viator, K. (1992). *The Influence of Testing on Teaching Math and Science in Grades 4–12: Executive Summary*. Boston, MA: Center for the Study of Testing, Evaluation and Educational Policy.

Marlowe, Bruce and Page, Marilyn. (1998). *Creating and Sustaining the Constructivist Classroom*. Thousand Oaks, CA: Corwin Press.

McCombs, Barbara L. *Twelve Learner-Centered Psychological Principles*. Midwest Center Educational Laboratory.

McElroy, Camille. *Middle School Programs That Work,* Phi Delta Kappan, December 2000.

McKnight, John. *Are Social Service Agencies the Enemy of the People?* Utne Reader, Jul-Aug 1992.

Meier, D. *Reinventing Teaching,* Teachers College Record, 1992–1993, no. 4.

Meier, D. (1995). *The Power of Their Idea: Lessons for America From A Small School in Harlem*. Boston, MA: Beacon Press.

Melchior, A. *National Evaluation of Learn and Serve America: Interim and Final Evaluation,* National Corporation For Community Service, 1996–1998.

Merrill, M. David. *Constructivism and Instructional Design,* In *Constructivism and the Technology of Instruction*. (1992). Duffy, T. and Jonassen, D. (Eds.). Hillsdale, NJ: Erlbaum Associates Publishers.

Miller, Ron. (1990). *What Are Schools For? Holistic Education in American Culture*. Brandon, VT: Holistic Education Press.

Mizell, Hayes. *Six Steps To An Achieving Middle School: Keynote Speech,* Charlotte-Mecklenburg Schools: NC, First Annual Middle School Institute, 1999.

Muller, W. (1996). *How, Then, Shall We Live? Four Simple Questions That Reveal the Beauty and Meaning of Our Lives*. New York, NY: Bantam Books.

Naisbitt, John. (1999). *High Tech–High Touch: Technology and Our Search For Meaning*. New York, NY: Bantam Books.

Newkumet, M.B. and Casserly, M. *Urban School Safety: Strategies of the Great City Schools,* Washington, DC: Council of the Great City Schools, 1994.

Noddings, Nel. *A Morally Defensible Mission for Schools in The 21st Century,* Phi Deltan Kappan, 1995.

Noddings, Nel. *Schools Face Crisis in Caring,* Education Week, 1988.

Ohanian, Susan. *News From The Resistance Trail,* Phi Delta Kappan, January 2001.

Ohanian, Susan. (1994). *Who's in Charge? A Teacher Speaks Her Mind*. Heinemann.

Paris, Scott and Ayres, Linda. (1999). *Becoming Reflective Students and Teachers with Portfolios and Authentic Assessment*. Washington, DC: American Psychological Association.

Pedersen, Jon E. and Digby, Annette D. (1995). *Secondary Schools and Cooperative Learning—Theories, Models and Strategies.* New York, NY: Garland Publishing.

Pert, Candace (1997). *Molecules of Emotion: The Science Behind Mind-Body Medicine.* New York, NY: Simon and Schuster.

Piaget, Jean. (1970). *Science of Education and Psychology of the Child.* New York, NY: Orion.

Piaget, Jean. (1950). *The Psychology of Intelligence.* New York, NY: Harcourt Brace.

Pipher, Mary. (1995). *Reviving Ophelia: Saving the Lives of Adolescent Girls.* New York, NY: Ballantine Books.

Postman, Neil and Weingartner, Charles. (1969). *Teaching as a Subversive Activity.* New York, NY: Dell Publishing.

Promoting Social and Educational Learning: Guidelines for Educators, Study Guide, Association for Supervision and Curriculum Development, 1998.

Reich, Robert. (1991). *The Work of Nations.* New York, NY: Alfred A. Knopf.

Resnick, M., Bearman, P., Blum, R., Bauman, K., Harris, K., Jones, J., Tabor, J., Beuring, T., Sieving, R., Shew, M., Ireland, M., Bearinger, L., and Udry, J. *Protecting Adolescents from Harm: Findings from the National Longitudinal Study on Adolescent Health,* Journal of the American Medical Association, 1997.

Rumi, Mathnawi of Jelahuddin. (1990). *Delicious Laughter: Rambunctious Teaching Stories.* (Coleman Barks translation), Athens, GA: Maypop Books.

Sarason, S.B. (1972). *The Creation of Settings and the Future Societies.* San Francisco, CA: Jossey-Bass.

Sarason, S.B. (1990). *The Predictable Failure of School Reform.* San Francisco, CA: Jossey-Bass.

Scales, Peter C. (1996). *Boxed in and Bored: How Middle Schools Continue to Fail Young Adolescents—And What Good Middle Schools Do Right.* Minneapolis, MN: Search Institute.

SCANS Report for America 2000—What Work Requires of Schools. (1991–1998). Washington, DC: Secretary's Commission on Achieving Necessary Skills, U.S. Department of Labor.

Schein, E. (1985). *Organization Cultures and Leadership: A Dynamic View.* San Francisco, CA: Jossey-Bass.

Sergiovanni, Thomas. (1994). *Building Community In Schools.* San Francisco, CA.: Jossey-Bass.

Sergiovanni, Thomas. (1996). *Leadership for the Schoolhouse.* San Francisco, CA.: Jossey-Bass.

Sergiovanni, Thomas. (1999). *Rethinking Leadership: A Collection of Articles.* Arlington Heights, IL: Skylight Training and Publishing.

Sizer, Ted. (1984). *Horace's Compromise: The Dilemma of the American High School.* Boston, MA: Houghton-Mifflin.

Smilovitz, R. (1996). *If Not Now, When? Education Not Schooling.* Kearney, NE: Morris.

Starhawk. (1997). *Dreaming the Dark.* New York, NY: Beacon Press.

Stoddard, Lynn. (1992). *Redesigning Education: A Guide for Developing Human Greatness.* Tucson, AZ: Zephyr Press.

Stolp, Stephen. (1994). *Leadership for School Culture.* ERIC Digest.

Swope, Kathy and Miner, Barbara (Eds.). (2000). *Failing Our Kids: Why the Testing Craze Won't Fix Our Schools.* Milwaukee, WI: Rethinking Schools, LTD.

Taffel, Ron. (1999). *Nurturing Good Children Now*. New York, NY: Golden Books.

This We Believe: Developmentally Responsive Middle Level Schools. (1995). Columbus, OH: National Middle School Association.

Thompson, Scott. *The Authentic Standards Movement and Its Evil Twin,* Phi Delta Kappan, January 2001.

Toffler, Alvin. (1980). *Third Wave*. New York, NY: Wm. Morrow.

Turning Points: Preparing American Youth for the 21st Century. (1989). New York, NY: Carnegie Council on Adolescent Development, Carnegie Corporation of New York.

Valliant, G.E. (1977). *Adaptation to Life*. Boston, MA: Little, Brown.

Wells, Gordon. *Dialogic Inquiry in Education: Building on the Legacy of Vygotsky*. Ontario Institute for Studies in Education, University of Toronto, 1996.

Werner, Emily and Smith, Ruth. (1992). *Overcoming the Odds: High-Risk Children from Birth to Adulthood*. New York, NY: Cornell University Press.

Werner, Emily and Smith, Ruth. (1989). *Vulnerable But Invincible: A Longitudinal Study of Resilient Children and Youth*. New York, NY: Adams, Bannister and Cox.

Wheelock, Anne. (1998). *Safe To Be Smart: Building A Culture for Standards-Based Reform in the Middle Grades*. National Middle School Association.

Windschitl, Mark. *The Challenges of Sustaining a Constructivist Classroom Culture,* Phi Delta Kappan, June 1999.

Wong, Caroline. *A Comprehensive Review of the Research Literature On Middle Level Education Provides Compelling Support for the Implementation of the Middle School Concept*. Honolulu, HI: Hawaii Department of Education, 1997.

Wong, Caroline. *Focus on Learning—Self-Study for Accreditation Report*. Honolulu, HI: Moanalua Middle School, 1998.

Yager, Stuart, Johnson, Roger, Johnson, David and Snider, Bill. *The Impact of Group Processing on Achievement in Cooperative Learning Groups,* The Journal of Social Psychology, 1986, v. 126.

Tribes Professional Development

TRANSFORM YOUR MIDDLE SCHOOL WITH TRIBES LEARNING COMMUNITIES® PROFESSIONAL DEVELOPMENT FROM CENTERSOURCE SYSTEMS

*T*ribes is a community building process—a culture and active learning pedagogy best learned by actively experiencing it. You can make the process come alive in your middle level school by scheduling training for your teachers, administration and support staff.

What Tribes can bring to a class is dynamite— what it can bring to a total staff is spectacular!
—LESLIE MCPEAK, PRINCIPAL
MODESTO CITY SCHOOLS

DISCOVERING GIFTS IN MIDDLE SCHOOL WITH TRIBES TLC®

The purpose of this training is to provide a research-based approach for middle level school educators to focus their schools on the critical developmental learning needs of young adolescents. The training illuminates how to transform the cultures of middle schools into caring learning communities that support the full range of students' growth and development as well as establishing academic excellence.

Middle school educators will…

- Recognize the critical importance of the middle level school to make as its focus, all aspects of the development of its young adolescent students
- Gain an understanding of four developmental tasks of young adolescents
- Learn what a *responsive middle level school* is—the gifts students discover and the meaningful learning that is achieved
- Learn how collaborative groups of learners (students, teachers, administrators and parents) can create and sustain a caring school culture
- Recognize the comprehensive studies that underlie the caring process of Tribes Learning Communities
- Understand why and how group learning supports adolescent development
- Learn how teachers can move through *sequential stages towards excellence* and into *responsive education* and discovery learning
- Design active group learning experiences that develop student-centered classrooms
- Realize the need for fairness, equity and social justice in middle schools and consider ways to reverse inequities
- Learn why democratic leadership is needed in a middle school that is focused on students' development and learning
- Understand the need for and power of *reflective practice* throughout all groups in the school community
- Learn how *authentic assessment* promotes learning and student development.

OTHER TRIBES TLC® PROFESSIONAL DEVELOPMENT TRAINING

CenterSource Systems has a network of licensed trainers who conduct professional development training throughout the United States, Canada and the Caribbean. Schedule an overview presentation or classroom demonstration at your school where the key concepts of Tribes are explained and demonstrated through typical training strategies and our videos. Give your administration, school board and staff the information they need to consider whole school training. In addition, conversations with Tribes TLC® school administrators and teachers can be arranged by contacting CenterSource Systems.

TRIBES TLC® I—BUILDING COMMUNITY FOR LEARNING

The purpose of this training is to prepare teachers, administrators and support staffs to develop a caring school and classroom environment, and to reach and teach students through an active learning approach that promotes student development, motivation and academic achievement.

TRIBES TLC® II—ACHIEVING EXCELLENCE

This training builds upon "Building Community for Learning" by providing school personnel with additional in-depth knowledge and methods to intensify the use of the Tribes Learning Community process throughout school classrooms and the community… and thereby achieve higher success for students and schools.

TRIBES TLC® III—UNIVERSITY COURSE

The purpose of the university course is to teach the theory, basic research, active learning process and cooperative group learning approach to pre-service and in-service teachers, graduate interns, administrators and other professionals who are committed to school improvement and education that is responsive to the developmental growth and learning needs of today's students.

TRIBES DISCOVERY LEARNING

This training is designed for experienced Tribes TLC® teachers who have become proficient in using the Tribes cooperative group learning process, and who are ready to move to the constructivist approach of learning which incorporates group inquiry, and student initiated research, planning, presentations, teaching, assessment and projects. The approach can be adapted to all age levels but is particularly appropriate for middle level and high school students.

DEVELOPING REFLECTIVE PRACTICE AND AUTHENTIC ASSESSMENT

This training for Tribes TLC® schools assures the success of the developmental process of Tribes throughout a school in two important ways. It establishes as an essential part of the school culture the on-going *practice of reflection* for learning, teacher collegiality, school improvement and educational excellence. Secondly, it provides realistic ways in which students and teachers working together can *authentically* assess and celebrate academic learning on a regular basis—long before year-end tests. *Authentic assessment* is motivational and promotes long lasting retention of learning.

MULTI-YEAR TRIBES TLC® TRAINING PLANS

CenterSource Systems can help you design a multi-year training program to meet the needs of your school by implementing several of the professional development opportunities mentioned above. When integrated into the whole school community, Tribes can effect system-wide change by creating a caring culture and cooperative learning community, which fosters student growth and achievement, strengthens staff relationships and collegiality, and effectively redesigns the learning community.

TRAINING-OF-DISTRICT TRAINERS

CenterSource Systems has designed a capacity building model for professional development so that your district or school can have your own certified Tribes TLC® trainers to provide on-going training, coaching and support to teachers, administrators, resource personnel and parent community groups. The CenterSource Training-of-District Trainers provides in-depth skills, knowledge, experience and quality training materials for your own qualified personnel.

FOR ADDITIONAL INFORMATION CONTACT:

CenterSource Systems, LLC
7975 Cameron Drive, #500
Windsor, California 95492
800-810-1701 or 707-838-1061
FAX: 707-838-1062
email: tribes@tribes.com
website: www.tribes.com

Descriptions of the Tribes TLC® Materials

TRIBES, A New Way of Learning and Being Together

by Jeanne Gibbs

Item 100 $32.95

This new edition shows teachers how to reach students by developing a caring environment as the foundation for growth and learning. Material details how to teach essential collaborative skills, design interactive learning experiences, work with multiple learning styles, foster the development of resiliency, and support school community change. 2000, 6th edition, 432 pages, 165 strategies/energizers, index and resources.

TRIBUS, una nueva forma de aprender y convivir juntos

by Jeanne Gibbs

Item 120 $32.95

The same wonderful Tribes book has been translated into **Spanish!** 1998, 1st edition, 448 pages.

Guiding Your School Community

by Jeanne Gibbs

Item 130 $14.95

In this 110-page book written with school Administrator's in mind, you will learn why and how the positive Tribes culture will develop community throughout an entire educational system. You will gain an understanding of how to initiate, support and sustain the Tribes process over time.

Discovering Gifts in Middle School: Learning in a Caring Culture Called Tribes

by Jeanne Gibbs

Item 140 $32.95

This new book motivates and supports middle level schools to make the full range of young adolescents' developmental growth and learning needs the over-riding focus of the whole school community. The author presents a lively synthesis of a wealth of research studies and effective practices, which underlie the *Tribes Learning Community* developmental approach. The major emphasis on middle level schools becoming *responsive* to the contextual basis of adolescent development leads not only to greater achievement and success for students but a new spirit, energy and the discovery of gifts throughout the whole school community. The book contains 440 pages, 138 active learning strategies, an extensive bibliography, resource section and index. 2001.

Discovering Gifts: Student Journal

Item 141 Call for price

This journal provides students with many ways to discover their unique gifts, talents, interests and new skills throughout the school year. The journal contains pages for daily reflection on discovered gifts and learning; materials on the tasks of the middle years, decision-making, setting goals, and the exploration of careers; personal & group assessment forms, multiple intelligence checklists, a monthly calendar and task organizer. The journal is recommended for all middle school classrooms using Tribes TLC®.

Video: TRIBES, A New Way of Learning and Being Together

Item 151 $22.95

See and show others what Tribes looks like in a classroom. Hear what principals, teachers, parents and kids say about the process. Revised 2000. 15 minutes.

Teaching Peace by Red Grammer
Item 153 (cassette) $10.00
Item 154 (CD) $15.00
A delightful set of 10 songs written, sung and played by Red Grammer. This music supports the same caring principles and fun enjoyed in Tribes.

Teaching Peace Songbook and Teacher's Guide by Kathy Grammer
Item 155 $15.00
Features piano, guitar and vocal accompaniment to the Teaching Peace songs and contains activity and discussion ideas for each song. The guide also contains a bibliography of over 100 books that relate to the themes of the songs. 1993, 85 pages.

Video: Creating Futures of Promise
Item 161 $22.95
Bonnie Benard and students describe the concept of Resiliency and Protective factors. 15 minutes.

Energizer Box
Item 162 $21.95
This colorful desktop card file contains 101 tried and true energizers that are a great way to revitalize students throughout the day.

Tribes Buttons and Magnets
(2¼ Inches)
Item 165 (50 Buttons) $20.00
Item 166 (25 Magnets) $20.00
Assorted Tribes buttons in English, Spanish or Hawaiian. Please specify. We also put the agreements with the teddy bear on a magnet for your kids to take home for the fridge. Great for the whole school, parents nights, Tribes Celebration days and just for fun.

Video: TRIBES—Learning for the 21st Century
Item 170 $22.95
Looking at Tribes as a process for systemic change from classroom to the whole school community. Voices of Administrators describe the wonderful benefits of creating a caring school culture for learning. 15 minutes.

Tribes Postcards
(Pack of 50, English or Spanish)
Item 173 $7.50
A full-color card to send to tribe members, other educators, and parents to announce events, stay in touch and keep expressing appreciation.

Tribes Book Bag
15" L x 12" H
Item 175 $14.95
A wonderful way to tote your Tribes TLC® materials. Vinyl lined with outside pocket. Blue and white with your favorite Tribes kids on the front. Great gift idea too!

The Tribes Assessment Kit: Reflecting on the Tribes TLC® Process
Item 400 $75.00
The Tribes Assessment Kit will help your school strengthen its implementation of the process and assess outcomes. The Kit includes four process assessment instruments and complete directions for use throughout classrooms of the school.

TRIBES TLC® MATERIALS ORDER FORM

ITEM NO.	DESCRIPTION	PRICE	QTY.	COST
100	*Tribes, A New Way of Learning and Being Together* by Jeanne Gibbs	$32.95		
120	*Tribus, una nueva forma de aprender y convivir juntos* by Jeanne Gibbs	$32.95		
130	*Guiding Your School Community* by Jeanne Gibbs (Tribes Administrators book)	$14.95		
140	*Discovering Gifts in Middle School* by Jeanne Gibbs	$32.95		
141	*Discovering Gifts: Student Journal*	Call		
151	*Video: Tribes, A New Way of Learning and Being Together*	$22.95		
153	*Teaching Peace* (audio tape) by Red Grammer	$10.00		
154	*Teaching Peace* (CD) by Red Grammer	$15.00		
155	*Teaching Peace Song Book & Teacher's Guide* by Kathy Grammer & colleagues	$15.00		
161	*Video: Creating Futures of Promise* (15 minute video on Resiliency)	$22.95		
162	*Energizer Box* (desktop card file with 101 Energizers)	$21.95		
165	*Tribes Buttons Assorted* (2¼ inches) Bag of 50 Specify: ❏ English ❏ Spanish ❏ Hawaiian	$20.00		
166	*Magnets* (Bag of 25) Agreements with Teddy Bear ❏ English ❏ Spanish	$20.00		
167	*Warm Fuzzy* (stuffed animal approx. 9" long)	$12.00		
170	*Video: Tribes—Learning for the 21st Century*	$22.95		
173	*Tribes Postcards* (Pack of 50) ❏ English ❏ Spanish	$7.50		
175	*Tribes Book Bag* (15" L x 12" H)	$14.95		
400	*Tribes TLC® Assessment Kit*	$75.00		

METHOD OF PAYMENT

Check enclosed for $_____

❏ MasterCard ❏ VISA ❏ American Express

#_____

Expiration Date: MM/YY _____/_____

Purchase Order # _____

Please attach purchase order to this form

SHIPPING RATES:	CONTINENTAL USA	HAWAII, ALASKA & CANADA
Up to $39.99	= $5.00	= $5.00
$40.00 to $59.99	= $6.00	= $8.50
$60.00 to $349.99	= 10 %	= 15 %
$350 or more	= 5 %	= 11 %

All shipping is via UPS ground or USPS Priority Mail
Call for international or rush shipping rates

★ California residents: include sales tax for your county

SUBTOTAL	
SHIPPING	
SALES TAX★	
TOTAL	

SOLD TO: NAME _____

ORGANIZATION _____

ADDRESS _____

CITY/STATE/ZIP _____

DAY PHONE _____

SHIP TO: NAME _____

ORGANIZATION _____

ADDRESS _____

CITY/STATE/ZIP _____

DAY PHONE _____

Index

About the Author

JEANNE GIBBS has spent her professional career studying, writing and implementing systemic processes and programs to support children's development and prevent youth problems. Her perspective on human development is a systems approach that encourages schools, families and communities to create healthy environments in which children can grow and learn. The developmental culture and educational process now known as "Tribes Learning Communities" evolved out of years of studies Jeanne has pursued to synthesize a wealth of literature pertaining to the ecology of human development and learning. She is convinced that well being and success for students is not a result of curriculum, instruction and assessment—nor of intelligence—but the result of a school finally focusing on the growth and whole human development of its students in all aspects of their individual uniqueness and brilliance. The vision takes on reality whenever a school system focuses first on creating and sustaining a caring culture in which children truly are able to discover themselves and succeed.

Jeanne supervised implementations of the community learning process throughout hundreds of schools and youth-serving agencies for more than ten years while managing a non-profit corporation, which she had founded. Though serving as the executive director, she continued to research, refine and author publications—until her first formal retirement. Since then, Jeanne has retired many times—none of which last long due to her passionate purpose. Ever-growing requests from schools throughout the United States, Canada and other countries for professional development and quality materials led her to establish CenterSource Systems in 1995 as "the home of Tribes."

Her primary interest now centers on the potential of school reform being achieved through reflective Learning Communities that are responsive to the developmental and learning needs of their students. It is no surprise that people across the country know Jeanne for her warm and generous spirit... and ability to build community wherever she goes.

Notes:

Notes:

Notes:

Notes:

Notes:

Notes: